AFTER MARXISM

CRITICAL PERSPECTIVES
A Guilford Series

Edited by
DOUGLAS KELLNER
University of Texas, Austin

POSTMODERN THEORY: CRITICAL INTERROGATIONS
Steven Best and Douglas Kellner

A THEORY OF HUMAN NEED
Len Doyal and Ian Gough

PSYCHOANALYTIC POLITICS, SECOND EDITION:
JACQUES LACAN AND FREUD'S FRENCH REVOLUTION
Sherry Turkle

POSTNATIONAL IDENTITY:
CRITICAL THEORY AND EXISTENTIAL PHILOSOPHY
IN HABERMAS, KIERKEGAARD, AND HAVEL
Martin J. Matustik

THEORY AS RESISTANCE:
POLITICS AND CULTURE AFTER (POST) STRUCTURALISM
Mas'ud Zavarzadeh and Donald Morton

POSTMODERNISM AND SOCIAL INQUIRY
David R. Dickens and Andrea Fontana, Editors

MARXISM IN THE POSTMODERN AGE:
CONFRONTING THE NEW WORLD ORDER
*Antonio Callari, Stephen Cullenberg, and
Carole Biewener, Editors*

AFTER MARXISM
Ronald Aronson

AFTER MARXISM

Ronald Aronson

THE GUILFORD PRESS
New York London

© 1995 The Guilford Press
A Division of Guilford Publications
72 Spring Street, New York, NY 10012

Printed in the United States of America

This book printed on acid-free paper.

Last digit is print number: 9 8 7 6 5 4 3 2

Library of Congress Cataloging-in-Publication Data

Aronson, Ronald, 1938–
    After Marxism / Ronald Aronson
        p.   cm.—(Critical perspectives)
    Includes bibliographical references and index.
    ISBN 0-89862-417-7 (hardcover).—ISBN 0-89862-416-9 (pbk.)
    1. Marxism. 2. Post-communism. 3. Postmodernism—social aspects.
4. Radicalism. I. Title. II. Series: Critical perspectives (New York, N.Y.)
HX44.5.A78   1994
335.43'7—dc20   94-23009
                                                                      CIP

*This is dedicated to Saul Wellman—
lifelong revolutionary,
dear friend, inspiration, mentor*

PREFACE

This book had its beginning during a period of mourning. The end of Marxism came as a shock to me, although for years we had spoken of its being in "crisis." Like most of my colleagues, comrades, and friends, I cheered the breaching of the Berlin Wall and awaited expectantly what might follow. No longer believing that a reformed Communism might fulfill Marxism's promise, I had become sure that its very existence blocked political energies in the West as well as the East, and eagerly anticipated that the end of this "sustaining menace" would release enormous emancipatory forces everywhere. But the opposite happened: the end of Communism instead became part of a stunning defeat of those social forces, ideas, structures, projects, and even values, which for two centuries have been identified with the Left.

A remarkable silence enveloped the Left after the fall of the Berlin Wall and the disintegration of the Soviet Union. How assiduously we have avoided mourning the fate of Marxism and socialism! Instead, we have become uncharacteristically quiet about who we are, what we are for, and what has become of our vision. Look at any recent *New Left Review*; attend the Socialist Scholars, or Radical Activists and Scholars, or *Rethinking Marxism* Conferences; read *The Nation* week after week; and it becomes apparent that the Left has fallen into a profound state of denial.

And no wonder. The very immobility and ponderousness of the Soviet Union counted for something positive in our collective psychic space, allowing us to keep hope alive that a successful socialism might still emerge. It provided a backdrop against which alternatives could be thought about and discussed, including, for some, the hope that other versions of Marxism remained viable. But now, no longer. Try as we may to rescue its theoretical possibility from Communism's demise, the great world-historical project of struggle and transformation identified with the name of Karl Marx seems to have ended. And, as the postmodernists know, an entire world view has crashed along with Marxism. Not only Marxists and socialists, but other radicals, as well as those regarding themselves as progressives and liberals, have lost their sense of direction

It is not surprising that this loss is not being explicitly and directly acknowledged by the Left; already besieged on so many other fronts, we continue to fragment and dissolve. But defeat turns into disaster when cloaked in silence and repressed, when its disorientations are ignored even as they are being absorbed. Isolated from a common mourning and thus denying their connection, individuals lose their sense of social being, and come to feel disoriented and impotent. Increasingly alone in the face of the world's evils, unable to think clearly about such issues as the rape of Bosnia, we can barely recall our onetime solidarity; it seems more a ruse of memory than any lived experience.

On the other hand, fully accepting the burden of mourning can catalyze us to look ahead, to reconstitute ourselves on the other side of the loss. This can happen as we consent to experience bereavement, to feel the pain, to let go. To mourn collectively thus has the potential to resurrect the hope that solidarity gave us. It revives the sense of sharing at the point of loss, but also perhaps a common need to work past it, to reaffirm and perhaps recast our identities, so as to find new bases for collective action.

Perhaps this is one reason why I have involved so many people in creating this book. Like any book, it is ultimately the sole responsibility of its author. But I have been much more than assisted by those who have responded to the ideas, propositions, and analyses that I have presented them. Some have agreed with me, some disagreed, but above all, they have together made *After Marxism* possible—by giving me the experience of the community for which I write.

Thanks to Phyllis Aronson, Saul Wellman, Steve Golin, and Raphael de Kadt, for sharing the entire journey. Thanks to Ernst Benjamin, Christopher Johnson, Douglas Kellner, Milton Tambor, Tom Lonergan, Robert Deneweth, David Fukuzawa, Charles Rooney, Jean Dietrich Rooney, Helen Samberg, Evelyn Millstein, Steve Shank, and Tony Rothschild–all of whom participated in the project. Thanks also to the Continental Philosophy Reading Group at the University of Windsor, especially Barry Adam, Walter Skakoon, Adrian van den Hoven, and Deborah Cook; the members of the Fall 1992 graduate reading course on the crisis of Marxism at Wayne State University, especially Frank Koscielski and Richard Weiche; and to Richard Schmitt, Debra Bergoffen, Hazel Barnes, Sonia Kruks, David Herreshoff, Francis Shor, David Wellman, William McBride, Joe Walsh, Christopher Ballantine, Lungisile Ntsebeza, Iris Young, Nancy Fraser, Eli Zaretsky, and Moishe Postone, for responding to the book's ideas in general and/or those of specific chapters.

While this book was in the last stages of production, two events took place that deserve mention in any study of Marxism today. South Africa's first free elections led to the inauguration of Nelson Mandela presiding over a coalition cabinet including several members of the South African Communist Party, most notably its longtime leader, Joe Slovo. While this remarkable fact did not change any of the dilemmas discussed in several places in this volume, especially in Chapters 2 and 3, it paid tribute to the unique role Marxists and Communists have played in the South African liberation struggle. Second, Ralph Miliband, one of the world's major Marxist thinkers died in mid-1994. His lucidity, integrity, and demanding intellect will be missed by all of us on the Left who, over the years, benefited so greatly from them. His loss further saddens me because I had keenly looked forward to his response to my argument with him in Chapters 2 and 5. If I will now be spared his stern criticism, I will also miss being able to continue the argument.

CONTENTS

Introduction   1

    A Farewell to Marxism   2
    On Our Own   4

PART ONE: FAREWELL TO MARXISM

Chapter One. A Marxist Itinerary   9

    Finding Directions   10
    Conversion   12
    The Movement   16
    Looking beyond Marxism, Looking toward Marxism   19
    Liberation of the Self   24
    Setback and Victory   29
    After the Movement   30
    The 1980s   33
    Why Hold On?   36

Chapter Two. Marxism Is Over   40

    The Argument   41
    Marxism as Science: Theory and Practice Unified   45
    From Theory to Practice: The Underlying Condition   47
    Marxism as Project   50
    Appreciating Marxism as Project   52
    Is the Project Over, or in the Doldrums?   55
    The Case for Marxism's Obsolescence   56
    The Case for Marxism's Continued Relevance   58
    What Both Sides Acknowledge   59
    Why Not Wait?   60
    South Africa and the Marxist Project   61

The Strengthening of the Working Class?   63
Marxism as an Idealism   66

Chapter Three. Why Now?   68
Reformism and Lenin's Recasting of Marxism   69
At the Margins   71
Marxism's High Tide?   73
Signs of Decline   75
Disintegration   76
No Return to Revolutionary Goals   78
Socialism in One Country?   80
The End of Postcapitalist Society   80
No Surviving Revolutionary Inspiration   81
Marxism as Idea   82
Mourning Marxism   83

Chapter Four. Marxism and Modernity: 87
   A Contemporary
   Critique
The Need for a Contemporary Critique   90
Critiques of Marxism: Eschatology   91
Eschatology in Bad Faith   95
Critiques of Marxism: Scientism, Objectivism, Indifference to the
   Subjective   97
Marx's Objectivism   99
The Missing Practice of Subjectivity   101
Subjectivity's Decisive Role   104
Critiques of Marxism: Authoritarianism   107
Marxism-Leninism and Authority   111
Evaluation: Marxism in Its Time   113
Evaluation: The Obsolescence of Marxism   115
Postmodernism or Mature Modernism?   119
The Modernist Critique   121
Marxism and the Transition to Modernity   122

Chapter Five. The Marxist–Feminist Encounter   124
Feminists Encounter Marxism   125
Socialist Feminism   127
The Short Career of Socialist Feminism   130
The Impossibility of Socialist Feminism   134
In the Wake of Socialist Feminism   136

Chapter Six. Marxism without Marxism   140
The Moment of Analytical Marxism   140
Reconstructing Marxism   143
What Remains of Marxism?   151

Why Hold On?   153
Marxists after Marxism, 158

PART TWO: ON OUR OWN   161

Chapter Seven. The New Situation   165

No New Marx   166
Losing Universality   168
Loss of Alternatives   171
Loss of Faith in Progress   172
Losing a Sense of History   174
Losing Faith in Human Nature   175
Losing Our Bearings   177
Parameters of a New Radical Project   179

Chapter Eight. A New Radical Project   181

Bases for a Single Movement: Collective Identities   182
How Wide a "We?" 184
Taking Oppression Seriously: Dionne's *Why Americans
   Hate Politics*   187
Taking Oppression Seriously: Cohen and Arato's *Civil
   Society and Political Theory*   189
Why *Radical* Change   192
Realism and Radicalism   193
What's in a Name   198

Chapter Nine. Emancipating Modernity   203

Toward an Emancipated Modernity   204
Modernity's Dark Side: *Dialectic of Enlightenment*   205
Modernity's Dark Side: Foucault   208
Going beyond Horkheimer and Adorno: Marcuse   210
Going beyond Foucault   212
Modernity at Century's End: Habermas and Cohen
   and Arato   215
Emancipating Modernity: Tasks and Complexities   219
The Ambivalence of Emancipation   223
A New Paradigm?   225
Theory as Tool, not as Framework   227

Chapter Ten. We Should Be Talking about Right and Wrong   231

Morality in the Center?   232
Marxism's Ambivalence toward Morality   234
The Contemporary Crisis of Morality   236
Moral Bases for Radical Change: Immanent Critique   239
Moral Bases for Radical Change: Judging Societies by
   Their Possibilities   241

Moral Bases for Radical Change: The History of
    Freedom   242
Universal Rights   247
Difference   250
Connecting Difference and Universality   252
An Adequate Moral Basis?   255

Chapter Eleven. Sources of Hope   258
The Problem of Hope Today   260
Ernst Bloch and *The Principle of Hope*   261
Hope without Reason   264
Herbert Marcuse and the End of Utopia   266
The Uses of Utopia: Homage to Marcuse   269
A Despairing Hope: Critique of Marcuse   271
A Five-Hundred-Year Perspective   275
Action   276
Creating Utopia   278
Hope   279
The International   281

Notes   283

Index   315

INTRODUCTION

Marxism is over, and we are on our own. Until recently, for so many on the Left, being on our own has been an unthinkable affliction—an utter loss of bearings, an orphan's state. To genuinely think and act beyond Marxism means embracing this new situation, being on our own deliberately and even with enthusiasm. Only then can new radical projects, incubating over the generation in which Marxism has been ending, find their proper shape. Many of us will discover ourselves anew without our albatross, free from the need to think increasingly post-Marxist thoughts and confront an increasingly post-Marxist situation within the reassuring but confining parameters of an obsolescent holistic, teleological, and synthetic unity.

Accordingly, we will be able to develop ways of conceiving radical thought and action that are fully modern. "Fully modern" may seem an odd way to characterize the future of radical thought, but I am envisioning thought free from Marxism's premodern eschatological attitudes, as well as from its early modern reductionist, scientistic, and authoritarian strands. Only a *fully modern* radical project can embrace fully the task of understanding and radically transforming this contemporary world.

As Marxism's last generation, we have been assigned by history the unenviable task of burying it. Those of us who continue to be committed to radical change did not expect this; we have been surprised and shocked by the sweeping and demoralizing effects of the disintegration of Eastern Europe and the Soviet Union. Many of us looked forward to transformations in these countries, which we expected would herald an end to their deformed types of Marxism and make it possible to agitate for a more humane and authentic socialism. Yet, quite startlingly, in the face of movements often led by our comrades, the overthrow of the party-states did not revitalize Marxism, but turned out to be its death knell.

In what follows I argue that Marxism is indeed over. In mourning this ending, trying to make sense of what it means to be on our own today, and examining what we have lost, the first part is a personal and political, as well as philosophical and historical account. It entails autobiographical and historical narrative, history of ideas, and philosophical and political argument. It is an exploration that begins from within Marxism.

A Farewell to Marxism

I do not apologize for writing as an adherent, for having experienced the end of Marxism from that most insular and intimate of places—as a Marxist. I have not concluded that Marxism was wrong, and this book is not intended as farewell and critique from a newly achieved distance, by someone who has seen another light. This is why I begin by saying that Marxism is over rather than with what, for generations, has been the customary statement: "I am no longer a Marxist." That by now conventional personal disavowal assumes a continuing theory and movement, by saying which the individual has broken, and which she or he now views from the outside. In the course of this century many have thus abandoned Marxism—in anger, in disillusion, in intellectual dissatisfaction, in dramatic political breaks with various Marxist parties. Their books and articles have gone on to show us what is wrong with Marxism, where it is mistaken. This is not what I am saying; what follows is not that kind of book. In spite of everything, I would have preferred the survival and flourishing of the Marxism to which I was philosophically and politically committed, and within which I thought and acted for thirty years. Only when it became clear that Marxism had disintegrated around me, did I reluctantly accept and then embrace, being on my own. If I fail to denounce it, if I stress that capitalism has not ended, if I retain certain Marxist approaches that I still consider useful, if I sound ambivalent about its end, it is because I remained within Marxism for what I regard as good reasons, and in certain respects I would have preferred to continue to remain within it.

I have thought it important to begin by discussing my own involvement with Marxian thought and political practice. I started writing Chapter 1 as a preliminary essay in self-clarification, and it grew into an explanation of Marxism's potency for the generation of the 1960s. In it I describe what Marxism meant to many of us personally, philosophically, and politically. I do so by showing how, in my own case, Herbert Marcuse provided the critical, skeptical, and dialectical approach needed to revitalize historical materialism to fit our generation's experience, and how Jean-Paul Sartre provided the insistence on, and tools for, relating social oppression and social structures to individual choice and action.

My efforts at constant revision, deeply influenced by Sartre and

Marcuse, are reflected in my first book, *Jean-Paul Sartre—Philosophy in the World* (1980). There I present a reading of Sartre heavily influenced by Marcuse, but one that embraces Sartre's emphasis on individual action, freedom, and self-determination, while insisting on integrating these with an analysis of our fundamental sociality. In *The Dialectics of Disaster: A Preface to Hope* (1983) I used a historical materialism influenced by both Sartre and Marcuse to analyze the catastrophic social irrationality that has marked so much of the twentieth century, and is especially evident in the Holocaust and Stalinism. I have not gone beyond these explanations today. In writing *Stay Out of Politics: A Philosopher Views South Africa* (1990) I stressed both the dimensions of individual responsibility and of socioeconomic determination, and probed the construction of irrational national identities that serve socioeconomic interests. At the same time I tried to situate apartheid in the larger sociohistorical dialectic of the European encounter with the non-Western world. If in the end I gave perhaps too much credit to constructed forms of identity such as the *volk*, a corrective stress on specific class interests would still not adequately explain the violence that has wracked South Africa since Mandela's release.[1] Still, the Marcusean and Sartrean Marxism I employ in all of these books remains a powerful tool of analysis and explanation, and helps account for Marxism's remarkable persistence as a radical philosophy.

And yet, I argue, Marxism is over. The reader will, nevertheless, find me still referring to useful aspects of Marxism, to other individuals who remain Marxist, perhaps even to the few and dwindling Marxist movements, parties, and governments. If these remain among us, how then can I insist that Marxism is over? My second note of warning involves stressing what I mean by Marxism. I am *not* primarily, talking about Marxism as a theory, or as a set of tools, or as an analysis, or as a badge of identification that some individuals, organizations, and even societies continue to hold dear. If it has included these, Marxism has above all been a movement of societal transformation. More sharply defined, Marxism has been a *project*. As a project it has united a certain philosophy of history with a specific ethical outlook; with an analysis of societal dynamics based on the centrality of class and the economy; with an understanding of how capitalism functions; with a partisanship on the side of a particular social class, the proletariat; and with a revolutionary vision of that class achieving power and then abolishing classes. It has been all of these, united in a struggle aiming at the overthrow of capitalism by a movement of the workers: a theoretical–practical project. While it may still continue today as an analysis or a theory, a Marxism that is not taken up by workers or is not embodied in a movement stops being a distinctive project of social transformation, and becomes something else.

When I say that Marxism is over today, then, I mean it is over in precisely this sense: as a *project* of historical transformation. I cannot object if some people want to continue propounding and studying the theory, as philosophy or political economy, or employing it, as societal analysis, as philosophical critique of capitalism, or using any other of its fragments. They may even want to call themselves Marxists when they do so, but they must understand that they are no longer Marxists in the original sense of being partisans of, and allied to, a Marxian project of social transformation. All such theoretical Marxisms are, in fact, post-Marxisms that refuse to admit it. By mistaking the continuing vitality of one or more fragments, such as the Marxian analysis of capital, for what was once an integrated theoretical–practical movement of revolutionary transformation, they mistake sentiment for reality, the part for the whole, its steadily weakening hold on life for the flourishing world-historical movement. The starting premise of this book is that none of the surviving strands is Marxism as Marx intended it and as the world-historical force it became. In whatever ways its many fragments may live on, this Marxism is over.

On Our Own

The phrase "on our own" characterizes the central theme of Part II of this book. It means that after Marxism, we can expect to remain without the guidance of any holistic theory, without being directed by an authority (Marxism was, after all, named for its founding father), without the faith that our actions for a better world join a larger current destined to become an overwhelming force. "On our own" means the end of a happy childhood vision that united all aspects of life into a single, coherent outlook able to answer emotional, social, ethical, and world-historical questions, as well as claiming to guide revolutionary political practice. This holistic vision belongs to an earlier age, and I call for going beyond it in a rigorously modern outlook. At its best, this is what "postmodernism" seeks to do, and many of its features are essential to what I regard as a mature modern outlook. But its confusion about the project of modernity, its lack of historical grounding, and its bad faith, reflected in being quintessentially modern yet denying this, makes it as incapable of comprehending itself as it is of comprehending the modern condition. Comprehending our condition means no longer to lament being on our own, or to long for an all-embracing theory, but rather, as Marshall Berman has argued, to embrace the radical openness of modern life and our own indeterminacy. The condition of being "on our own" means, for better or worse, that we are thrown back on our own powers and energies. This is reflected in the post-Marxist outlooks-in-the-making of the New Left and new social movements, as well as, a generation before, in such a quintessentially modern philosophy as existentialism.

Without abandoning the insights of historical materialism, my argument still insists on the *new* character of any future radical project of thought and action. This includes accepting the inevitable heterogeneity of the social field and the autonomy of diverse social movements. It also includes refusing to take for granted the necessity that there must be a *single* project of radical transformation, asking whether as well as how and why the movements might become unified into a single movement. It equally means questioning the very need for *radical* projects, demanding that a new radicalism justify its goal of systemic transformation. I explore what kinds of commitments, values, and approaches to social realities may be still described as radical today. They include a determination to change attitudes, behaviors, and structures and systems when necessary. They include a commitment to justice, solidarity, unsparing social critique, and a determination to speak about right and wrong.

What hopes propel these efforts? How do we move past the discouragement and disillusion accompanying Marxism's end? What becomes of hope in the reversal of priorities between theory and practice, in the kind of pluralistic and open radicalism that I am sketching? Indeed, what is there left to hope for? What becomes of such tantalizing, and inspiring, images as Marx's "beginning of history," of the "free development of each" being the condition for "the free development of all"? What happens to the vision of a classless society, and its theme of universal liberation? A contemporary radical theory and politics will place utopian hope at its center, but unlike Marxism, it cannot pretend that its objects are coming into being. To appreciate the fully relationship of hope to radical politics it is necessary to recognize that such great utopian visions as those of Ernst Bloch and Herbert Marcuse are projections well beyond where historical reality itself seems to be heading, and thus in the strict sense are, and always were, *unreal*. But this unreality constitutes the necessary boundary to all social reality, and in this sense is profoundly real. As a vital dimension of the human adventure, utopian visions need discussion, clarification, and debate. They need to be stated explicitly, kept alive as criticisms of the established order and projections of a possible alternative, and so understood as "unreal realities." Freed from the illusion that it is being realized, linked with the kind of movement I describe throughout Part II of this book, radical hope may find new ways to inspire projects of social transformation into the twenty-first century.

Part One

Farewell to Marxism

Chapter One

A MARXIST ITINERARY

Marxism is over.

This has not been an easy conclusion for someone who has spent his entire adult life within its orbit. I was not raised in its aura, or drawn to Marxism as a worker whose experience its tenets closely fit, or guided to it as an activist discovering its power to illuminate my political struggles. Rather, I came to it as a young man searching for philosophical, moral, and personal bearings. I embraced the Marxian project because of its stunning explanatory, ethical, and inspirational power. It allowed me to share in a sense of collective might and right, of acting with and for all humanity, beginning with the oppressed and exploited. It drew me into a larger "*we*"; it allowed us to think that we were grasping the world's central structures and evils, to act with the sense that history was with us and we with it. From the beginning I knew that this Marxism had limits, weaknesses, and holes, but for thirty years it remained coherent and compelling. The Marxian project was at the center of my life, my thought, my action; it explained, guided, justified, and consoled. Now that Marxism is over, in its place stands—nothing.

Even if its end is a kind of liberation, it is simultaneously a profound loss, painful and difficult, which I cannot avoid mourning. I want to trace my own path through it, in order to articulate what Marxism has meant to me: how and why I came to it, why I stayed with it for so long. Then, in a more generalized argument, I will explain why I have finally concluded that it is over, my sense of loss at this ending, and what direction the settling of accounts might take. The first, personal, part of this story will be presented in this chapter, the rest in the remainder of Part I. Mine is, obviously, only *a* story, by someone who remained with Marxism until the end. But I think my path opens onto a wider road.

Finding Directions

At first blush it may seem puzzling that I ever came to Marxism at all, especially during the Cold War, and from my Detroit Jewish lower middle-class family background. My socialist and trade-unionist grandfather had given speeches in Yiddish denouncing the capitalist system, but the boy who listened to them with pride, amazement, and ambivalence, my father, did not reflect them in his life or thought. And even my grandfather, the man who once told his fellow cap makers that the Constitution should be torn up, grew old as a shopkeeper, then a janitor, and a supporter of Roosevelt. In any event, he died three years before I was born. And for all his own native brilliance, his high-strung son, the only boy in a family of nine, never finished school. My father ended up earning a decent living selling car insurance to Polish, Appalachian, and Italian automobile workers, and spent much of his time at the race track and (with me) rooting for the Detroit Tigers. He sensed that there was more to life than working and following the herd, but he left me to find out what. My mother, orphaned at birth, instinctively sided with all underdogs and taught me to do so as well. If she was one of the world's little people, and he was upright and fair-minded, they left me believing in equality but not in politics, and they never doubted that I would find and follow my own way, whatever it was.

Deciding not to rejoin my high-school friends in a fraternity at Wayne State University, instead I immediately embraced the critical, literary, and intellectual atmosphere of college, becoming one of those students for whom talking with professors and reading into the night were most important. I discovered reading and writing fiction, and studying history and philosophy. When I first learned about Marxism, neither inclining nor feeling hostile toward it, I got high grades. I had a powerful drive to succeed, but equally powerful drives propelled me toward writing and thinking and away from the conformity I saw all around me.

Politics interested me less than the bohemianism of the Beat generation, with which I identified myself. With his rough lyrical energy and refusal of all elitism, his willingness to attack convention and hypocrisy, his insistence on submitting all dimensions of social life to a human standard, and his willingness to tell America to "go fuck yourself with your atom bomb,"[1] Allen Ginsberg reflected my reality more than did the socialists I met in college.

After graduation in 1960, my search for points of orientation intensified. I decided to postpone thinking about graduate school. I married someone who equally wanted to travel, search, and find herself, and we went off to Mexico and California, planning to write, read, and work part-time. I briefly flirted with religious Judaism and Zionism, but neither satisfied what I have since realized was a very Jewish universalism and a slowly dawning drive to "mend the world."

Religion said nothing I could really grasp about the *future*; its meaning seemed to lie in a past for which my parents had instilled no reverence. Jewish religion also seemed to have little to say about the Holocaust, memories of which more than once reduced my father to incoherent raving. While Zionism focused on this recent history, it saw the rest of the world primarily as antagonists. Although it truly spoke to a part of my identity, in laying claim to the whole it brushed aside my other dimensions, leaving behind the American, the budding citizen of the wider world, the young would-be novelist, the young intellectual looking for universal patterns of meaning. And so I chose the wider world, via a circuitous path: my wife and I lived briefly in San Francisco, and then went searching for ourselves in a remote mountain valley in northern California, teaching in a country schoolhouse. The vision of the twenty-two-year-old was, in retrospect, amazingly simple: to find a secluded and beautiful place, reduce life to its essentials, and then to read, take walks, write, and think about self, history, and the world. The natural beauty contrasted sharply with the social reality of a world of poor loggers' families and prosperous ranchers who owned the valley, a little society of inherited wealth and poverty, of isolated people suspicious toward outsiders (although not hostile to Jews), and filled with intrigues and legendary resentments toward each other. We were lonely there, relied heavily on our own resources, made friends only with a single poor logging family who, like us, were regarded as "transients."

In this my first adult job I became painfully aware of how little I could accomplish. No matter how hard I tried as a teacher, some students just weren't able to learn. It seemed that it was already too late for them, that they were living out problems beyond their control or my intervention. I remember asking myself whether their limitations were hereditary or due to their family's social and economic situation. I concluded it was the latter, that it was not only unfair to be born poor or rich (which I must have always believed), but that one's starting point was usually decisive for one's finishing point. During our stay in San Francisco I had met a young man who was the first radical peer I ever talked with. I had argued with his self-assurance, but I had also listened carefully, feeling that he had something I wanted. He had told me about *The National Guardian*, and six months later, living in the Mattole valley, I bought one of the seven copies on sale at the Eureka newsstand nearly two hours away.

Looking for a coherent world-historical picture, not yet knowing what I would write about, or even in what forms, I began to become politicized and radicalized. Moving along an irresistible path, I hatched a rudimentary kind of socialism out of my own head. Justice and equality demanded, in the name of equal opportunity, that children not be forced to inherit their parents' disadvantages. Everyone's starting point should be the same. I was groping, as I entered the world, to find a meaningful explanation of what I was encountering and of the confusions and tensions I brought with me. I was struggling to unite and focus my alienation, my urge to understand, to figure out what to do and what I believed. Years earlier I had begun to disbelieve the Cold War demonization of Communism, deciding that the Khrushchev who pounded his shoe on the podium at the United Nations was no less a human being than Eisenhower—and certainly not my enemy. Now, in the early 1960s, I began to be attracted to the very otherness of the Other: I began to once more appreciate the Castro who had inspired my closest friend and me to dance with joy when he and his movement entered Havana on New Year's Day, 1959, and whom I had begun to dislike when he nationalized American businesses. Now I realized that he was trying to do the things I thought should be done.

I read Sartre's *Existentialism Is a Humanism* during these months, but it made little conscious impression. Although I would later make a career of my deep engagement with Sartre, at the time I found his message of freedom, responsibility, and self-determination to be interesting, even self-evident, but to offer little direction. Free for what? What should I do? I recall the night I let go of religion, driving down a mountain into Weaverville, California, with my wife asleep next to me as I pondered the meaning of meaning. The Judaism I encountered seemed to separate the meaning of life from our present-day actions, and seemed to look back to the past rather than centering itself in the present. I realized, as the lights of the town miles below slowly grew closer, that my life's meaning would have to be alive in daily action rather than lying somewhere behind it, had to be in the present and future rather than the past. My life's meaning would be a human construction rather than one given by God or drawn from the past.

I wrote several stories and a novel in our hideaway, but I kept asking philosophical and historical questions. How does the human world hang together, over time? Where is it going? I craved direction, particularly in relation to the main lines of world history and the main movements of Western thought. It was not enough to know, à la Sartre, that I was on my own. I wanted to feel that my increasingly subversive thoughts about American society were valid, to connect these with a larger picture, and to find a way to make sense of, perhaps even break out of, a feeling of isolation I carried wherever I went.

Conversion

I arrived at Brandeis University in September 1962. I recall watching wide-eyed as the silver-haired, hawk-nosed Herbert Marcuse lectured in his grey double-breasted suits. He taught Marxism but also the classics: Plato, Aristotle, Kant, Hegel, eighteenth-century liberalism and nineteenth-century social theory. And he taught the perspective that integrated them all: the hopes of humankind, from Plato to Marx, were of a piece and must be taken seriously. From Plato to Marx and Marcuse, that is: he sternly and self-consciously saw himself as continuing this great tradition of Western rationalism, referring to each of his predecessors as "the old man." Thus was Marx gilded with the authority of Plato, Kant, and Hegel; thus did Marcuse assume their mantle, thus did he gild Marxism with *his* authority. As he spoke, everything I had been wrestling with, all my interests and needs, and my budding socialism, easily drew together. The human and historical world, my ideas, my interests, my hopes, my alienation, even my despair all came together in a single, coherent vision.

By November I had converted to Marxism. This single way of seeing and living the world very suddenly provided what I had been looking for in northern California and before: a philosophical perspective; a way of giving coherence to human history; an explanation for inequality, privilege, and other social evils (including my former students' difficulties in learning); an understanding of the fundamental social evils and the path to overcome them; a vision of a meaningful future; a sense of belonging to the community of those who pursued this; an explanation for my sense of being an outsider in the middle-class world that awaited me; and a direction for my own life. Marxism helped shape and focus my beliefs about people and about history; it simultaneously explained the feeling that something was wrong and that humans were at bottom cooperative, rational, and equal, and it allowed me to project these feelings into a history to be deciphered not only as a story of human and technical development, but of oppression and uneven progress in overcoming it. My new sense of coherence, of understanding, of purpose, of being part of the new world in the making was dazzling.

Adhering to Marxism turned around my entire being, and I soon found its analogue in Plato's description of the process of discovering the Good in the *Republic*. I had been preparing myself for it, I pursued it eagerly, even while being keenly aware of the paradox—which Marcuse would never let us forget—that Marxism was the theory of a practice absent from the United States. Still, no other theory covered as many bases or went as deep. If it would take another two years before I would be ready to move into political activity, I was aware that this Marxism that joined itself to all of human history, and built on the entire prior movement of Western thought from the Greeks through the Enlightenment and Hegel, located me in the midst of a world-historical process. Even its isolation from current American political reality was momentarily an advantage for me, because for the moment I was urgently drawing my internal grounding from these new philosophical, historical, and moral bearings.

Marxism spoke to my feeling that something was wrong with the life that lay ahead. By joining me to a deeper, truer mainstream and helping me find my own purposes, it gave point to my studies, nurtured my ambitions without seeming to, sharpened my sense of critique, and promised me something to write about. In retrospect I see that I might have been more skeptical, perhaps submitting Marxist tenets to a stringent analysis; what, for example, became of the theory of proletarian revolution without a revolutionary proletariat? But I *felt* Marxism focusing my experience, needs, and longings, and *felt* it providing the outlook I had been searching for. Conversions are like that.

At this decisive moment in becoming an adult, I shaped myself as an oppositionist in a world that now made sense, explaining the evils I hoped one day to participate in changing. It was a powerful synthesis. My vision of the future stretched backward in time to the beginnings of human life and spanned the earth, encompassing the universal processes of industrialization, imperialism, capitalism, and socialism. I absorbed all this as value, as moral commitment, more than as idea. "What shall I do?" became tied to understanding and in turn to morality, history, and the hopes of the entire human race, as expressed in philosophy and literature, and to knowing that one day I would act on it.

Stressing that the proletariat had not succeeded in creating socialism as Marx had anticipated, Marcuse spoke of the countervailing mechanisms used by capitalism to avert crisis, especially imperialism, monopoly, welfare reforms, and the warfare state. Marxism had become embodied in the Soviet Union in a way that distorted and transformed its promise, but this was no accident of history, and no willful betrayal. The source of Soviet deformation was the failed revolution in the West, which imposed upon a backward country the task of finding its way to socialism alone and without support.

In his own books, never discussed in class but read on our own, Marcuse tried to explain capitalism's stabilization and its consequences with reference to Freudian theory, the Bolshevik Revolution, and consumer society. Unlike his colleagues Theodor Adorno and Max Horkheimer, Marcuse continued to insist on the prospect of human liberation, even if no agency was demanding it, and continued to search for those who could make that hope real. Marx's own eschatological vision, he told us, was no longer radical enough: the actual capacities of advanced industrial society far exceed any emancipation Marx might have imagined.

In this sense he gave us Marxism through post-Marxist eyes. History, he argued, had made many major Marxist categories obsolete without abolishing rulers or ruled, capitalists or working class. Capitalism overcame Marx's predictions of massive crisis by creating a system able to deliver the goods to those who mattered most at its center, visiting its terrors on those on its margins. Yet Marcuse doubted that this was temporary: the change in the consciousness of the working class pointed to a change in its *being*. Thus in place of "exploitation" Marcuse spoke of "domination" and "repression," instead of "class interests," "particular interests," while the various "ruling classes" became "forces." In this process, the burden of opposition shifted from the industrial working class to outsiders, who now represented the expanded possibilities for human liberation and called down upon themselves the full fury of the forces seeking to contain it.

Through these changes, in the advanced industrial societies Marxian theory had been deprived of the practice that once gave it its historical force. If it was no longer, as Marx announced even before shaping Marxism, "the work of our time to clarify to itself [critical philosophy] the meaning of its own struggle and its own desires,"[2] theory now had a more desperate function: to "recall and preserve historical possibilities which seem to have become utopian possibilities."[3] Recall and preserve: Marcuse left us with the task of demanding and protecting the space for conceiving root-and-branch opposition, even if no such opposition currently existed. Would workers one day return to the possibility of seeing and contesting the system? Or had capitalism evolved well beyond such a possibility—had Marxism become obsolete? Marcuse verged on such a conclusion but avoided pronouncing it definitively.

In the early 1960s such a perspective did not yet speak openly about a historical dialectic within which Marxism had occurred, but that led beyond Marxism and toward the explosion of *contemporary* contradictions. In other words, it did not point to new nonproletarian forms of action, although it confirmed a profoundly sharp sense and suffocating mood of alienation. If Marcuse gave us the logic of that alienation, he did not encourage the activist impulse in his descriptions of a closing universe, of declining possibilities, of a hopeless hope, of socialism returning to utopia.

Thus we learned Marxism as agnostics, as skeptics, able to use it without even the hint of confidence in how history was turning out. Flexibility and subtlety came to be self-consciously built into this theory without a practice. It was also clear that Marxism could not be used to explain everything—it only went deeply into certain areas and scanned the main lines, and in Marcuse's hands became part of a larger way of explaining the entire process of civilization, tied as well to Freudian theory and to the great tradition of Western aesthetics. Thus universalized, Marxism even explained our hopelessness. Pointing to no action, it described our situation, elucidating the workings of the world with impressive reach and depth, and confirming our own impasse.

Still, its decisive predicament was that this theory called for the unity of theory and practice and was unable to offer it. It was presented to us with the pain of its incompleteness, as self-consciously lacking. As it was given, as I absorbed it, it had a hole at its center. History had split theory from practice. But how, logically, could I accept a Marxism that contradicted its own essence as a project of societal transformation? How could I say, "I am a Marxist," when I knew that my very commitment was a kind of internal contradiction? How could I be a Marxist if I couldn't even imagine proletarian revolution?

I nevertheless became a Marxist in 1962 and remained so for thirty years. No matter how sophisticated my Marxism seemed to be, in embracing it I absorbed less skeptical and more optimistic beliefs *between the lines.* Hidden even from my own conscious processes of thought —and thus always capable of causing confusion since they motivated me but vanished under scrutiny—were a series of powerful beliefs that informed my experience but were not drawn from it. Between the lines I acquired the faith that objective forces beyond my or anyone's control were persevering toward human emancipation; that this was promised by the authority of the founding fathers of Marxism and their disciples, such as Marcuse; that at the end of this process human existence would be wholly transformed. Progress, liberation, all based on scientific authority: between the lines of the most skeptical and open Marxism, even against it, I absorbed a belief in history with a capital "H," based on theory with a capital "T."

One basis for my faith was that Marxism was being practiced elsewhere: distortedly in the Soviet Union, but we had that country to thank for our Marxist texts; under conditions of anti-imperialist and anticolonial struggle in places like Cuba and Vietnam, in creative applications; in movements seeking to transform less advanced industrial societies such as Italy, that might educate us about our own possibilities. And soon an even more powerful historical current would sustain my Marxism: our own political activism. In a sense, having absorbed his analysis and the force of the Marxian promise, it was against Marcuse, the Marcuse of *One-Dimensional Man,* that we developed our hope and our action, for the sake of our own survival in the totalitarian universe he had described. The answer was, always, to act, to resist, and to create and find centers of resistance. In other words, we had to provide the practice that the theory called for, by ourselves if necessary, and then to extend the theory to explain the practice. Embracing such a Marxism, however it had come to decisively diverge from practice, did not cause despair but rather stirred us to fulfill the promise we absorbed between its lines—by challenging the system.

The Movement

I remember lying by the radio in in our apartment in Highland Park, New Jersey, one night in late 1964, listening to the WBAI account of the Free Speech Movement in Berkeley. The room was dark, and the radio brought into my life the news of its next turning point. After a two-year period of theoretical incubation at Brandeis, my radicalism joined that of other students, who were acting by the thousands. I recall hearing the account of the police dragging them from Sproul Hall, hearing about their heads banging against the stairs as the police pulled them down. I was infuriated by the police violence, awed by the commitment of my brothers and sisters. Yes, brothers and sisters: I was discovering my people. More than anything, I responded with solidarity and love. They were in California and I was three thousand miles away, but for the first time in my life, I belonged to a movement. The heads banging—did I hear them or did a reporter simply talk about them? Since then it seems, always, as if I hear them banging down the stairs. The sound crystallized my anger at the hypocritical system, my admiration for my comrades' commitment, my desire to be with them. Odd though it may seem, those banging heads were my first political image of hope.

Joining "the Movement" completed the process of conversion begun at Brandeis. Hope involved understanding and commitment, but also action with others. Thus began a lifelong career as a political activist, intimately bound up with a career as a political intellectual. My activist career started with community organizing in New Jersey, and continued with deep involvement in the Movement until it collapsed after 1970. I remained active in one political group after another throughout the 1970s, and then agitated on behalf of Israeli–Palestinian peace and against apartheid in the 1980s and even into the 1990s. Keeping groups alive, organizing meetings, attending demonstrations, writing newspaper articles, stuffing envelopes, giving speeches, leading and participating in study groups: these forms of activism became part of my life in 1965 and have remained so ever since. Then, as now, hope was inseparable from action.

But action on behalf of what? Ultimately I it was motivated by a sense of right and wrong. I *believed* that all people were created equal. How then could those who unctuously intoned such phrases defend a system that made them unequal? A lower middle-class drive to be as good as those above me fused with anger that the children of workers could be destined for even lower rungs on the social ladder than myself, blacks yet lower, and women beneath any men of the same class and race. Blaming the system rather than the victims, it was marvelous to find myself amidst people who agreed, and who were ready to fight.

In the mid-1960s, many of us who began as Marxists and completed our identity in the Movement did not yet hope to change the system. We drew hope simply from standing up and discovering ourselves acting together. In the black ghetto of New Brunswick, New Jersey, a group of us, mostly graduate students, set up a small office in a former kosher meat market, knocked on doors, talked with people about their problems, held meetings, and organized demonstrations against the city administration. We were relating to blacks as outsiders; a newspaper called me "the bearded boy" from Highland Park, across the Raritan River. We were political missionaries to the ghetto, but we organized around *their* problems, helped them develop *their* movement. We had long conversations, developed friendships, and came to love and respect people who showed enormous courage and political sense.

I had been raised both to fear blacks and to identify with them; now I overcame the fear with a rush of pleasure, sharing my days with people who confirmed my fervent sense of equality. I'm not sure what sense of possibility less theoretical activists felt during the early days of the New Left, but as a Marxist I was convinced that what we were doing remained far from the possibility of real social transformation. Yet I did it anyway—eagerly, desperately; and in so doing the Movement confirmed and deepened the hopes that Marxism had focused for me, that ordinary human beings could take charge of their own fate, could act on behalf of, and would flourish in, a genuinely equal society. These people did not deserve to be poor.

I felt strongly the gap between the theory that led me to act and the actions themselves. This was the substance of my very first published article in *Studies on the Left*, "The Movement and Its Critics," in which I stressed the core problem within which the New Left created itself: a theory without a movement, a movement without a theory. As a Marxist doing community organizing in a northern ghetto, I explored the tension between these poles in a situation where theory was not confirmed by practice, nor practice by theory. I tried to depict the mutual irrelevance and incomprehension of Marxist theory on the one hand and Civil Rights organizing efforts on the other, stressing the Movement's consequent moralism and anti-intellectualism. I also tried to explain why some Marxist intellectuals had to criticize the Movement, but why the problems they criticized stemmed from the Movement's situation itself.[4]

The Movement lacked a theory in the Marxian sense because of the socioeconomic location of those who were being organized: as members of residential communities in northern ghettos, for example, they were denied a grasp of root economic institutions and relations of power, even though they might protest against undemocratic and unresponsive political systems. Remaining remote from revolutionary political possibilities, Movement organizers were unable to develop long-range goals, analysis, and strategy. They could not even develop *in themselves* a genuinely radical political consciousness. This situation displaced future revolutionary longings onto the present, leading to utopian community building and agonizing over the "manipulation" of those being organized.[5]

How to resolve the mutual incomprehension between Marxist theoreticians and Movement activists? I tried to show the concerns of each to the other. Locating myself simultaneously in both camps, I ended my first article with a Marcusean reading of our achievement and limits: until the Movement could see the connections between its "gut reactions" and the socioeconomic structure, I wrote, "many of us shall continue to organize, to reject and oppose the system. Obviously we shall be doing it more for personal and moral reasons than because of objective possibilities of success. At least the possibility—and dignity—of opposition has been reborn."[6] What I had discovered by 1965 was the possibility of acting if not yet of succeeding, and I embraced this.

Looking beyond Marxism, Looking toward Marxism

As a result of that first essay, in 1966 I became an editor of *Studies on the Left*. I had discovered that my graduate study mattered, that theory mattered. My ambitions began to be satisfied in the Movement; and so I continued to push my Marcusean reflections further. The structural inability of the movements to sight the systemic roots of the problems we were battling against turned on another fact, namely, that by and large the American working class was politically passive. At what point did we have to conclude that this long-term passivity was permanent? And if so, what became of Marxism? I wrote, again in *Studies on the Left*, that without its orientation toward practice, historical materialism was no more than a guide for social analysis."[7] What we needed, I argued, was a "post-Marxian" analysis that focused on American capitalism's "current and emerging opponents. The conclusions and prescriptions of earlier social theory must be changed as the society itself changes, and so Marxism can hardly be passed as doctrine from generation to generation."[8] Insisting on the unity of theory and practice, I maintained that however valid and historically relevant Marxian theory may have once been, "events have passed it by. While much of its method and analysis remain pertinent, it has, as revolutionary social theory, become irrelevant."[9] And during this time new radical movements had emerged.

The point was not that Marx or Marxism had been wrong, but that advanced capitalist society's ability to provide a previously unimaginable standard of living to key sectors of the working class had undermined the traditional revolutionary role of the proletariat, and as a result posed a number of new questions. What are the possibilities for revolution in an advanced industrial society? Is material need the only radical need? What social dynamic made possible the rise of the New Left? Is American society shaped by an underlying socioeconomic structure, or has the process become inverted insofar as the control of consciousness is necessary to sustain production?[10]

I quote at length from the final section of this 1967 article, "Reply to Oscar Berland," because of its sharp sense of the limits of contemporary Marxist commitment, its hope for the New Left, and its call for a new post-Marxian theory to account for and illuminate it. Above all, I have not improved on it.

A new revolutionary theory will never be built without first facing the consequences of the historical changes in American capitalism and the American working class. That is, Marxists must begin by facing themselves and their own irrelevance. This would mean, for example, taking seriously the fact that current radical politics has virtually nothing to do with the working class, and less to do with socialism. Socialists or

Marxists may be active, even in key leadership positions, but hardly because they are working for socialism. However they may understand the workings of the American economy and the general movements of current history, Marxists can hardly claim to be engaged in socialist activity. The objective economic and political conditions for such activity do not exist.

No doubt it is possible to admit the apparent internal stability and the quiescence of the American working class and yet continue to call oneself a Marxist. This is precisely what most of us do. But what does it mean? Certainly it reflects our intellectual orientation, our analysis of American society, and our personal desire for socialism. But being a Marxist today in the United States has little more objective political meaning than being an existentialist. It is not a political identity, but a personal one. With the decline of a working class movement, Marxists have lost their connection within the only historical force that can give political meaning to their commitments. Socialism in America has become a question of personal conviction, a belief in what is good and right, identification with the revolutionary forces overseas, but no more than this.

The mistake is to make it more, to identify personal commitment with historical necessity. If one wishes to remain a Marxist in America, and presumes this to be more than an act of personal faith or commitment to a set of analytical principles, it is necessary to separate theory from practice, to minimize the now meaningless concepts of Marxism and so distort its meaning. Thus the Marxist can continue to write and read articles, to give and listen to talks, to criticize and claim to guide political activity—without facing for a moment the nature of his abstract and unhistorical commitment to a socialism without a proletariat, without seeing that he represents only a theory and not an objective historical force.

By mistaking his personal commitment to socialism for a real historical trend, the Marxist can view his role as making Americans "see the relevance" of socialism, as working to bring about "socialist consciousness"—whatever that might mean at a time when proletarian class consciousness no longer exists. Although the class whose exploitation and strategic relationship to the means of production made it the agency for revolutionary change is solidly "in" the system, socialism is still taken for granted as the "right" and "necessary" goal of radical political activity. To thus assume socialism, to confuse one's personal commitment with historical necessity is, after all, to be unhistorical. It is to regress to a Platonic conception of a political vision formulated apart from present historical currents and then applied to reality. If we have read Marx, we should know better.

Now to face these facts is to admit we are at zero. It is to realize our political irrelevance. We may understand a great deal, but little of it is related to the actual prospect for a movement. Only by seeing this can we ask the questions which matter most today. Not, "How do we spread our view?" and "How do we create socialist consciousness?" but rather,

"Is socialism historically relevant any more?" and "How does the concept of socialism make sense without being rooted in the producing classes?" If our theory is committed to practice, if we are, after all, revolutionary historical materialists, we must face the long-range tendencies, contradictions and possibilities of *this* society—and not one corresponding to the categories of classical Marxism.

No doubt this appears to be a flat and uninspiring conclusion. It offers no insight into how socialism might be relevant, not even the hint of a new theory for a new movement. I have argued for Marxism's irrelevance and said that we have no objective political basis for a commitment to socialism. This is a negative analysis, but being positive in this situation is to be dishonest. It is to perpetuate illusions. It is to avoid entering the uncertain process of reconstituting our identity.[11]

With this last remark I proposed a step beyond the tension between theory and practice that I had been living in my own political work. I advocated a reexamination of both Marxism and capitalism as Marx described it that looked to the transformations of the second for indications of necessary alterations in the first, with an eye toward understanding theoretically and clarifying the nature and positions of the New Left and its possibilities. This proposal had come from my absorption of Marxism through the eyes of Marcuse: beginning with the historical–materialist dialectic that led to capitalism and the proletariat, exploring how the exploitative, profit-centered economic basis of social life pushed *beyond* that stage, tracing its further evolution, its new contradictions, and its generating of new grave diggers. The new activism would find its theory in a historical materialism that went beyond Marxism, yet kept alive its tenets. I remained optimistic that a historical dialectic was propelling us toward liberation. I still placed the socioeconomic realm at the center, still saw capital and its pursuit of profit as the driving social force, even if capital it now led to unanticipated conflicts and contradictions: mine would be a thoroughly historical–materialist post-Marxism.

Applied rigorously, such a historical–materialist critique of Marxism would lay to rest its very hopes for proletarian revolution, abandoning a primary commitment to the working class. A project that began within Marxism led beyond it, pointing to its obsolescence. And I could say so because I was part of *another* movement, a New Left emerging in response to contemporary American capitalism's current contradictions: its inability to solve the problems bequeathed it by slavery, its imperialist interventions overseas, and its need for the Cold War. With ideas like these—some drawn from theoretical reflection on my own experience—why did I still call myself a Marxist? A central reason for retaining this label lay in the fact that I was making use of Marxist tools to explain the non-working-class character of the New Left.

In an article I wrote with John Cowley for *The Socialist Register*, "The

New Left in the United States" (1967), we stressed the ideological character of consumer capitalism. Its imposition of a one-dimensional society, we argued, is necessary to convince people to buy goods that they don't really need, resulting in a struggle over every individual's consciousness.[12] The New Left was a natural response to capitalism containing its contradictions by displacing them onto other levels. In short, we maintained that as long as exploitation and oppression continue, a dialectic of oppression and resistance will continue, even in changed forms. If the working class was contained and bypassed, we believed, this historical process would produce other agents of change.

Accepting this dialectic implied shifting from the centrality of workers' oppression and, eventually, insisting that the oppression experienced by relatively privileged white students was no less important than anyone else's. Not self-evident at first, this went against Old Left dedication to the workers. Our own political initiation had come through joining the black struggle for equality, which was far from the point of production. Accepting its legitimacy, acknowledging that there was no radical workers' movement, led to seeing that our rebellion was not only on behalf of blacks and Vietnamese, but also *on our own* behalf.

The Movement's growth was astonishing, but even as it seemed to lead away from Marxist tenets, its very existence anchored my Marxism. First, because many activists shared a Marxist starting point. Second, because we were inspired by, and linked with, an increasingly worldwide movement. If we were struggling on our own behalf, we could equally point to, and connect ourselves with, Marxist revolutions overseas, notably in Vietnam and Cuba, and Marxist workers' movements, notably in Italy and France. Indeed, the line between wanting American troops out of Vietnam and ending that obscene war, and supporting the Vietnamese Communists, was a line crossed by many of us. Vietnamese Marxism, and the conditions of its struggle, were drastically different from our movement, particularly because we were living in the most advanced of industrial societies, while they were still struggling against imperialism. But we were all part of the same revolutionary spiral.

The *bad* socialism and *distorted* Marxism practiced in various countries around the world nevertheless lay within the universe of socialism and Marxism, and held out promise that the real thing was possible. If the Soviet Union (because, against Marx's anticipations, it had applied Marxism to a largely preindustrial country) had constructed a deformed socialism, many of us hoped that it might evolve into a more truly egalitarian system, and might one day become the democratic and bountiful society we dreamed of *in the name of Marxism*. We knew that as critical intellectuals, we would not survive there at present, nor in Cuba, China, or Vietnam. But all of these governments proclaimed themselves as Marxist, which inclined the loyalties of many of us toward them as the American atmosphere became increasingly polarized. We knew that the official Vietnamese, Cuban, Soviet, and Chinese Marxism usually had the character of rote and dogma. But we also knew the Vietnamese and Cubans were under siege, building socialism under the near-impossible conditions imposed by our own government. As activists we sided with them, often publicly apologizing for (and privately criticizing) their distortions of socialism. We expected that throughout the Soviet world there were many people like ourselves, not in open opposition, of course, but at least reading the real texts, seeing their revolutionary potential, and waiting for their moment. Accordingly, we undertook countless hours of studying and alternately justifying, explaining, and criticizing the Communist societies.

Their Marxism–Leninism belonged either to the conditions of underdevelopment or to a previous revolutionary generation, that of 1917. For the worldwide New Left 1968 was our 1917. Nothing was more appropriate, in this great year of the New Left, than its variety of political expressions: from the Tet Offensive to ghetto rebellions, from the Prague Spring to the Red Guards, from the Columbia University sit-in to May in Paris. Everywhere, not only at the protests against the Democratic Convention in Chicago in August, the whole world was watching. I passed my Ph.D. orals at Brandeis in April, was active at Columbia University in May and June, watched in horror as Martin Luther King and Robert Kennedy were killed in April and June and as the Soviet tanks rumbled into Prague in August, and moved back home to Detroit in that same month to begin teaching at Wayne State University and to plunge into its cauldron of political activity.

The hope for revolutionary change seemed to have ignited the entire world, and Marxists of my generation could not help but see this as validating our theorizing. Indeed, the various radical currents seemed to be the tangible proof of a half-century of unorthodox Marxism and critiques of capitalism: those of Lukacs, Gramsci, Adorno, Horkheimer, Marcuse, and Sartre. The worldwide movement, with its explosion in the United States and France and flaming in Italy and Germany, its brief moment of a new kind of communism in Prague and even, it seemed, in Peking, pointed toward an open Marxism that would liberate even the neo-Stalinist societies themselves.

No longer a single coherent, indeed, mandated doctrine, Marxism as a set of complex, overlapping, vital currents had become *the* outlook of opposition: in its many forms, it inspired the various Communisms, the youth of Paris, the New Lefts of Britain and Italy, workers' control in Yugoslavia, and tens of thousands of young Americans, including those streaming into Detroit in solidarity with its black working class in response to the 1967 Rebellion and to organize among the white trade union rank and file. The theoretical and activist flowering included the old, doctrinaire Communist Marxism, various dialectical anti-orthodox yet still Leninist or proletarian Marxisms, and Marcusean and other New Left theories focusing on recent trends in capitalism. As a broad oppositional mood Marxism was manifestly a living political force, even though there was still no radical working-class movement in the United States. Here it accounted for youth rebellion, there workers' movements; here it inspired anti-imperialist peace movements, there anticolonial revolutions.

We became swept up in the sense of possibility we had helped create, even against the basic fact that most white American factory workers remained politically passive throughout the 1960s, and some became supporters of the Vietnam War, hostile to the student movement and counterculture, and supporters of racist reaction. Not all white American workers took this stance, of course; we exulted at the militancy of teachers and social workers, for example, and defined ourselves as radicalized members-in-preparation of the "new working class." As the Civil Rights movement became the black movement, and as that movement became increasingly radical, large numbers of blacks also found their way to Marxism. This was clearest in Detroit, with its Dodge Revolutionary Union Movement (DRUM) and its various other RUMs, especially during the intense period (1968–1969) when Wayne State's student newspaper, *The South End*, becoming the mouthpiece for these black Marxists, was handed out at factory gates emblazoned with the slogan "One class-conscious worker is worth a hundred students."

We applauded ingenious analyses of how the black working class, centrally located in key industries and increasingly radicalized, was going to become the strategic agent of revolutionary change. And we cheered as further radicalization did happen, often causing explosive tension at workplaces and in unions. Furthermore, we kept up links with those who went into the factories, hopeful that white as well as black workers might catch hold of the electricity sweeping the country. Indeed, didn't many working-class whites begin to grow their hair long, and smoke marijuana; and didn't all of us listen to the same music? Whether or not American capitalism's downfall would be the exclusive work of the working class, it was certainly producing revolutionaries, even among workers, many of whom called themselves Marxists. If some of our experiences and ideas pointed beyond Marxism during these years, across the world, in the United States, and perhaps above all in Detroit, the Petrograd of the coming American revolution, there were strong reasons for remaining within it.

Liberation of the Self

For a period my strongest preoccupations were the kinds of "liberation" everyone was talking about in the late 1960s and early 1970s, as we followed our impulses and again and again challenged and crossed lines that we had always thought impassable, as we sought immediately to translate our ideas into experience. We lived with the sense of adventure, of becoming new, of violating traditional barriers and in doing so of discovering ourselves. At Wayne State we closed the university in May 1970, but were unable to build sustainable structures to capitalize on the explosion. Convinced that the "personal was political," I focused much of my energy on my teaching at Wayne State University's Monteith College, and on my efforts to transform my personal life in keeping with new possibilities.

The energy of the time combined with my own experience, between 1965 and 1968, of having been in psychoanalytic psychotherapy in New York. If Marcuse's *Eros and Civilization* had given me theoretical warrant for dealing with personal conflicts, other pressing needs—a full-time college teaching job, the strains of marriage, increasing political involvement, the writing of my dissertation—made it necessary. Like many other new activists, I worried that this pursuit of self would lead me away from the political–intellectual project that was increasingly becoming the center of my life. My therapist, however, turned out to have been a member of the Abraham Lincoln Brigade and of the Communist Party, and still saw himself as a radical; he encouraged my activism. I'll never forget him giving me survival advice when I had blundered into a crisis by defiantly opening my classroom to two suspended student radicals where I was teaching in 1966, or actively supporting me during a controversial presentation of "Dear Herbert" at the Socialist Scholars Conference three years later. As I slowly, painstakingly labored to identify and understand my own feelings, he stressed that "weak egos will never overthrow capitalism," fueling my drive to integrate the personal and the political.

I became convinced that more and better theory was less important than integrating existing theory with our emotions, than looking into our experience and seeing the structures of oppression there, along with the paths to liberation. If workers and blacks were oppressed in specific ways, it stood to reason that middle-class white people like myself would be oppressed in our own equally systemic ways. Just as analyses like *Capital* illuminated workers' experience of oppression under capitalism, so did we need to develop ways of throwing light on *our* experience, without being shy about the personal, emotional, or psychological dimensions. Thus when I encountered Women's Liberation in 1969, I was almost immediately sympathetic to it—not only for its insistence on women's freedom and equality, but also because of its determination to begin with personal experience, to talk about other forms of oppression than those of workers, blacks, and colonial peoples.

For many of us the women's movement confirmed our sense of how deep and widespread was the oppression we were fighting against. It encouraged many of our efforts to live differently, to become different. Along these lines, some of the central new themes spawned by the women's movement included: being true to what one feels, integrating thought and feeling, and neither being nor bowing to external authority. In the summer of 1968, after the

Columbia sit-in, I led a workshop at the "Liberation School" the intent of which was to continue and deepen the movement; my goal was to show the connection between long-suppressed feelings and our emerging grasp of oppression and liberation. I continued these explorations after moving back to Detroit. If feelings carried a unique kind of truth, I realized, this should allow space in our political deliberations for those not skilled in traditional forms of radical discourse, and should encourage exploring nonintellectual forms of political action, such as guerilla theatre.

As an activist young professor I grappled, painfully, torturously, with my role as authority in the classroom, at first trying to use it to promote emancipatory learning, then questioning it to the point of turning the classroom over to my students. I remember one meeting of all the students and faculty in Humanistic Studies at the end of the semester, assembled during class time to report on what the different sections had done. For my colleagues this separation of our large class into student-defined interest groups had already been a major concession to the spirit of the time; my own students carried it much further. Having spent the term exploring nonintellectual paths to liberation, they decided to "turn the lecture hall into a musical instrument," drumming and singing their way around the bemused crowd to celebrate and share their spirit of liberation. As I discovered when it came time for my tenure decision, some of my colleagues never forgave me.

This was just one kind of experiment during these years. The air we breathed was filled with political experiments, experiments in communal living, experiments with sexual freedom, with drugs, with dropping out, and with an intense preoccupation with liberating ourselves in the here and now. In the process, theory took on a bad name: wasn't it an effort to guide people from above, another form of authority? After all, weren't people capable of figuring out on their own what to do, if they could only recognize and move beyond patterns of thought that had been imposed by the system in order to keep them out of touch with themselves, with their needs, with their bodies, with their feelings? In response to this mood and to the Summerhill vogue, my belief that humans intuitively *want* equality, democracy, and solidarity became yet more simplistic: I explored the idea that, freed from the distortion of unnatural institutions (which functioned to impose privilege and hierarchy), humans will also find the paths leading to the realization of these ideals.

But after being attracted to it by my own desire to integrate thought and feelings, I was frustrated by my students' desire to avoid rational thought altogether. And I still felt responsible for what went on in my classrooms, which remained mine no matter what I consented to let the students do. I eventually assumed authority consciously and deliberately. Nor did I abandon Marxism or theorizing about our situation. But the new work I envisioned followed the spirit of Marcuse's *Essay on Liberation* and Murray

Bookchin's *Listen, Marxist!* and was to be called "The Anarchist Manifesto." It would be antitheoretical theory, tracing the historical–materialist dialectic that was generating these new movements to transform our existence. In so doing it would reconcile our anarchist impulse, our concern for personal liberation, our transcendance of Marxism's basic class premises, with our respect for the Marxian synthesis and the heritage of Marxism. This was, after all, the dialectic of advanced capitalism, pointing to a *directly* universal liberation beyond the class liberation Marx wrote about, taking in all social and individual spheres. Wasn't it happening, inside us, between us, all around us?

Thus I had written of my revolutionary politics in 1969 in "Dear Herbert," which caused a sensation at the Socialist Scholars Conference that September:

> It's not my politics that are at stake, or my ideas. My whole being is at stake. My experience is of being lost in the smiling sick sea and of needing to wrench myself out step by step; my goal is to avoid and destroy all of *Their* categories in my life, to live joyously, to reject bullshit in all its disguises, to let America have none of myself, to get whole and to become a guerilla.[13]

In this essay, denounced on the front page of *Barron's* in September 1969, I spoke of coming of age in the consumer society, and responding by demanding a "total break with America" as a means of psychic survival. I spoke of coming to one's own deepest needs and feelings—becoming oneself—as a radical process that, repeated millions of times, would lead to a revolutionary transformation demanding a new way of life, "in working, in loving, in thinking, in feeling, in eating, in joking."[14]

Being radical meant no more than being oneself, but also no less. Whether stemming from the larger society or the Left, oppression meant being separated from oneself—alienation. The Movement's pressures to deny oneself were to be combated no less than those coming from the society it was fighting. My targets convey the flavor of the times:

> Not only bourgeois morality oppresses, but any morality which imposes oughts from outside. Not only the bourgeois contempt for ignorance, but the radical reliance on a higher culture. Not only the bourgeois domination of feeling by reason, but the radical insistence on the priority of theory, the correct position. Not only the middle-class role-playing is oppressive, but accepting any kind of role, even the role of radical intellectual. I have become revolutionary because America, while willing to sell me everything, won't let me be myself. Should I give up any part of myself in order to oppose America?[15]

Thus did I construct a theoretical justification for the kind of life-style anarchism that was to permeate the Movement of the late 1960s and early 1970s, the personal explorations that insisted they were political. It was a first effort to carry out the project I had called for earlier, of developing a radical theory anchored in the present. I paralleled this theory with Marxism's description of the experience of capitalism. Its facts, such as hunger amidst plenty and business cycles, hit with self-evident force. Today, however, many people can deny their oppression.

> If your survival needs are met well and you can keep busy, self-deception is possible in a way that it's not if you're hungry. America keeps going as everyone draws a veil over his own life. If so, to show the truth is no longer merely to locate the structures behind what everyone admits to be a problem, but rather to tear away the veil.
> Yet the veils don't hide only the system—they hide each and every one of us from ourselves. And each of us distorts his experience in a different way, according to his own particular situation. Because of this peculiar historical situation a critique of America which tries to get inside the key place where it affects us must first be personal. It must begin as a series of attempts to reveal the different kinds of experience possible in America. The opposite of remoteness: talking about ourselves. And since tearing away the veil is hardly a matter of convincing people's intellects, revolutionary thought must engage the whole person: his feeling, his imagination, his sense of being lost. Not only tracing the structure of capitalism, but also blowing people's minds. Disrupting, shattering, springing people loose: we need to be personal, poetic, disturbing. To make people want liberation.[16]

This was my version of what so many of us were doing at the time. There were efforts to talk about "youth as a class," to describe the "new working class," and to situate anti-imperialism, the peace movement, the black movement, feminism, the student movement, and cultural and sexual liberation—including rock music and the drug culture—all in relation to our only truly comprehensive theory, Marxism. Staying within it insofar as we insisted on developing a historical–materialist dialectic, we went beyond Marxism to the degree that the dialectic led us to abandon the primacy of class and a specifically working-class revolution.

From the Beatles to the youth culture, from the peace marchers to the ghetto rebellions, from gay liberation to feminism, we were *all* responding to the new potentialities humans had created, but that were contained within an advanced capitalist society. I wanted to unite all these levels with a world-historical perspective and a revolutionary purpose, a project in keeping with Marxism but going beyond it because of the emphasis on making the personal political. The coherence of this New Left project was exhilarating and exhausting, integrating all aspects of life—be they child rearing, leisure, lovemaking, or political activity—giving high seriousness and purpose to even the most inconsequential distraction. We justified politics as psychotherapy, psychotherapy as politics, guerilla theater as revolutionary praxis, and self-revelation as social change. I was to practice every one of these, all with a sense of revolutionary purpose.

But I never wrote the full-scale manifesto that would have spelled all this out. Those I was closest to simply weren't interested in the theoretical project in the first place, or if they were, they rejected these thoughts as anarchistic. Moreover, my own drive to theorize the need to get beyond theory was ambivalent. And the Movement began to dissipate. If some of my concerns remained relevant for several years, most eventually lost their force and point. Against the fact that the Movement was losing steam, it was difficult to find the heart to construct a new all-embracing theory. The problem was that the Movement's dialectic of liberation seemed to be grinding to a halt.

Setback and Victory

My awareness of this was delayed. I was turned down for tenure at Wayne State University in 1973, and then mounted, with close friends and political comrades and by means of our chapter of the American Association of University Professors (AAUP), an all-absorbing struggle to reverse the decision. The struggle came naturally to us, and we relied on the fact that I had been deeply involved in teaching courses to graduates of the university's Labor School. Political discrimination *had* to be the reason for my being turned down: my Marxism, my activism, and my support for labor, women's, and Chicano programs. One of the courses, a seminar on Marxism, was attended by a number of trade unionists, more than one of whom later became national labor leaders; one of these students now helped me make contact with local labor figures. In addition, a United Automobile Workers (UAW) activist from another class complained to the UAW Education Department about my being denied tenure, and after an interview at Solidarity House, I received their support.

Collective bargaining had just begun at Wayne State, and the AAUP immediately involved itself in my case. We filed a grievance which, combined with a campaign that included student rallies and political pressures, resulted in my winning grievance hearings in the summer of 1974. The arbitrator decided that my First Amendment rights had been violated. It came out that one of the letters from a colleague in my department made explicit mention of my "Marxist politics"; another well-known anti-Communist made veiled Cold War references to "political orthodoxy." The arbitrator paused over these remarks to indicate that while these raised First Amendment issues, their relevance had been denied by all who opposed me. But, in denying that they turned me down because of my personal politics, key people involved in the decision spoke freely about opposing my commitments to programs for blacks, labor, women, and Chicanos, clearly a violation of First Amendment rights.

As a result, the President reopened my case, sent my writings to colleagues at another university for review, and promised the restless members of the Board of Governors—which after the 1974 elections now included both the student leader of my struggle and a longtime UAW activist—that a positive evaluation would lead to granting tenure. In January 1975, the President received a strongly positive evaluation, and I was immediately awarded tenure—after six months of unemployment and eighteen of struggle and misery. An open Marxist, I had won tenure at a large state university, with the decisive support of my own union as well as the city's major labor unions. It was the victory of a lifetime.

After the Movement

Although it was carried on in the name of the Movement, my intense struggle and ultimate success enabled me to ignore the Movement's disintegration until 1975. The one-dimensional society required by capitalism's evolution was no longer producing the sense of "one struggle, many fronts" that we had thrown ourselves into in the late 1960s and early 1970s. The mounting, slowly cohering, steadily radicalizing opposition stopped mounting, no longer cohered, and lost its radicalism. Local rebellions persisted, but remained local. Radical analysis interested fewer and fewer people who were not already radicals, and as a result it became less exploratory, drawing closer to original sources. The spread of opposition to various social groups at different sites, spiraling from Paris to Peking, to Prague, to American campuses, to ghettos, to kitchens, and to Washington, D.C., ground to a halt.

I remember what it felt like to realize that the Movement was fully and finally dead. Evenings, there was no place I *had* to go; daily, no organizing efforts for which I was responsible. The global demand that had shaped my life since the mid-1960s was gone. I was free from its pressure, no longer compelled to live by it—and yet I was alone. Although I had just been awarded tenure at Wayne State I felt a bit empty. I was a free agent. Directly connected to no historical force, in May 1975 I celebrated the fall of Saigon by myself, aware of contributing to it, able to share it only in passing with a few close friends. If I spoke of it as a world-historical victory, *our* victory, no one listened.

Within a year, with others, I organized the Detroit chapter of the New American Movement (NAM), gathering a number of activists together in an organization that we first called "revolutionary–democratic socialist," then "socialist–feminist." Many in the New Left had withdrawn from political activism entirely; others had joined various Marxist–Leninist organizations. But a broad current of deeply committed activists still saw ourselves as socialists and even Marxists, yet were not orthodox Marxist–Leninists. Two dozen old Leftists, old New Leftists, trade unionists, college instructors, students, social workers, and former VISTA volunteers came together in Detroit NAM.

On the one hand, we believed deeply in the "participation of all people in shaping their own lives and the direction of society."[17] On the other hand, we saw ourselves as the kind of more-or-less Marxists that I and others had been since the early 1960s. Marxism provided the best overall view of history, society, and our goals and tasks. It also linked us with movements overseas. If the U.S. industrial working class did not seem to be revolutionary, many in NAM hoped that our struggles would expand the meaning of the working class to include all of us, and that after the lull that class might ignite into radical consciousness and action.

Writing about our Marxism in a debate with Marxists–Leninists both within NAM and outside of it (specifically Irwin Silber, in the *Guardian* of October 15, 1975), I stressed our efforts to be faithful to the reality in which we had struggled rather than to the abstract "correct line" laid down by Leninism. If we were committed to democratic control, emancipatory politics, and the various movements from which we had sprung, it was clear that none of these ideas or movements stemmed from the working class acting as workers—neither the industrial working class nor the broader working class to which we all claimed to belong. I attacked Marxism–Leninism as a doctrinaire, religious, and indeed preposterous outlook, wholly out of touch with these realities. And I argued that our movement was far from traditional working-class concerns and issues.

I was still reconciling Marxism and a post-Marxian dialectic by arguing for a politics that *included* the working class but that also reached beyond its historical moment, an open, exploratory radicalism based on contemporary social reality:

> A new American movement for socialism will include people who see socialism as the answer to pollution of the atmosphere; who want to control the cancer-causing adulteration of our food; who demand the liberation of youth, who want, as blacks or Chicanos, their own autonomous political and social units; who demand an end to capitalist control of industry; who understand that to be themselves and become happy requires a new society; who insist on humanly designed living places and cities; who see the need to overthrow the influence of the automobile in our lives; who want to be freed from stultifying sex roles. And it will include many others—as workers, consumers, minority group members.[18]

The various movements of the 1960s and 1970s, the industrial working class, and the yet to be defined groups and movements, would together have to become a majority movement for a new kind of socialism. An essential feature of such a movement would be its freedom from the need to identify itself with a parental authority, such as that of Lenin or Marx. I returned to the theme of my very first article, arguing that becoming radicalized in relation to no particular ongoing socialist movement keeps unsatisfied many people's need for a sense of security and direction. To be tentative and open-ended when the situation calls for it can become too great a strain. Thus some found their way to Leninism—a clear, simple doctrine that offered security, even if it only barely corresponded to reality.

In local discussion papers within NAM I was attacked for "utopian socialism" and "anarchism," for "petit-bourgeois individualism," and for "substituting the fragmentary observations of bourgeois facticity for the historical dialectics of Marxism–Leninism." Marxism was still *the* defining pole, even if NAM was sufficiently commodious to accommodate both my version as well as versions of Marxism–Leninism. We were unable to bid farewell to Marxism and move on to another revolutionary theory because there was none that had even remotely equal force and coherence, and because some of us, like myself, had become preoccupied with enlarging Marxism to accommodate who we were, where we originated, and what we had experienced during the 1960s.

Was Marxism of any help in our day-to-day organizing and strategizing efforts? In NAM Marxism continued to give us a sense that we were going somewhere, that we were part of a larger, worldwide movement with a universal field of vision. It made day-to-day routine and setbacks tolerable. There was an obvious gap between theory and practice, but the tension it caused us stimulated both thought and action. And Marxism's concept of class provided to many a key for looking at our situation and our society: it gave point and direction to our analysis and explained important areas of our experience. The Marxism that seemed to be verging on obsolescence fifteen years earlier had achieved a powerful reality by the late 1970s—as *the world's* one uncontested revolutionary outlook, as explanatory tool, and, increasingly, as academically legitimate. As an activist group, many of whose members organized unions in their workplaces, we continued to give this theory practical life.

Through Marxism we thus had a common home in NAM. I continued to be drawn to the post-Marxist project I had begun earlier, but my own skills were needed to keep the organization going in a daily way and I was, after all, an expert on Marxism. My comrades wanted me to teach it to them, not to develop new theoretical directions. Thus, unlike my counterparts in the women's movement, I let slide my earlier theorizing and desire for more total change. I had lost much of the aggressive, self-confident spirit of ten years earlier, and instead let my thoughts move within the confines of Marxist theory, even where they clearly led beyond it. We were trying to cling together as a "socialist family" in the face of a more general collapse.

If most people had not even mastered the classics, I thought, how could I move beyond them? My comrades were certainly not going to read Marcuse before they had developed a working knowledge of Marxism and socialism. So we concentrated energies there, on learning from the solid body of basic theory. I recall teaching one session of our study group in which I challenged our members to name a single area of life that defied explanation by a historical–materialist analysis. They couldn't.

During this same time, I also turned to a more scholarly reflection on the relation of ideas to social reality in the work of Jean-Paul Sartre, and that project had its own highly demanding and absorbing logic. This did not involve the further exploration of post-Marxian possibilities—quite the opposite. The New Left had generated an enormous young, international constituency of Marxist activists and intellectuals, and we together had been exploring the various implications of our chosen worldview. In my case, analyzing Sartre's critique of and additions to Marxism involved, first, evaluating Sartre in Marxist terms—reasserting, against his perspective, the importance of theory. Second, it meant absorbing Sartre's insights. He argues that human beings make themselves, always and everywhere, even if it be under conditions they have not made. All social realities thus become internalized and reexteriorized as *projects*; all forms of oppression rest ultimately on the complicity of the oppressed. A worker accepts and internalizes the identity of worker, or else rebels against it: one *makes him- or herself* from what he or she has been made.

Placing such reflections within Marxism, as many of us were doing during these years, meant confirming theoretically what we had done in practice since the 1960s: removing mechanical determinism, making room for human spontaneity and intention. Whether human actions were socioeconomically conditioned "in the last instance," or unfolded within boundaries or parameters imposed by fundamental socioeconomic structures, or took place within a situation decisively shaped by class dynamics, we always sought to preserve the twin realities of self-determining human action and determination by the social system. Absorbing such outlooks as existentialism into Marxism expanded its capacity for intellectual and political understanding, permitting us to remain Marxists while stressing how far we were from the one-sided determinism of Communism's "dialectical materialism."

The 1980s

When, in our study group, I challenged anyone to come up with an area that defied historical–materialist explanation, I secretly feared that someone might. In the back of my mind I was not thinking about women's oppression, for example, because I felt sure *that* area of experience could be accommodated, but about other themes that were coming to dominate my life: hope, evil, my own jewishness. During the late 1970s my writing raised the question of hope for the first time. "Is there reason to hope today?" was intended as a provocation. Of course there was reason to hope, and my strategy was to get people to see how much human beings had accomplished toward humanizing the world. But I was unconsciously placing in question my very faith in humans and history—my Marxist faith. How can it be that humans—who, it must be assumed, ultimately want freedom, solidarity, and equality can produce the disasters of the twentieth century such as the Holocaust or Stalinism? What made possible these catastrophes? Is progress, even in Marxian dialectical terms, still a meaningful concept? Was it ever? Is socialism still possible? Was it ever? Little by little I became absorbed in what has turned out to be a life project: to explore whether and how hope is possible, after catastrophe, after progress, after Communism.

As a political organization, NAM slowly, valiantly, withered, even as it provided a nurturing environment for its individual members' personal and political growth. Somewhere along the way the New Left finally and definitively ended as a movement, and my own interests took over completely. I had put my "Jewish Question" on the shelf in the early 1960s. Twenty years later, increasingly lacking a movement or an organization around which to center myself, when I was asked to reply to Edward Said's discussion of the Palestinians in an early issue of *Social Text*, I could no longer avoid it.[19] Absorbed in my hope project, concerned to educate my children about their roots, I began to rediscover both the Holocaust and Israel.

I did not go back on my original intellectual–political conversion, but I began to interrogate the faith that lay between its lines. Being committed to an increasingly remote good was no longer enough; I increasingly struggled to explain evil. As I explored the issues of hope and despair, I continued to use my Marxist tools. At the same time, in order to explain the century's "dialectics of disaster," it was necessary to sensitize these tools to its social irrationality by focusing on irrational collective behavior—actions that were decisively *not* system-functional, paths taken toward massive self-destruction and genocide because no better paths were available. I also chose new ways to use Marxism's illuminating power in dealing with the Israeli–Palestinian conflict. The original reasons for Israeli displacement of Palestinians had little to do with conventional Marxian notions of class and political economy, but a great deal to do with *national* identity and survival.[20]

The hope project took me far from the tension between theory and practice that had preoccupied me during the 1960s and early 1970s. My larger goal became sifting through the wreckage of our movement, and then of the century itself, in order to see what grounds for hope continued to exist. My activism persisted, on behalf of the Jewish peace movement and later, after a visit to South Africa, against apartheid. In the one case, the possibility of a meaningful Jewish identity for my children and their children was at stake, along with finding a secure basis for both Israeli and Palestinian self-determination; in the other, the pain, generosity, and heroism of South African blacks, oppressed by the world's last openly colonial regime, motivated my involvement. The Marxism I employed to illuminate these situations became yet broader, now stressing the Afrikaner identity project and its material basis, now stressing the five-hundred-year-old world-historical process of capitalist colonial expansion. And, in spite of everything, it continued to nourish my activism, still providing a universal vision and broad narrative within which to think and act.

While using Marxism as a guide to understanding these situations, I moved in a direction opposite to the one I pursued in the 1960s and 1970s. Then, the Movement had been challenging, confirming, and shaping my unorthodox Marxism; now, the century's "dialectics of disaster" did the same. Then events had reaffirmed a Marxian commitment as fast as they undermined it; now, it was growing clearer and clearer that Marxist personal commitment and analysis had little infuence on the actual shapes of 1980s political activism. At the same time, it was no longer possible to argue on behalf of a single dialectic of oppression and emancipation. Whatever their ultimate systemic root, various social and political problems demanded to be understood and struggled against *on their own terms*.

In spite of retaining Marxist commitments and tools, then, I was coming to conclude—in *New Left Review* against Perry Anderson's too-sanguine view in *In the Tracks of Historical Materialism*—that Marxism was in a terminal crisis.[21] Marxism, I argued, described a stage in both human and capitalist development that had been partially superseded. I say "partially" because this had taken place without the overthrow of capitalist economic institutions, without removing capitalism's fundamental contradictions, and within a social order still based on class and profit. By pointing beyond Marxism, I finally resumed my argument of fifteen years earlier.

I began, very much in keeping with my earlier work, by distinguishing Marxism as a particular theory appropriate to an earlier stage of capitalist history, when the proletariat was potentially *the* revolutionary class, from historical materialism, a more general outlook still awaiting a *contemporary* and *post-Marxist* specification. I regarded historical materialism as the way out, an outlook that makes possible a layered developmental analysis of today's social forms. It can thus incorporate classical Marxism *and* the systemic changes since its heyday, while seeking to identify the forces capable of transforming late capitalist society. These forms and forces—such as feminism and other new social movements—may have evolved historically due to displacements and partial resolutions of capitalism's fundamental problems, or in part owing to advances in productivity and technology. But these movements now functioned, and now had to be treated, autonomously.[22]

Thus did I begin to look beyond the Marxist post-Marxism I had been thinking within for so many years. Perhaps the various forms of oppression can still be located within some single world-historical dialectical spiral, but the movements opposing them are autonomous and plural by nature, each seeking to undo specific, however interrelated, forms of oppression, each requiring an understanding that respects its specificity. The fundamental fact is that any large-scale movement today or in the future, if it is to be *a* movement, must be kaleidoscopically diverse in principle. To be politically effective, it will be a radical coalition—or nothing at all. And although such a coalition is the single conceivable force capable of transforming contemporary society to its roots, it can only take on the systemic source of each of its components' specific struggles by developing a communal vision in which each struggle is joined to every other.

Any movement that would aim at transforming the most basic contemporary oppressions, any such radical coalition, will have to strive for socialism *and* an end to patriarchy *and* an end to racism *and* gay liberation *and* a transformed relationship to nature *and* nuclear disarmament *and* a profound settling of accounts with the once-colonized and native peoples— *without prioritizing one struggle over another.* Such a movement will have to incorporate a Marxist component, a feminist component, a native peoples' and a peoples of color component, a gay and lesbian component, and an ecological component. None of the components should pretend to speak for all of humankind. This post-Marxist universalism must differ from that of Marxism by placing on the agenda the liberation of all oppressed peoples, of the overwhelming majority—*in their specificities* as well as in their commonality. Or it will not happen.

Why Hold On?

I formulated these thoughts in 1984. Giving up on any notion of necessary or even likely progress, adding *social irrationality* to my conceptual armamentarium, letting go of a single dialectic of oppression and liberation, seeing the need for any future radical politics to be coalitional on principle, and stressing environmental and nuclear dangers, why did I not say, "Therefore, I am no longer a Marxist"? Why still formulate these ideas so that any departure from Marxism was a short trip indeed, still trying to hold onto the larger historical–materialist dialectic within which Marxism had developed?

Since the declaration of martial law in Poland, I had already been thinking in terms of what would happen "after Communism," and wrote some unpublished thoughts about it. I had even predicted that the demise of Communism would begin by the end of the 1980s. As a Sartrean, I knew that every system of oppression is dependent ultimately on the acquiescence of the oppressed, and as a Holocaust scholar I strongly believed that the second generation after the original trauma—the children's children—would begin to shake off the paralysis induced by Stalin's rule. Why did it take another several years, and spectacular events, before I would take the simple step already implied in these ideas, and draw conclusions about the end of Marxism? Today, as I reflect on some of the many genuinely post-Marxist writings of the 1970s and early 1980s—for example, those of Jürgen Habermas, Cornelius Castoriadus, Albrecht Wellmer, André Gorz, Rudolf Bahro, Ernesto Laclau, and Chantal Mouffe—at first blush I feel a bit embarassed to have held on for so long.

One turning point came when reading my daughter Pamela Aronson's senior essay for James Madison College, Michigan State University, in December 1989. It was "A Feminist Critique of Marxism," based on writings from the early 1970s to the present, in which she stressed the need for socialism *and* for an independent feminist presence on theoretical and practical grounds. Not tied, as I was, to a single all-embracing dialectic, she easily saw autonomous developments where these in fact existed. My daughter's feminism persuaded me, rather late in the game, to finally and fully accept its autonomy from Marxism.

The second moment was a lecture I gave in South Africa, in August 1990, which is the first statement of the idea of this book, namely that the fall of Communism was the last of a series of trends and events that force radicals to be "on their own" and to rethink everything.[23] On a day-long hike circling Cape Town I excitedly sketched a second essay about the ways socialism was and was not on the agenda in South Africa, emphasizing the urgency of creating a climate in which struggle and disagreement were possible without resorting to violence.[24] Being tied to South Africa led me to understand how well Marxism explains that reality, how important the working class and Marxists have been in preparing the ground for a postapartheid order, how relentlessly the dynamics of capitalism have been transforming that country—and the yawning gulf between these understandings and the possibility of a socialist transformation.

The last straw came at the Central Meeting of the American Philosophical Association in April 1991, when I heard Nancy Fraser deliver an eloquent paper, "The Future of Marxism in the Postmarxist Field." Fraser left no doubt that Marxism was over as a project of societal transformation, even though it remained vital as a critical and analytical tool for understanding the capitalist layer of contemporary society and its oppressions. Here was another feminist self-confidently breaking the same ground I had been exploring more tentatively and gingerly. She pushed me off the fence.

Why did I cling so—until I could no longer ignore the autonomous reality represented by women's oppression and the feminist movement, until I sorted out the ways Marxism is and is not central to postapartheid South Africa? I let go only when it seemed to me that Marxism as a revolutionary project had made its final exit from history. Why were others like Wellmer and Gorz drawing conclusions that I long refused to draw, although I had both the tools and the disposition to do the same? Marxism is over: If such thoughts seem self-evident once one comes to them, why does it take so long to get there? Why do others still resist?

There are, of course, reasons for persisting that bear on personal history and psychology. These have to do with Marxism's (and Marx's) still-powerful authority, with the need to belong to a world-historical movement such as Marxism still offered, with my refusal to betray a sinking ship and thus give another iota of comfort to the apologists of the system, with close friendships and loyalties developed over the identity-forming politics of the past twenty years, and with what Sartre called one's "ideological invest-ment" in a certain set of ideas.[25] But some of the reasons indicated in this itinerary are so transparently a reflection on the situation of the Left and radical theory itself, and bear so directly on the argument I make in the next chapters, that they can be mentioned without any translation from the personal to the political.

First was the palpable reality of Marxism. If the proletariat seemed integrated into advanced capitalism, our Marxism spoke of still other contradictions, still other dialectics. Didn't we ourselves, the New Left, reflect this stunningly? Didn't the Third World revolutions that inspired us, and that we supported instinctively, give proof of Marxism's continued viability? One quarter of the world was officially Marxist, was being edu-cated in Marxist ideas, used Marxist texts, and still paid homage to Marx, Engels, and Lenin. These societies were at least *beyond* capitalism, and allowed us to hope for other, better ways of going beyond capitalism. Shorn of their specific faults, they made a Marxist alternative thinkable and believable, and they nourished Marxist faith. I have said that I had absorbed this faith between the lines, that despite all insistence on skepticism and openness I believed in history with a capital "H," as grasped by theory with a capital "T." As long as various justifications for this faith could be found in reality, Marxism gave me hope.

Second, my attempts to sketch a revolutionary theory were nourished by Marxism's considerable intellectual riches and power. From the begin-ning, my tools and concepts were developed as an extension and correction of Marxism, even when they proposed a broader historical dialectic than that of Marxism. Using these tools and applying them more broadly as an activist and intellectual brought me face to face with some of the most challenging issues: the Holocaust, Stalinism, the nuclear threat, the Israeli–Palestinian conflict, apartheid. Extended to include such themes as the dynamics of societal irrationality, historical–materialist analysis had a depth and reach that remained unequalled.

Third, after twenty years of thought and action, none of us in the New Left had come up with a convincing replacement for the proletariat as revolutionary actor—no matter how many times we marched. If we added, say, blacks, women, and office workers to the industrial working class in our revolutionary scenarios, we still were unable to conceive socialist revolution without workers as its central actors. Our search still turned on the Marxist conceptions of revolutionary agency, theory, and the appropriate relationship of theory to practice. This meant that all new candidates for revolutionary actor had to speak the original lines and perform the original roles. We remained haunted by the power of the original drama, dwelling on the memory of the original script and its actors.

Fourth, the richness of historical materialism and the power of Marxism's revolutionary scenario were at the heart of a project that dominated the field for good reason. At once emotional, moral, political, existential, philosophical, eschatological, intellectual, and active, Marxism's compelling synthesis dwarfed the alternatives. Our New Left Marxism may have renounced much of Marxism's self-confidence, hope, drama, and even coherence, but it retained, or was perhaps parasitic on, Marxism's synthetic power. As long as Marxism remained a living historical force, each and every unorthodox or hyphenated Marxism unfolded within its aura. However qualified or attenuated, each and every Marxism absorbed the fundamental self-confidence, explanatory power, prophetic force, scientific bent, and stress on objective processes that I discuss in the next chapter as characterizing the Marxian project.

For these reasons, then, I continued to remain within Marxism even as it was collapsing around me. I do not regret participating so fully in a great world-historical project, right up to its end. Some saw the end coming earlier, some are still holding out, and the reasons of each bear listening to with respect. It seemed that one could have debated forever whether an officially Marxist country like the Soviet Union one day might be recalled to radical and democratic Marxist impulses. But now that its people have taken matters into their own hands and abolished official Marxism, the time for such debate is over. Similarly, in both the West and the Third World, the possibilities of Marxism as a transformational project have also been exhausted.

Thus it is not merely necessary to rewrite the play entirely; because we are on our own, we must forget about the play. It is time for those of us who have struggled to make a home "within" this project, and its theory, to change our center of gravity entirely. Marxism as a revolutionary project, compelling as it has been, belongs to an earlier age. Any new radical project, for all its continuing commitment to emancipation and social justice, will look and feel very different.

Chapter Two

MARXISM IS OVER

Nearly a century and a half after *The Communist Manifesto*, Marxism no longer threatens capitalism. It is scarcely any longer embodied in societies proclaiming themselves to be an alternative to contemporary capitalism, or in movements struggling for revolutionary change. Whatever its interest to students and scholars, whatever continuing analytical importance it may have concerning the society, economy, and work process, whatever its dwindling sentimental significance as a standard of radical identity, if we judge Marxism from within, by its own stringent standard of validity, it is over. By its own standard: having become a theory without a practice and, increasingly, lacking a social base oriented toward a possible Marxist project, Marxism has fallen victim to history's most withering judgment. Its time has passed.

Because Marxism has so dominated the field of oppositional thought and action, projects of radical change that seek to be contemporary must self-consciously situate themselves *beyond* Marxism. As such, they must not only be new, post-Marxist projects, but new *kinds* of projects. If we cannot think or act without Marxism's terms and concepts, these have been absorbed into the common cultural stock and no longer characterize a unique project. Our new projects will take account of the fact that capitalism has not ended and is indeed more hegemonic than ever, but they must be rooted in the social orders they would seek to change, as was Marxism in the world that produced it.

Why is it so difficult to pronounce the conclusion that seems so obvious to so many—namely, that Marxism is over? The death of Marxism has, of course, been celebrated as well as mourned throughout the twentieth century. Since its birth, among those who feared it and those who placed their hopes in it, no statement about Marxism has been able to be expressed without being fiercely contested. There is no academic detachment where Marxism is concerned: as a theory and movement Marxism sought the overthrow of capitalist society. On behalf of the working class it intransigently revealed and simultaneously attacked the class interest, and the class oppression, at the heart of an economic and social order that has always pretended to be the embodiment of civilization's highest values. On its theoretical side, it presented not just a specific socioeconomic analysis, but an entire outlook, including a philosophical anthropology, an ethics, a philosophy of history, and a theory of truth. On its practical side it encouraged, and attempted to illuminate, the class conflict between worker and capitalist that accompanied the appearance of the industrial revolution. It confidently placed capitalist society in an historical progression of socioeconomic forms, each of which had its definite function and limits, and each of which was destined to give way to a higher form. It proclaimed capitalism's workers as the agents of that higher form, in their deepest class identity the enemy of the society dependent on their labor. And then, for a short while for many and for a longer while for some, the partial fulfillment of Marxism was proclaimed in the Communist societies that had overthrown capitalism and/or colonial and neocolonial rule. Thus Marxism was at the heart of the conflict between the good and evil on both sides that became the Cold War.

Discussing that conflict has always meant entering a terrain where rational analysis was proclaimed central to the self-identity on all sides, and where all sides have fallen habitually into the most extreme forms of dismissal and denial.[1] This clouds any attempt to make a definitive statement about Marxism today. Has dusk really fallen on its historical project, allowing it to be painted retrospectively in its true colors? Is it really time to mark its passing and mourn it? It seems impossible to speak at all about an end of Marxism, in the face of the fact that Anglo-American Marxist intellectual culture is more diverse than ever; that social systems still inspired in part by Marxist ideas and texts continue (in 1994) to rule over one quarter of the world's population; for all the reaction against Marxism of the past few years, the dust from seventy-five and forty-five years of Marxist rule has certainly not yet settled in the Soviet Union and Eastern Europe, leaving the full practical accounting of its positive and negative heritage still to be accomplished.

The Argument

In short, it seems self-evident that in spite of everything Marxism is still palpably real in today's world—as a leading idea, as a major force that has shaped our world. If there are so many Marxists who act and think and write, doesn't it stand to reason that Marxism continues to exist? If capitalism remains with us, doesn't Marxism? My response is drawn from, in a sense *is*, Marxism itself. Marxism no longer exists in the peculiar way it itself always claimed as decisive: not as theory or idea or analysis, but as *project of transformation from capitalism to socialism.*

This unique status is conveyed in one of the most celebrated of Marxist aphorisms, the second "Thesis on Feuerbach," written in 1845: "The question whether objective truth can be attributed to human thinking is not a question of theory but is a *practical* question. Man must prove the truth, that is, the reality and power, the this-sidedness of his thinking in practice. The dispute over the reality or nonreality of thinking which is isolated from practice is a purely *scholastic* question."[2] When talking about Marxism more than a hundred years after Marx's death, Marxism itself poses the question: What practical results can we point to? The "reality or nonreality" of Marxism needs to be assessed not as idea, but, after generations of practical activity, as historical fact.

This need to point to what has been created by a practice embodying the "reality and power, the this-sidedness of [man's] thinking" is essential to Marxism; to point to actual social forces, to real historical tendencies, to results, to demonstrable alternatives. This need to point to its own practical results has always been immanent in a Marxism describing itself as a *unity of theory and practice.* It never presented itself as a set of ideals or values separable from their embodiment in reality, or as merely a class analysis or an economic study or philosophical argument or historical theory, but more fulsomely—as a description of the world unfolding before our eyes, in struggle, and with our active participation. That is, of the conflict-laden pathway from capitalism to socialism.

Marx and Engels wrote, "Communism is not for us a stable state which is to be established, an *ideal* to which reality will have to adjust itself. We call Communism the *real* movement which abolishes the present state of things."[3] But if that movement, the project of change, no longer exists in practice, then Marxism no longer exists. Marxian theory that is "just" a theory is not Marxist, but something else.

The early Marx distinguished his outlook from Hegel and his fellow young Hegelians by looking for, and finding, social forces that would make his philosophical critiques true in a practical as well as a theoretical way. Marx and Engels drew their self-confidence from being able to point to the English working class in Manchester and other industrial cities, to the awe-inspiring human and natural powers released by the Industrial Revolution but thwarted by class society, to the French working class and its remarkable political capacity, to the revolutions of 1848, to the immiseration caused by capitalism wherever it touched, to the first International, to the great and tragic Paris Commune, to the steady growth and increasing strength of the German working class. Marx and Engels assumed that history itself had to bear out, and *was* bearing out, their projections and analyses.

For over a century Marxism has remained true for this reason. It has remained present as a transformative historical force in this irrefutable practical sense: in class movements, in major political parties, in social revolutions, in national movements, in socialist states, and as inspiration of radical movements. But as we look around us and look back, what conclusions can we draw about the Marxist reality that has unfolded in the century since Marx's death? To ask this is to ask what the class struggle has produced that we, living today, can point to as a viable alternative to capitalism. In asking this question after so many generations of Marxist struggles, we should certainly be able to insist on viable rather than potential alternatives, on achieved realities rather than possibilities. We should certainly insist on seeing what successes have been produced in the name of the theory that sought not to comprehend, but to change, reality. Above all, is there a single socialist society that might serve as a model and source of inspiration, if not as material support for the building of socialism elsewhere today, say in South Africa?

We know that the concrete influence of Marxism has made for many revolutionary experiences, many inspiring movements, but few successes. For all their partial achievements and modifications, neither parliamentary nor revolutionary paths have produced a contemporary working alternative to capitalism. At their best—and from the standpoint of the United States they can seem quite remarkable—Scandinavian socialisms have stabilized and humanized life under capitalism. But, with all its profound problems, capitalism reigns supreme politically and ideologically as never before. This historical fact cannot leave untouched a theory whose hallmark has been to be so firmly rooted in facts.

As a project of social transformation based on a union of theory and practice, Marxism concerns itself with a given state of affairs that is in the process of being radically transformed. As such, it is both a historically based comprehension of what is happening and a guide to make it happen. Thus it is not simply a description of a given social reality or an idea of a better social reality, but a theoretical and practical guide to the transformation of the one into the other. Its claims to validity are dependent on the realization of the entire process and project. Thus, if after a reasonable length of time, socialism has been nowhere achieved, if world-historical trends are moving away from, rather than toward, socialism, these facts can only undermine Marxism's claims to be true.

But how long is a reasonable period of time? Well over one hundred years after Marx's death, three generations after the high tide of the great European socialist movements, two generations after the first Marxist revolution, a generation after Marxism's zenith as a worldwide call to arms, we are in a position to draw some conclusions. The facts are not with Marxism; history has been rendering a judgment. If we cannot find a successful socialism as we near the twenty-first century, can we at least find a working-class majority, struggling toward socialism? If not a majority, a significant movement? The fact is that nowhere in the world has the industrial proletariat ever been the numerical majority.[4] Moreover, industrial working classes everywhere seem to be *shrinking* under the new techniques of advanced capitalist production. And where can one point to a working-class movement unifying rather than fragmenting, becoming more class-conscious, and moving toward, rather than away from, an alternative to capitalism? At what point do we ask, with Herbert Marcuse, whether a long-term change in working-class consciousness isn't also a "corresponding change in [its] 'societal existence' "?[5]

Yes, there are explanations, time-honored and more recent Marxist explanations, that the capitalists too have studied the *Communist Manifesto* and *Capital*, and have strategized accordingly; that the prosperity of a (wide or thin) layer of the working class, in the industrial West, has been bought at the expense of the absolute immiseration of the vast majority in the Third World.[6] Other explanations include that the Cold War stabilized capitalism and allowed the creation of a coalition between labor and capital[7]; and that partially successful workers' struggles, institutionalized in stable union–management relationships, have drawn a decisive portion of working class loyalties into the consumer society. Still others argue that capitalism has revealed a remarkable capacity to use its own contradictions, distorted into consumer needs, to stabilize itself[8]; or that popular socialisms, whether in Cuba or in Chile, never really had a chance to succeed. These are not illogical attempts to explain the phenomena. Still, all such efforts come up against the fact of facts: socialism is *not* en route to becoming a dominant trend. Indeed, it is no longer even a major trend.[9]

In the face of this overriding fact it is certainly possible to remain committed to Marxism as a theory and body of analysis and *potential* movement. But to do so is implicitly to split (or recognize the split in) what Marxism saw as unified. It is to remain *personally* committed to a possible social system, but no longer to an emerging hegemonic movement or project. Such commitments have become subjective ones, moral ones, sentimental ones, normative ones; even if fiercely defended, they are no longer commitments to a world-historical process that can be *pointed to*. Marx was able to explore the logic of that process and decide to serve it; we cannot. We may argue over the exact moment when the crisis of Marxism began—that is, when actual historical trends diverged decisively from revolutionary goals[10]—but as we near the end of the twentieth century, we can no longer point to a world-historical revolutionary process or project whose agents we can become.

If Marxism claimed to be science *and* action, the two were joined together by history itself. It was economic analysis and study of class struggles, joining, as Perry Anderson has said, an intellectual system, a theory of history, and a call to arms.[11] Its intellectual power has been inseparable from its political force, and this in turn was built on a conviction about history's direction. The Marxist project as we know it is the *unity* of these philosophical, historical, economic, and political moments. Take away any of these elements—as Marxists today are forced to do by history itself—and the whole of Marxism becomes transformed into something else. Thus does history itself reveal to us the frail character of the unity first proclaimed in the "Theses on Feuerbach." For in the end, Marxism's characteristic joining of theory and practice is not an intellectual operation; it depends on events and on human action to hold it together. And when abandoned by its agents, when events turn out otherwise, its theory diverges from practice, so that it can no longer be called Marxism.

Marxism as Science: Theory and Practice Unified

What then *is* Marxism, this unique force that has set its sights on understanding and changing the basic structures of social reality, on diagnosing its ills and overcoming them, on understanding social classes and abolishing them, on grasping the sweep of human history and fulfilling its deepest purposes, on being science and guide for revolutionaries? What is its special character, that we may say of it, in spite of so many Marxists, in spite of surviving Marxist parties and even governments, and also in spite of the continued flourishing of capital and its continued exploitation of workers, that Marxism's day has passed? My argument contains a number of points that now demand a more systematic treatment, and that rest on an understanding of Marxism's uniqueness. It stresses two central themes: that Marxism is a *unity* of several dimensions, levels, and elements, beginning with theory and practice; and that as such it is a *project* of social transformation. After clarifying these themes I will develop the argument that it is precisely as unity and as project that Marxism has ended.

Two somewhat different but overlapping self-conceptions have reigned among Marxists. The first, drawing its direct warrant from Engels' *Socialism: Utopian and Scientific* and prevalent in Second International Marxism as well as orthodox Communism, has seen Marxism as a predictive but committed *science*, grasping what inevitably is going to happen.[12] Such a science might well be invalidated by events in much the same way that any scientific theory can be eventually invalidated—by the accumulated discrepancy between its predictions and observed experience.[13] Indeed, Marxism has often been critically evaluated this way. For example, one list of such predictions, by Daniel Little, focuses on "the law of the falling rate of profit, the creation of an industrial reserve army, the polarization of classes, the concentration and centralization of property, and the increasing severity of cyclical crises."[14] Contrary to Marx's predictions, it has turned out that the rate of profit is relatively stable, that classes are less polarized, that labor unions have achieved power to protect their members and affect social policy, and that "the capitalist state seems more capable of managing the economic crises of capitalism than Marx expected; and socialism seems to be beyond the horizon for the Western capitalist nations."[15] In a similar vein, one remarkable book, containing analyses of each of the 172 economic predictions made by Marx, evaluates the scientific basis for each of them.[16] Because, so the argument goes, its predictions of specific historical changes are without foundation and in many cases have been falsified by events, it would seem to retain little force.

Taken as a predictive science, Marxism could be accused of trying to foresee the unforeseeable; no rigorous social science would extend itself so rashly as to project the form and direction human action would take to end social systems and replace them by other social systems. Indeed, the full list of Marx's predictions can be taken as indicating how wildly speculative Marxism has been in predicting not only objective trends, but also human struggles in response to these trends, as well as the results of these struggles.[17] But all such approaches ignore the fact, stressed throughout its history, that Marxism is predictive in a special way and from a special point of view: of the social reality in which the working class intervenes actively, and that they change.

In other words, we are wrong to evaluate Marxism as a science in the usual sense, as a predictive description of the workings of some independent, objective reality. After all, the validity of its predictions turns not only on the occurrence of certain processes, but also on the success of specific forms of highly complex human behavior interacting with equally complex socioeconomic trends. In short, the predictive power of Marxism turns on class struggles, which it both foresees and, as a partisan, illuminates and guides. In this sense, Marxism is a situated, self-conscious, and politically committed science that sharply distinguishes itself from social sciences that profess neutrality and wish only to "observe" their object of study, which they regard as constituted independently of them. In their very concepts and goals, such sciences conceal definite class standpoints. Marxism tried not so much to foresee as to *bring about* an entire chain of events stretching over years. To select just three of those 172 predictions, Marx attempted not only to predict that "class consciousness among the proletariat will develop as they become more numerous and as the modes of production develop," but to *make it happen*; not only to observe that "the proletarian revolution evolves from the class struggle," but to *bring it about*; not only to anticipate that "the proletariat will ultimately defeat the bourgeoisie," but to offer itself as a tool in this project.[18]

Confounding all efforts to see Marxism primarily as a conventional science is its goal of drastically transforming the given state of affairs into a wholly different state of affairs. Above all, Marxism calls upon its subjects, the working class, to carry out the changes it anticipates, through extended struggle and ultimately through imposing their will on the capitalists and their supporters. This is the reason why Marxism undertakes its situated and committed scientific analyses: to develop tools *for guiding the proletariat*.

If it is not a traditional science, then, as "Western Marxists" empha-sized, Marxism is a unity of theory and practice. The projected process of transformation involves a committed but objective study of the social reality *and* an active effort to transform that reality. To speak of "theory *and* practice" is to also speak of theory which is motivated by practice as well as theory which guides and culminates in practice. In other words, the theory, which taken by itself is committed to being scientific, finds its fulfillment only in practice; and the practice, whose goal is human liberation, is informed and directed by the theory. They constitute a unity: each is unthinkable without the other.

Any particular objective, "scientific," analysis of the system may well be theoretically sound, and may be developed from the point of view of the working class, but this has little long-range significance for Marxism if it does not eventuate in decisive action by the working class. To say this is not to equate Marxism with philosophical pragmatism, because Marxist thought insists that there is such a thing as an objective and valid analysis of the essential aspects of capitalism's functioning—a scientifically correct or adequate theory. But the purpose of this analysis, performed in the name of working-class emancipation, is not primarily to describe capitalism adequately, but rather to illuminate the practice that would overthrow it. Because its ultimate test is not its scientific adequacy for purposes of theoretical comprehension (i.e., "a purely scholastic question"), but its ability to serve those who would change the system (i.e., its "reality and power, [its] this-sidedness"), Marxism thus from the outset characterizes as *academic* all forms of "critical theory" that do not try to locate the social force, and the practice, that would realize their predictions.

The young Marx shared the desire for a radical transformation of existing society with his young-Hegelian colleagues. Like them, he began with the call for "a *ruthless criticism of everything existing*."[19] But what distinguished Marx was his conviction, first expressed in his "Contribution to the Critique of Hegel's *Philosophy of Right*," that criticism "leads on to *tasks* which can only be solved by *means of practical activity*."[20] This entailed making his critique genuinely effective: "It is clear that the arm of criticism cannot replace the criticism of arms. Material force can only be overthrown by material force; but theory itself becomes a material force when it has seized the masses."[21] The masses are the "*passive* element," the "*material* basis" for the theory, but "theory is only realized in a people so far as it fulfills the needs of the people."[22]

From Theory to Practice: The Underlying Condition

Nevertheless, as I said above, Marxism's unity cannot merely be willed: it depends on events. Already in the essay just quoted, written in 1843, Marx has the key insight that an essential condition must be met for theory to be realized in practice. Aware that critique does not happen to grip the masses either by chance or longing, or, above all, because of the theoretician's efforts, he points to the need for a historical concordance between all of these and the actual evolution of social forces. "It is not enough that thought should seek to realize itself; reality must also strive toward thought."[23]

In searching for the ways in which reality is indeed developing in the directions indicated by critique, Marx locates the particular social class whose aims and interests make it the "general representative of this society." The attention given to his famous formulation about the proletariat as the class with "radical chains" and his equally famous remark about religion[24] has tended to obscure his equally original insight: *only the actual evolution of social reality itself can make it possible to unite critical analysis with a social movement.*

Unlike Hegel, Marx refuses to wait until dusk for the owl of Minerva to depict accurately what has already happened. In fact, the opposite: he seeks to use wisdom not contemplatively, to give its proper colors to the world that has already come to be, but actively and projectively, exercised by masses of human beings, to give the world that is becoming its proper shape. But this means that the union of theory and practice depends on more than the "purely scholastic" correctness of the theory; it also rests on the existence and actual motion of social forces gripped by the theory. Its success depends on the actual contours, the historical development, of social reality itself—meaning both the objective systemic tendencies whose laws Marx would seek to understand, and the human beings oppressed and set in motion by them. As Nicholas Lobkowicz puts it, Marx stressed, in an almost "ontological" transformation, that theory's actualization "depended on whether reality itself pressed for it." But this means that, inasmuch as reality strives "toward thought, reality and its potentialities, not knowledge, were the ultimate source of man's emancipation, of salvation."[25] Obviously, theory must be scientific. Less obviously, but equally essential, history must smile on the project.

What role does this give to theory, to human will? What relationships are entailed among the theory, the historical development of the political economy, and human action—the action both of the intellectuals articulating the theory and of the proletariat? What is the relationship of human willful activity to the scientifically described movement of social reality? What becomes of the unity of theory and practice if history does not turn out as anticipated? If theory fails to comprehend events and trends? If theory ends up hatching the un-Marxist project of drastically *assaulting* social reality?[26] Obviously, Marx's first formulations cannot be expected to answer such questions, which have remained thorny issues throughout the history of Marxism. They lead us into the conflict, for example over "fatalism" and "voluntarism"[27]—that is, in its most extreme form, between the view that history alone will produce the anticipated transformations without the active intervention of human will or indeed, without the theory itself, and the view that human will has wide, virtually limitless scope to alter social reality, regardless of underlying conditions.[28]

If Marx's early writings tend to stress subjectivity and the active role of theory in reshaping reality, as Lobkowicz notes, many writers point out that over time the mature Marx lays greater stress on objective mechanisms—the actual development of capitalism—than either on the role of theory or the tasks of developing a revolutionary response. The fact remains, however, that Marx the social scientist, who spent his years at the British Museum studying the dynamics of capital, also as revolutionary leader devoted enormous time and energy to paying close attention to and trying to guide the movements emerging in response to capitalism. Marx intended his studies to aid, and to guide, the proletarian movement to which capitalism was giving rise.

Despite famous remarks to the contrary about "necessity" and "inevitability," Marx never acted in a way suggesting that one could simply let the economic machine destroy itself and then effortlessly "expropriate the expropriators." The correct theory was necessary as well as a working class guided by it—yielding conscious revolutionary action. Even Lobkowicz, who criticizes Marx for turning the revolutionary drive "into sheer facts" and the history of practice "into a necessity" and stresses Marx's emphasis on the "more or less automatic actualization" of his ideals, also emphasizes the limits of Marx's reliance on predictions and laws: "Contrary to the old Engels, and in spite of a few misleading phrases which in later writings he himself used, Marx always seems to have known that the effectiveness of his 'laws' depended on man's willful doing, at least in some respect."[29]

I will return to this question in Chapter 4, when exploring the question of Marxism's weaknesses. For our purposes here—to understand the premises of Marxism's "unity of theory and practice"—it is important to stress that the "willful doing" in turn depended on not only correctly grasping and acting on capitalism's "laws" but on the historical processes so described moving in the direction of proletarian revolution and socialism. Marx fiercely combated those who believed that capitalism could be transformed at will, before both objective and subjective conditions made revolutionary change possible—that is to say, before capitalism had not only appeared but matured, and before the proletariat had also matured. A deep faith in history lay behind Marx's attacks on all those "Jacobins," from Gottshalk to Bakunin, who sought to make revolution *prematurely*, before the masses were ready. Marxism assumed as a foregone conclusion that the dynamic of capitalism was moving, on its own, in a direction making socialism possible. A falling rate of profit, deepening proletarian immiseration, a simplification of class structure—these were specific historical tendencies on which

Marxism's hopes and anticipations were pinned, which would lead to an intensification of class struggle and growth in working-class consciousness.

Marxism as Project

If Marxism demands not to be judged as a traditional science, but as a committed unity of theory and practice, it is from the beginning dependent on events. The proletariat's "willful doing" uses the theorist's understanding of the system's laws in responding to a dynamic fully expected to generate a proletarian revolution. But this is not yet Marxism as we know it, not without a decisive further dimension. If Marxism's description of capitalism was required to be adequate to the main tendencies of the system,[30] from the beginning its practical task was never simply bringing a subjective agent to bear on an objective series of events, grasped through correct analysis, but much more. This "more" is usually passed over in silence by Marxists today, in part because it is patently not scientific, nor logical, nor accessible through a study of political economy; indeed, strictly speaking it is neither theory nor practice. It eludes such categories, in fact, and dissolves under the efforts of Marxists to sharpen their analytical tools.[31] Yet from the beginning it entered into the other dimensions that I described above, only then yielding the project of revolutionary transformation that we recognize as Marxism.

We can gain access to this *more*, the "soft" but essential side of Marxism, by reflecting, for example, on the fact that, as a situated project of political and social transformation Marxism has depended not simply on theory and on the actual development of the economy, but also on human numbers, knowledge, organization, persistence, and will. But what happens when the social force on which Marxism is based becomes defeated or demoralized? The Marxian agency is not an instrument uniformly and infinitely available for revolutionary or even trade-union action. Workers may not see themselves *as a class* but rather in terms of traits that divide them. They may be cowed by the power of capital or cease to believe in themselves or their mission. They may lack sufficient vision to see beyond the structures oppressing them or the forces needing to be overcome.[32] Or sufficient self-confidence to believe that they will inherit the earth. How they perceive social reality and how they regard themselves are decisive components of their struggle, and require constant tending and encouragement—based on analysis, understanding, and experience, but also based on hope and conviction.

Proletarian unity and self-confidence depended in part on what has been variously described as Marxism's prophetic, eschatological, chiliastic, religious, or moral dimension. Anderson evokes this dimension by describing Marxism as an intellectual system, a theory of history, *and* a call to arms.[33] The third term conveys something less hard-edged and scientific, more clearly evocative and subjective, than the other two. While depending on accurate theoretical comprehension and a favorable unfolding of events, Marxism became a practice only by articulating these into a stirring and compelling call to arms that encouraged struggle. Sustaining the struggle required projecting vision, hope, confidence, and a sense of righteousness. Marxism did this by being prophetic, by projecting well beyond what was realistically, "scientifically" predictable toward an alternative that would inspire and draw together all those who were actually or potentially part of the struggle. And in posing their victory as "necessary" and "inevitable," Marxism prophesied not just a better world in the distance, but a new world in the making. It projected a powerful belief in its rightness, a sense that history was realizing human dreams of justice, and a readily comprehensible and persuasive vision of the meaning of all of human history. These inextricable components of the Marxian project were not patched together arbitrarily, but rather stemmed from actual human longings and real historical possibilities.

To those who would reassert Marxism today, this prophetic dimension, so patently unfulfilled 150 years after Marx began to articulate it, so out of keeping with our contemporary modest hopes, appears as a vaguely embarrassing and disconcerting relic of an earlier age. Indeed, it is Marxism's critics, such as Leszek Kolakowski, rather than Marxism's defenders, such as Ralph Miliband, who want to stress this aspect of Marxism in debate.[34] As discussed in Chapter 6 the renewal of Marxist thought that took place in the 1980s largely abandoned this prophetic dimension. For the moment I want to accent not this contemporary issue, but the structural one: that this dimension, infused with theory and practice, makes Marxism recognizable.[35] Only when this dimension enters into and is unified with the others I have been describing, does Marxism take on the character it assumed in its heyday as a *project of revolutionary social transformation*.

To call Marxism a *project* is to speak of a conscious, intentional activity that is developed at a certain historical moment.[36] As such, it bears a specific set of goals with it: it undertakes to unite and mobilize masses of people to change radically the social orders in which they live. If Marxism calls on humans to overthrow their oppressors and freely and collectively fulfill modern social, economic, and human trends, its appeal stretches from explaining world history to guiding the individual's action; from redefining good and evil to explaining how the one will be realized and the other overcome; from accounting for the fundamental traits of the world, including its misery, to promising human redemption; from offering itself as *the* scientific realism to proclaiming the advent of the first real utopia on earth. Intrinsic to the Marxian project is both a scientific theory of bourgeois society and a stirring narrative of the entire sweep of Western history, all waiting to be brought about by the working class.

Thus Marxism wedded scientific scholarship to action on behalf of a coherent vision of history, society, and the future, in the name of a specific social class. The Marxian project joined not only theory and practice, but also universal and particular, science and value, prophecy and struggle, all previous history with this particular moment and the future. It united its broad intellectual vision and its detailed scientific analyses with a prophetic commitment to revolutionary social transformation by the oppressed and exploited themselves.

Above all, the Marxian project focused on economic exploitation as the central feature of capitalist accumulation, saw it giving rise to class conflict, and tried to trace the logic of a class struggle that would heighten the tendencies leading to its undoing. If the labor process lay at the heart of bourgeois society, the labor theory of value was at the center of Marxism. The crux of the labor–capital relationship was the pursuit of surplus-value, which indicated and measured the extent of the laborer's exploitation. In Marx's projection, the specific liberation of the proletariat meant universal human liberation, not only because no classes were beneath them, but because they were the reproducers of society, its material backbone; because their counterpart, modern technology, created the precondition for a life of wealth and culture for all; because all previous modes of oppression that had lasted into the contemporary world came to depend on this one; because the working class was becoming the vast majority of society. Thus all other struggles were increasingly subsumed by a workers' movement expected to carry every oppressed group along with it. Its mission lay in this universality: the workers' liberation was to be everyone's.

Appreciating Marxism as Project

Marxism is a powerful, compelling vision. Its genius and historic force lies precisely in the fact that it is a single coherent theoretical and practical project. In one narrative it has given us the meaning of human history, the essence of human strivings, the roots of the most fundamental of moral conflicts, a vision of the solution unfolding in our midst, a clear sense of which side is right and which wrong, and the path we ourselves should choose. Social science, economics, philosophy of history, ethics, ontology, as well as political theory all culminate in revolutionary practice. Marxism as we know it is this holistic project, unimaginable without prophecy and mythmaking, *a priori* projection and eschatology, careful scientific study of actual trends, and rigorous analysis of social reality.

Seeing Marxism as a project should help explain some of its notorious confusions, contradictions, inconsistencies, and tensions. In fact, as I will argue in Chapter 4, many of its greatest strengths are precisely those features that, over the years, have come to be recognized as its greatest weaknesses.

Such features were demanded of a revolutionary project in capitalist socie-ties during Marx's lifetime and Marxism's heyday, between 1848 and 1917. To "seize the masses" Marxism had to be eschatological vision *and* its positivistic disavowal. It had to be prophetic exhortation concealed be-neath claims of scientific necessity. It had to be close analysis of economic dynamics not susceptible to any human intervention except revolutionary action. It had to be a critique of reification succumbing to a belief in progress with a capital "P." It had to be an account of objective processes entailing subjective emancipation. It had to be a celebration of human power that encouraged a profound confidence about the unfolding of history. It had to be an assault on external authority in the name of its founder. And it had to incorporate deep insight into the social–structural dynamics of oppres-sion without considering the complex social–psychological dynamics of liberation.

On the one level it appears totally contradictory for Marxism to be so wholly committed to science while containing such an immense infusion of eschatology—to talk, for example, about "the beginning of history" and to reach toward overcoming alienated labor. But what happens if we suppress the contradiction? To do so dismantles Marxism (as does calling it "marxism," in the lower case). We can see this dismantling taking place in efforts to talk about an "early" (dialectical) and a "late" (scientific) Marx that claim the one or the other to be more authentic. The point is not only that, being one and the same person having developed over time, the "late" Marx himself fully incorporated, and thus presupposed, the full force of his "early" vision. More important, *both* dimensions became inextricably inter-twined components of Marxism as a historical project, the second likewise presupposing the first.

It is, after all, a project that made central use of science, but but also became *scientistic* as a way of nourishing its hope. Science, scientism, hope: if the first dimension was needed to adequately grasp the capitalist system, the second, a quasi-religious fetishism of science that extended its claims to areas where they remained wholly inappropriate, was inevitable in any effort to create a nineteenth-century movement. Its faith that an alterna-tive was unfolding depended on the sense of certainty given by the magic word, "scientific"—even when that term gilded what we now see was so patently a quasi-religious expectation. To be sure, hope is necessary for any significant social movement, at any time in history. But, as I will argue in Part II, ways of hoping are historically conditioned: ours will be different from Marxism's. In its heyday a quasi-religious belief in science anchored the sense of redemptive possibility needed to call forth heroic sacrifice and sustained struggle. A child of its time, Marxism was both unsuited to and incapable of the more tentative and stringent hope that has become necessary and possible for a generation living at the turn of the twenty-first century.

In Chapter 4 I will further discuss the appropriate outlook for a revolutionary project rooted in the late nineteenth and early twentieth century, and in Part II I will explore the appropriate outlook for a contemporary radical project. My present argument is that the term *project* is decisive for our understanding of Marxism's special character: in projecting the purposive action of a social class based on specific insight into historical reality, Marxism's goal was to realize itself by bringing into being an alternative society, socialism. In studying capitalism's essential structures and tendencies, including the active force of the proletariat, Marxism forecast and called for proletarian intervention to transform these structures. Thus, will and action are decisive in the project of Marxism, although the project is also dependent on events.[37] As project, it made use of prophecy, but was much more than prophecy, both because it was necessary to understand the tendencies and structures Marxism would transform and because Marx called upon humans to do this. Similarly, if the Marxian project made use of science in trying to forecast the main lines of history and to depict accurately the specific tendencies of capitalist society, Marxism could no more be equivalent to science than to prophecy. Suppressing its nonscientific elements will not "correct" Marxism, but rather transform it into something else. As I will demonstrate in Chapter 6, to "correct" Marxism, as analytical Marxism attempts to do, is to abandon its character as project.

Thinkers who appraise Marxism often wander in the confusions involved in taking its prophetic statements as scientific claims; thus they fail to comprehend the logic of many of its paradoxes and contradictions. Did Marx's predictions come true? Were his prophecies borne out by events? Was his description of the proletariat correct? Is socialism inevitable, and if so, what is the role of individual human action?[38] How far were Marxism's economic analyses correct? Focusing on whether Marxism successfully gave us empirical truth about historical or economic reality ignores its primary and unique character as project. As a project, Marxism had its own standard of verification, and its own set of tasks. If from the beginning the tendencies Marx studied were subject to human action and will, this meant that the agent was inseparable from the investigator, and was slated to intervene in the experiment. If Marx wrote assertively and categorically about the coming proletarian revolution, this was not a rhetorical carryover, but was meant projectively. As leader, he sought to create a movement cloaked in the aura of scientific self-confidence. But in his historical and scientific writing Marx could never, and actually never sought to, validate the prophetic sense of certainty he projected as leader. As scientist he identified certain historical tendencies; as leader he tried with every means at his disposal—including using the mantle of science to declare what was only possible to be necessary and inevitable—to help bring these tendencies to fruition.

This is not to suggest that any modern project of social transformation has to take place "beyond" scientific analysis, exempt from its judgments. Nor is the social area a realm of shifting indeterminacy capable of absorbing the imprint of any project that happens to be imposed on it.[39] As Marxism teaches us, a project must correspond to certain definite, verifiable tendencies and the needs of specific actors in order to be taken up historically.[40] And these can be debated, and validated, according to their own appropriate rigor. But Marxism's understandably sweeping claims to be scientific have confused the fact: such analyses are only components of the much larger unity I have been describing, which includes social forces, intention, vision, will, and action. *This* is the project. When Kolakowski criticizes Marxism as prophecy (and dismisses Marx's other claims),[41] he ignores both the performative character and the historicity of prophecy. To become one of the modern world's major projects, Marxism not only succeeded in unifying the needs and currents described above, but did so only to the degree that it accurately grasped, reflected, and voiced some of the modern world's central features and forces, hopes and aspirations.

Is the Project Over, or in the Doldrums?

The success of Marxism's project was to express and focus the actual features and attitudes of its period, in both its strengths and its weaknesses. It no longer expresses and focuses ours. My argument is simply that nowhere in the world today does Marxism remain a significant historical project. This is the exact sense in which Marxism is over: as project. The end of the Second World of Communism, combined with events in the First and Third Worlds, leave us so few and such scattered actors for Marxism's project that for the first time in its history, the capitalist system is unopposed. In this sense, Marxism is over.

From the beginning Marxism depended on events. When a historical project is no longer reflected in the existing forces and secular trends, what else can we say but that the project no longer exists? When its traditional actors refuse their roles not just once, but again and again and over the long term, the project must be deemed definitively at an end. When the main social movements over the span of a generation emerge *outside* of the traditional project, that project has lost its historical salience. When no existing party, society, or movement any longer testifies to the project's continued relevance, the project is practically irrelevant. When its only relevance is as critical analysis, not as practice of transformation, the project identified by its transformational practice has, by its own definition, failed.

But perhaps Marx's beloved mole of history remains at work, still burrowing beneath the surface in ways that will only appear suddenly and spectacularly one day when least expected. Europe's great twentieth-century years of world-historical upheaval—1917, 1936–1937, 1968, 1989— presupposed vast but slow cumulative changes, taking place against and seemingly in spite of the dominant trends. Mindful of this historical pattern, some continue to wait and see, anticipating the next thunderbolt, perhaps even hoping for not only a revitalization of working-class struggles, but even a sudden breakthrough to revolutionary class consciousness, the coming collapse of capitalism, the advent of socialism. And why not? In the 1850s the prediction that capitalism must inevitably terminate in proletarian revolution seemed just as far from realization as do the expectations of today's most dogmatic radical sects. And yet such revolutions did occur, even if in ways and with outcomes that differed substantially from Marxist projections.

When making broad historical arguments such as I am doing, how can we be sure that we're not merely adrift in history's doldrums again? What internal and structural evidence justifies talking about Marxism in the past tense so definitively, and dismissing as wishful thinking claims of an eventual Marxist revitalization and even culmination? After all, we are certainly not beyond capitalism, beyond its chaotic and destabilizing effects, its drive to commodify and transform everything in its path, its creation of vast industrial reserve armies. We are certainly not beyond the need for Marxian analysis of the system. The working class still exists. South Africa, for example, has an important Communist party which, having played a major role in the liberation struggle, is rethinking its Marxism with an eye toward developing a working-class movement appropriate to the post-apartheid situation. How then can we be beyond Marxism as a meaningful project?

The Case for Marxism's Obsolescence

There is in fact much evidence in support of the argument that the Marxian project is over, because of structural transformations in capitalism and even in the working class itself. The centrality of Marxism's cardinal category, labor, has been placed in question by capitalism's own evolution, as has the primacy of class. Capitalism's evolution has not only transformed the nature of labor and the nature of the working class, but also the character of its experience. These transformations have been much studied by, among others, Marxist or former Marxist writers, who focus on fundamental changes that have slowly brought about the current situation. They include the following:

1. The continued and deepening immiseration of the working class— anticipated by Marx as a precondition for revolution—has not taken place, nor has the anticipated breakdown of the system. Instead, through capital-

ism's unanticipated productivity, workers' struggles, state intervention, the strategy of mass production and mass consumption that has come to be known as Fordism, and the postwar development of consumerism, capitalism has stabilized. The industrial working classes of all industrial societies have struggled for, and won, a standard of living unimaginable in Marx's time.[42]

2. Class structure has not simplified in the twentieth century, leaving essentially two classes facing each other in a situation of increasingly polarized conflict. Rather, intermediate strata between the bourgeoisie and the proletariat have proliferated.[43]

3. While enormously increasing productivity, the transformation and restructuring of industrial labor processes have infinitely subdivided manufacturing processes. Consequences have included: (a) reducing the number of industrial workers needed; (b) diminishing their consciousness of a more and more technically intricate manufacturing process in which they have become less and less significant agents; (c) lower skill requirements; and (d) fragmentation of workers rather than their unification. The outcome is a significantly diminished potential for workers' control over these processes.[44] The proportion of highly skilled, prosperous workers has shrunk, yielding large numbers of under- and unemployed.[45]

4. The general shrinkage of the industrial working class deserves special emphasis. While Marx anticipated that the working class would become the vast majority, the traditional factory working classes of advanced industrial societies have declined to less than one quarter of the gainfully employed population. This demographic change has been accompanied by a shrinking of labor's social weight. Rethinking this transformation of the working classes might yield equal numbers of "new" workers, but the nature and conditions of their work, as well as their self-conception, are such as to make them unlikely candidates for class consciousness and class struggle.[46]

5. Correlatively, workers' experience has changed to the point where identification as worker has become less and less important. Drastic changes have not only been taking place at work but also in workers' relationships with their trade unions and in decisive areas beyond the workplace. Where, as foreseen by Marx, being a member of the working class was once a central feature of social identity under industrial capitalism, today being a worker is at best one dimension among others. Residential, social, consumption, recreational, and even employment patterns have changed so considerably as to amount to a virtual change in the identity of those who once regarded themselves as workers.[47]

The cumulative argument of these points is that capitalism and its working class have changed in ways that make key premises of Marxism obsolete. Contemporary capitalism has achieved, and depends on, the integration of the working class into the socioeconomic and political system—as well as the broad acceptance by the working class of its priorities and values, including its cultural and consumption patterns. Capitalism has long since ceased to be constructed by the labor of an alienated and impoverished majority of workers with "radical chains," who could also claim to be the universal class. As a result, in the West, contemporary workers no longer work like Marx's workers, no longer live like Marx's workers, no longer suffer like Marx's workers. As a result, they no longer think like Marx's workers. The fact that, since the 1960s, new social movements have pressed other causes—including those of women, minorities, the environment, and peace—only accentuates the long-term trends among workers, which have led to demobilization, demoralization, and defeat, resulting in the further weakening of unions, left-wing parties, and the working class as a whole.

The Case for Marxism's Continued Relevance

If many Marxists have followed this line of thought all the way out of Marxism,[48] others have challenged it in analyses that emphasize continuities rather than changes:

1. Most of the world is living in far worse conditions today than at the beginning of the capitalist transformation of the globe.[49] In Marxist terms what has happened can be viewed as a *displacement* of capitalism's contradictions overseas onto an increasingly growing Third World population at home. Decisive sectors of the metropolitan proletariat may have once achieved a high standard of living (which has been on the decline since 1980), but the hundreds of millions torn away from traditional village lives and dumped into urban slums and townships on the edges of the Third World's exploding cities have suffered capitalism's most dire human consequences.

2. Changes in the working class and in the labor process have been taking place since the beginning of capitalism, but they have not altered the fundamental character of capitalist society. The working class has been going through a constant process of recomposition, as can be seen, for example, in the increasing number of service workers and declining number of industrial workers. But the most plausible Marxist interpretation of what it means to be a worker stretches far beyond industrial or "productive" workers, either to all those whose labor is exploited for profit,[50] or to all those whose whose income comes from the sale of their labor power and keeps them among the lowest or lower income groups.[51] Thus the working class today amounts to between two thirds and three quarters of the population of the advanced industrial societies.

3. Recent changes in the labor process, such as "flexible accumulation"

(giving rise, for example, to talk about a "postmodern" economy), do not affect the fundamental dynamics of the capitalist system's operation. A variety of exploitative labor processes seem quite able to exist alongside each other in the new global economy, each of them in keeping with capitalism's basic needs and tendencies. Even if modes of experience seem to change drastically under new conditions of "time–space compression," fundamental structures and problems remain unchanged.[52]

4. The jury is still out on whether technological changes in the labor process are inexorably reducing skill levels among the working class and, as a result, transforming its power and capacities for struggle. There is evidence that new skills are created as old ones are made superfluous; at the same time some have argued persuasively that all such technological change is part and parcel of the class struggle, on which it in turn has an effect.[53]

5. Workers continue to wage class warfare and to press their demands on employers and the state. A variety of historical changes have changed the conditions and terrain of the struggle, but there is no reason to believe that it will not continue.[54] The working class remains "primary" in any future struggles for social transformation because it has "a greater potential strength, cohesion, and capacity to act as a transformative force than any other force in society."[55] And its claim to be a "universal" class stems from the specific ways in which it alone is capable of challenging capitalist society's "*distribution of power, property, privilege* and position."[56]

What Both Sides Acknowledge

Clearly, there are strong arguments on both sides. But both sides implicitly or explicitly acknowledge the same starting point: *something* profound has changed, leading us to debate in the first place. Neither capitalism nor the working class has developed as Marxism anticipated. Capitalism has achieved unimagined levels of productivity; its workers have achieved an unexpectedly broad distribution of wealth, and have not become revolutionaries. These are not only the conclusions of those of us who argue that Marxism has ended. Ralph Miliband, for example, recognizes that the Marxian project has not been realized. Misery and working class homogenity have not increased as Marx expected they would, and workers have not carried out a revolutionary overthrow of advanced capitalism or even developed revolutionary consciousness. The organizations created to advance their cause have lost any possible socialist vocation in pursuit of "moderation," fostered by working within the bourgeois–democratic system.

A nondogmatic Marxist such as Miliband advocates a less inevitabilist, more tentative and open-ended kind of Marxism—a Marxism whose only certainty is that class struggle will continue. But a Marxism built on such foundations is hard-put to justify its faith in a transformation *carried out by* the working class. If Miliband continues to place his full confidence in the working class, he provides no warrant for this faith. While Miliband persuasively diagnoses capitalist class society, the premises he shares with post-Marxists leave him no basis for explaining why or how the working class might be capable of overthrowing capitalism and creating a new order. In other words, his sober and exceedingly clear restatement of certain of Marxism's fundamental ideas, shorn of all triumphalism—indeed, even of Marxism's confidence in history—is unable to convincingly project beyond capitalism, to explain why it might still be a project that is "grounded" in material conditions, human will, and historical experience."[57]

Marxists can do no better than post-Marxists on this score. Insofar as they acknowledge the same facts, they are unable to give us a project or a movement any longer. Thus Marxism becomes a theory deserted by its practice, kept alive by thinkers shoring up the diminishing faith that its agents will become rekindled.

Why Not Wait?

Even so, why hurry to resolve such a profound issue and declare that Marxism is over? After all, if the transition from feudalism to capitalism took five hundred years, why expect the transition from capitalism to socialism to take any less time? And why not be prepared to rise and fall with its vicissitudes? This means, so the argument goes, weathering this transition's periods of defeat and retrenchment, sitting out its doldrums, such as now, without losing hope. It also means finding encouragement in those places such as South Africa where significant political organizations continue to declare themselves to be Marxist. Surely the mid-1950s was a similar time of gloom. Shouldn't a long-range and global view temper the impatience that wants to turn away from Marxism?

A common Marxist response to recent trends is to focus on structural restraints that will sooner or later make capitalism incapable of avoiding a major crisis. In this view Marxists studying long-term economic trends may not be able to predict the exact character of working-class response, but stress that capitalists may be running out of ways to head off a drastic reckoning. Perhaps then, as the fragility of working-class economic well-being is revealed, workers will rediscover their socialist and even revolutionary vocation. From this point of view, any argument not developed on the ground of political economy cannot begin to address the real issues facing Marxism. Such a perspective could conceivably admit almost every point I have argued in the previous pages while still maintaining that capitalism's constricting structures and undermining trends eventually must lead to the breakdown of that system.

What sort of reply can be made to those Marxists-in-waiting, and specifically to those who await a new crisis? The point is that in order to preserve faith in the face of an unfavorable reality, they too have tacitly redefined their Marxism. Abstracting from the various struggles and acts that have created the current network of socieconomic relations, and from those relations themselves, they seek out an *underlying structural process* that they hope will one day prevail. A severe economic crisis will produce a new working-class mobilization: this objectivist faith abandons Marxism's unity of objective trends and "willful doing," of theory and practice, by waiting for events to bring about renewed movements. Unable to point to Marxism as a social and political trend created by the working class, their Marxism becomes study of "objective" trends of political economy, and concentrates further on "underlying" processes.

Inasmuch as such arguments always concern the next crisis, they are always irrefutable. In response, we cannot dispense with the need to point, but Marxism always meant pointing to manifest as well as underlying economic trends, pointing to a project becoming realized, and joining that project. Those who insist on waiting have whittled down their Marxism from a project to only one of its strands. Waiting replaces motion toward working-class parties, movements, and societies. What keeps Marxists-in-waiting from seeing that they have let go of the Marxian project? The Marxist tenor of their concepts and anticipations conceals the distance separating their faith from Marxism itself.

South Africa and the Marxist Project

What would we need, as we near the end of the twentieth century, to make this faith in the proletariat into a genuine hope—that is, to ground it solidly in actual achievements and empirical tendencies? First, we would need to be able to point to places where Marxism is clearly still alive as a project. I have mentioned South Africa more than once in this chapter: a non-Western society with a large, prestigious, and explictly Marxist movement, a communist party that has developed deep roots among the masses, in the African National Congress (ANC), and in the country's leading trade-union federation, the Congress of South African Trade Unions (COSATU). The South African Communist Party (SACP) in fact was the key organizational force behind the ANC's guerilla army, as well as one of the main ideological sources of its nonracial philosophy—which are in themselves immense historical accomplishments no matter what else the SACP achieves. After it was unbanned along with the ANC it enrolled a membership in the tens of thousands, continued to play a major role in the ANC and in COSATU and in national politics, and addressed both the collapse of Communism elsewhere and its own dilemmas with openness and realism. Far from shrinking to an insignificant sect or changing its name after the collapse of Soviet Communism, the SACP remained popular *as* a communist party, for its revolutionary heroism and continuing radicalism. It appealed, of course, to workers in this society because they live in a nation characterized by high levels of industrial modernity alongside extreme poverty; it also appealed to vast numbers of marginalized and militant youth, and, paradoxically, to those white, Indian, and mixed-race intellectuals who drew hope from its universalism for overcoming the racialized fragmentation imposed by apartheid.

It is precisely its great achievements that made the impasse of the SACP appear so striking as it sought to become a mass working-class party aiming at national liberation through socialism, under conditions of open and public struggle. The problem was not merely, as a 1993 discussion paper acknowledged, that its greatest geographical strength and core membership came from a relatively small sector of organized industrial workers, and that beyond these lay the marginalized, "characteristically scattered, disorganized, and unskilled" vast proletarian majority.[58] After all, we would expect that in a society urgently needing programs of literacy and rural development, a major goal would be building the strength, numbers, and self-confidence of the working class "as a force which is capable of leading our society in every respect, capable of solving the crisis that reaches into every aspect of our society's fabric—economically, culturally, morally and politically."[59] Equally, we would expect a party so near to sharing power as a minority member of a multiclass national liberation coalition, to be ambivalent about the "class bias and character of the ANC,"[60] even while accepting the need for a provisional accommodation with capitalism.[61]

Being forced to grapple with such questions as South Africa neared majority rule was a token of the SACP's success. But at least two other problems testified to its loss of moorings in the post-Communist world, where its external sources of inspiration, material and ideological support, as well as its models for a future South African economy, had ceased to exist. First, its acknowledgment that it no longer has a clear sense of what socialism is, or how it might conceivably get there. Thus its forthright criticism of Soviet socialism looked forward to achieving a "coherent approach to the kind of socialism we are trying to build," while admitting that "our criticism of the administrative command system, of bureaucratism and our support for representative and participatory democracy ARE *implicitly* part of a coherent approach to socialism. But we have not yet adequately developed this."[62]

Second, the SACP remained caught between traditional communist ideology and a fresh and open appreciation of the new situation: it still talked about the working class becoming "the hegemonic, the leading class" but also stressed a "more pluralistic approach to the struggle for socialism." It insisted on its own vocation to represent the working class while acknowledging their backwardness in Marxist terms. It emphasized being ideologically and analytically open yet relapsed into talking about "the correct way forward." The SACP spoke about "a more *pluralistic notion* of socialism" drawing in "[civic organizations], trade unions, churches, youth and students, rural people, cultural workers, other political formations, etc."[63] It firmly stated: "We do not aspire to a monopoly of power, either in the making of the socialist revolution, or in an ensuing socialist state."[64] In short, having suggested that its role was to represent the workers in an implicitly post-Marxist coalition, the SACP remained a contradiction in terms—paying homage to "the leading role of the working class" *and* calling for "the organized power of all sectors of the oppressed masses."[65]

To be sure, as majority rule came to South Africa, the SACP retained its strength as an example of nonracialism, militancy, courage, and a working relationship between a disciplined party and a larger mass struggle. But a good part of the SACP's ideological self-confidence, and its own salience in the struggle against apartheid, had always depended on its privileged relationship with the Communist world. It was precisely this world's passing that gave South Africa's rulers their chance to move toward negotiations: the weakening of socialism as an alternative for South Africa gave F. W. De Klerk his opportunity to release Mandela and unban the ANC and SACP. Paradoxically then, the SACP was allowed to emerge as a visible public force at the moment when all sides, including, as we have just seen, its own spokespersons, agreed that its status had drastically declined as a force for a socialist alternative.

The Strengthening of the Working Class?

Locating a basis for continuing Marxist hope also depends on exploring the *subjective* fruits of a century and a half of working-class struggle against capitalism. One way to explore this realm would be to trace whether and how the concrete social and political changes brought about by workers' struggles have strengthened the self-consciousness and confidence of workers' movements. A second way would be to look at the evolution and current state of the political parties calling themselves socialist and communist. A third way would focus on workers' relationships with their own self-defense organizations—trade unions—and the vicissitudes of these organizations themselves. And finally, although it is more difficult to assess and rarely studied, we might inquire into the current state of workers' class consciousness.

We would want to point to positions won, from which new offensives might be launched—concessions, in Marx's words, to "the political economy of the working class"[66] *that are experienced as such* and thus become sources of strength that nourish the class' sense of itself and its will to struggle. We would want to point to organizational structures developed by the working class from which it might draw energy and within which it might take refuge.[67] We would want to show progress toward wresting cultural hegemony from the bourgeoisie—not only growing alienation from the capitalist order but creation of an alternative culture and value structure.[68] Thus we would want to discover "strategic reforms" that, in the words of André Gorz's influential 1960s analysis, prepare the workers' movement "to assume the leadership of society and which will permit it in the meantime to control and to plan the development of the society, and to establish certain limiting mechanisms which will restrict or dislocate the power of capital."[69] Above all then, we would need to demonstrate clear development of working-class self-confidence—an increase, however slow, in the workers' sense of their own mission and capacity to rule.[70]

Alas, the sad reality is that no matter what kinds of objective changes we can show—indeed, even tendencies toward absorbing socialist principles into capitalist society,[71]—nowhere in the industrial world can we speak about a long-term growth of working-class strength, self-confidence or autonomy, much less cultural hegemony, or revolutionary outlook. On balance the opposite is true.[72] Workers are not more but much less likely today than one hundred years ago to see themselves as opponents of the capitalist social order, as proponents of a new and different society, as confident of their right and ability to rule. Their parties have everywhere lost their original bearings. As Stanley Aronowitz says, their unions "have taken their place as a vital institution in the corporate capitalist complex."[73]

None of this shatters the faith of those Marxists who believe that class consciousness "is a necessary byproduct of economic crisis."[74] The reason why Marxists do not dwell on the various processes I just indicated is not simply because they seek to avoid bad tidings; rather, their very conception of this subjective side of the struggle has distorted their insight into the issues I am raising. Marxists have tended to neglect the necessity for a lengthy and complex, indeed multigenerational, historical process in which workers slowly develop the will to take power. As I will discuss in Chapter 4, they instead tend to think in terms of a mechanistic and narrow view of subjective capacity as *depending on* objective processes and events. Instead of studying closely whether workers are becoming and making themselves willing and able to rule—the alpha and omega of Marxism—Marxists primarily stress the objective processes that retard or enhance the occurrence of the appropriate subjective response. Eventually a fixation develops: to show how capitalism is running out of ways of displacing its contradictions, and how the workers' situation is worsening; to show how the next downturn (or the one after that) will bring a new and sudden breakthrough.

These problems characterize Bertell Ollmann's discussion of class consciousness in *Dialectical Investigations*. In defining class consciousness he gives us no sense of a complex, difficult, and lengthy existential process in which self-confidence, autonomy, and determination are won in the course of generations of struggle. What appears is rather a largely cognitivist process in which classes achieve in reality what they already possess in potentiality: "the appropriate consciousness of people in that position, the consciousness that maximizes their chances of realizing class interests, including structural change where such change is required to secure other interests."[75] Ollmann divides class consciousness into objective and subjective sides (the actual structure of the workers' position, and their consciousness of this), and then in turn he divides their subjective consciousness into its subjective and objective sides. His thoroughly objectivist look at the subjective dimension stresses "the barriers and pressures rooted in the objective situation of workers, in their work, life, and world, against their becoming class conscious."[76] For Ollmann, because Marxists ask about "something that they believe is already there, in one sense, and not there, in another,"[77] they are preoccupied with questions like, "why *haven't* the workers become class conscious?"[78]

Rather than a multigenerational struggle requiring a lengthy and complex series of developments before workers see themselves as willing and able to rule society, Ollmann gives us "the unfolding of a potential"[79] that is "expanded" by certain developments and "restrained" by others. And this analysis is undergirded at key points by faith: that this is "a journey with an end"; "that class consciousness has *a* future is incontestable";[80] and that with worsening conditions, "as the objective forces propelling workers toward full class consciousness become overwhelming, it is difficult for any worker to retain his old outlook."[81] The fitting response to Ollmann's faith is the old Yiddish expression: "Halevai"—It should only be so.

Instead of concern for the lengthy processes required for workers to arrive at the capacity and will to rule, Ollmann stresses "one of the most neglected aspects of class consciousness"—"the speed at which it can develop (and also, unfortunately, undevelop or come apart)."[82] Arguing that it can "spread with the speed of a forest fire" leads Ollmann further from the study of consciousness, to stress yet one more time the objective causes that make this happen. Thus does Ollmann completely ignore, perhaps as irrelevant, the various subjective historical processes mentioned above, and their negative cumulative development—the *waning* of class consciousness. His "forest fire" analogy unwittingly expresses the problem: if they are not preceded by long-range and complex processes in which workers might slowly develop capacity, self-confidence, autonomy, and hegemony needed to bid for power, all revolutionary uprisings are fated to burn themselves out, to "undevelop or come apart." Not because forest fires burn themselves out—an objective and natural process—but because if such momentary outbursts of rebelliousness are to have long-range effects, they need to eventuate in new structures, institutions, attitudes, and values.

If it is to be more than faith or stubbornness, belief in the proletariat as revolutionary class today must demonstrate its basis not simply in structural arguments about the workers' role in production, but in the lived history of the past century and a half, and in its actual results as experienced today—in workers' actual progress toward becoming *willing and able* to rule. To believe in the proletariat today means overlooking too many blank spots. Those who still consider themselves Marxists fill in the blanks with faith, sentiment, or nostalgia, rather than demanding that the project be justified empirically. Or they may hope for explosions in which workers suddenly slough off submissiveness, lack of confidence, and their acceptance of capitalism, and to become radicalized.[83] This last belief leads to a waiting for the revolutionary proletariat, which will come sooner or later. It is no less irrefutable—and no less an article of faith—than that which keeps some Marxists waiting for capitalism's collapse. It is, indeed, faith and stubbornness.

Marxism as an Idealism

In the past, "idealist" was one of the most withering terms in the Marxist armamentarium. It applied to those who disregarded the centrality of the material historical processes discovered by Marx and believed instead in the historical efficacy of what were "mere" ideas, purposes, and designs. When Marx wrote, he could point to the coming together of a new growing social force, the modern industrial working class, a revolutionary economic system, capitalism, and the theoretical comprehension he provided of the class' struggles against the system. As I argued earlier in this chapter, only *this observable coming together validates Marxism as a project.*

Yet many of those who hold tightly to Marxism today, such as Ollmann and Miliband, have paradoxically moved toward idealism. Not that they ignore that Marxism was a project rather than a mere idea;[84] nor do they argue that ideas are the motive force of history. Indeed, their writings testify to the continuing analytical power of Marxist intellectual tools. They betray an unconscious idealism, however, in assuming that that Marxism's continuing theoretical vitality designates a viable Marxist political project. It is as if the undeniable vigor of the former evokes memories of, and then arguments for the possibility of, the latter. And so Sartre's statement made in 1957 proclaiming Marxism to be "the philosophy of our time" is often cited: how can Marxism be obsolete if the world that gave rise to it is still with us?[85] But as we approach the year 2000, can we say that the project, and not just the analysis of the system which is only one of its components, is still alive? Do we have not merely hopeful memories, but rather evidence within the lifespan of a generation of the proletariat as an earth-shaking social force, one capable of proclaiming and carrying out a mission of universal liberation?

Fragments of the old project, some of its onetime components, remain with us—but not the project as a whole. Its vision, of working classes becoming indomitable, revolutionary, of universal social forces capable of carrying through the structural transformation of their societies has passed. As strong as Marxist memories may be, as useful as Marxist ideas and analyses are, workers in advanced industrial societies today lack the class consciousness, the will, indeed, the universality, and perhaps even the numbers to carry through such a transformation.[86] Throughout the advanced industrial world, they have long since accustomed themselves to accepting the capitalist system's logic, its values, its ideology, its priorities, and its ethos. They have largely abandoned seeing themselves as embodying and pointing toward an economic, social, political, and cultural alternative. They have long since lost confidence in themselves.

In this situation, Marxists like Miliband and Ollmann substitute ideas, analyses, and perhaps memories, for Marxism as a viable historical project. Marxism's ultimate grounding appears fated to become more and more biographical and sentimental as its proponents await objective economic crises that will "sooner or later" produce subjective breakthroughs and revivify the original project. For some, Marxism's unrivalled intellectual coherence and emotional force, underscored by its alternating stress on looking beneath appearances and being thoroughly based on reality, still removes doubts raised by history and observable fact. After all, no other theory answers as many questions, works on as many levels, indeed seems designed to meet as many needs. Consequently, in the face of a recalcitrant reality, Marxism can become a kind of Platonism: a set of commitments (once anchored in historical trends) lying behind a set of analytical tools that now function as a priori norms against which the real world is measured. To keep its hopes alive, an idealist shifting of the terrain of Marxism takes place—from historical project, needing to be legitimated by forms of validation appropriate to it, to theory and analysis, with its Platonic and essentialistic bias. Marxist-idealists ask: if workers are structurally alienated or exploited, will they not one day *see* this and *act* on it? Won't capitalism's structural barriers and tendencies one day lead it into a crisis that will change everything? As Ollmann says, "sooner or later the worsening problems of the system, together with the reduction and eventual disappearances of system-approved alternatives for dealing with them, will drive most workers to embody the consciousness of their class."[87]

This "sooner or later" Marxism marks the end of the great Marxian project of social transformation. Along with some theoretical approaches and analytical tools, this faith is what remains of Marxism. Its hopes are based on abstractions and memories, not on living, breathing workers, movements, and parties. At its peak, Marxism was an effort by significant forces, both theoretical and social, to make the world over in certain specific ways that corresponded to its main fault lines. But today, these forces have been depleted and scattered, deprived of their universal claims and sense of strength. The project is over, even if the idea of it lives on hauntingly.

Chapter Three

WHY NOW?

Why is Marxism over only now? Why not at any of several decisive moments of fragmentation, passivity, defeat, or discouragement since Eduard Bernstein first signaled that Marxist expectations were being refuted by historical reality one hundred years ago? Why wait until the turn of the twenty-first century to draw this conclusion, until all but the very last nails are in the coffin?

Marxism was very much alive as long as it was spreading in the world and being adapted to a variety of conditions, as long as it was being recast in response to previous disappointments and new possibilities. Only at this historical moment is it clear that these are exhausted. I emphasize *this historical moment*: our generation has seen the definitive end of the several twentieth-century incarnations of the original Marxian project. First, the reformist road, although followed with waning attachment to Marxism, was viable through the high tide of Swedish social democracy, the moment of EuroCommunism, and into the first months of Mittérand's government in France. Now it seems completely dissipated. Second, Soviet Communism, based on Lenin's recasting of Marxism in response to reformism and to the revolutionary conditions of a backward capitalism, has run its course. Third, Third World socialism and Communism, inspired by the victory of the Bolsheviks in Russia but shaped in response to conditions of colonial domination and extreme underdevelopment, moved from strength to strength in what seemed an ineluctable march to power from the 1940s to the late 1970s—from China, Vietnam, and Cuba, to Nicaragua, Angola, and Mozambique. Now it is almost everywhere overthrown, in retreat, or on its last legs. Fourth, in the 1960s and 1970s various revised and modernized Marxisms—including the theories of the Frankfurt School and the French Existentialists, as well as Trotskyist and Maoist activist permutations, were tried out as *political* projects in the West by the various New

Lefts. These had their moment, climaxing in May 1968, and then disappeared.

Can these versions of the Marxian project be revived, or can others be imagined? This renewal would have to occur under conditions no Marxist has ever faced: all the existing variations are depleted, no new ones are on the horizon. Each existing version has been tried, and has run its course—as movement, as party, as government, as revolution. From its adoption by the German Social Democrats in 1891 until the Soviet Union's dissolution in 1991, Marxism's permutations took place within, drew energy from, and reshaped, a continuous historical wave. Today this is spent; any future renewal faces a void. By erasing its last, lingering hopes, the dissolution of the Soviet Union closes the eyes of the Marxian project.

Reformism and Lenin's Recasting of Marxism

The original Marxian project had already entered into crisis shortly after it was codified in 1891. Unexpected conditions, including imperialism and monopoly, but also increasing democratization and institutional strength, allowed the German proletariat to avoid impoverishment, cooperate with their class enemies, and begin to reconcile themselves to life under capitalism.[1] Karl Kautsky spoke of the party as "a party which, while revolutionary, does not make a revolution."[2] Even so, Marxism continued to generate meaningful theoretical–practical projects after Bernstein's *Evolutionary Socialism*, the original bible of revisionism, abandoned key Marxian ideas— notably predictions of the working class' increasing immiseration and growing revolutionary consciousness. The world's most developed and organized working class split during the upheaval following World War I, as the Social Democratic Party (SPD) achieved a share of political power and violently imposed order on revolutionary workers. Here and elsewhere, Central and Northern European Social Democrats tried to preserve remnants of a waning nineteenth-century Marxist faith, now become "classical," as they rose to power intent on rationalizing and reforming capitalism.

Beginning with Lenin's response to the reformist trend, every recasting of Marxism had to solve the same basic problems: (1) account for the declining possibility of revolution; and (2) reformulate the Marxist project by locating new objective possibilities and subjective capacities. As time went by, each recasting of Marxism had also to explain the failures of the previous ones. The key questions were: why hasn't the working class made a revolution, and then how and by whom will socialism be brought about?

In *What Is to Be Done?* and *Imperialism* Lenin concluded that under conditions of "economism" and imperialism a vanguard party would be required to bring class consciousness to the proletariat "from without." But if this strategy, carried out systematically, would have involved converting the proletariat from revolutionary subject to tool—wielded by a cadre of professional revolutionaries—Lenin himself saw beyond it in time to lead a workers' overthrow of capitalism.[3] As Lenin developed his strategy in the actual conditions of Russia in 1917, the Russian working class was clearly too small to rule on its own. It was, however, capable of joining with revolutionary peasants to fill the vacuum left by the collapsing old order and a weak domestic bourgeoisie.[4] As the only strategy that actually led to the creation of a worker's state, ruled over by a Marxist party, Lenin's approach utterly recast the field. Henceforth Marxists would be able both to wait on objective possibilities *and* to develop the organizational capacities to take advantage of them. Lenin's success in achieving power gave his party pride of place among claimants to the "correct" Marxist project, even while fundamentally transforming it.

It cannot be stressed too highly that Lenin preseved the Marxist hope of revolutionary transformation by *inverting* central Marxist tenets, with momentous consequences. As Herbert Marcuse later commented, the great task of all Marxists beginning with Lenin was to account for the apparent rupture between "the proletariat and progress."[5] Lenin, who saw both his theoretical and his practical efforts as having European and not just Russian implications, closed this gap by reversing Marxism in at least three immediate ways and one less obvious and long-term way: (1) he called for a vanguard party to lead the proletariat to assume power; (2) he called for it to do so at the head of a coalition with peasants; and (3) he thereby initiated the displacement of revolutionary struggles from the advanced capitalist world to its less developed and semicolonial periphery. These moves implied but never theoretically acknowledged that advanced proletariats were "overripe" for revolution. They also asserted the possibility of making a minority revolution. These apparent tactical shifts recast Marxism decisively: the revolutionary subject was resituated from proletariat to party; and revolutionary strategy shifted from industrialized societies to the capitalist chain's weakest links.

The even more fundamental reversal of Marxism projected a direct leap from conditions of backwardness to socialism—or rather, socialism was redefined. The Bolsheviks would lead Russia into the modern world rather than building the kind of postcapitalist society Marx anticipated.[6] The Marxist revolution's task would *not* be to realize the fruits of socialism, but to establish its preconditions: factories, literacy, a working-class majority, urbanization, and a modernized agriculture. This real meaning of "socialism in one country" had been grasped years before Stalin's formulation by Martov, the leader of the Mensheviks, at the fateful moment in October 1917, just before he led his party out of the Congress of Soviets: the Bolsheviks were assuming the bourgeoisie's task of presiding over Russia's industrialization. They would henceforth have to call into being a working-class majority—and extract the necessary surplus from them. Having proclaimed themselves agents of universal liberation, their actual role would be to push a peasant population into the twin maelstroms of urbanization and factory life. The Communist Party became the Soviet Union's bourgeoisie.

Why were these reversals of Marxism widely accepted as being no more than its clarification and adaptation to new conditions? As I suggested above, Lenin offered a way out of the reformist crisis that led Bernstein to abandon Marxism and its revolutionary hopes. Indeed, after Engels' and the SPD's embrace of electoral politics, his was the first coherent and effective Marxist strategy for achieving power. And in this he succeeded. He not only fulfilled Marxism's primary validity test—practice—but also thereby seemed to validate Marxism itself. Moreover, Lenin drew on the authority of Marxist tradition and its texts, which turned on proletarian revolution.

Insofar as Soviet Communism became the arbiter of what was and what was not Marxism, this had incalculable consequences: the Marxism of democracy and total confidence in the workers and their political development, devoted to creating a world of milk and honey from the building blocks left behind by the capitalist stage of development, became a Marxism of minority domination, workers' submission to a party acting in their name, and forced modernization. These new emphases recast Marxism in a most peculiar way, allowing "Leninism" to retain Marxism's original promise and simultaneously to contradict it. We can see the theoretical results in such documents as Stalin's *Dialectical and Historical Materialism*. While concisely rendering Marxism's main ideas, it presents the dialectic as a *natural* law "applied to social life, to the history of society,"[7] dogmatizes the logic of revolution, and treats human beings primarily as the objects of scientific laws. The cult of the party completes this theoretical transformation: it becomes *the* agent of history, interpreter of its stages and requirements, and above all, guardian of the proletariat's will and revolutionary consciousness.

At the Margins

Presiding over the world's largest land mass and its third-largest population, Soviet Marxism understandably became the dominant revolutionary theory and practice. Equally understandably, given its isolation and the defeat of revolutions elsewhere, Soviet Marxism used its hegemony to bend Communist parties everywhere to its survival requirements. Only many years later, and in the wake of the Chinese Revolution, would unorthodox and Third World Marxism become serious political alternatives.

Unorthodox Marxism incubated in the margins of, and sometimes in antagonism to, Soviet Marxism. At first seeking to be responsive to the revolutionary potentialities of the Western proletariat, the writings of Korsch and Lukacs were soon to be cut off by Stalinism from any possible practice[8]; the Frankfurt School devoted itself to understanding why imperialist war and the Bolshevik Revolution, and later the Depression, failed to bring about proletarian revolution in the West. After Trotsky's exile from the Soviet Union, an activist unorthodoxy emerged that tried to incite an alternative sense of revolutionary possibility. If such recastings of Marxism had to account for working-class quiescence in the West, project an alternative revolutionary force and scenario, and account for the Soviet Union's negative features, they had to so with an equal authority to Lenin's. On the activist side this authority might be drawn from other great revolutionaries such as Rosa Luxemburg and Trotsky, as well as from appealing to Lenin against Leninism. On the theoretical side, it was possible, especially as previously unknown material was published for the first time, to appeal to Marx himself.

Trotskyism immediately assumed the mantle of the revolutionary alternative to Stalinism. It presented an attractive argument that the Soviet Union would be set right by a more enlightened and democratic leadership, as well as by more militant revolutionary policies—without challenging the minority revolution or the vanguard party. If they could be appealed to over the heads of their reformist or Stalinist leadership, workers would show their revolutionary character. A second but even more marginal activist orientation maintained this as well, based as it was on the words and actions of Rosa Luxemburg. Devoted to the revolutionary force of the proletariat, activists inspired by Luxemburg's writings and martyrdom argued that changes within the working class registered by Lenin were either temporary or affected no more than a thin layer. This current of Marxism abjured a vanguard role and instead banked all hope on the proletariat's spontaneous class consciousness and continuing revolutionary will.

The other Marxists willing to put the *failure* of revolution at the center of their work were theoreticians without a movement like Adorno, Horkheimer, and Marcuse. If their outlook had been shaped by the crushing of the revolutionary German Left and the catastrophe of Nazism rather than the triumphalism of Stalinism, their research reflected their distance from radical politics. In effect, they sought a Marxian explanation for the failures of Marxism, incorporating non-Marxist tools (e.g., psychoanalysis) as necessary. Still, essays such as Horkheimer's "Traditional and Critical Theory," written in 1938, continued to foresee the union of theory and practice, based on the expectation that capitalism "must necessarily lead to a heightening of those social tensions which in the present historical era lead in turn to wars and revolutions."[9] In the face of the Depression and fascism, and in spite of its deformation-cum-success in the Soviet Union, Marxism was still seen as having the potential to inspire and guide the masses.

Marxism's High Tide?

Although Horkheimer was to abandon this hope by the mid-1940s, other thinkers and movements were inspired by the Soviet successes against Germany, as well as by other revolutionary victories. The Marxist movements that took power in the 1940s in the wake of World War II—in the former Yugoslavia, China, Korea, and Vietnam—went a step beyond Bolshevik practice in mounting successful revolutions in the context of foreign occupations. And they were even farther from representing a sizable proletariat in an industrial society. Communist movements gained hegemony over workers in France and Italy during these years, after having played decisive roles in partisan movements. By the war's end, then, parties of industrial proletariats once again laid claim to the Marxian project, new revolutionary governments faced the need to construct the prerequisites of socialism, and the isolation of the Soviet Union was definitively overcome.

At the same time, however, its exclusive ability to define *the* Marxian project and marginalize all other contenders was coming to an end, as the sheer existence of China and Yugoslavia pointed to other roads to socialism. As a result, it was no longer possible to think in terms of a single Marxian project. Unorthodox Marxism moved away from the margin, and the various Third World Marxisms began to inspire the world.

The various unorthodoxies, eventually grouped under the name "Western Marxism," and often stressing cultural or subjective dimensions tabooed by orthodox Marxism, slowly developed, including not only Trotskyism, the heritage of Luxemburg, the writings of Korsch, Lukacs, and the Frankfurt School, but also the writings of Antonio Gramsci and Jean-Paul Sartre. These would all enter into the formation of the New Left, and all over the West by the 1960s and 1970s a variety of Marxists would enter factories, neighborhoods, minority movements, community organizations, and schools, and would freely and self-confidently agitate and organize. Unlike the Leninist Old Left, the New Left would never be a coherent project, but rather many projects stemming from many different perspectives and sets of circumstances.

The Movement was, of course, inspired by the wave of Third World revolutions taking place throughout the 1950s, 1960s, and 1970s. These diverged drastically from Leninism, even while depending on its authority and, usually, on a vanguard party. Almost everywhere, the focus of struggle was against imperialism and colonialism, meaning that virtually every Third World movement began as, or became, a struggle for national self-determination against an imperial power. The movements in turn assumed a variety of forms. Both the Chinese, victorious in peasant war, and the Vietnamese, victorious in guerilla war, may have regarded themselves as Leninist; but each, centered in the countryside and not the city, recast Marxism no less than did Lenin. The Cubans, on the other hand, only turned to Marxism–Leninism after a guerilla army that was ideologically rather unformed seized power. Marxist or Marxist-influenced guerilla organizations fought successful anticolonial wars in Mozambique, Angola, and Zimbabwe, but never became orthodox communist parties when in power. Other movements, such as the Sandinistas in Nicaragua, the Farabundo Marti Liberation Front (FMLN) in El Salvador, and the African National Congress in South Africa were Marxist-oriented or coalitions of Marxists and non-Marxists. The South Africa Communist Party, for example, was a vital member, but never the dominant component, of the African National Congress. In short, for all its diversity Third World Marxism faced distinctly different conditions—and accordingly shaped itself into a distinctly different project—from either the Soviet Marxism to whose Leninism it paid such homage, or the New Left Marxism that it so inspired.

Since I am inquiring about the Marxian project's subsequent disintegration, two facts are worth noting about this period of Marxism's great expansion. First, I have already called 1848 to 1917 Marxism's heyday, meaning that during these years the development of capitalism and working-class opposition seemed to bear out its analysis and justify its project. Second, the three decades after the 1940s witnessed the high tide of the Marxian revolutionary project—even though the actual shape of events in the 1940s and after had less and less to do with Marx's anticipation of increasing class-consciousness pointing toward proletarian revolution under advanced capitalism.[10] In the sensational rise of Marxist rule, allegiance, and influence during these years, a startling fact went largely unnoticed: the spread of this project ostensibly based on workers' revolution had less and less to do with revolutionary workers.

Marxism's great paradox was that although it was not spreading in the form in which it was originally conceived, it was widely believed, even by its antagonists in the 1960s and 1970s, to be the wave of the future. It seemed to achieve intellectual as well as political hegemony virtually everywhere outside of the advanced industrial societies, and briefly made political and theoretical inroads even there. Even if the proletariat and progress were growing further apart than ever during this period, another "reality and power," another "this-sideness" was replacing the original union. From the beginning of the Vietnamese revolution in 1946 to the fall of the white settler regime in Zimbabwe in 1980, the world saw a steady succession of anticolonial and anticapitalist struggles that put in power movements with a strong Marxist bent—from Santiago to Saigon, from Havana to Harare, from Peking to Pnom Penh, from Managua to Lorenço Marques, from Addis Ababa to Aden. EuroCommunism became a serious current in Southern Europe, and Marxist influence became a major force throughout Latin America, as well as in the Southern African liberation movements.

Western Marxism received its first real trial in the movements of the 1960s, gaining support among students and intellectuals for a nondogmatic, nondeterministic, democratic, genuinely dialectical political philosophy. A thousand Marxisms seemed to bloom in the wake of May 1968, including those of Marcuse and Sartre, and they added important theoretical depth to this new Left's remarkable political energy.

A worldwide struggle was clearly taking place on dozens of fronts between capitalism and its alternative. Socialism, illuminated by the many Marxisms, guided by Marxist intellectuals, and resting on popular struggles was in the ascendancy. This rising tide saw many great moments in the 1960s and 1970s, but perhaps its most unforgettable image is of the helicopters evacuating the American embassy in Saigon, as South Vietnam fell to the Vietcong and North Vietnamese on May 1, 1975.

Signs of Decline

How is it possible that this thirty-year high tide, from the late 1940s to the late 1970s, should overlap with another equally dramatic period, from the early 1960s to the early 1990s, during which the *disintegration* of Marxism took place? How is it possible, in fact, that a signal event of both could be one and the same moment: the May 1968 uprising in Paris? Of course, the deeper problem was not only never resolved, but continued to worsen: the absence of a revolutionary working-class movement, and the integration of the best-organized and most advanced working classes into capitalist society. May 1968 led to a near-revolution, and was certainly deeply indebted to the general diffusion of Marxism in France, the Vietnamese struggle against neocolonial rule, and the influence of thinkers such as Marcuse and Sartre. It was, that is, the product of *all* the currents we have been exploring. Yet, most paradoxically, it confirmed the deeply nonrevolutionary character of the French Communist Party and its stranglehold on much of the working class at the moment of their potential breakthrough, marking the beginning of the end for French Marxism.

Furthermore, when Communist reform in Czechoslovakia was repressed by Soviet troops in August 1968, it became clear that the Marxist systems held no chances of being democratically transformed from within, by Communist reformers.[11] And by the mid-1970s it had been demonstrated again and again that no underdeveloped society—not only the Soviet Union under Stalin, but also China and Cuba—had any chance of building a socialism in anything like the sense envisaged by Marx. Underdevelopment, a minority working class, and perhaps above all, American hostility, guaranteed that a Marxist victory in Vietnam—or in Zimbabwe, or Angola, or Mozambique, or Nicaragua, or Grenada, or Laos, or Cambodia—would lead to the same dismal outcome as Marxist victories elsewhere. In more advanced societies, coalitions or parties winning electoral victories—such as in Chile—would be faced with destabilization and ultimate overthrow by a combination of American intervention and their own ruling classes. And, in the advanced industrial societies, after brief flashes during the late

1960s, any talk about the working class desiring socialist transformation would be greeted with snickers.

Of course, even if these multiple signs of Marxism's weakness were there for all to read, the enormous energy of the historical moment and the apparent vulnerability of capitalism had made it possible to look elsewhere and see otherwise. Even if the worldwide revolutionary wave was overwhelmingly *not* based on proletarian movements, Marxism as a revolutionary outlook and practice reached its peak. Indeed, Lenin's strategy of destroying the chain of capitalism at its weakest link, in its empire, seemed still to hold the chance of success. With defeat in Vietnam, American capitalism seemed more vulnerable than perhaps at any time in its history: the fall of Saigon was accompanied by Portugal's defeat in Africa and followed a few years later by the dramatic fall of Managua to the Sandinistas, the American humiliation in Iran, and the victory of the guerrillas in Zimbabwe.

If by 1980 the American New Left had fragmented, Marxism was winning converts in all the Western universities, and the most deeply rooted movement to emerge from the New Left, the women's movement, was involved in sustained theoretical and practical interaction with Marxism. In Southern Europe, parties devoted to EuroCommunism still sustained hope for a non-Stalinist, indeed, a democratic communism. The early actions of the Sandinistas and Mugabe's government in Zimbabwe held out the possibility that successful revolutionary movements could benefit from the experience of Stalinism and the availability of Communist aid, and avoid the worst excesses. Mittérand's early actions in France suggested that other paths of change lay open. Dissidents from the East such as Rudolph Bahro in East Germany and Roy Medvedev in the Soviet Union articulated nonauthoritarian paths of socialist reform for their societies. A working-class revolutionary movement erupted in Poland.

Disintegration

The promise of 1975 stayed alive well into the 1980s. Despite unmistakable signs of Marxism's growing irrelevance on the most fundamental theoretical and practical level—where the working classes of advanced industrial societies were concerned—significant projects calling themselves Marxist were still being attempted, other socialist offensives were launched, capitalism continued in deep crisis, and the Marxist world remained a powerful counter to capitalism and continued to give inspiration and support to revolutionary movements. Today, all this has changed. Capitalism has won the Cold War, and Communism has done what seems unimaginable, namely, ceasing to exist. The shocking collapse of the Soviet Union was the final nail in the coffin of Marxism; the near-universal flight from Communism that followed was its funeral.

There have, of course, always been nonparty Marxists who argued that Soviet Communism was not Marxism. Trotskyists, reform communists with a small "c," non-Communist Marxists, anti-Communist Marxists—generations who have insisted that Marxism was fatally deformed in the Soviet Union, indeed, perhaps even overthrown by a Stalinist counterrevolution. Many have even looked forward to its collapse. In the words of Alex Callinicos, what has died in the Soviet Union and Eastern Europe "is not socialism, of however a degenerate and distorted form, but the negation of socialism."[12]

But wasn't this "negation" begun by a united Bolshevik party and further carried out by narrowing coalitions of Bolshevism's original leaders and in its name?[13] Callinicos stresses Stalin's many undeniable ruptures with the original project: the expulsion of Trotsky, the liquidation of the Kulaks, the purges and Great Terror, the creation of a new ruling-party class. But he ignores Stalin's many *continuities.* After all, however purged and dominated by Stalin, it was the Bolshevik Party and no other that carried out (however distortedly) "the building of socialism," which included the collectivization of agriculture, the creation of a working class, and the industrialization of the Soviet Union, as well as vast campaigns of literacy, education, and health care. The West's hostility was based on reality: private property had been expropriated and transformed into a form of collective property; a new and noncapitalist form of collectivity was created. If this was also nondemocratic, and thus nonsocialist, didn't Lenin's fateful embrace of the notion of a vanguard party and minority revolution, as well as the patent fact that the Soviet Union was besieged and engaged in an urgent process of self-transformation, explain such deviations? As the West's unending hostility indicated, the Soviet Union's unwavering insistence on realizing Marxism and building socialism was more than mystification: day in and day out for nearly seventy-five years it paid homage to Marxism and to the Bolshevik Revolution, reflecting the ruling party's need to legitimate itself by constant reference to the revolution's starting point and goals.[14] As Isaac Deutscher described it, the Revolution's betrayal and its fulfillment were tragically inseparable.[15]

Rejecting this interpretation out of hand, Callinicos hopes that the Soviet Union's disintegration may allow "the authentic Marxist tradition, long driven underground, to return to the light of day."[16] He speaks of the revolutionary tradition "founded by Marx and Engels and continued principally by Lenin and the Bolsheviks, by Trotsky and the Left Opposition, by Luxemburg and by Gramsci."[17] Obviously by "return" Callinicos means the possibility of revolutionary movements being reconstituted around non-Stalinist Marxism now that the model and deterrent, "official" Stalinist Marxism, no longer dominates the field. Yet while such a return is abstractly conceivable, it is increasingly clear that the collapse of Soviet Communism heralded the demise of all Marxisms. After decades during which working-class movements claiming loyalty to Marxism continued to shrink, the period after 1989 witnessed a wholesale stampede from not only Communism but Marxism. To retain any shred of credibility, most Communist parties and movements outside Eastern Europe and the former Soviet Union scrambled to distance themselves from anything sounding like Communism or Marxism. Once-Marxist governments in Africa embraced capitalism, as did the Chinese Communist Party. By 1994 the holdouts could be counted on the fingers of one hand.

No Return to Revolutionary Goals

But is this a defeat for non-Communist Marxists like Callinicos, who *opposed* these regimes and parties? The answer lies not only in the many continuities between the October Revolution and the Soviet Union. Nor does it lie in the fact that the movements overthrowing Communism did not seek to create a new and democratic socialism, nor that the people's victory over Communism has unleashed every manner of right-wing impulse. Unexpected as was the turn of events, something even more unexpected has happened, reflected in a generalized depression that came over the Left virtually everywhere after August 1991. The end of the Soviet Union signaled the end of a wide range of hopes and possibilities that were, perhaps often unconsciously, parasitic on its continuing existence. Even if it incarnated Marxism in a totally rhetorical, mystified way, even if it did no more than *mock* Marxism, it thereby kept Marxism alive, encouraging Marxists in their Marxism even as it infuriated them. Even independent non- and anti-Communist Marxisms were confirmed in their Marxism by this solid, palpable legatee-cum-betrayor of the great revolutionary past, tradition, and theory. Its collapse generated an undertow that has swept away a whole range of radical hopes that depended on its stable, if repugnant, reality.

This happened on at least three levels, which reflect the hopes of very different political currents. First, as I suggested above, many on the Left who saw the continuity between Marx, Lenin, and Soviet Marxism still anticipated that undemocratic and authoritarian Soviet-style Communism might one day evolve or be reformed into democratic and humane Communism, perhaps through a workers' movement.[18] As Isaac Deutscher speculated when Stalin died, "freedom may once again become the ally and friend of socialism; and then the forty years of wandering in the desert may be over for the Russian revolution."[19] History, so the hope went, might some day place the story of Bolshevism, even Stalinism, as stages along the way of the difficult passage to humane, democratic socialism. By combining its socialist but party-dominated achievements with democratic workers' control, the Soviet Union might one day, through evolution or revolution, fulfill its revolutionary promises.

In a 1987 study of Jean-Paul Sartre's analysis of Stalinism, I wondered whether some kind of revival might be conceivable that could recreate, at a higher level appropriate to an industrialized socialist society, the Revolution's original compelling vision.[20] Throughout his extended study of Stalinism, Sartre stressed that it was the Bolsheviks' urgency about constructing a modern industrial society that was the source of Stalinism and the Bolshevik Revolution's deviation from its original goals. *Deviation* is his key analytical concept, pointing not only to a turning away from the revolution's original goals, but to a change in the very consciousness of the revolution's heirs.

At the end of his study Sartre strikes a note of optimism that the extent and nature of the deviation might be limited by *the purpose* of this enormous apparatus. His final words suggest that humanity might still remain resilient in the face of its creations and that the persistence of the needs for which the revolution was originally undertaken give us hope for a reawakening of the original revolutionary longings. This resiliency, Sartre argues, arises from the fact that there are limits to deviation: even if human beings redefine reality, forget their past, live monstrosities and barbaric lies, they cannot totally repress their memories or their needs. No amount of deviation could completely erase a revolutionary history that became institutionalized into a practico-inert layer of social life. Each citizen of the Soviet Union, as a member of that society, shared in its world of rights, traditions, institutions, and expectations. The deviations were rooted, in spite of all the rewriting of the past, in heroic ancestors and liberating ideas. Indeed, even Stalin's *Dialectical and Historical Materialism*, for all its universal laws governing all of reality and its being taught dogmatically, retained a subversive, revolutionary thread: the notion of bringing history under the conscious, collective control of its subjects.

Marxism retained a liberating core that remained a constant thorn in the side of Soviet rulers who taught it, lived by it—and denied it in their daily practice.[21] This is, after all, one reason why Marxism became so compelling to the worldwide wave of New Left activists, in spite of repeated revolutionary betrayals, as well as its histories of deviation.[22] I wrote in 1987, "One whole side of it, with all its gaps, weaknesses and omissions, remains revolutionary and liberating—in Moscow even when taught as catechism, at Harvard even when studied as falsehood."[23]

Now that the long-awaited upheaval has happened, of course, it turns out that the founding Revolution has not been completed, and there remains scant ideological basis within the life of the successor societies for "recalling" them to Marxist promises. Even so, as the election of former Communists in such places as Poland testifies, there may be limits to how far Communism may be reversed. Those intent on overturning the Revolution's accomplishments will inevitably stumble against, and paradoxically may find themselves deviated by, the stubbornness of the expectations with which they began.

Socialism in One Country?

What effects would Communism's collapse have on those few Communist movements that retained their vitality? As I mentioned in Chapter 2, the South African Communist Party surfaced just as events in Eastern Europe and the Soviet Union were making it a political orphan. If the ANC had become mother and father to thousands of exiles, in many ways its heart and soul had been the SACP, and in turn the Soviet Union and its satellites had been the SACP's material as well as spiritual parents.

In one of history's most ironic twists of fate the SACP was forced soon after its unbanning to ponder the fateful question that had split Marxists in Russia seventy years earlier: Is socialism possible "in one country?" That is, is socialism possible under conditions of backwardness and capitalist encirclement? Is socialism possible, to put it more precisely, in a world dominated by the International Monetary Fund and without Soviet and Eastern European material, political, and moral support? If, unlike Stalin in the 1920s, the SACP leadership was able to accept reality and conclude that pursuing such a course was unthinkable, this did not, however, give it a clear alternative. Along with the factors cited in Chapter 2, its sense of suddenly being orphaned ruled out any push toward socialist transformation.

As a party discussion paper pointed out, South Africa did not even possess the advantanges of the Soviet Union seventy years earlier: vast territory, resources, and population, as well as the capitalist disarray brought on by the world wars and the depression. Adding this to the related facts that the SACP no longer had a coherent vision of socialism, that the South African working class faced an extended process of development to become capable of leading South Africa, that revolutionary politics in South Africa henceforth had to be pluralistic, and the SACP's conclusion was inescapable: "The advance to socialism within our own country depends considerably on the regrouping and resurgence of Left forces world-wide in the face of [capitalism's current] challenges."[24] In short, without wallowing in passivity or defeatism, socialist transformation in South Africa had to wait on events elsewhere: "the construction, deepening and defense of socialism is, at best, highly improbable within our own country *on its own*."[25]

The End of Postcapitalist Society

The SACP's plight highlights what the collapse of Communism will mean for those who identified with it. Secondly, there were those who saw the socialism embodied in the Soviet Union as false or incomplete. But these many critics, enemies, and friends based themselves on, and drew hope from, its existence *as a society that had overthrown capitalism*. For seventy years anti-Communist socialists have pointed to the Soviet Union as deformed socialism, or as a mockery of socialism; but many thought that Soviet Union, however weakly or distortedly, had gone *beyond* capitalism. A bad socialism represented an historical advance, even if that progress remained to be completed by radically democratizing the Soviet system. Even when they regarded it angrily and oppositionally, many who opposed the Soviet Union were nourished in the belief in an actually existing world beyond capitalism, thus the real historical existence of a *potential* alternative to capitalism.

In a weaker version of this mood, Communism, even when it was hated, remained solid, stable, and real; one could point to it and excoriate it. This meant using what it claimed to be, as a prod to think toward *another* alternative. To say, as so many have, that this Communism was not socialist, was to continue to anticipate that beyond the false socialism lay a true one. Even as false socialism, even as bureaucratic state capitalism, the Soviet Union's experience of doing away with capitalism encouraged this belief. But today, after the overthrow of Communism, we can no longer point to even an ugly alternative. Today, no significant society or movement exists that continues to proclaim itself as being beyond capitalism. The hopes that were openly or secretly, consciously or unconsciously, nourished by the existence of the Soviet Union have disintegrated along with it.

No Surviving Revolutionary Inspiration

Even many of those Marxists most critical of the Soviet Union have conceded that it was built on, and it paid homage to, an original workers' revolution over seventy-five years ago. Callinicos, for example, argues that a genuine socialist revolution took place, and was in turn overthrown by a Stalinist counterrevolution that installed bureaucratic state capitalism.[26] It is from the original revolutionary experience that Callinicos draws outlines of a future postcapitalist society.[27] Others equally hostile to calling the Soviet Union "socialist" at least agree[28] that its deepest memories and portions of its constantly rehearsed ideology kept alive a vision of human action and power that, however belied by the reality, retained a subterranean subversive force in Communist societies.

Thus even many hostile Marxist critics of the Soviet Union hoped that the masses in revolt might recover the original emancipatory meanings of ideas and texts that had been jammed down their throats by Communist education and culture. As long as these masses did not yet decide that they had had enough of any and all kinds of Marxism, Marxism was not yet over. Now all those texts, in Russian, in German, in Czech and Slovak, in Romanian, in Bulgarian, in Hungarian, all those volumes churned out by the tens and hundreds of thousands by official state publishing houses, are no longer valued and thus carry no more possibility, suggest no more hope. By the 1990s, they represented no more than the sheer physical detritus of Communism, fated to burden libraries, bookstores, and used book tables in Eastern Europe and the former Soviet Union for decades to come, or (more likely) to be used to heat apartments and houses. The entire official Marxist cultural apparatus, along with any revolutionary inspiration it still contained, was swept away at one stroke and consigned to history's rubbish heap.

For all of these reasons the Soviet collapse was followed by a more general exodus from Marxism, a fin-de-siècle feeling of exhaustion and the end of an era. The remaining dwindling hopes for Marxism in the West and the Third World were now deprived of the actual incarnations of Marxism, no matter how ambiguous and even negative these had become. And so, far from emerging from this debacle with the kind of energy and enthusiasm Callinicos tries to muster, non-Communist Marxists found themselves now isolated as never before, now discouraged and depressed, because in a fundamental sense the collapse of the Soviet Union suddenly revoked the sense of *beyond* that so many had been living with. Rather than capitalism being in its final stages, threatened and ranged against this brutal and incomplete but still young historical current, it now appears that history has passed beyond its "next stage." What was once *the* ascendant world-historical trend belongs to the past. The rout is complete.

Marxism as Idea

Or rather, it is almost over. There are still a few who, in Callinicos' words, believe that "it is time to resume unfinished business."[29] For him this means reviving classical Marxism in the face of Stalinist Marxism's collapse; in the case of others it means rethinking or reconstructing Marxism so that it is once again an adequate tool of understanding and guide to action. But a close reading of Callinicos' *The Revenge of History*, which seeks to explain the breakdown and lay foundations for the revival, reveals the prototypical weakness we will encounter in all such efforts: a fatal detachment from any social force that might make it true. As I argued in Chapter 2, such efforts transform what was originally theoretical–practical project into an *idea* that lives in the minds of a few intellectuals.

Followers of Trotsky have always been forced to defend a distinctively idealistic Marxism, given the fact that since the Bolshevik Revolution workers overwhelmingly have been oriented toward self-proclaimed Marxist states and movements on the one hand or social-democratic and even more reformist movements and parties on the other. If Trotskyists rejected the various self-proclaimed socialisms as not really being socialism, their goal could only be glimpsed fleetingly and in rare historical moments, such as among the original Soviets in 1905. One had to argue not only for the basic analyses of Marxism, but also against all existing socialisms, on behalf of the *idea* of a more authentic socialism. To sustain hope it was also necessary to argue that workers were ready and eager for such a socialism and on the verge of casting off their false leaders.

If Callinicos takes most of these steps he leaves out a Marxist (or any other) analysis of the current state of workers' or socialist movements. Capitalism, he tells us, "stands condemned." He maintains,

> a different form of society is required which would eliminate exploita-
> tion, overcome the anarchy inherent in capitalism, and achieve the kind
> of collectively regulated relationship to our natural environment with-
> out which humankind may perish. Marx believed that these require-
> ments would be fulfilled by Communism, the rule of the associated
> producers.[30]

"Condemned" by whom, "required" by whom, we might ask. Why does a Marxist haul capitalism before the bar of reason? The obvious answer is, because its grave diggers are nowhere to be found. Likewise, Callinicos argues for the ideas of communism and of soviets (as a form of socialist democracy), but without pointing to any currents that indicate that these remain historically realizable. And so, arguing the idea of socialism, he gives a plausible set of abstract projections beyond capitalism, utterly separated from any agents struggling to get there. In response to the collapse of Communism, Marxist ideas camouflage a strikingly non-Marxist commit-ment.

Mourning Marxism

These are the reasons why I say Marxism is over now, and was not over until now. In 1975 the New Left, the Third World struggle against imperialism, and the Communist world seemed to belong to the same complex and contradictory, but ascendant, field of force, while the capitalist world appeared more vulnerable than ever. Today this field of force has disinte-grated, and the deeper structural issues plaguing Marxism for nearly one hundred years appear as the underlying cause. One could have said that the Marxian project had been over for several generations, because almost none of its reformulations seemed able to revive a sense of revolutionary possi-bility in the industrialized societies. But having traveled the earth and been recast time and again, only today has Marxism finally exhausted its possi-bilities.

Marxist renewals are not conceivable in the former and still-Commu-nist world where Marxism served a vital role as the theory and practice of anticapitalist "modernization." Marxist-led struggles for national liberation have run their course and were by and large about neither socialism nor the working class. The New Left was unable to successfully unite its undoctrinaire and dialectical Marxism with its various social movements; and even the most ideologically radical of advanced industrial proletariats, the French and Italian, have overwhelmingly abandoned Marxism. The one-hundred-year wave has spent its force: just as all radical thought and action between 1891 and 1991 took place within the field Marxism shaped and defined, so today must all radical thought and action take place *after* Marxism. It is finally time to declare that, whatever value its intellectual tools may still have, the Marxian project has been tried everywhere and reveals no remaining possibilities. It is over.

Should we mourn its passing? There are powerful reasons not to. After all, its end is as much a relief as a loss, freeing those of us who have been radical and socialist from the endless burden of explaining away the Soviet Union and its satellites. It ends the hours many of us have spent in study groups, in discussions, in arguments, learning and explaining why Soviet Communism did not reflect the original Marxian project, why its political structure was not socialist. Freed from our albatross, are we not, as André Codrescu said in celebrating the fall of the Romanian leader Ceausescu, finally free once again to dream of socialism?

Another reason to not mourn is to show sympathy for the millions who died in the name of Marxism—in the Soviet Union, of course, but also in China, in Kampuchea, in flimsy boats in the South China Sea. We should also remember all those who have not only been killed but oppressed and bullied and straitjacketed in its name—throughout Eastern Europe, in Cuba, elsewhere in Asia. If Marxism became the ruling ideology in all those societies, there must have been something about it that can be linked to how and where and why it was used as it was. It may not have caused Stalinism, but Stalinism was after all a form that the Marxian project assumed under certain determinate conditions. It is absurd to argue that nothing about the one is implicated in the other.

Another reason for not mourning Marxism's demise is the fact that many millions more have felt and thought and lived Marxism's vision of human liberation through solidarity and have been disillusioned by their leaders, their hope destroyed. If we still wish to pursue that vision, at the very least we need to share and understand their loss. And to see how frail hope is, and that it must be forever renewed; something vital is lost when it dies.

Yet was the Marxian project to blame for this wreckage, and not those on the other side, who fought with all the weapons at their disposal to retain every last one of their class privileges? And not the social systems that made these privileges seem like second nature? Should the countless millions not have struggled against capitalism, colonialism, and imperialism over the past hundred years? Should they not have taken this radical vision to their heart as a coherent and meaningful project? Should they instead have accepted lives of oppression and exploitation, for themselves and their children? Once deciding to fight, could they have devised a better project, one not needing power to fight power, one not susceptible to corruption, one immune to defeat, and worse, to defeat in victory? Could their revolutionary project have avoided the illusions and evils of their world while they were in and of that world? Should they have not hoped so powerfully?

Even under Communism, its dogmatic texts, imposed and learned by rote, travestied daily, contained revolutionary messages about human life and human dignity. Some learned them well, well enough to overthrow Communism. And even its most corrupt, nepotistic, cynical hierarchies served, along with themselves, a sense of community, the destruction of which is disastrous. What now will happen to the hope that Marxism inspired as that vision of community is torn apart by nationalisms, as the former Marxist societies are delivered over to the mercies of a new war of all against all?

No, do not regret Marxism, in spite of all the regrettable acts committed in its name. For there are reasons to mourn its end: it gave hope; it made sense of the world; it gave direction and meaning to many and countless lives. As the twentieth century's greatest call to arms, it inspired millions to stand up and fight, to believe that humans could one day shape their lives and their world to meet their needs.

It lent coherence to human history, explained inequality and privilege—regarding these as the fundamental social evils—projected a meaningful future, and shaped and guided millions of lives. Committed to the view that humans were at bottom cooperative, rational, and equal, it said that all of human history could be deciphered not only as a story of human and technical development, but of progress in overcoming oppression. Now, after Marxism, most of this has vanished. Without it, without the sense of collective might it gave, of a coherent and shared picture of the universe, of all humanity joined together pursuing right, can we help but be forlorn? Scattered groups will continue to fight for their good, but will we ever again see people regarding themselves as no more and no less than people, fighting for a common good? And we have lost, along with this vision of universal solidarity, the sense that its victory is possible. Optimism about where history is headed is denied us after Marxism, as social orders predominate that give most people just enough, that are just flexible enough at the last minute to avoid fundamental change. A world racked with pain, its people mystified, lost to themselves, with its evils having become more and more acceptable: is this our fate?

Marxism nourished a sense of human collectivity, of humanity capable of becoming a vast we—and thus the sense that the problems facing us could be solved. This is no longer the case. Without it we are alone against profound inequity and oppression—our sense of justice diminished, our strength sapped, our self-confidence undermined, our picture of the universe shattered into multiple, contending, and overlapping perspectives, lacking even the right to talk about we. After Marxism we are, cannot help but be, desolate.

But perhaps we have lost no more and no less than our illusions. After all, those who presided over the *we* silenced many voices and gave us the humanity of a specific culture, race, and gender masquerading as humanity in general. And wasn't this humanity's confidence in history mythical, and its sense of coherence based on erasing all that didn't conform to its simplified picture? Didn't reducing human activity to labor, and deriving culture from the socioeconomic process, drastically misrepresent and misunderstand all that humans do? And didn't the particular universal good being pursued leave out many less privileged goods of particular people? In short, weren't the comforts and hopes of this *we* bought at too great a cost, and isn't its end, however sad, to be welcomed as is the loss of any great illusion?

For all its negative aspects, Marxism was nevertheless a powerful, positive reality with powerful, positive effects. The sense of collective strength it encouraged and tapped was real. It might not have been enough to solve all of the problems all of the time, and it might not have even been enough, at any give moment, to win specific demands over the ruling powers, given their control over the means of survival, culture, values, and state apparatuses. But its vision of collective solidarity was made into reality, not only in song and incantation but, time and again, in struggle. Its strength became real, as did its hopes, as did its sense of right and justice. Even if the *we* it nourished and from time to time realized was not broad enough, or diverse enough, or complex enough, it was more and other than an illusion.

We can see how much more by glancing at the collective gloom and loss of energy after Marxism. The strength of its universal vision, it turns out, encouraged strength; the depth and breadth of its hope encouraged hope; it was the main alternative, and its ending leaves us with no alternative. We now lack the sense that the victory of justice and equality is likely, or even possible. Without its collective strength, anger, and sense of justice we now lack a sense of how our world may be significantly improved.

As a result, Marxists or not, we all suffer from the end of Marxism, at least for the time being, until other visions and projects rekindle the sense that we can tackle, and solve, our most pressing problems. The end of Marxism is accompanied by a general loss of social will: we are left with overwhelming social difficulties, no sense of amelioration, no paths to solution, no identifiable force capable and willing to act. If we have no feeling that good is winning out, neither do we any longer believe even that it *can* win out, or what it is, or how to find it. We do not even have a sense of the collective body that could do this. Marxists or not, with the end of Marxism we have lost all this. Alone among evils, with no clear answer to them or comprehension of them, for everyone's sake we will have to reconstitute the who and how and why and "we" of radical opposition. Until then we are at a loss.

Chapter Four

MARXISM AND MODERNITY: A CONTEMPORARY CRITIQUE

One of the many striking moments of the great revolution that swept Communism from Eastern Europe and destroyed the Soviet Union was the return of Leningrad, Russia's "window on the West," to its original name, Saint Petersburg. By the vote of its residents, the city became renamed for its founder and his patron saint. What does this return to the past say in response to the inherent, self-conscious intention of Marxism (even Soviet Marxism) to move the Soviet Union into the future, to its devotion to technical and human progress, to modernity? Marxists have always viewed themselves as proponents of *the* modern political outlook, typified by the "reactionary"/"progressive" distinction they, and virtually all those on the Left, have always stressed. Marxism has offered itself as *the* tool for social progress, and, at the same time, as *the* expression of modern science and industry, focusing above all on modernity's most characteristic creation, the industrial proletariat. Even to many of its critics, Soviet Marxism was seen as a force for bringing old Russia into the modern world. Is its passing, as the renaming of Leningrad would suggest, a turning back in time?

The debates between Mensheviks and Bolsheviks before the October Revolution explained why Julius Martov and his supporters walked out of the Congress of Soviets that ratified the Bolshevik seizure of power in 1917. These debates turned on whether Russia was ready for the most advanced form of economic and social life, socialism. Socialism meant the socialization of the means of production, but this was meant as a way to harvest the fruits of human productive development and human history. It meant rationally administering a modern industrial society that had developed, but could not capitalize on, the capacity to overcome poverty, whose working class had achieved high levels of technology, skill, literacy, and political self-organization. Socialism's historical function was not to *create* the economic and technical prerequisites for a full human life; that was the historical function of oppressive and exploitative class societies—of capitalism, above all. Rather, socialism would take the next step, of organizing the democratic use of these prerequisites for the general well-being. For this to happen, the workers, called into being and exploited by capital, would themselves have to become thoroughly modern.

Marx saw them attaining considerable freedom from superstition, religion, and belief in traditional hierarchies and authorities, until, as the famous line goes, man is "at last compelled to face with sober senses, his real conditions of life, and his relations with his kind."[1] Thus Marxists assumed that socialism presupposed a high degree of industrialization, a high level of technical skill, modern forms of ownership, and above all, centuries of *human* development. "We know," Marx said, "that to work well the newfangled forces of society, they only want to be mastered by newfangled men [*sic*]—and such are the working men. They are as much the invention of modern time as the machinery itself."[2]

For Martov and the Mensheviks, the Bolsheviks' intention to seize power over Old Russia portended disaster because the country had a preponderance of illiterate peasants and traditionalist forms of production. The Russian working class was far from having achieved the fundamental prerequisite for exercising this power: the technical, economic, and human development necessary to build socialism. Rigorous Marxists, the Mensheviks insisted that Russia would take decades to develop enough modern machinery or modern men to make this modern society possible. And, unlike the Bolsheviks, the Mensheviks refused to bank on revolution elsewhere coming to the aid of what was fated to be a minority revolution. Thus they foresaw disaster if the Soviets, led by the Bolsheviks, took power. A few modernizers would confront millions of illiterate, backward, impoverished, Russian peasants just two generations from serfdom, farming with wooden plows, living in the countryside. Walking out of the Congress at the decisive moment, Martov and his followers heard one last ringing taunt from its president, Leon Trotsky, a taunt that recent history has given new irony: "Go now into the dustbin of history."[3]

One of the great interpretations of the revolution's fate, by Isaac Deutscher, stresses the tragic encounter between the modernizers and those they would modernize: "Indeed, Stalinism may be described as the amalgam of Marxism with Russia's primordial and savage backwardness."[4] Stalin strained mightily to bring Russia into the present, but through the premodern means at his disposal; and in using those means he built that primitiveness into the society itself. In other words, there was no possibility of using more modern methods of debate, discussion, consensus, obeying norms of democracy. Rather, the situation of encirclement by hostile powers and the social conditions of devastated Russia's backwardness led to it reaching back into its past and brutally imposing terror on masses of the Soviet people. Lenin himself saw the problem in the same way: the culture of the vanquished imposed itself on its conqueror. Thus, Deutscher argues, the backwardness the Bolsheviks strove to overcome simultaneously overcame them, and they beat and brutalized old Russia into the modern world. They used, and themselves absorbed, its authoritarianism, its religiosity, its respect for hierarchy, its submissiveness to arbitrary rulers.

The flaw in this interpretation lies in its uncritical view of the Bolsheviks and its blind spot toward their Marxism. It sees the Bolsheviks as already fully modern in the best sense, their Marxism as already mature, rational, democratic, realistic, self-critical. But was there nothing in Marxism itself that adapted it for its fated role? Instead of liberating an already modern society—Marxism's proclaimed task—there was some element in Marxism that, when in power, enabled it to be very effective in forcefully modernizing a traditional society. What in Marxism enabled Marx's rather paradoxically gentle characterization of violence as midwife for creating the new society to become supplanted by the reality of violence as constitutive force of the new society?[6] Rather than being the guide for achieving proletarian democracy, why was Marxism able to become the justification for rule *over* the proletariat, in its name, by a party elite? Instead of being the inspiration for a new critical and inventive culture, how did Marxism lend itself to becoming a set of dogmas forced down people's throats? Instead of opening to the full richness and complexity of the modern world, how did Marxism allow itself to become a way of forcing that world into a series of reductive straitjackets?[7]

Of course it may be argued that any outlook can be deformed in its application—above all a theory whose test is practice. In this case, however, the distorting process was able to make use of several features of Marxism that were rooted in the old world it was trying to transform: its eschatological thrust, its objectivism, determinism, and sense of necessity and an authoritarian bent that would serve well the new authoritarian society. *Pace* Deutscher, the ways in which Marxism and the new order reciprocally defined each other turned on Marxism's ambivalent tie to modernity.

Although it has so strongly presented itself, and come to be known, as the quintessential modern outlook, there is much that is less than fully modern about Marxism, and indeed about Marx himself. As a result, certain of its features make Marxism more congenial to situations demanding the transformation of a traditional culture and society into a modern one than for liberating the potentialities of a modern, capitalist society. If Marxism is less than fully modern, it is no wonder that its main historical role became, contrary to its founder's intent, to act as a bridge between two worlds, traditional and modern, *both of which* it belonged to and expressed.

The Need for a Contemporary Critique

A contemporary critique of Marxism must understand both its weaknesses and its strengths in terms of its unique historicity. But, having observed and declared from within the fold that Marxism is over, why is it necessary for me to point to faults and weaknesses that made this happen? After all, history has performed its own withering critique, as I stressed in Chapters 2 and 3. Still, the question of what it was about Marxism that made for its demise imposes itself persistently as we sift through the ruins. We seem compelled to find out what went wrong, and to trace this to what was wrong.

Indeed, what was wrong? I have a single, decisive "criticism": Marxism was developed between 1840 and 1870, and reached its flowering as a movement between the 1880s and 1917. Marxism's great failing was no more than its great strength: being profoundly rooted in its time and place. But its time and place was the early modern world. Expressive of it, bound to it, it illuminated certain characteristic tensions and struggles of that world. Marxism may well be the most forceful and most coherent expression of modernity, but today we can see that it contained many early modern and even premodern elements. To the degree our world and its people have remained the same as when Marxism took shape, or have entered into its moment and structures, Marxism has remained vital. To the degree both have changed, it seems old-fashioned and out of place—so much so that there is no possible way of bringing Marxism back to life by removing those of its features that have become obsolete, and adding new, contemporary elements. Now, at the end of the twentieth century, its early modern project has aged, meaning that in decisive ways the world has passed beyond Marxism.

These are the key terms of a contemporary critique of Marxism, an analysis that cannot avoid engaging with, and participating in, the spirit of postmodernism. What is it that we are beyond, after all? Isn't it not only Marxism, but also key aspects of the world in which it took shape and to which it helped give an identity? Continuing my insistence on describing its end from within—and now in retrospect, from a half step beyond, and looking back—I argue in what follows that Marxism's weaknesses were not only inseparable from, but indeed were identical to its strengths. This is why it cannot be modernized or revitalized by the adding or subtracting of elements: all Marxisms in some profound sense rest on these features, powerful strengths that became glaring weaknesses. A contemporary critique of Marxism must then eventually become reflexive, a critique of the historical world in which it first emerged, and a self-critique of the period in which it is being superseded. It demands understanding why Marxism "took" when and where it did, and not since or elsewhere. Rooted in a relatively early modernity, Marxism was, after all, the single most forceful and coherent formulation of both the modern project and modern attitudes.

Looking back, at least three features of Marxism, underpinnings of its every variation, demand exploration. First, Marxism promises a "beginning of history" and an end of alienation—that is, an earthly salvation. Second, it stresses focusing on objective trends and the structural processes that determine them. Third, it is a scientifically and theoretically based project demanding enormous study and interpretation. My argument is simply that each of these essential features of Marxism, so apparently modern, contains an attitude that is less than modern. These traits have been central to its appeal, part of its force, and, today, are implicated in its collapse. Marxism has been criticized as a religion in bad faith, proclaiming an earthly salvation it refused to submit to analysis; it has been reproached with failing to have taken adequate account of human subjectivity; and it has been criticized for tending toward authoritarianism, as evidenced by its being named for its founder and by the succession of dictatorial regimes and undemocratic parties it has produced. Although none of these criticisms is new, hindsight adds a special weight to each one. Marxism may have been manipulated and deformed in order to impose a brutal modernization on the Soviet Union, but this very employment betrays its mooring in an earlier age. This side of Marxism kept it, like the Soviet Union, suspended between its original starting point and the full embracing of the modern world.[8]

If it is not already clear enough, let me emphasize that I am talking not only about the "classical" Marxism of the Second International or the "orthodox" Marxism of the Comintern. I am addressing equally all efforts to revitalize and modernize Marxism, such as those of Sartre, Marcuse, and other Western and New Left Marxists. I am speaking about my own Marxism, for all its proclaimed sophistication and subtlety. What follows is not simply a critique of the crudities of an orthodoxy still observed only by one or two parties and governments and a few dwindling sects; it is rather an attempt to understand, and historically situate, traits that are part of Marxism's political and intellectual force. My discussions of these traits in this chapter will be followed by two arguments. The shorter argument, concluding the chapter, is that these features have been part of the appeal of all Marxisms. The longer argument, developed in Chapters 5 and 6, is that recent efforts to modernize Marxism to respond to new realities and modes of thought have produced something other than Marxism.

Critiques of Marxism: Eschatology

The first criticism turns on Marxism's basic impulse and starting point: the belief that a revolutionary transformation of bourgeois society is taking place that is leading both to a fundamental reversal *and fulfillment* of the main trends of human history. A transcendence of class exploitation, toil, impoverishment, and alienation were believed to be in the offing, and with them would appear a new human being and a genuine beginning of history as a conscious process controlled by its subjects.[9] Hindsight based on the fact that this has not happened and is not happening reveals a good deal about Marxism's early modern character, especially about the nature of its hope.

Marx's vision of a turning point of human existence remained present throughout his life, uttered in published as well as unpublished writings. It appears in his discussion of the proletariat as the universal class in his "Contribution to a Critique of Hegel's *Philosophy of Right*" (1843); in his portrayal of alienated labor in *Economic and Philosophical Manuscripts of 1843–1844*; in his and Engels' discussion of the communist future in *The German Ideology* (1845–1846) and the revolution to bring it about in *The Communist Manifesto* (1848). It is present in his discussion of the future possibilities of freedom and labor in the *Grundrisse* (1858); in his reference to the end of class society as the end of "prehistory" in the Preface to *A Contribution to the Critique of Political Economy* (1859); in his analysis of the forms of rule devised by the Paris Commune in *The Civil War in France* (1871); and in his remarks on communism in the "Critique of the Gotha Program" (1875). These well-known statements of Marxist philosophical anthropology differ markedly from the restrained and unrevolutionary words of Marx's Inaugural Address of the Working Men's International (1864), with its celebration of the victory of the Ten Hours' Bill as "the first time in broad daylight [that] the political economy of the middle class succumbed to the political economy of the working class."[10] Still, if the Ten Hours' Bill is the first victory of the proletarian political economy, what will its ultimate victory look like? If the First International's great step toward realism[11] involved speaking soberly about the workers' duty "to conquer political power," where would workers' power lead? In short, the most sober strands of Marxist analysis are propelled by deep, powerful commitments to ultimate goals.

Throughout the history of Marxism, communism was never foreseen as merely a more rational and less exploitative state of affairs, but always as a transformation of human existence, "the riddle of history solved."[12] Thus it is striking to see how the prosaic and sober Frederick Engels describes the future society in *Socialism: Utopian and Scientific* (originally the third part of *Anti-Duhring*, which was written while Marx was still alive and in part with his collaboration).[13] Visualizing the future whose formulation he and Marx shared, Engels characteristically sees it in terms of "an unbroken, constantly accelerated development of the productive forces" and an end to crises, waste, and the capitalists' "senseless extravagance." He cannot help rhapsodizing about "an existence guaranteeing to all the free development and exercise of their physical and mental faculties—this possibility is now for the first time here, but *it is here*." Then, after a note stressing the great quantity of wealth already available under capitalism but squandered during its crises, Engels' productivist vision foresees the future transformation of human nature itself:

> With the seizing of the means of production by society, production of commodities is done away with, and, simultaneously, the mastery of the product over the producer. Anarchy in social production is replaced by systematic, definite organization. The struggle for individual existence disappears. Then for the first time man, in a certain sense, is finally marked off from the rest of the animal kingdom, and emerges from mere animal conditions of existence into really human ones. The whole sphere of the conditions of life which environ man, and which have hitherto ruled man, now comes under the dominion and control of man, who for the first time becomes the real, conscious lord of Nature, because he has now become master of his own social organization. The laws of his own social action, hitherto standing face to face with man as laws of Nature foreign to, and dominating him, will then be used with full understanding, and so mastered by him. Man's own social organization, hitherto confronting him as a necessity imposed by Nature and history, now becomes the result of his own free action. The extraneous objective forces that have hitherto governed history pass under the control of man himself. Only from that time will man himself, more and more consciously, make his own history—only from that time will the social causes set in movement by him have, in the main and in a constantly growing measure, the results intended by him. It is the ascent of man from the kingdom of necessity to the kingdom of freedom.[14]

Here, shorn of Marx's rhetorical power but still stirring enough, is the *vision* animating Marxism: human beings will attain lordship over nature for the first time, make their history for the first time, become free and thus fully human for the first time.[15] What is Marxism without this eschatological and unscientific starting point, its commitment to transforming the world root and branch, and its underlying conviction that these unprecedented changes were indeed *taking place*?

Was it "religious"—that is, irrational and unrealistic—to anticipate such a world, such a transformation of the human condition?[16] In the summary judgment of Leszek Kolakowski, "Marx's faith in the 'end of prehistory' is not a scientist's theory but the exhortation of a prophet."[17] What Kolakowski calls prophecy is a vital dimension of what I have called the project of Marxism. Kolakowski is highlighting the fact that Marxism reaches beyond what we know—beyond employing scientific knowledge of trends and possibilities—to inspire, consciously mobilize, and direct social forces. And it does so while claiming to be scientific on all levels and in every way. Since an eschatological dimension, an ethical layer, and an existential determination to begin from historical trends and *to change the world* are patently not scientific, for Kolakowski this self-contradiction refutes Marxism.

But the Marxian project, as I have described it in Chapter 2, contains *intertwined with each other* science, prophecy, morality, and the determination to create a new social order. As a meaningful sociopolitical project it contains an analysis that corresponds to main lines of historical evolution, a vision of the goal to be realized, a description of how this fits into the larger human adventure, *and* ways of motivating and justifying the actors who are supposed to struggle to realize this vision. Is it intrinsically irrational to be motivated by an eschatological vision, based on the hope of giving history a totally new direction? Not at all, if certain conditions are met and questions answered: Is the vision presented *as* vision—as possible, but contingent? Or does it hide its real nature behind various forms of necessity? Does the vision correspond to actual possibilities and tendencies? Does it anticipate a plausible historical project? Are there agents who are, or might become, disposed to struggle to make this vision into reality?

The very first formulation of historical materialism in *The German Ideology* explains why the possibility of an eschatological transformation arrives only with, and because of, capitalism. Otherwise, in any communist revolution "*want* is merely made general, and with *destitution* the struggle for necessities and all the old filthy business [*die ganze alte Scheisse*: all the old shit] would necessarily be reproduced."[18] For the first time in history, in other words, world-historical and universal intercourse exist, as does a sufficiently high level of productivity—meaning that human beings have collectively learned to harness nature and to organize themselves socially to produce a genuinely human world. Until now, any rebellions on behalf of a just society remained just that, hopeless against an imperious nature that had from time immemorial decreed general want and suffering. Scarcity meant that a genuinely human life could be only lived by the privileged few, at the expense of everyone else. Only today, Marx and Engels concluded in the 1840s, does the possibility exist for the first time for all human beings to assert their humanity and take collective control of their social life. That is to say, the technical capacity has been achieved for the first time in history for all to live a fully human life. Industrialization, based on the latest stage of class society, made possible a society beyond scarcity. Thus, for the first time a classless society is materially possible. Our relationship to nature, to our own social creations, to our own individual lives, need no longer be governed by brute necessity or its displacement as social necessity, and instead we may preside over each of these—collectively, to be sure, but consciously and deliberately—in freedom. And so the project that draws all previous history to an end, the eschatological project of creating a socialist society, is not at all irrational, not at all "religious," even if it is fueled by longings that have historically been expressed in religion. It is a plausible goal of a meaningful collective project.

Eschatology in Bad Faith

The problem is not *that* Marx injects the "beginning of history" into his thought and into the Marxian project, but *how* he does so. Look at its underlying premise: human development and human history make possible an end of alienation and a beginning of a new kind of history; and this is based on powers, freedoms, and experience so different from what went before that we are truly talking about new kinds of human beings. This striking possibility needs to be thought about, demonstrated, argued. The changes Marxism foresees demand to be explored, explained, and analyzed for its vision to be made clear and its possibilities and preconditions established.[19]

And in fact Marx began this task, in his *Economic and Philosophical Manuscripts* and, with Engels, in *The German Ideology*. Neither of these pre-1848 works were published during either of their lifetimes. Had he continued along this line, however, and published the results, Marxism as we know it would never have seen the light of day. Marx would have taken a very different path. Giving sustained attention to this ultimate end of the struggle would have decisively diverted energy from the tasks needed for the struggle. Instead of making clear the conditions for a utopia, instead of arguing and developing its possibility, Marx created Marxism. He sought to understand how this utopia was *being brought into being* by the evolution of capitalism and the class struggle; *these* became most important. Once having stated it, he presupposed the goal, and turned to the more essential task of understanding the objective processes moving toward it. Scientific rather than utopian socialism was called for, showing workers the basis for their exploitation.[20] For Marx it was unthinkable to be just a prophet against prophets: first against Hegel and Feuerbach, Bauer and Hess, and then against Saint-Simon and Comte, Owen and Fourier; and then against Proudhon and Bakhunin. Rather, Marxism's defining trait was its insistence on premising itself on the facts, being historically grounded in real tendencies, as opposed to all of these prophets who invented castles in the air.[21] To Marx's mind these idealists were both preindustrial and preproletarian. Against them he argued for science, with full nineteenth-century confidence in its theoretical power to grasp the curves of empirical reality and predict where it was headed.

The new world remained alive as Marxism's animating impulse, and appeared in its rhetorical flourishes, its tone and verbal coloration. The problem is that Marx never quite knew what to do with such essential unscientific and undemonstrable carryovers from his early wars with the young-Hegelians. Because they were not put forward explicitly as prophetic vision or animating force, but rather had to be seen in the process of being made real by history, his starting points were not openly and systematically thinkable. Nor were they criticizable. In fact—and this is Kolakowski's

point—Marx would have been unable to demonstrate that such an eschatological transformation was actually underway. The new human being that
Marx *sensed* in the French and Industrial Revolutions and the new proletarian movements would after all flower only as the result of a thousand
other transformations that would follow proletarian revolution.

Thus for several reasons the eschatological goal became "rhetorical"—
believed deeply, invoked from time to time—but remaining a realm beyond
the facts. And Marxism's vision of emancipation, as Albrecht Wellmer
observes, was repressed and even fundamentally contradicted by Marxism's
characteristic stress on science and the facts.[22] But once repressed, it wound
up becoming inexplicable. It both gave meaning to the facts and daily
struggles and gilded them with its power. And it became yet more powerful
because it remained virtually unmentionable even though reality was
heading toward it. Hidden, almost but not quite buried, Marxism's eschatological vision forms a haunting center of reference—an ever-elusive basis
for commitment, giving meaning both to the struggle and to all of human
history, yet fundamentally unarguable and unanalyzable. It thus remains
safely beyond question or criticism.

Simultaneously, then, Marxism was eschatological at its core and yet
in bad conscience about it. And this repression was intensified by the many
pseudoscientific threads in Marx. In his own terms, Marx was being
unscientific, and echoed religion, by claiming to see an eschatological
transformation happening before his eyes. Speaking accurately, he might
have observed that it was *not yet* taking place, and that conditions were just
then provoking thought about how it might one day take place. The
preconditions of an eschatological transformation were indeed beginning
to unfold, and in this sense the Marxian vision is neither whimsical nor
arbitrary. But the Industrial Revolution did not *entail* the dialectical reversal
Marx prophesied —that is, the emancipation of human beings and human
experience.[23]

Because it depended on human will and action, such an emancipation
could never be predicted with any degree of confidence. To call it any more
than possible, and to do any more than understand its preconditions and
work for its coming into being, was a gross violation of the very ideas
embodied in the "Theses on Feuerbach." Yet the power of Marx's eschatological vision cloaked these changes not just with possibility, not just with
moral urgency, but with *necessity*. A total world-historical transformation
was indeed conceivable (and it is certainly possible today), but it was always,
as Wellmer has said, "a *vérité à faire*"[24]—a truth to be made. Until it has
been made its status can never be more than hypothetical or provisional,
hence it deserves to be presented prophetically. But this must be done
self-consciously and critically; Marx always confused categories and kinds
of thought in asserting that this transformation was actually taking place,
and even more so, that it was doing so necessarily.

Beneath its veneer of science, such dogmatic prophecy reveals its deeper and premodern kinship with religious anticipations of a world redeemed by a divine power beyond our control. Thus did a legitimate vision, an entirely plausible one, inspired by actual historical trends, become distorted by its being repressed while being infused with science and necessity appropriately belonging to other parts of the project. Thus did Marxism, proclaiming the whole as science, become an almalgam in bad faith of the visionary, the scientific, the premodern, and the modern. And in the process it became a powerful rallying cry and call to arms.[25]

When later looking away from what was being realized to study the ways in which it was being realized, Marx and Marxists retained this eschatological mood. Now undergirding hard social science, it appeared to be supported by that social science. Everything would change in a wave of total emancipation—to be brought about by calculable, measurable processes. This eschatological faith in history as a story of liberation with the proletarian revolution as its climax, is Marxism's unscientific and ahistorical starting point. Repressed but absorbed by Marxism's scientific and historical side, eschatology gives it much of its emotive force. Marxism's stress on science thus hides, but also reflects, this absolute faith in sweeping historical redemption.

Critiques of Marxism: Scientism, Objectivism, Indifference to the Subjective

For all its eschatological impetus, what continues to distinguish Marxism from other radical projects is the effort to root it in the historical shape and direction of social forces and events. In *The German Ideology* Marx and Engels stressed that their "premises are men, not in any fantastic isolation and rigidity, but in their actual, empirically perceptible process of development under definite conditions." Marx again and again made war on socialists who "make sheer *will* instead of real conditions the driving-wheel of the revolution."[26] Whether battling against Weitling in 1848 or Bakunin in 1871, Marx sought to align revolutionary strategies with objectively ascertainable possibilities. As Marx explained his activity during 1848 and 1849, "Our task was not that of trying to bring any kind of utopian system into being but was that of consciously participating in a historical revolutionary process by which society was being transformed before our eyes."[27]

As a result, it became necessary to take the further step of placing socialism on "the only tenable theoretical foundation, namely scientific insight into the economic structure of bourgeois society."[28] This task consumed most of Marx's energies for the next twenty years. Scientist dedicated to grasping the curves of the political economy, revolutionary leader guided by the close study of long-range trends and possibilities—these were Marx's self-assigned roles.

But Marx is often accused of writing and thinking as if events and trends could bring about the revolutionary transformation all by themselves, without an active, subjective human force—the proletariat—deciding on such a transformation, struggling for it, and carrying it out. Or acting as if the processes leading to its decision and action were unproblematic, being essentially the subjective result of objective workings. Or as if history itself, all by itself—that is, virtually without human intervention except to lessen the new order's birth pangs—was bringing about the proletarian revolution and the new social order. This is the side of Marx that uses and attracts terms like "inevitable" and "necessary," is accused of being scientistic as well as scientific, and is criticized for being fatalistic, objectivistic, or positivistic. These accusations are not only made by anti-Marxists: some of the most telling analyses of a Marxist blind spot toward the subjective determinants of social transformation have come from those arguing within Marxism and seeking to revitalize it.[29]

These criticisms have become major battlegrounds, with much ink being spilled over three related topics: the issue of science, the question of inevitability or necessity, and the problem of Marx's view of the proletariat. By looking at one after the other, we can see that they imply each other and raise deeply connected issues. The first accuses Marxism of being like positivistic philosophies and social theories in seeking to imitate the natural sciences. The second stresses that the processes this science would discover and describe are said mistakenly to be leading, on their own and with a necessity similar to natural processes, to the overthrow of capitalism and the advent of socialism. The third criticism focuses on the agents bringing this about, arguing that Marx largely treats them as the objects of this transformation rather than its subjects, never taking fully seriously their active revolutionary role.

Paul Thomas has replied forcefully to what he regards as the misreading of Marxism as a pseudoscience by stressing Marx's essentialism and antipositivism, his critical, value-charged approach to political economy, and his emphasis on the historically grounded rather than timeless and universal character of the laws he discovered. Indeed, Marx disdained the idea that he was seeking to fashion a "science of society." Thomas writes, "There is, in other words, in Marx's writings no general law formulated by abstraction from the principle of interaction itself."[30] The reason for this is intrinsic to Marxism: "Marx's analyses of society do not subordinate society to permanent laws like those of physics because society is seen by Marx as being in transition, as moving toward a new arrangement in which the 'laws' of classical economics *will no longer apply*."[31] In other words, the goal of Marxism is to move humanity beyond the realm of necessity, where humans are determined by forces beyond their control, to the realm of freedom, where they self-consciously and freely decide their own fate. Historical materialism's goal is to cancel itself out.

Yet Thomas expands this strong argument about why Marxism is not a positivism or a scientism into an ever more tenuous set of claims that verge on denying the scientific character so essential to it.[32] He writes as if Marx never sought to discover the "natural laws of capitalist production" or did not speak in Volume I of *Capital* of these laws as describing "tendencies working with iron necessity toward inevitable results."[33] And Thomas ignores many passages in Marx where "science" is used positively as a key term or idea,[34] overlooking the fact that Marx, if he rejected positivism, equally rejected all of the various socialisms that refused to base themselves on historical trends and possibilities. Marx prided himself on grounding *his* approach on a close and accurate reading of the larger contours of history (such as the necessity for bourgeois revolution and for the development of capitalism to precede the development of a worker's challenge to capitalism) as well as on a systematic investigation of the functioning of capitalism. This revolutionary realism was characteristic of the group around him in Cologne in 1848–1849 and in London immediately after, of those close to him during the First International, and, toward the end of his life, of his followers in France, Germany, and Russia. It is what "Marxism" began to mean during his lifetime.

Marx's Objectivism

Marxism thus incorporates science in a special sense which distinguishes it from the natural sciences, as the theoretically clarified, selective, and systematic "study of the actual life-process and the activity of the individuals of each epoch."[35] As Daniel Little points out, it is a *science of tendencies*, and includes struggle, strategy, and choice.[36] Since this science can be sharply distinguished from the positivism or scientism of the mid- and late nineteenth century, what criticism can be made of it, especially if we incorporate it into the larger Marxian project of social transformation, of which it is a decisive component? Albrecht Wellmer argues that Marxism contains "latent tendencies" toward scientism, objectivism, and positivism, tendencies that are implicated in some of its most deplorable twentieth-century incarnations.

Wellmer constructs an ever-sharper tension between the scientific and deterministic side of Marxism and its critical and revolutionary character. He argues that Marxism is split by a fundamental contradiction: *either* the labor process, and economic life in general, shape the various superstructural features of capitalist society, including the possibility of the critical consciousness that would overturn it, or these emerge out of an active, indeed willed, political praxis. The very nature of this praxis would have to be open and indeterminate. Either capitalism itself evolves toward revolution and socialism, which are thus objectively determined, or the socialist transformation is unthinkable without the active participation of the proletariat, which begins with the very act of critically thinking about capitalism—that is, of penetrating the society's ideology.

Wellmer provokes us to ask, as Maurice Merleau-Ponty did in his farewell to Marxism in the 1950s,[37] about the relationship between two of Marxism's most essential features: determinism on the one side, and critical consciousness and self-determination on the other. The problem is that if free space is to be possible within capitalism, then not only a genuinely emancipatory revolution must be possible, but also various kinds of reforms short of revolution, and the deliberate creation of new and yet unimagined countervailing tendencies—as well as the proletariat's acceptance of capitalism. Both human nature *and capitalism* would then have to be so modifiable that many other outcomes are equally possible, outcomes far short of socialism. On the other hand, if we are in the midst of a deterministic, objectivist process that is indeed unfolding on its own, the transition to socialism would never bring about a qualitatively different reality. Human beings would never truly be liberated from the general law of historical materialism that the socioeconomic base determines the political and cultural superstructure. It would be patently absurd that the free world foreseen by Marx could unfold through historic necessity, a function of economic changes,[38] unrelated, as Engels (following Hegel) said, to the actors' conscious intent.

What has history taught us about these mutually exclusive alternatives? Wellmer overemphasizes an important insight, namely that Marxism contains a bias toward objectivism, and overplays its built-in tension between the determining character of economic and historical processes and its insistence on the proletariat's historic break with such determinisms. In fact, contrary to Wellmer's oppositions, today it seems more and more arguable that *both* points are true. Certainly the hypothesis has been borne out again and again that under any social system there exists a considerable subjective space in which all social classes and groups can not only take stock of themselves and their position but formulate ways of modifying reality. We need only mention the plasticity shown by capitalism, the system's adaptiveness, the inventiveness of its rulers in the face of challenge, or, more recently, the inability of apartheid to control its subjects, and the total collapse of Communist "totalitarianism."

At the same time, the subjective capacity to change or overthrow oppressive social systems seems again and again to be overtaken by the grinding weight of those systems. After all, the world remains, more firmly and completely than ever before, dominated by capitalism. Every breach in this system has been closed, transformed into its negative mirror image, or eventually absorbed. Not only has its overwhelming power and ability to undermine and set limits to projects of change won out again and again, but its recent triumph over Communism confirms the surrender of human conscious control to the "invisible hand" of market forces—letting economic necessity govern human social life. Thus all the many and important alterations and adaptations of capitalism remain within its dominant logic, which has indeed become more fully international than ever and has extended its transformative reach across previous frontiers, deeply into nature as well as the human psyche.

In the consumer society capitalism's shaping processes have become so powerful as to transform the human subjects themselves: their needs, their values, their psychic constitutions. It depends on a selling and buying that have long ago penetrated far beyond vital material needs and into peoples' fantasies, wishes, and deepest hopes—thus the centrality of marketing and advertising for convincing people about what they really need and who they really are. Yet if the system's priorities seem to dominate more totally than ever before, it is through active human will and consciousness. Paradoxically, both the dominance of a system and the activity of human will have achieved centrality—at one and the same time. These are the two sides of Marxism's constitutive tension, erected by Wellmer into opposing poles: determinism or self-determination. In a way, *Capital* stands as a monument to both sides of the process, embodying the act of emancipatory consciousness in a study that sets out the system's overwhelming dynamic, the logic driving its human agents.

The Missing Practice of Subjectivity

The core of Wellmer's criticism nevertheless remains: Marx did not adequately appreciate the subjective side of the revolutionary process. The plain fact is that most of his scientific attention was biased toward the objective processes leading to the establishment and transformation of capitalism. Most of his theoretical formulations stressed the role of these processes. Marx devoted himself to studying and understanding the objective processes because ultimately he regarded proletarian revolution as the more or less unproblematic result of these processes. This bias gave Engels, Kautsky, and later, Lenin and Stalin, support for their ever more systematically objectivist readings of Marxism.

Erica Sherover-Marcuse has shown how "two opposing models of emancipatory subjectivity" can be reconstructed from Marx's remarks and practices. They are a dialectical and a dogmatic perspective, "one which regards emancipatory consciousness as contingent and problematic, and one which regards emancipatory consciousness as inevitable and unproblematic."[39] While a dialectical perspective is never totally missing from Marx, as I have suggested above, by and large the dogmatic conception dominates. In Sherover-Marcuse's assessment, the dogmatic conception "haunts" Marx's thought, being present "in certain formulations of the thesis of historical materialism, in Marx's own understanding of the scientific character of his work, and in a particular conception of the nature of the transition to socialism."[40] What will make a subordinate and exploited class, the proletariat, want to overturn capitalism and see *itself* as capable of doing so? According to Marx's dogmatic conception, the "quasi-automatic development of emancipatory consciousness" is produced by the dynamics of capitalism. This perspective can be seen in the celebrated Preface to *A Contribution to the Critique of Political Economy*, where Marx regards consciousness as a superstructural reflex of the socioeconomic base.[41] Once the structures and situation creating false consciousness are abolished, it seems, a new and correct comprehension of actual conditions will follow.

But, as Sherover-Marcuse stresses, how is a revolution even thinkable without the proletariat taking major steps toward emancipation beforehand? These would include rejecting the system's ideology and the fetishization contained in daily experience, sloughing off age-old reflexes of submission to domination, developing the self-confidence and the *will* to rule. In other words, no revolution is possible unless the revolutionary class consciousness of the proletariat has reached the point where it sees itself needing and able to overthrow capitalism and rule in its own name. Sherover-Marcuse's insight, which was articulated in her tragically shortened life project, is that such emancipation is a long-term project in its own right, not merely a quasi-automatic function of "objective" processes. She reveals what is at stake when explaining why it is not enough to see emancipatory consciousness as simply involving the theoretical comprehension of the laws of capitalism, as Marx sometimes suggests.

> This perspective fails to recognize the semi-autonomous nature of the consequences of oppression: namely, it fails to recognize that the patterns of thought and action inculcated through the experience of oppression take on a substantiality and a life of their own. This view of the matter fails to acknowledge what I would call the *materiality* or the *sedimented nature* of mystified consciousness. Namely, it fails to recognize that mystified consciousness is not merely a set of false ideas or illusions but that it encompasses modes of being, ways of acting and of experiencing oneself and one's existence to which people have become accustomed, attached and even "addicted" on an affective level. The sedimentation of mystified consciousness congeals into "character structures" and "personality types"—naturalized and normalized cages for the individuals who inhabit them. The habits engendered by domination become forms of life through which individuals reproduce the system of domination.[42]

Marx's most dogmatic early perspective regarded workers as fundamentally outside the social order, uncorrupted by it, and perhaps for this reason embodying a fully human universality.[43] Unless we likewise consider workers as having from the outset escaped these systematic negative effects of the social system in which they live, we have to accept that, in Sherover-Marcuse's words, a "transformative practice of subjectivity" is needed to overcome the deep, systematic, and often unconscious effects of domination. In suggesting what might be included in such a practice today Sherover-Marcuse underscores its distance from Marxism.

> The arena of a practice of subjectivity would include not only explicitly articulated beliefs and values; it would also include the unstated assumptions which are embodied in people's lived experience, as well as the affective underpinnings of oppressive character structures and behavior patterns. A practice of subjectivity would seek to implement the *affective unlearning* of the habits of oppression. Such a practice, undertaken as a form of subversive self-education, would seek to interrupt *both sides* of the dialectic of domination; it would strive for the *affective undoing* of the introjected "perpetrator" and the introjected "victim." Thus it would address both "internalized domination" and internalized oppression. A practice of subjectivity would aim to prevent the continual re-creation of "psychic Thermidors" even as it attempted to foster the emergence of the "social-psychological presuppositions" for the transition from capitalism to socialism. At its best, it would encourage the development (inevitably in partial and limited form) of modes of interaction which would *prefigure* and thereby promote the achievement of a liberated society.[44]

With his great confidence about the direction of events, Marx never said much about what precisely it would take for the proletariat to slough off the dead weight of submission and domination and "to train [themselves] for the exercise of power."[45] It was an unshakeable assumption that over time the proletariat would lose its illusions about any possible subordination to the bourgeoisie and would come to see itself as the new society's rulers—both through witnessing and living capitalism's chaotic development, and through struggling against exploitation. For example, such an optimistic assumption pervades Marx's account of the 1848 revolution in *Class Struggles in France*. There, the working class is being educated by the repeated betrayals by bourgeois and petty-bourgeois politicians.[46]

In any case, if Marx mostly stressed and studied the objective side of the process, he did not view it as entailing any sort of simple determinism. And certainly, Sherover-Marcuse deduces her contrary argument from Marx's own economic and historical analysis: that the capitalist order, once established, might strengthen a widespread system of *self-sustaining* controls and cause it to be internalized. Thus the brilliant discussion in *Capital* of how bourgeois equality, freedom, and self-interest turn into their opposite once the capitalist hires the worker[47] might be coupled with his early remark about Protestantism installing an "internal priest" in every person.[48] Together they provoke us to explore how capitalist oppression depends on the self-submission of politically free people. Thus, Sherover-Marcuse stresses, Marxism itself would seem to require a "practice of subjectivity" to unlearn the habits of oppression.

Subjectivity's Decisive Role

But Marx himself, and the Marxism that followed, did not follow this path. If Marx was not inclined to problematize class consciousness, we have seen that Engels was even more confident that objective processes would produce a subjective transformation of human capacities. Karl Kautsky, the great codifier of German Social Democracy, shared Engels' optimism. And most striking, Lenin, who witnessed the reconciliation of decisive strata of European workers with capitalism, refashioned his tactics accordingly by calling for and creating a vanguard party—but without drawing the theoretical conclusions of this move or seriously reconsidering the objectivist analysis.[49] In other words, just when historical trends themselves seemed to be posing proletarian class consciousness as a problem, and just when Freud had opened the terrain *within* consciousness to systematic study, Marxism's main exponents seemed able to respond only by strengthening their dogmatic interpretation of revolutionary consciousness.[50]

As we near the end of the twentieth century, no advanced industrial proletariat has seen fit even to attempt the overthrow of capitalism, and—although we know a great deal about how capitalism functions as an economic system—we do not adequately know why. Why, for example, didn't the Depression, when the capitalist system virtually ground to a halt, provoke or generate the kinds of revolutionary response that Marxists anticipated? Marxists have not had even the beginning of an appreciation of the subjective processes that make revolutionary change possible, necessary, or unthinkable. Indeed, Marxism as a whole has insisted on staying moored in the prepsychological early modern world, remaining virtually illiterate about, and hostile to, the entire vast subjective territory first mapped by Freud. In place of a genuine modernist commitment to using all available tools for understanding why and when people act as they do, Marxists have by and large tabooed discussion of such questions and continued to wait for the Godot of proletarian revolution, or have despaired of its ever happening, without even knowing why. In a twentieth-century mode of thought claiming to be revolutionary, such obtuseness and passivity are unforgivable.

What appears passive and obtuse from a twentieth-century perspective, however, makes more sense in a nineteenth-century mode of thought claiming to be scientific. Marxism was formulated as a coherent and systematic project of asserting itself against various "sentimental socialisms" and those who "make sheer *will* instead of real conditions the driving-wheel of the revolution." For an early modern revolutionary like Marx, whose formation took place between 1818 and the early 1840s—who was writing at a time when only Britain, the Low Countries, and the United States had fully completed the bourgeois revolution and when only the first two had moved into the industrial revolution—the idea of a "practice of subjectivity" would have been unthinkable. It would have meant abandoning the revolutionary project for a haphazard politics of personal transformation. Marx sought objectivity and was biased toward it because basing revolution on scientifically comprehensible *real conditions* at that moment in history meant focusing on, and fully understanding, the socioeconomic soil in which capitalism and then socialist revolution germinated. The Enlightenment had done battle with irrationality and false consciousness, especially that of religion; Marx sought to explain these and look beneath them to discover the logic producing them, the dynamic leading toward social upheaval. From Marx's heyday to Freud's, insisting on real conditions meant considering the subjective world as derivative, as secondary, as a function of the "objective" world, and demanded instead looking to the economic and social forces that determine the subjective world to explain cultural and political practice.

Claiming hegemony over a mid- and late-nineteenth-century movement based on real conditions ruled out focusing on subjective processes, for another reason. Its participants must have been not only unsure of their ultimate victory in such a totally new and historic undertaking, but also filled with uncertainty about their own adequacy to the task—as well as burdened by the immensity of the reversal they were expected to bring about. If they were moved by a premodern belief in total transformation and an early modern objectivist bias and confidence in science, and if they were simultaneously repressing their doubt, one natural response would be a rhetoric of certainty and necessity. The genuinely scientific and historically grounded dimensions of Marxism were thus extended illegitimately to areas where they had no application, in order to inspire confidence in the movement's eventual victory.

Marx, after all, spent a considerable amount of his time as political leader, in the 1860s as well as the 1840s, counseling patience. His message was that the great transformation toward capitalism *was happening*, that socialist revolution depends on conditions being ripe, and it should not be be forced. Such an emphasis would lead naturally to erring on the side of triumphalism of the long run rather than on the side of premature action or crippling self-doubt.

Then, too, and perhaps above all, Marx's relative indifference to the complex process of attaining class consciousness was rooted in his thoroughly Enlightenment premises, which have more in common with a Voltaire than a Freud. Marx seems to have believed that once his writing and lived history had made the essence of capitalism self-evident, any intelligent worker would see this, draw the appropriate conclusions—and act appropriately. His conception of reason was thoroughly rationalist. Bourgeois ideology did not correspond to reality; bourgeois political economy did not accurately describe that reality, which was inherently self-contradictory, exploitive, and chaotic. The spirit of Marxism was saturated with Enlightenment self-confidence in rational observation. This rationality, and the workers' comprehension through experience and theory, would make the steps to take and the shape of the future society self-evident.

This faith in reason is inseparable from Marx's faith in the dialectics of history. The dazzling unleashing of human productive power only meant that the bourgeoisie was "incompetent to assure an existence to its slave within its slavery."[51] Marx firmly expected life under capitalism to become materially unbearable, workers driven to the brink by its major objective tendencies—including the tendency to keep wages at a minimum, to replace workers with machinery, and thus to create an industrial reserve army. No human agency would be capable of significantly and enduringly improving the condition of the working class within such a system. And as the logic of this development reached its climax, the workers would rise up and expropriate the expropriators. Given such a conviction, no wonder Marx saw the dynamics of class consciousness as being unproblematic.

One of the four countervailing tendencies mentioned in Volume III of *Capital* involves depressing wage levels *below* the cost of survival. But what if the human beings living within the system, on both sides of the class divide, intervened to ameliorate living conditions and economic cycles? Why didn't Marx see that it was possible for wage levels to rise well *above* the cost of survival? Or for capitalists to perceive the vital survival need for yielding an adequate living to some of their workers in order to head off revolution? Or for workers' struggles to win a long-term higher standard of living? Or for profits generated elsewhere, in colonies for example, to be used to grant some of the demands of workers at home? In each of these scenarios human force modified basic tendencies of the system. Marx erred on the side of objectivism by not anticipating that human responses would be able to offset the system's dynamic.

Yet clearly, in one form or another, all of these scenarios have actually occurred. The system's iron logic is more fluid than Marx anticipated, having proven amenable to sufficient human adjustment to win broad workers' loyalty to the system in every advanced capitalist country. Of course this tendency was clear at the beginning of the century, giving rise to the debates in Germany over revisionism and in Russia over the need for a vanguard party. As we have seen, this process has many implications, but only one of them concerns us at the moment: even well before the Depression showed that catastrophic objective trends were not enough to produce the subjective will to make a revolution, the Marxist faith that life under capitalism *must* worsen and *must* lead to revolutionary consciousness was effectively discredited. In each case, however, a decisive, and ignored, factor was human subjectivity.

Ironically enough, it was in its greatest celebration of modernity, its affinity for scientism and objectivism, that Marxism was least modern and misfired most seriously. The success of reform in making life bearable within capitalism, the proliferation of countervailing tendencies beyond those named by Marx, the ever-increasing commodification of physical and psychic space that we know as consumerism, testify that capitalism has been able to transform itself to meet its most vital challenges, and these trans-formations have redefined the political and cultural space in which we live. Not only has a certain type of consciousness become constitutive of the system itself, but we have seen some writers argue that reality has been plastic enough to allow for the redefinition of proletarian identity itself. The key to the defeat of Marxist anticipation has been the unexpected capacity of subjective forces to alter structures and trends once perceived as objective and necessary.

Critiques of Marxism: Authoritarianism

Lenin's determination to create a vanguard party, and the subsequent rise and eventual collapse of Marxism–Leninism, point equally to another widely discussed and perhaps fatal flaw of Marxism: its alleged tendency toward authoritarianism. Did Marxism encourage individuals to surrender their decision-making power and submit themselves to a higher authority? At first, nothing would seem farther from the truth. Although Marx himself was famous for his intolerance of other points of view, he never claimed a purely personal authority. His arguments, as we have seen, appealed to the shape of history, to the facts. And they were arguments, not pronounce-ments. His deeply scientific orientation entailed understanding, and re-specting, the contours of lived reality, and he spent his life demonstrating these tendencies. What significant internal connection can there be be-tween what evolved as Communist authoritarianism, the doctrines and practices of a new ruling class, and Marxism itself?

The answer is that there is a structural bias toward authority in a project that leans so heavily on the kind of scientific understanding accessible only after long training and study. In this sense, Marxist authoritarianism would not necessarily be one based on a unique personal authority, but an authoritarianism of science and its findings, of history and its forces—of theory. It would be an authoritarianism of the individuals claiming to have developed the skills and the wisdom to interpret them. This is the modern form in which the issue of authoritarianism appeared during the French Revolution in the tragic career of Condorcet, a scientist in politics who rejected his own elitist conclusions and sought to develop mathematical bases for entrusting decisions to democratic processes. Philosophe become moderate republican politician, the author of the Girondist constitution became painfully aware that something other than enlightened reason was motivating events and the masses, but tried to resist the authoritarian implications of his belief in a "social physics." After the Jacobins came to power he was sentenced to be guillotined, and, after writing his great paen to progress while in hiding from the Committee of Public Safety, apparently committed suicide.[52]

If Condorcet grasped but resisted the authoritarian conclusions latent in believing that politics and social life must be understood scientifically, Auguste Comte embraced them wholeheartedly, openingly calling for a technocratic elite to understand, and administer, the new industrial order. The masses, who were not expected to grasp historical and technical processes, were to be ruled over, pacified by his positivist religion.[53] It is when we compare him with the founder of "sociology" that we can see how unique—and democratic—was Marx's conception of theory. Marx saw the social theory he was developing being used for quite opposite purposes than that of technocratically managing the masses: his critique of political economy was intended as a scientific tool to be used *by the masses themselves* in overthrowing bourgeois society and creating a genuinely democratic order.[54]

Even so, it may be argued that Marx himself became, and was granted the status of, an expert. Occupying this position, he constantly trod the thin line between the authority granted to the expert because of the content of his ideas and the authority granted him as such, *qua* expert. Even so, it is remarkable that, in spite of his legendary intolerance of opposing opinions, it was Marx himself who insisted in 1871 that "the International propagates no particular *credo*."[55] And this was his consistent approach, not only in order to accommodate as many tendencies as possible within the International, but because of his deep commitment that the workers must follow *their own* development.

How could Marx be simultaneously intolerant of other theorists' points of view and tolerant of workers' views, with which he so obviously disagreed?[56] There is no contradiction here: if he fought fiercely against other intellectuals about the appropriate direction for the workers' movement, Marx was committed to ensuring that the workers *themselves* evolve the appropriate strategy and tactics for their pursuit of power. His faith in the workers, and in history, contained the implicit proviso that the workers not be diverted by false leaders with fanciful theories. That is, as long as they were not deflected from politics or propelled into premature revolution his faith in them was enduring. As leader of the International, then, Marx's purpose was not to prescribe a direction for workers' movements, but to give them the space to follow their own authentic impulses, and to battle fiercely those who would block the space. Nothing could be more anti-authoritarian. Of course, Marx never doubted that these authentic impulses were anticipated theoretically by his own interpretation of history and study of capitalist political economy, and in turn that they would validate *his* reading of events.

What role in the movement did this give to his own intellectual work? Marx accepted leadership of the International and never doubted the importance of scientific knowledge and clear thinking in the struggle against capitalism. He was the prototype of the intellectual as revolutionary leader, chosen for his position by virtue of his superior theoretical insight into the reality needing to be changed. But he often deferred to workers and never claimed that intellectuals *as such* ought to be their leaders. In his view and in his practice, theory should not automatically guide practical activity, but those with the correct theory were under the obligation to combat false theories.

Yet, as we have seen, not all parts of his theory had emerged from equally careful study. The eschatological undergirding of Marxism was an unverified presupposition; his faith in the proletariat received no analysis. As I stressed above, these were nevertheless presented and understood as being no less scientific than Marx's analysis of capitalism. Similarly, Marx's always dubious proclamations about certainty or inevitability were equally gilded with the authority of science. Thus Marx's own practice left an ambiguous heritage. Close scientific study, on principle accessible to anyone, justifies many of his claims; but not all of his claims stem from close scientific study. The intellectual does not automatically command deference from workers; but the intellectual who has the "correct" understanding of history heaps scorn on all contenders.

A Janus-faced perspective stems from Marx's deep faith in the workers' long-term responses to capitalism on the one hand and his awareness of the vital role played by correct understanding on the other. Condorcet tried and failed to bridge this kind of tension two generations earlier, and was destroyed by it. Understandably, Marx would have said, since today's situation is entirely different because the proletariat is making the theory true. Thus if the importance Marx gave to theory suggests as one consequence the authoritarianism of the theoretician, this is counteracted by faith that the proletariat would carry out the role revealed by history and political economy.

Naming the Movement for Marx

Yet very early on Marx's project became Marxism, a theory and practice named for its founder. This could not help but carry authoritarian overtones. We may ask why it is that, in contrast, other great thinkers of the nineteenth and twentieth centuries, while certainly establishing, say, a Darwinian or an Einsteinian theory and science, have been able to bequeath equally widely used ways of describing their approaches that are not encumbered by their own names. If Marx himself had been able to choose, he would probably have named his theory and movement "critical materialist socialism." Why did we not inherit this term, or Engels' preferred "critical and revolutionary socialism," or, indeed, Engels' "scientific socialism"?[57]

It is striking that "the use of personal epithets and the personalization of the currents of ideas"[58] should take place in a modern movement for human emancipation—where attitudes toward such personalization might be expected, if anything, to be far more negative than in science. Writing in 1873, Henri Perret, a member of the International from Geneva, appropriately rejected the use of "Bakuninists" and "Marxists" to describe the opposing currents: "The fact that sections have grouped around proper names is deplorable, contrary to our principles and the interests of workers' emancipation."[59] He called for an end to factions naming themselves for "uprooted members of the bourgeoisie" and instead wanted to see "a sincere and real alliance of the *workers*."

According to Maximilien Rubel, the "illicit and unjustifiable" practice and "universal scandal" of naming the movement for Marx is due to Engels, who used his authority to sanction it, but who might equally have vetoed such an "abscess."[60] Yet the practice of calling his followers Marxists predated Marx's death and the systematizing efforts of Engels. Did such a practice foreshadow the similar, and even more pronounced, process of personalization developed around the dead Lenin and the living Stalin?

Insofar as eponymous movements derive their authority from their namesakes, they assume a certain cast. While the founder's original meanings may be interpreted and debated, proclaiming oneself and being accepted as an authentic follower rather than a revisionist becomes essential to claiming leadership in such a movement and to setting its direction. Because considerable study is needed to understand the founder's works, and to keep them consonant with current developments, second-generation leaders naturally lay claim to being the most correct interpeters, naturally seek to establish their place in the line of succession. In a certain sense, then, they become priests.

Since such a movement inevitably develops a greater or lesser tone of ritualized adherence to the founder's purposes and understandings, all new analyses must become extensions of his thought, demonstrably laced with quotes indicating their provenance. In short, in the process of being adopted as the official outlook of the German Social Democratic Party in 1891, Marxism was fated to develop a strongly reverential bent. Its interpreters—chief among them being Kautsky, August Bebel, and Willhelm Liebnicht—were versed in the science of the founder, using it to develop an up to date understanding of economic developments since his death. If this is a characteristic early modern phenomenon, as the modern world has continued to evolve such reverence seems more and more a throwback to an earlier age. Instead of relying on the demonstrable authority of reason, or scientific study, or new approaches to understanding, or even on individual conscience, Marxists have tended instead to base their authority on the words of the Founding Father. This may be a "scandal," as Rubel says, but it is part and parcel of Marxism as we know it.

Marxism–Leninism and Authority

But "Marxism as we know it" can hardly be separated from its dominant form in the twentieth century, Marxism–Leninism, with its explicit enshrining of the commanding role of theoreticians. (Indeed, the various unorthodox Marxisms are if anything even more theoretically based.) In a much celebrated and much denounced passage of *What Is To Be Done?* (1902), Lenin quotes the "profoundly true and important words of Karl Kautsky"[61] about why socialist consciousness was not created in England by economic development and class struggle, as their "necessary and direct result":

> Of course, socialism, as a doctrine, has its roots in modern economic relationships just as the class struggle of the proletariat has, and like the latter, emerges from the struggle against the capitalist-created poverty and misery of the masses. But socialism and the class struggle arise side by side and not one out of the other; each arises under different conditons. Modern socialist consciousness can arise only on the basis of profound scientific knowledge. Indeed, modern economic science is as much a condition for socialist production as, say, modern technology, and the proletariat can create neither the one nor the other, no matter how much it may desire to do so; both arise out of the modern social process. The vehicle of science is not the proletariat, but the *bourgeois intelligentsia* [Kautsky's italics]: it was in the minds of individual members of this stratum that modern socialism originated, and it was they who communicated it to the more intellectualy developed proletarians who, in their turn, introduce it into the proletarian class struggle where conditions allow that to be done. Thus, socialist consciousness is something introduced into the proletarian class struggle from without [. . .] and not something that arose within it spontaneously [. . .].[62]

It could not be more striking that Lenin calls for a vanguard party to bring political consciousness to the workers *from without*. But, as I mentioned in Chapter 3, in so doing, and in so justifying this tactical shift, Lenin is decisively abandoning Marx's faith in the unproblematic development of class consciousness. He no longer believes that it will emerge from and in struggle with the dynamics of capitalism, as foreseen in Marx's historical and economic analyses. Lenin abandons this without confronting the full theoretical implications of this profound change. Lenin was indeed forced by history to face the problem that Sherover-Marcuse stresses, and that Marx largely ignored, namely that the development of revolutionary class consciousness among the proletariat has become *problematic*. While Marx wrote and acted during capitalism's early stages, Lenin acted and wrote in the midst of the debate over revisionism, when the reformism of growing sectors of the German working class was beginning to pose a theoretical challenge.[63] The momentousness of Lenin's recasting of Marxian theory is hidden by the fact that it is done in bad faith, being presented as a *tactical* modification. But here, and in his essay on imperialism—equally far-reaching in implications but similarly obscuring, to avoid rethinking Marxism's central theses—a Marxist practice is posited that betrays a loss of faith in "the coincidence of the proletariat and progress," and yet that remains revolutionary to its core.

Contained within Lenin's innovation of the vanguard party is a fundamental decision: he overcomes Marx's ambivalence about whether theory or the workers should predominate, and fully shifts the locus of consciousness from the workers to bourgeois intellectuals. Theoretical consciousness thus takes precedence over workers' consciousness born of the struggle with capitalism. And this theory is lodged in an insulated center of revolutionary consciousness, protected from the meteoric rises and falls of spontaneous proletarian consciousness. Such a recasting would only intensify any existing tendencies toward authoritarianism.

But of course Marx is not Lenin, and Lenin is not Leninism. It was Stalin who concocted a full-scale cult of Lenin's embalmed body, and intensified and pushed to their limit the escalating tendencies toward authoritarianism in Marx, Marxism, and Lenin. Under Stalin, Marx's and Lenin's writings became fully canonical texts, and Marxism became the official ideology of an authoritarian state. Within the Bolshevik Party, Lenin himself was remarkably unauthoritarian, and was capable of arguing his position and being outvoted. He wrote a remarkably democratic revolutionary text, *State and Revolution*. In fact, it must be stressed, against all contemporary Leninists, that the vanguard party was more idea than reality until *after* the revolution. Still, any final judgment on Lenin will have to include the fact that—against equally Marxist Mensheviks—he argued for and carried out a minority revolution in 1917. He also ordered the dispersion of the democratically elected Constitutent Assembly in 1918, with its anti-Bolshevik majority, as well as the crushing of the Kronstadt workers' and sailors' uprising in 1921. It was Lenin's leadership that set Russia on the unthinkable path of minority rule—a direction opposed by Marx in 1848 and by Mensheviks in 1917. Moreover, Lenin embarked on this path in a society that had not yet undergone its bourgeois revolution and industrialization, equally unthinkable in Marxist terms. In other words, the practice of the man who developed the idea of the vanguard party opened the pathway that led to the twentieth century's nightmare of Stalinist Communism.

But these developments did not take place in a vacuum. Although cloaked with the appropriate objectivist logic, they resulted from difficult choices in nearly impossible situations. Ultimately a crisis lay behind Leninism—the profound crisis of the European working class that found expression in revisionism and World War I. In responding to the crisis, where Marx had created the possibility of but never proposed a theoretical elite, and where the Marxism of the Second International encouraged it but also resisted it, Lenin gave to such an elite its organizational formulation and theoretical rationale. The minority revolution he carried out created the conditions in which vanguardism would become "official" Marxism after his death. The Leninism of the Soviet Union was fittingly launched in the tone and words of Stalin's oration at Lenin's funeral:

> On his departure from us, Comrade Lenin commanded us to revere and maintain the purity of the name of the party member. We swear, comrade Lenin, that we will faithfully carry out this command! . . . On his departure from us, Comrade Lenin commanded us to safeguard like the pupil of our eye, the unity of our party. We swear, Comrade Lenin, that we will faithfully carry out this command.[64]

How much of a distance lies between Marx, Marxism, Lenin, and Stalin's Leninism? The medieval character of Stalin's incantation gives fuel to the argument that Marx, or even Lenin, was turned on his head under Stalinist Communism, that Stalin's authoritarianism is not drawn from the original founders. Yet if each step I have explored does not lead inexorably to the next, it contains the next as a tendency, a plausible path. The path might perhaps have been taken reluctantly under pressure, but then became justified as *required by the circumstances* when it was never more than contained within Marxism's range of possibilities. Marxism is not in this sense "responsible" for Stalinism, nor does it contain it "within itself," waiting to be actualized, conceived as Marxism was years in advance of the Bolshevik Revolution. But, in Wellmer's judicious language, each step in the authoritarian misunderstanding of what Marx would have named "critical and materialist socialism" can be seen to "find support in a theoretical relationship latent in Marx's theory."[65] And, we must add, it became placed on the agenda and justified by the historical situation in which Marxists found themselves.

Evaluation: Marxism in Its Time

What does this retrospective account of obsolescent features of Marxism—its repressed eschatological thrust, its penchant for scientism and objectivism and neglect of subjectivity, and its tendency toward authoritarianism—

add to the arguments of Chapters 2 and 3? One way of focusing the cumulative point of these analyses is to ask whether Marxism is over *because of these three weaknesses.*

I have argued, first, that they were in fact prime sources of Marxism's immense historical impact. A chiliastic appeal was appropriate, but also had to be repressed, in a world that was in the process of displacing religion from its central role. If the new demands of rational discourse and scientific consciousness made it difficult to trumpet too openly the promise that history itself was leading to the peaceable kingdom, that promise was nevertheless read in the explosion of human powers brought about by the Industrial Revolution. Visions of redemption would strike a ringing chord to those whose outlook took shape within the Judeo-Christian tradition: the still-powerful demands of the receding religious consciousness made unthinkable any mass movement that did *not* promise the land of milk and honey.

Moreover, the inner conviction that history itself was fulfilling this promise helped to give point, purpose, and self-confidence to a movement that must have been deeply uncertain of its inner capacity to triumph over not simply capitalism, but the fundamental conditions of exploitation and domination that had pervaded all of known history. The profoundly authoritarian baggage of this history was not at all swept away by the coming of capitalism, bourgeois democracy, or the socialist movement. Indeed, appeals to authority—but to a modern, scientific authority—helped guarantee the line of march for millions who had been brought up scraping and bowing before authority, in traditions lasting hundreds and thousands of years, and who, thrown back on their own resources and consciousness, may well have had their doubts.

These weaknesses, then, were sources of strength for Marxism. And indeed, it remains to be seen whether a mass political outlook can inspire heroism and self-sacrifice without the kind of bad-faith eschatological appeal that undergirded Marxism, whether a radical movement might seriously undertake the necessary "practice of subjectivity" without becoming fatally distracted from its goal of changing society, and whether adequate consensus and self-confidence might be possible among participants not bound together by a certain amount of reverence for authority. If these are questions to be explored in the second part of this book, our concern at the moment is how to appreciate these weaknesses historically. I maintain that they were vital to Marxism's great success, but we cannot forget their disastrous consequences. They led Marxism toward authoritarianism, profound illusions as well as equally profound disillusionment, and gradual abandonment by its social class. In other words, these features of Marxism are not simply theoretical weaknesses, but are implicated in the catastrophes and defeats it suffered in the twentieth century.

If we change our location for a moment, and resituate ourselves in the late nineteenth and early twentieth century, the problem becomes more complex. Marxism was once an appropriate project for this period because it fit a certain historical situation, as well as people's experience and sense of themselves in that situation, and their attitudes. But at the same time, I am arguing that Marxism was incorrect in not appreciating the subjective factor that was to become so decisive, was mistaken in not scrutinizing its eschatological commitments, tended to be undemocratic in its bowing to authority. In short, I am asking whether such a criticism is retrospective only: wasn't it equally true during Marxism's heyday? And if so, what does this tell us about Marxism's chances of success *in its own time*? If these have become obvious as failings of twentieth-century Marxism, was it not always so? Didn't they then undermine Marxism from its beginning? Wasn't Marxism therefore incapable of the emancipatory revolution it proclaimed?

These questions tell us much about the historical period that Marxism so powerfully expressed and focused. The great movement of emancipation of the late-nineteenth and early twentieth century could not help but have these flaws—indeed, in some sense it needed them to become dominant. Marxism fit its situation, this movement based on apocalyptic expectations and pseudocertainties, unwilling and unable to look too deeply into the subjective side of oppression. The paradoxical conclusion this suggests is that if the world of the nineteenth century found appropriate expression in such a movement, it *was not ready* for the transformations it demanded.

In the end, if it fit its world tightly, Marxism was utopian in its call for a general human emancipation, based on the struggle of the working class against the bourgeoisie, using the human and material resources generated by the early years of industrialization. The world was not ready for emancipation. Marxism was incapable of fulfilling its mission because (among other reasons), like itself, its world was still too authoritarian, too close in time to domination by religion, too needful of, yet uncomprehending of this need for, a long subjective practice of emancipation. Since Marxism so closely fit—so fully expressed, focused, and gave shape to—its time, its promised liberation was itself premature. Like its historical period, its hopes were stimulated by real events and trends, but not grounded in them. The early modern revolution, containing, as it had to, so many premodern remnants, could never lead to transforming history as Marx envisaged it, even if it produced the vision of doing so.

Evaluation: The Obsolescence of Marxism

It remains to ask *which* Marxism is over. The question, of course, contains an argument on behalf of those who, for three generations now, have worked to make Marxism adequate to the contemporary world. Such a modernization is implied in Sherover-Marcuse's stress on an emancipatory practice of subjectivity; the same impulse marks the Marxist itinerary I recounted in Chapter 1. As I indicated in Chapter 3, recastings have been going on for a century, and each of them has aimed at bringing Marxism in line with the evolving historical reality. As a result, so the argument goes, it is necessary to say that there are today many varieties of Marxism. Perhaps then my evaluation best fits Second International and Marxist–Leninist orthodoxy. Merleau-Ponty distinguished between two strands; a Western Marxism featuring a soaring sense of human possibility, fostering "universal criticism"; and an orthodox Marxism that encouraged a crude naturalism, stressing the weight of a world seemingly moving on its own, its dialectic imbedded in things.[66] The critical, dialectical Marxism, is, in Russell Jacoby's term, a "dialect c of defeat"; it never held power, was never enlisted in constructing a new society or creating new relations of domination.[67]

Didn't the New Left spurn orthodoxy and self-consciously seek to create a Marxism that was free from eschatology, scientism, and reliance on authority? In Chapter 1 I have related how, following Marcuse or Sartre or Gramsci, my generation of Marxists persisted without despair in the tensions between theory and practice, between commitment to working-class revolution and to particular movements. Why now proclaim that not only orthodoxy is dead, but this Marxism as well? Since capitalism is surely not over, won't we, as Sartre said, continue to need Marxism as long as "we have not gone beyond the circumstances which engendered it"?[68] And above all, why stress Marxism's obsolescence—for example, its premodern and early modern characteristics—as if these undoubted features of orthodoxy are still present in the critical, open Marxism practiced so widely by our generation?

Since the 1960s the attempts to rethink Marxism have continued: to clarify and criticize it, to render it more solid, effective, and durable, to modernize or postmodernize it, and to render it compatible with the theoretical and practical current that has recently challenged it most fundamentally—feminism. How should we respond to these efforts to take account of, to engage, and to resolve, Marxism's central problems?

In Chapter 1 I indicated that despite the skepticism and openness of the Marxism I embraced thirty years ago, between its lines I found, *and also embraced*, faith in history as a process of emancipation, of the good being realized, guaranteed by the authority of theory. Unconsciously, but no less forcefully, the features explored in this chapter have been essential features of my own Marxism. Must any Marxism contain such a faith, either explicitly or between the lines? My reply here and in the next two chapters is that the experience of Marxism's ending, described in chapter 1, applies to *all* Marxisms. In arguing in Chapters 2 and 3 that Marxism is over, I aimed at essential features shared by any and all Marxisms, and without which Marxism becomes something else. In describing its eschatological, objectivist, and authoritarian tendencies in this chapter, I am speaking of features that *all* Marxisms either consciously espouse or unconsciously absorb—or which they throw over completely only in defining themselves outside of Marxism.

Absorb how? Marcuse's subjective, Hegelian Marxism had its origins in Lukacs' *History and Class Consciousness*. It is Lukacs who places the proletariat's self-understanding at the heart of the revolutionary process and, along with it, the cultural, ideological, and subjective dimensions denied both by Second International and Comintern orthodoxy. Lukacs, like Marcuse after him (recognizing the dilemma described by Wellmer above), stresses the task of conquering a space beyond determinism, the space for freedom and self-determination that makes human emancipation possible. But achieving this space amounts to a fundamental human transformation denied all other classes: the working class overcomes experiencing the human universe as dominated by blind forces, and recognizes the human labor at the heart of all social processes. Overcoming reification entails "transforming society consciously"[69]—becoming the new human beings we saw Engels speak of above, achieving the moment when human beings self-consciously and freely make their own history. Fully understood, class consciousness *is* the proletariat's awareness that their labor is the active, human source of social life, as well as their assertion of the capacity freely and consciously to control it.

This powerful analysis unites Marxism's distant goal and its philosophical underpinnings with the proletariat's immediate struggles. It is worth noting that in so doing, Lukacs is consciously exploring, and not merely assuming, Marxism's eschatological vision. Objective events are no longer realizing it; achieving this not merely depends on, but in a profound sense *is*, the conscious activity of the proletariat. If in this discussion Lukacs gives the proletariat superhuman tasks, painting it as larger than life, it is because he is posing Marxian eschatology in good faith, and asking what possible earthly activity can realize it. But in the process, Marxism's flirting with the myth of objective history realizing itself is abandoned for a new flirtation: burdening the proletariat with tasks that can only be carried out by mythical heroes.

Another, equally serious problem appears in this first statement of Western Marxism: Lukacs was forced to recant it in 1933 in order to be able to survive in the Soviet Union. Lukacs himself, as late as 1967, continues to condemn this contemporary, sophisticated Marxism, as being "colored by an overriding subjectivism," "a relapse into idealistic contemplation,"[70] "overriding the priority of economics."[71] However we might criticize his self-criticism, the more important fact is that his unorthodox Marxism was never conceived as existing by itself but only in relation to official Marxism, to the point of bowing before it. Whether as a supplement or as a rebellion, Western Marxism is inconceivable without ortho-doxy. Merleau-Ponty understood this in *Adventures of the Dialectic*: Lukacs and Luxemburg's Western Marxism fit those moments of revolutionary soaring, Leninism those long periods of state power and socialist construc-tion. Neither was self-sufficient. Lukacs' Marxism was an assertion of subjectivity *within* or *alongside* a primarily objectivist Marxism. By itself it could not survive.[72]

Every Marxism since 1917 has emerged *in relation to* orthodoxy, which has thus framed it, completed it, provided its emotional cement, becoming the Other against which it has shaped itself.[73] And this has been true both practically and theoretically, with a crude, authoritarian, and oppressive— but solid and established—Marxism provoking, justifying, and underpin-ning its more subtle and sophisticated variants. In some sense it was the very institutional force of the ugly Marxism, the hollowness of its still-ring-ing appeals, alongside the continuing existence of revolutionary Marxist possibilities, that gave alternative Marxisms their historical legitimacy. They were part of orthodoxy's field of force, natural responses and alter-natives to it that nevertheless depended on it for their very existence.

Think of orthodoxy's claims. Was the beginning of history at hand? Was it being brought about by objective processes, scientifically ascertain-able, which would drive the proletariat to make a revolution? Was all this happening in the name of, and certified by the authority of, Marx and Engels, Lenin and Mao, even Stalin? In a world where these are proclaimed by great movements and revolutionary states, even skeptics draw on and are nurtured by the force of such beliefs. If, as Marcuse insisted, Marxism is social theory and not science, the established belief that it is science underpins and nurtures the unorthodox belief that it is social theory; the first frames and becomes part of the second.

Imagine, on the other hand, a fully post-Communist Marxism—one that had successfully overcome the historically untenable beliefs described in this chapter. It would be tentative about the proletariat's capacity to master its oppression and struggle its way to the kinds of strength and self-confidence needed to overthrow capitalism. It would be humble and limited about its claims to knowledge; it would be unable to point to any force realizing its vision. It would be unwilling to insist that history was on its side. It would rename itself according to its goals or point of view rather than resting on its founder's name; and it would try to combine a respect for theory with a skepticism toward authority. At the same time it would insist on the necessity to pursue proletarian emancipation as the key to human liberation; it would continue to focus on the labor process and the economy as its central areas; and it would continue to stress exploitation and class struggle.

Such a Marxism would lack the certainty needed to proclaim itself *the* movement of our times? It would be deprived of its dynamic force, its original sense of self-confidence, its power to unite all social movements under *its* universal rubric. It would approach the movements that have been at the center of history over the past generation as the representative of no more than a single important force among others. The working class would be unable to reclaim, in practice and theory, the universality that powered nineteenth-century Marxism. In short, this new, fully contemporary Marxism would face the task of squaring the circle. It is hard to imagine how such a project might "take," due to its being either internally inconsistent or inadequate to the theoretical demands of a contemporary consciousness and recent social struggles. It is difficult to see how such a "critical materialist socialism" might become a theoretical and practical force in the next century.

Postmodernism or Mature Modernism?

What then does it mean to say that some of Marxism's decisive features were premodern and early modern, and that our consciousness, additudes, modes of perception, and expectations have gone *beyond* Marxism? As we near the twenty-first century, human awareness, life-experience, and social conditions have evolved in a number of significant ways, germinating into what many describe as a postmodern phase—or becoming what I would prefer to describe as more fully modern, or in the words of Anthony Giddens, "high modern."[74] Of course neither term can be used unreflectively. Both "postmodern" and "high modern" reflect what Zygmunt Bauman has described as a "necessary stocktaking," in which we distance ourselves from accustomed projects and ways of perceiving in order to understand and evaluate them.[75] Both, while pretending to be descriptive, contain their own kinds of normative appraisal. If "high modern" refers to a specific periodization of human history, and is a highly charged way of evaluating its products and alleged residues, "postmodern" takes up the same cudgel—that is to say, the same appeal to *progress*—but with somewhat changed contents.

If the unqualified vogue of modernity is being replaced by the equally unqualified vogue of postmodernity, it was always more appropriate to distinguish between contradictions and phases *within* the vast historical space of modernity. Modernity has first of all always been profoundly contested, divided and dividing between radically different ways of experiencing and thinking about the world. Modern life has created the most extreme tensions, including what Ernst Bloch called "nonsynchronous contradictions,"[76] its invasive processes of uneven and combined development placing the most inconceivable strains on traditional cultures, social groups, and social classes.

Moreover, this great world-historical modern period has itself unfolded in phases. Much of what postmodernism rejects, or declares itself beyond, is what I would regard as early modernity. Indeed, postmodernism celebrates trends toward ambiguity, difference, specificity, complexity, and respect for individuality. These trends are fully modern trends and are now gaining strength against other, earlier, features of modern life. But proponents of contemporary consciousness lose track of such continuities by celebrating themselves as "beyond" the world in which they emerged, or thinking of their world as "beyond" modernity. These continuities can better be grasped by thinking in terms of premodern, early modern, and "high" or mature modern phases—thus by drawing less definitive lines, rather than stressing a rupture between the modern and the postmodern worlds and sensibilities.

In any case, if Marxism is over today it is not *because* it is modern, but rather because it is insufficiently so.[77] From the beginning, the modern sensibility included skepticism about the traditional centrality of religion, tradition, and authority; a strong reliance upon reason and science; a demand that social practices justify themselves, whether in terms of social justice or utility; a growing insistence on democratic modes of social decision making; and respect for the right and capacity of individuals to act freely and make up their own minds, which encompassed a growing stress on workers' freedom to shape and control their work.

In short, whatever else it involves, modernity insists that human beings are *on their own*. "Enlightenment," said Immanuel Kant, "is man's emergence from his self-incurred immaturity."[78] While we might quarrel with Kant's explanation of the causes of immaturity, or disagree with the clear political limits he places on humans coming of age, his determination to link maturity with the capacity and freedom to act is clear. Marxism's commitment to science and "real conditons" and its enthusiasm for modern industry mark it as modern. Marxism is also modern in that it projects humans who are capable of overthrowing their oppressors to create freely and collectively the consummation of modern social, economic, and human developments: a democratic, egalitarian industrial society.

But as it has further matured, especially in the century since Marx's death, the modern sensibility has further freed itself from what André Gorz calls the irrational, religious, and absolutizing contents it inherited.[79] Paradoxically, this continued development of modernity has meant an awakening from the dream of modernity: its belief in progress, and the once-totalizing religions of science, technology, and politics. These are all characteristic early modern illusions. Today, our experience calls out to us to beware, to be humble, and to count costs. After the century's many catastrophes, after progress, after Communism, a fully modern consciousness (or, to avoid continuing skirmishes with postmodernism, a *contemporary* consciousness) would reject early modern illusions and myths about modernity.

Living in the late twentieth century has meant learning to accept diversity, multiplicity, and complexity; it has meant giving up the dream of absolute knowledge or of grasping with any degree of certainty the fundamental principles governing natural or social reality; it has meant further and more fully undermining externally imposed authority; it has meant critically analyzing universalizing presuppositions and chiliastic hopes; and, perhaps above all, it has meant accepting the centrality of human subjectivity and subjective experience. If, in all of these ways, we are living "the postmodern condition," we are equally preparing ourselves for the fullest acceptance of modernity. And however we regard what we are doing, we can begin to realize that, for all its structural continuities with our world, Marx's time was closer to Mozart's than to our own.

The Modernist Critique

Yet, as Marshall Berman has so stirringly pointed out, Marx is probably our greatest guide to modernity. He discovers and presents, more than any other writer, its enormous promise. He presents an unrivaled description and analysis of the modern world's dynamism, as well as of its contradictions and their source. He celebrates modernity and breathes its spirit, as does the movement that bears his name. In describing the flux of modern history, in discussing specific historical events, in analyzing capital's drive for change, Marx gives us some of the main contours and the main ambiguities of the modern world.[80]

And yet if it leads us to that modern world and bids us to behold, Marxism is less than fully modern, for all the reasons detailed in the critical analyses in this chapter. It counsels waiting for an end (or a beginning) of history, and expecting not just a better world but a resolution of the most fundamental of human conflicts. Marxism is also named after, and bases its authority on, the words of the founding individual (and his most illustrious followers). Marxism excludes subjective action and decision from its scientific study of society. The Marxian project rejects debating goals and values because these are supposed to be unfolding in history. It is "unscientific" to discuss them; Marxists expect one class of people, the proletariat, to liberate all of those who are oppressed.

Marxism has been a powerful and compelling vision and project, but in drawing together in a single coherent outlook all these dimensions, wishes, and needs, it not only flew far from science, but, as I have already suggested, did so by placing much of itself beyond the bounds of critical analysis. It is, indeed, astonishing how much modernist mythmaking and a priori assumptions are presented as study of actual trends and hard analysis of social reality in this holistic vision. As I describe its revolutionary project, Marxism makes as much use of prophecy and morality as historical and scientific analysis. Insofar as it suggests that the good is coming into being independently of human actions, that human progress is somehow taking place on its own, it has replaced the Judeo-Christian God with History with a capital "H"? Insofar as Marxists regard it as a "science" but still claim that it holds the key to the most important existential understandings, presents an answer for the central human conflicts, and grasps the meaning of history, Marxism operates in bad faith. Thus its passionate embrace of modernity has tended in the direction of a scientistic, and thus irrational, cult. In all of these respects Marxism has been less than modern, in the name of modernity importing needs, expectations, and mental habits from an earlier period into the scientific study of society and a modern political project.

Authority, whether of science or of individuals, religiosity, reductive simplicity, a vision of redemption to come, human dependency on enormous, seemingly superhuman forces, the failure to appreciate subjectivity: these features of Marxism are pre- or early modern inasmuch as they keep us from being *on our own*. Marxism places us in a modern world that is in constant flux and transformation, but with the key questions answered, our values already decided, ends posited, and historical processes unfolding toward their conclusion.

Are these then the reasons for Marxism's obsolescence? Its greatness was to fit its time closely, and its time is still very much like our own. Dominant structures and dynamics remain with us, so that Marxism remains not only a useful guide to key aspects of our world, but the best introduction to its origins. But it is no longer adequate as it presents itself, as an all-embracing interpretation of our world, as that world's project of transformation. Its project can no longer be our project.

Marxism and the Transition to Modernity

If the project of proletarian revolution was doomed to fail, what then was Marxism's historical function? For over one hundred years it united the oppressed and exploited of many societies into forceful, coherent movements. It has forced alterations within capitalism in the industrialized societies, helping labor movements at least partially to humanize their societies. It has led to alternative modes of development—for example, in the Soviet Union and China—permitting great societies to find ways of achieving basic steps toward industrialization and modernization outside the capitalist orbit, and free from its particular forms of domination and distortion. And, finally, Marxism has assisted other societies—for example, Cuba and Vietnam—to create modern national identities, first, in mobilizing to free themselves from the vise of colonialism and neocolonialism, and second, to begin embarking on their own paths of national development.

In reality Marxism's actual revolutionary goal turns out not to have been to build socialism from capitalism, but first to create the space for independent development, and second to do the work of capitalism. It has industrialized traditional societies that were originally dominated by imperial powers. Thus the Marxian project has actually operated as a link between traditional and modern life. It did so in the authoritative manner so characteristic of early science. And it has spawned centralized governing forces that have taken control of virtually all aspects of social life in the process of modernizing. Marxism told newly revolutionary societies where they were going and how they would get there.[81]

Sartre's description of the Soviet Union's slogan "Socialism in One Country" may be generalized to describe the role of Marxism in underdeveloped societies: "It became the simple signification of the way in which this still-traditionalist country, with its illiterate population, absorbed and assimilated at once the overthrow of its ancient traditions; a traditional withdrawal into itself; and the acquisition of new traditions, through the gradual absorption of an internationalist, universalist ideology that helped the peasants sucked into industry to comprehend the transition from rural to factory labor."[82] In the name of modernity, Marxism replaced traditionalist holistic visions with a new holistic vision, replaced an earlier faith and authority with a more modern faith and authority, replaced earlier forms of oppression with newer forms of oppression, and provided simple guidelines and catechisms for the newly modernized or modernizing to grasp their social reality. As such, it has acted as the cement unifying newly revolutionary societies around a coherent purpose. Instead of inspiring the liberation of advanced industrial societies so that "the free development of each is the condition for the free development of all,"[83] Marxism has unified societies in the transition to modernity, helping bend all possible energies to their transformation—with results that have been both beneficial and catastrophic.

In short, we must go beyond Deutscher's and Sartre's notion that Marxism was a modernizing project whose proponents were forced to make use of traditional means *because of the situations in which they found themselves.* My point is rather different: that it was precisely because of its transitional character, as an early modern outlook integrating many pre- and early modern features, that Marxism was able to become the project of transition. For many in both undeveloped and advanced societies, it became a kind of religion of modernity, incorporating an organized faith in science, in the working class, and in History, and dedicating individuals to work for an emancipated future. Inasmuch as modernity reaches beyond religion, inasmuch as its real thrust is to place us on our own, this is a living contradiction. Contradictory or not, this religion of modernity was the cement that held together Marxian socialism and the worldwide Communist movement.

Chapter Five

THE MARXIST–FEMINIST ENCOUNTER

Feminism destroyed Marxism. Not alone, to be sure, but in connection with other theoretical forces and political realities, it (and its socialist–feminist offshoot) contributed decisively to relativizing Marxism. Before the encounter, Marxism enjoyed unchallenged hegemony on the Left, proclaiming itself the answer to humanity's problems. Afterwards Marxism had become one narrative among others, and certainly no longer the most interesting one. When *the* answer becomes *an* answer, it is no longer what it was; like the featured speaker at the tail end of a banquet, it now scrambles, amidst the general din, to be heard by whomever will listen.

With the development of the women's movements of the 1960s it was inevitable that the proponents of Marxism and feminism would enter into a sustained and mutually challenging interaction, sometimes clashing bitterly, sometimes adjusting to each other, sometimes trying wholly to absorb each other. Inevitable, that is, because Marxism became a dominant political force within the antiwar and student movements, and because women decided that *their* liberation *as women* was no less an issue than peace, self-determination for the Vietnamese, or black liberation. This began a contestation, as it turned out, not only of women's subordination within the 1960s movements, but also of those movements' very goals. Marxists entered into this encounter enjoying unchallenged hegemony on the Left, indeed looking forward to worldwide intellectual and political ascendancy, perhaps within the foreseeable future. But by the time the encounter had played itself out, Marxism would be shaken to its roots, deserted by many of its main adherents, theoretically and practically enfeebled by its inability to incorporate the elemental radical force of women contesting their oppression as women. If it was unable to accommodate feminism and the other new social movements within *its* project, neither was Marxism recast so that it could exist alongside them in a new coalition, in relations of mutual respect, or find a way to recover its original explanatory resonance and political energy in a world distinguished by such movements.

Well before being challenged by feminism, Marxism had an honorable theoretical and practical history of taking seriously "the woman question."[1] But it did so *within* its paramount commitment to the liberation of the (overwhelmingly male) working class, and over the years continued to subsume, in Heidi Hartmann's words "the feminist struggle into the 'larger' struggle against capital."[2] Confident that their theory and method grasped the central and determining forms of oppression, Marxists have always expected that socialist revolution would usher in universal liberation. As I argued in Chapter 4, this universal and eschatological mood, mistaken or not, was at the heart of the Marxian project and its enormous appeal. It seemed self-evident that women, both as wage workers and as members of working-class families, would join, and be liberated by, the proletarian struggle. As workers in the classless society, they would enter the world on equal terms with men—for the first time.[3]

This universalist conviction was no doubt based on, and deformed by, what by the 1980s would widely come to be seen as gendered, patriarchal premises, allowing the family to be ignored as a site of oppression as well as neglecting the power relations hidden in gender identities. Nevertheless, by the 1960s Marxists had become quite used to and quite effective at carrying their universalism, their sense of grasping the fundamental human contradiction, their anchoring in the one area from which the decisive human oppressions flowed—class and capital—well beyond the advanced industrial proletariats. Above all, Marxist parties rallying the countryside had liberated China, North Vietnam, and Cuba from colonial and neocolonial domination. These struggles showed the utility and flexibility of Marxist categories of thought and methods of organizing. Marxism allowed us to critically understand the First World according to its situation, had become the reigning ideology in the Second, and was applied—with ever-increasing success—by revolutionaries in countries in the Third World according to their situations. No wonder, then, that the entire world had become polarized along the lines of a bitter struggle between socialism and capitalism. Marxism had by the 1970s become a world-historical field of force within which other problems and modes of thought were quite spontaneously expected to fit.

Feminists Encounter Marxism

It was only natural, during this time of Marxism's greatest influence, that many Marxists would approach feminism with the easy self-confidence that subsumed *all* significant issues within its embrace—and would think creatively in the process.[4] It was also natural that feminists would feel the need, as Lourdes Beneria describes it, to use Marxist analysis to make feminist concerns legitimate.[5] Its theoretical prioritization of production and the model of base and superstructure only increased this tendency: after all, weren't all significant social realities either directly bound up with essential structures, relations, and dynamics of capitalism, or decisively shaped by them? If any issue mattered, anywhere in social life, a common expectation was that Marxism could explain it from its central categories and dynamics, as a function of the development of capitalism.

If "everything" fell within Marxism, this centripetal force was soon met by the centrifugal force of feminism; from its determination to attack the oppression of women *as women*. This irrepressible drive broke with full force against an older habit, women allowing themselves and their oppression to be dissolved into other, sex-neutral and more universal categories. Since Western women had long since won the vote, and thus formal political equality, their attention in this "second wave" was now turned toward their social, economic, and cultural oppression, and was destined to aim at overturning any and all subordination of women and women's issues. Once "man" was dethroned as the accepted term for the species, for example, it became clear that ostensibly gender-neutral terms, and ideas, and movements—like Marxism—actually expressed male-gendered orientations and implicitly reflected male domination. As Alison Jaggar says, both liberalism and Marxism approached women's problems "in terms of the categories and principles that were formulated originally to deal with other problems."[6] But this meant that while "male dominance pervades every area of life under capitalism, . . . it is little more than a footnote to Marxist political economy."[7]

Thus Marxism's vision of universal liberation might well mask continued women's subjugation, or at the very least, the kind of complicity with male domination that would ignore it as a major issue. To contest, at all sites and on all levels, what came to be called "patriarchy" was made unavoidable by women's determination to find and speak in their own voice, of necessity inventing the very language with which to get to the bottom of their oppression. This ever more powerful and ever more radical force would eventually lead women to challenge Marxism at virtually every site and level: as theory of exploitation, as account of human production and reproduction, as philosophy of history, as vision of human liberation, as theory and practice of universal emancipation. Beleaguered on so many fronts, the Marxism that emerges from this encounter is so profoundly diminished and so relativized that it will never be the same.

The Marxist–feminist encounter, as described by Michèle Barrett in *Women's Oppression Today*, turned on the fact that "Marxism, constituted as it is around relations of appropriation and exploitation, is grounded in concepts that do not and could not address directly the gender of the exploiters and those whose labor is appropriated. A Marxist analysis of capitalism is therefore conceived around a primary contradiction between labor and capital and operates with categories that . . . can be termed 'sex blind.'"[8] Capitalism may indeed exploit women, or children, or racial minorities, or colonial peoples—but whether and how each of these happens is a matter of specific and contingent processes and, unlike the fundamental structural relationship between capitalist and workers, is not built into the capitalist system as such. Barrett continues, "Feminism, however, points in a different direction, emphasizing precisely the relations of gender—largely speaking, of the oppression of women by men—that Marxism has tended to pass over in silence." There may be many possible feminisms, just as there many be many possible Marxisms, "But what is clear is that any feminism must insist on the specific character of gender relations." However they are treated, all feminisms "must surely pose them as distinct."[9]

And indeed, a number of feminisms have done so. Radical feminists, often focusing on biology and psychology, tended to formulate the issue in terms of a timeless conflict between women and men, based on fundamental differences. Distinct both from liberal and radical feminist formulations and the traditional Marxist response of subsuming women's oppression (and the struggle against it) within the struggle against capital's exploitation of labor,[10] Marxist and socialist-oriented feminists stressed the autonomy of women's oppression and the struggle to overcome it *as well as* the need to overthrow capitalism. Above all, the distinct approach that its proponents called socialist feminism sought to combine Marxism with feminist analyses of patriarchy. Whether regarding these as dual systems of oppression operating within the same social space or as synthesized into a single historical system, socialist feminists insisted that a new political outlook and practice were called for to accommodate both feminist concerns and key themes and goals of traditional Marxism. This approach represents one of the most sustained and original efforts to reshape Marxism to date.

Socialist Feminism

Not all feminists sought a new approach. Some used Marxism's capacities for incorporating the specific character of women's oppression within its analyses of capitalism: following the lead of the feminist movement, they no longer restricted the central category, labor, to that activity leading to the production and exchange of commodities. As Lise Vogel argues in *Marxism and the Oppression of Women*, women's household and child rearing activities are a form of labor, even if they are not socially remunerated because they do not directly contribute to capitalist profit. She then presents, in a Marxism that takes feminism seriously but still stresses the labor process, a reconceptualization of labor to include both capitalist production and the *reproduction* of the class of wage laborers, the first taking place publicly and the second in the family:

> Given that this [second] task has historically been carried out primarily by women, in a context usually characterized by male supremacy, the working-class family becomes a highly institutionalized repository of women's oppression. As domestic laborers in the private household, women seem to devote much of their time to performing unpaid services for wage-earning men. . . . It is responsibility for the domestic labor necessary to capitalist social reproduction—and not the sex division of labor or the family per se—that materially underpins the perpetuation of women's oppression and inequality in capitalist society.[11]

To socialist feminists this Marxist solution remains too traditional. While accepting their redefinitions of labor, it begs precisely the question that must be answered: why is the context "usually characterized by male supremacy?" Indeed, if capitalism itself operates in a "sex-blind" way, why is it that male domination seems virtually coextensive with history itself? By absorbing women's oppression into a sophisticated analysis of capitalism, Vogel fails to explain *why* men dominate women not only in working-class families but throughout capitalist society, and why they have done so not only under capitalism but under earlier social forms. In a sense, for feminists the greatest failing of Vogel's project is probably the project itself, seeking as it does to continue deriving gender oppression from the gender-neutral operation of capital without acknowledging its *gender-specific* character.[12]

Other feminists sought to understand and combat both the "apparent gender-blindness of traditional Marxist categories [that] is in reality a gender-bias,"[13] *and* radical feminism's reluctance "to search for theoretical explanations of male dominance, [which] thus leads naturally to a political practice of separatism."[14] Jaggar called for a theoretical and political approach "that will synthesize the best insights of radical feminism and of the Marxist tradition and that simultaneously will escape the problems associated with each."[15] Jaggar and other socialist–feminist thinkers attempted to do just this in the 1970s and early 1980s, formulating a coherent theoretical perspective for those committed feminists who equally sought to integrate key Marxian insights and a commitment to socialist transformation.

The fresh and undogmatic spirit of socialist–feminist theorizing was part of the creative New Left Marxism I described in Chapter 1. Theoretically sophisticated Marxists active in the womens' movement, in community organizing, in the struggle for black liberation, in the student and antiwar movements, all lived their political experience in creative tension with their Marxism. Aware that they were far from the decisive site of the labor process and its class struggles, they often organized according to the sense of a larger dialectic, inclusive of capital and labor, propelling their movements; or they assumed that the class character of their sphere would eventually clarify itself and predominate; or they remained hyphenated and self-confident Marxists expecting that the entire process would find its theoretical clarification later. The remaining alternative was chosen particularly by socialist feminists: they set out to create that theoretical clarification themselves. Like other New Left activist Marxists, socialist feminists sought to respond to lived history and to give voice to a vital political movement. They wanted to use Marxism inventively and without regard for doctrinal purity, developing and transforming it as necessary. Beginning with the categories of Marxism *and* with their own experience, socialist feminists endeavored both to learn from their situation and to remain theoretically consistent, while retaining Marxism's radical temper and historical method.

In this spirit socialist–feminist writers produced a strikingly self-confident and original body of work. Jaggar's impressive *Feminist Politics and Human Nature* (1983) represents one of socialist feminism's theoretical high points, painstakingly showing as it does the strengths and limitations of liberal feminism, traditional Marxism, and radical feminism, en route to demonstrating that socialist feminism is their dialectical synthesis. Throughout, Jaggar emphasizes the new and incomplete nature of the socialist–feminist project, which is, in Margaret Page's words, "a commitment to the *development* of an analysis and political practice, rather than to one which already exists."[16] That project laid claim to being solidly Marxist insofar as it based itself on the principle that human nature—including male and female gender types as we know them—is produced in human practical activity. Thus men and women are historically and socially constituted, and in activities that embody *power* relations. While it was Marx and Engels who originally articulated this, they, and most Marxists, failed to carry their insight far enough, tending to treat private, family relationships as natural and given, while casting their deconstructive light on public, economic relationships.

In contrast, socialist feminists insist on seeing both procreative and nonprocreative labor historically, and thus claim

> that our "inner" lives, as well as our bodies and behavior, are structured by gender; that this gender-structuring is not innate but is socially imposed; that the specific characteristics that are imposed are related systematically to the historically prevailing system of organizing social production; that the gender-structuring of our "inner" lives occurs when we are very young and is reinforced throughout our lives in a variety of different spheres; and that these relatively rigid masculine and feminine character structures are a very important element in maintaining male dominance.[17]

If a contemporary individual is thus formed by "her sex and gender assignment," her experience is also "shaped by her class, race, and nationality."[18] Unlike Marxism, socialist feminism refuses to take an a priori position on which of these is more important. Nor do socialist feminists believe "that the sexual and procreative aspects of production are determined ultimately by what is defined ordinarily as 'the economy'; in other words, sexuality and procreation are not part of the superstructure."[19] This means that, in order to adequately characterize *both* kinds of labor required by contemporary society for its survival and the centrality and pervasiveness of relationships of male dominance, socialist feminism redefines traditional Marxist conceptions of the economic base so that "procreation and 'production' are mutually determining but that one is not a more 'ultimate' determinant than the other; that both are part of the economic foundation of society."[20]

Jaggar is, to be sure, presenting a program and not a finished analysis. She recognizes that this redefined political economy based on gender *and* class remains to be conceptualized, that the relationship between the productive and reproductive systems needs to be established, especially in order to avoid the notion, current among other socialist feminists, that these are semi-autonomously operating "dual systems."[21] In undertaking the enormous task of "trying to synthesize the insights of radical feminism with those of traditional Marxism,"[22] socialist feminism needs to develop "a comprehensive theoretical framework for interpreting its scattered insights into the reasons why men have sought to control women's labor, the means they have used to do so and the ways in which women have resisted men's control."[23] Thus she calls for a socialist–feminist equivalent to Marxism's stages of historical development, taking into account not only the development of the forces of production but also related transformations in the sexual decision of labor.

The Short Career of Socialist Feminism

This then is the research program of socialist feminism, as interpreted by Alison Jaggar. There were numerous complementary and competing contributions to socialist feminism in the late 1970s and early to mid-1980s. In a justly celebrated article, for example, Heidi Hartmann called for a dual-systems approach to improve "the unhappy marriage of Marxism and feminism," a marriage in which "the two are one, and that one is Marxism."[24] Iris Young critiqued the dual-systems approach and called for "*a thoroughly feminist historical materialism which regards the social relations of a given historical social formation as one system in which gender formation is a core attribute.*"[25] Zillah Eisenstein, "using the Marxist method, transformed by feminist commitments,"[26] developed an analysis of "capitalist patriarchy," whose goal was "to emphasize the mutually reinforcing dialectical relationship between capitalist class structure and hierarchical sexual structuring."[27]

Michèle Barrett's version of the dual-systems approach argued that women's oppression took place on the semi-autonomous plane of ideology.[28] Ann Ferguson conceptualized the space within which women's oppression takes place as the "sex-affective mode of production" and women's oppression as that of a "sex-class."[29] Nancy Hartsock, in seeking to lay the bases of a feminist historical materialism, presented a powerful argument for a feminist epistemological standpoint providing unique insight into oppression and liberation.[30]

Surveying these and other socialist–feminist writings of the period, one cannot avoid the forceful impression that they make; they are a brilliant beginning at articulating a genuinely original approach to politics. They were intended to illuminate a political practice in which socialist feminism would seek to be a socialist force within the feminist movement and a feminist force within the socialist movement, bringing to each the insights, and the hard realities, represented by the other. Whether her own or other formulations would be drawn into this theoretical–practical process, Jaggar, upon completing her synthesis in 1983, could at least have expected that the collective project would continue to gain clarity, adherents, and strength. But, a decade after Jaggar's articulation of its parameters, what has become of socialist feminism? After its creative and self-confident beginning, the answer is astonishing: socialist feminism has virtually disappeared.

Already in 1985 *Socialist Review* published an interview entitled "The Impasse of Socialist-Feminism" in which three of the four feminists interviewed had abandoned the project of combining class and gender politics.[31] According to Lynne Segal, a British socialist feminist still loyal to the original project, "In the early seventies, radical socialist politics of some sort were integral to a feminist outlook" in Britain and perhaps even the United States. Yet by 1987 Segal had to admit, "The voice of socialist feminism is now remarkably silent in popular feminist debate, a change which has taken many feminists by surprise."[32] Michèle Barrett, author of the pioneering *Women's Oppression Today* (published in 1980), in a new introduction to the revised edition only eight years later, not only notices the "steadily declining" influence of Marxism within feminism, but effectively revokes the main premise of the book by questioning the desirability that the two be integrated. The project of reconciling Marxism with feminism "could be said to have been shelved—it was abandoned rather than resolved."[33] This is reflected in Barrett's new subtitle, changed from *Problems in Marxist Feminist Analysis* to *The Marxist/Feminist Encounter*. And in 1990 Zillah Eisenstein could reflect on, and try to account for, the "absence of socialist feminism as a political discourse."[34] In fact, socialist feminism has virtually vanished as a significant political–theoretical direction. As Anne Froines said in a 1992 call for reviving socialist feminism, "Attempts to establish socialist feminist women's organizations ended by 1980, and socialist feminist activism as such largely became socialist feminist theorizing in university Women's Studies programs."[35]

Of the writers just mentioned, Lynne Segal and Ann Ferguson have continued squarely pursuing the socialist–feminist theoretical project. Some who might continue to use Marxism, such as Nancy Fraser, are committed to socialism *and* feminism as components of a broad and plural "postMarxist field" rather than as a coherent project.[36] To better comprehend social reality in the one case and to better articulate projects of transforming it in the other, Barrett and Young, influenced by postmodern thinkers, have left the orbit of Marxism.[37] Eisenstein, similarly, now denounces the phallocratic assumptions behind any and all socialisms—"a stance that privileges the economy and the public sphere while using abstract notions of equality that assume the male body as referent."[38] Certainly such changes of interest and position are to be expected, but it is revealing that few new recruits have taken over from the pioneers and extended their work *within* socialist feminism. Or rather, those who have, have done so from outside of the Marxist rubric.[39] Insofar as the explorations originally initiated by socialist feminism have continued as a significant current in feminist thinking, many of their authors have decamped from Marxism and entered a new and more accommodating theoretical home, postmodernism. As Eisenstein says, socialist feminism has lost political status, while current feminist dialogue has incorporated "many of the earlier concerns of socialist feminism while moving through and beyond them."[40] "In the early to mid 1970s," she continues, "it was important for many of us who were leftists as well as feminists to theoretically define the relationship between socialism and feminism. In the later eighties many who in the past identified with this concern became involved in feminist politics outside its theoretical debates with socialism."[41]

Why the change? One might explain this in the language of former socialist feminists themselves: Marxism is blind to *difference*, is phallocratic, is an obsolete totalizing and falsely universalizing project, is incurably permeated with male-gendered assumptions and logic.[42] But these criticisms avoid the key question: why did the synthesizers abandon their original efforts to transform Marxism? After all, as Jaggar and other socialist feminists pointed out from the beginning, traditional Marxism had these faults before and during the encounter, as did virtually all thought and discourse. Indeed, one purpose of the encounter was to fashion a *new* Marxism, without the weaknesses of the original. Why give up on this effort?

Circumstantially, it is worth noting, most other kinds of political activism generated during the 1960s and 1970s had also dissipated by the 1980s. If socialist feminism emerged in response both to the women's movement and to the New Left, the first was in profound retreat by the mid-1980s and the second had disappeared. A wave of conservatism, partially in reaction to these movements, had swept the advanced industrial world that had produced the New Left and feminist movements. Further-more, the ebbing of socialist feminism corresponds to the decline of Marxism as a powerful theoretical and practical force field. As Eisenstein points out, the demand that feminists identify themselves in relation to socialism has faded: "The specification of feminism *as* socialist has little *political* context today."[43] Socialist feminism was unable to survive the general disintegration of socialist politics. As Marxian theory was challenged and supplanted as the dominant intellectual framework by postmodernism, the New Left continued to dwindle. As the French Communist Party atrophied and the Italian Communist Party continued its self-transformation, Communism in power was paralyzed by the impasse that led to the revolutions of 1989 and 1991. In short, Marxism was no longer a political or intellectual current that had to be dealt with—by feminists or anyone else. As Eisenstein says:

> Identifying as a socialist feminist in the mid-seventies meant something very important and strategic at the time. But today, unlike the early 1970s, socialism seems to hold out little new theoretical or political promise for feminism. This was not true when some of us were first trying to articulate the relationships between capitalism, racism, and patriarchy. But we are not trying to *first* do these things any longer. And as the analysis of feminism has deepened and focused more on the politics of sexuality, gender, and race, socialist theory and practice has not reinvented itself. It has not fundamentally revised itself by bringing sex, gender, and race to the "center." Socialism has become stale, while feminism remains in flux and vital.[44]

Although Eisenstein is talking primarily about a political process beyond the control of feminists—the present impossibility of socialist politics—this process had a theoretical side in which feminists played a decisive role. After all, it was feminists who sought to "reinvent" socialism by placing sex, gender, and race in the center, and it was feminists who gradually lost interest in the Marxist–feminist encounter—indeed, in socialist feminism itself. At first, many feminists needed to legitimate their analysis by placing themselves within Marxism's embrace and authority. Then, many of them more and more freely began to *use* Marxism, claiming loyalty to it, but employing it along with other approaches developed elsewhere. Then, in carrying out this second process, they looked at Marxism, now half from the outside and half from the inside. One doesn't look at *the* project; one is inside it. Marxism, now, had become *a* project: it would be evaluated, its limits tested, its weaknesses explored. Its insights would be retained while moving on to other projects. Placed alongside feminism, as explaining some important areas but not others, Marxism was consequently relativized by the encounter. In freely combining Marxism with feminism, socialist feminists were in fact continuing the undermining efforts begun by the women's movement. In this sense, socialist feminism ultimately helped to destroy Marxism rather than to revitalize it. Far from being a stable and historically meaningful project that would give Marxism a new coherence within a larger synthesis, socialist feminism turns out to have been a temporary resting point, a way station out of Marxism.

The Impossibility of Socialist Feminism

To put the underlying theoretical paradox inherent in socialist feminism most simply, a coherent Marxian project must argue that the capitalist labor process is central; but a coherent feminism must argue that it is not, and focus instead on male–female relations of domination. The two theoretical–practical directions are intrinsically opposed. It is a matter not of a simple tension, each side of which enriches and stimulates the other, but rather of polar claims about the central human problem and its resolution. Many of us were taken by surprise by this, because we had been able to retain our hyphenated Marxisms during the 1960s and 1970s by soft-pedaling Marxism's claim for primacy and universality. Hoping to dissolve our tensions in a larger synthesis, we looked forward to reconciling what we *theoretically* knew to be true with what we *experientially* knew to be so. In contrast, determined to get to the bottom of women's oppression and to speak in women's voices, feminism exploded such efforts at reconciliation.

Since each step in recasting Marxism further weakened its theoretical coherence, Marxists can hardly be blamed for not trying harder to rethink Marxism in a manner in keeping with feminist insights and demands. If we appreciate Marxism as a coherent project, and the reasons for its great historical power are understood, it becomes clear that to contest its identification of the capitalist labor process as containing the decisive social contradiction is also to contest its vision of history, its diagnosis of oppression, its projected solution, its explanation of the dynamic leading to change, its identification of the social force that will bring about the change, its ethical and existential messages, and the prophetic sense holding the entire project together. Marxism may be attacked today for falsely universalizing and claiming hegemony for its area of concern, and still-radical thinkers may seek more pluralistic alternatives. But such efforts need to appreciate that the hegemony of class and labor are precisely the reasons for Marxism's own long hegemony.

Socialist feminists, whether or not they saw the goal of their project as a dual-systems theory or an integrated theory, usually sought to accord male domination equal explanatory force to capitalism. This demand, inevitable inasmuch as it sprang from feminists' determination to grasp and overthrow women's subordination to men, at best places Marxist explanation and action alongside feminist explanation or action, whether en route to a larger synthesis in which Marxism would be only a single element, or in a theoretical and practical alliance of more than one autonomous force. This displaces Marxism from its accustomed pivotal role, cancelling its claims of theoretical and political hegemony for the labor process, class, and workers' struggles. Some socialist feminists even relegate Marxism to subordinate status. Hartsock, for example, in constructing a feminist historical materialism, turns the tables by proclaiming that the female experience is "*deeper and more thoroughgoing* than that available to the worker."[45]

Whatever its new reference points, the historical materialism thus construed is no longer historical materialism as we have known it. In this and other socialist feminisms, including "materialist feminism,"[46] Marxism is deprived of its claim to be the single most important answer. With its own synthetic and reductive power diminished, Marxism can only illuminate an important, but no longer the key, dimension of the human situation. Thus relativized, it may offer insights about a specific aspect of social life, but without commanding the field. Marxism's own gripping vision of the human adventure is now only one story among several. Thus demoted within socialist feminism, who can blame Marxists for failing to initiate a larger outlook, a more embracing political and theoretical perspective containing both Marxist and feminist theory?

Nor did feminism create that larger outlook. Characteristically, the various socialist–feminist theorists have been concerned to focus on *women's* oppression and liberation, but have left the general and Marxist side of things relatively untouched. Notably missing from Jaggar's effort at synthesis, for example, is any extended discussion of the relationship of socialist feminism to possible political movements advocating socialism. These movements, presupposed by socialist feminism, are seemingly taken for granted.[47] Presenting itself as a new synthesis, socialist feminism was really half of that, the half dealing with patriarchy. Its salience depended on the continued flourishing of a Marxist politics and culture that its presence and theoretical pressure would transform.

Theoretically, socialist feminism alternately claimed to recast Marxism and to be true to its deepest insights. No longer adhering to Marxism as *the* unified theoretical–practical project, it abandoned that without attention to the consequences. Where Marxism had been based on a close study of the socioeconomic dynamics that were leading the working class to demand the overthrow of capitalism, socialist feminism was unable to tie itself to any similar process. "It is one thing," says Jaggar, "to say that class and gender must be abolished, of course, and quite another to say how that abolition should be achieved."[48] She uses "must," no doubt, to express determination to transform the social relations that oppress women and exploit workers. The question following Jaggar's "must" reveals the impasse of socialist feminism. The Marxian revolutionary project used "must" in a very different sense, one that did not encourage wondering about how its goals would be achieved. The ethical imperative was contained within, and seen as being realized by, the actual sweep of world history, and was embodied in an objective process that was actually taking place and a subjective force whose coming to revolutionary consciousness could be pointed to. In contrast, the idea of marrying Marxism and feminism may indeed be a worthy one, but it is only an idea.

Socialist feminism was not able to point to the objective social dynamics that were pressing toward its realization, nor to the subjective dynamics that were creating the grave diggers of capitalist patriarchy. Although it sought to combine two major world-historical movements, it did so on the theoretical level only, without being able to specify the concrete conditions of their interaction, the processes that were bringing them together, or the unifying vision that they were generating. Socialist feminism contained rich insights drawn from two movements, important new ideas, fragments of analyses, and strong hopes, all brought together with the purpose of igniting a new movement. But as reasonable and even exciting as its proposed synthesis seemed to an important segment of the New Left, socialist feminism did not really capture the deepest meaning of an emerging world-historical process. It was a hope, with only momentary purchase on sociohistorical reality. On the one side, socialist feminism reflected the prestige but dwindling life of Marxism; on the other it was a way station for a number of creative activist thinkers finding their place between Marxism and radical feminism. They would continue to develop their analyses, beyond Marxism and socialism, "through an endless dialogue which continually reinvents the way we understand the politics of sex, class, and race."[49] Yet the theorists of socialist feminism could never point to the processes that were making it *real*. As a promising theory without a concomitant social dynamic, it could never be more than a good idea.

In the Wake of Socialist Feminism

One revealing response to socialist feminism came from a number of Marxist thinkers who, even while reasserting Marxism's hegemony, reflected the fact that feminism and the new social movements diminished its universality. Marxists such as Perry Anderson and Ellen Meiksins Wood sought to theoretically decouple Marxism from feminism by systematically focusing on the limited and specific nature of Marxism's promises, while rigorously applying it to the economic terrain. Echoing Isaac Deutscher's comments to the American New Left in the 1960s, Wood argues that "there are strong and promising emancipatory impulses at work, but . . . they may not be active at the core of capitalist society and may not free us from its oppressions."[50] Wood asserts Marxism's centrality for overcoming *economic* oppression by arguing that these movements are distinct from Marxism in their demand for "*extra-economic* goods—gender emancipation, racial equality, peace, ecological health, democratic citizenship."[51] Although capitalism cannot help but continue to threaten world peace and is "unavoidably hostile to ecological balance," the fact that "it is uniquely indifferent to the social identities of the people it exploits" means that it has no inner need to oppose gender equality. Antisexist and antiracist struggles, then, will not bring down capitalism; theoretically, they might well succeed *within* capitalism. Wood reaffirms the class nature of the "principal mode of oppression" under capitalism while stressing that abolishing it will not liberate women but rather "eliminate the ideological and economic needs which under capitalism can still be served by gender and racial oppressions."[52]

Marxism does not claim to relieve every oppression, Wood argues, but its attack on capital will have a decisive effect in transforming the rest:

> Unless class politics becomes the unifying force that binds together all emancipatory struggles, the "new social movements" will remain on the margins of the existing social order, at best able to generate periodic and momentary displays of popular support but destined to leave the capitalist order intact, together with all its defenses against human emancipation and the realization of "universal human goods."[53]

Although Wood states here nothing more or less than classical Marxism, dismissive toward such movements as feminism, it is a curiously humble Marxism; it simultaneously softens and yet retains its traditional call for universal emancipation. While carefully restricting Marxism's promise, Wood still insists that its target is the "principal" oppression and the "core" of social life, and thus that it retains all its old political mobilizing force. At the same time, by stressing that overthrowing capitalism will not bring universal liberation but only allow us to begin the process, and by conceding that many forces other than workers, such as women, have been carrying on contemporary struggles for their liberation and doing so in non-Marxist terms, Wood leaves us doubting Marxism's continuing power to rally the necessary forces to accomplish its own goals.

This Marxist separatism from the new social movements forces us to wonder, along with Perry Anderson, "What bloc of social forces can be mobilized, in what ways, ever to undertake the *risks* of disconnecting the cycle of capital accumulation in our intricately integrated market economies?"[54] Anderson advocates, in Michèle Barrett's words, a "a comradely friendship of the two movements rather than the pursuit of anything closer."[55] Yet what force will a workers' movement have *without* the new social movements? Wood's confident statements about Marxism's relationship to the new social movements can be reversed and applied to the anticapitalist struggles she seeks to retain at the center: "They are unlikely to succeed if they remain detached from [extra-economic struggles]."[56]

Far more widespread than this Marxist separatism is a second, feminist, response to socialist feminism. Instead of embracing socialist feminism and moving it toward a new and expanded universalism, toward *the* new theoretical–practical project of revolutionary transformation, the most sophisticated feminist thought has moved in the opposite direction, toward increasingly theoretical efforts to articulate difference and plurality, nourished by postmodern theories that emphasize this. At least two inner dynamics of this process derive directly from socialist feminism itself.

First, writes Eisenstein, "By the early 1980s the self-critique of feminism, launched primarily by black feminists and other women of color, required a rethinking of the internal pluralism of feminisms; the radically important differences which exist among women."[57] If social life in capitalist patriarchy can no longer claim to be governed by a single logic, might not the presence and struggles of other oppressed groups, such as racial and ethnic minorities, argue for the existence of *multiple* logics, justifying *multiple* standpoints and struggles? Once those who began as Marxists accept the feminist standpoint as independent and valid and begin to view Marxism from the outside, differences among themselves provoke a new approach, one that poses a mortal issue for their Marxism. Why not accommodate and even embrace other standpoints and struggles? If so, can this best be done by retaining Marxism as a touchstone, or are other standpoints better equipped to show the way?

Once we begin to grasp women's issues as being autonomous, there seems to be no compelling need to tie them even to determination "in the last instance" by the socioeconomic base of society. In an intellectual and political climate in which Marxism was losing steam anyway, why struggle to relate other issues to political economy? As Jane Flax asked in 1987, "Why 'widen' the concept of production [to include housework and child rearing] instead of dislodging it or any other singularly central concept from such authoritative power?"[58] Lourdes Beneria explains that this may have been necessary during a time when feminism still needed to "legitimate feminist concerns by integrating them into the male order."[59] The domestic labor debate of the 1970s, using Marxist tools, did just this. But by the 1980s, an increasingly self-confident feminism had developed the tools and the will to "search for a distinctive female identity by challenging and confronting terms of traditional male discourse"[60]—arguing, for example, that household labor is a distinctively nonmarket relation where no law of value applies. Having stepped halfway outside of Marxism, socialist feminists needed less and less, and were increasingly hindered by, the symbolism of an identity whose key terms and commitments they had in any case already absorbed. Standing *outside* of Marxism in the "post-Marxist field," feminists who also happened to be socialists such as Nancy Fraser could *look at* and *evaluate* Marxism, taking what was still useful and discarding what was not.[61]

This may explain why socialist feminism gave way to an increasingly non-Marxist approach to feminism that, if often politically radical and sometimes still socialist, located women's self-understanding and struggles within the growing postmodernist field of force. Michèle Barrett describes this as a "paradigm shift" within feminist thought.[62] Indeed, according to Flax, feminist theory can now described as "a type of postmodern philosophy."[63]

Determined to expose the specific interests behind all claims of gender neutrality, feminists found Foucault's studies of power enormously fruitful. Trying to get beyond a universal vision of history that in fact spoke about the mostly male working class and discounted women's experience, they enthusiastically welcomed Lyotard's attack on totalizing metanarratives. Aware of socially constructed but decisively diverging patterns of male and of female experience, they found Derrida's discussion of difference to be a major new conceptual tool. And perhaps above all, they embraced the postmodern mood, with its stress on multiplicity and plurality as well as the postmodern theoretical projects, with their stress on sexuality, subjectivity, and textuality.[64] Turning away from economic exploitation, they looked at sexual issues and power relations in their must subtle psychological and linguistic nuances. And they incorporated these theoretical insights without a single agreed-upon theoretical touchstone. As Flax says, "There cannot, nor should we expect there to be, a feminist equivalent to (a falsely universalizing) Marxism; indeed, the epistemologies of feminism undercut all such claims, including feminist ones."[65]

It turns out, then, that socialist feminism, the effort to integrate Marxism and feminism, pointed the way to its own superseding, for both internal and external reasons. It ended up far from being a new and stable fulcrum of social transformation. Even as it sought to renew Marxism, socialist feminism continued the relentless work of feminism in undermining Marxism's foundations. Rather than replacing Marxism with a coherent new revolutionary theory, it accelerated the questioning of any and all revolutionary theories. A temporary resting point rather than a new center, socialist feminism challenged Marxism at its core and was unable to be further developed *as* socialist feminism. This once-promising project wound up having mounted a mortal attack on Marxism as we know it. In so doing, it completed the deconstructive process begun by the movement for women's liberation. It is in this sense that feminism destroyed Marxism.

Chapter Six

MARXISM WITHOUT MARXISM

Marxists trying recently to escape obsolescence have faced two fates. First, like myself, for all their presumed sophistication they have unconsciously absorbed the early modern and premodern traits they have tried to go beyond. And why not, since these have been part of all politically effective Marxisms. Second, they may abstractly free themselves from these limitations, but at a cost—that of recasting the project so that it is no longer Marxism. But how is it possible to decide what is and is not Marxism? Any answer has to include two features frequently ignored in recent efforts to rethink Marxism: Marxism is not a theory but a theoretical–practical project of social transformation; and Marxism focuses on the liberation of the working class as its central goal and as the key to human emancipation. Whatever else it may be, any new "Marxism" that abandons these traits loses its Marxist identity.

We have already seen how, in trying to remedy specific weaknesses of Marxism, socialist feminism contributed to fatally undermining it. This chapter explores a second effort to create a contemporary Marxism, analytic Marxism, and argues that by abandoning the project of social transformation it becomes a peculiarly non-Marxist Marxism. But what else are those with Marxist commitments to do? What future might there be for a chastened and humble but theoretically rigorous historical materialism? How might a relativized Marxism become useful? In concluding the first part of this book, I will explore what becomes of Marxists after Marxism.

The Moment of Analytical Marxism

Analytic Marxism emerged "alongside" socialist feminism in the 1970s, but unlike it, it was not tied to any movement. Nor has it shared socialist feminism's decline. In fact, just as Western Marxism was once seen by some of its proponents two generations ago as superseding the Marxism of the Second International (while providing an alternative to Soviet Marxism), so today is "analytical Marxism" being trumpeted by its proponents as "a style of theorizing that has effectively superseded Western Marxism."[1] This second major recent effort to rethink Marxism grew in strength and influence among Anglo-American academics throughout the 1980s. After its moment of public breakthrough in 1978 with the appearance of G. A. Cohen's *Karl Marx's Theory of History: A Defense*, it has been continued by a growing interdisciplinary current that includes Allen Wood, Richard Miller, John Roemer, Jon Elster, Andrew Levine, Adam Przeworski, and Eric Olin Wright. Influenced by analytical philosophy and mainstream "bourgeois" social science, analytical Marxists have been unapologetic in their "wholesale embrace of conventional scientific and philosophical norms"[2] and have prided themselves on their "no-bullshit Marxism." Their aggressive effort to free historical materialism from theoretical imprecision and obsolete baggage has also self-consciously sought to inject Marxist thinking into mainstream academic discussions. From this point of view, they might be seen as Marxist modernizers, bent on freeing Marxism from the "vague programmatic schemes of an all-encompassing sort and . . . views that elude precise formulation."[3] These "weaknesses" are intimately related to the characteristics I noted in Chapter 4 as distinctively premodern and early modern. Committed to contemporary standards of clarity and rigor, analytic Marxists have defended a more precise, more modest, less sweeping, less reductive version of historical materialism, hoping that "a reconstructed Marxism, less grandiose but also far sounder than any of its ancestors, will emerge from this period of theoretical transformation."[4]

Cohen began by defending the cardinal theses of Marxism, making a sustained case for the centrality of the forces of production. He argues that there is a tendency for productive forces to augment; that social relations must remain compatible with the forces; that when this ceases to happen, instability and conflicts result, leading to socialist transformation. He presents this in a closely reasoned, rigorously developed style of argumentation all too foreign to Marxist thinking.

At the same time, however, Cohen's Marxism has a deeply problematic side. In the face of all arguments to the contrary, he revives a Marxism that lays heavy accent on processes of cumulative technological development and systemic tendencies toward transformation. A hundred years after Marx, he tenaciously defends the centrality of objective processes and discounts the importance of subjective capacities. Three of the most debated features of Cohen's work show this objectivist bias. The first is his insistence on the priority of the productive forces over politics and working-class action: "In the Marxism I defend, class struggle has primary political significance, but the political dimension of society is not itself primary. The Marxist theory of history loses its coherence when it ceases to assign primacy to the development of the productive forces."[5]

Cohen's insistence on "primacy" flies in the face of the fact that since World War I any recasting of Marxism that has not given at least equal weight to the subjective factor has been crippled both theoretically and practically. We have become accustomed to an interactive and dialectical view that considers even the "objective" augmentation of productive forces to depend on the growth of and changes in a variety of other areas, including freedom, intellectual capacities, skills, discourse, stocks of knowledge, and struggles. This rules out a simple monism and argues for a reciprocal causality. And it makes Cohen's insistence that "the dialectic of forces and relations of production . . . governs class behavior and is not explicable in terms of it"[6] appear both reductive and simplistic.

A second debatable area of Cohen's Marxism is the argument that socialism is inevitable, "because of what enough people, being rational, are bound to do."[7] Cohen makes the mistake of treating Marx's claims to inevitability as serious, and valid, scientific statements. Thus his questions become, "In what sense is socialism inevitable?" and, "What are the consequences of this for individual action?" At our present stage in Marxism's career, however, it should be clear that as a scientific claim, inevitability was always wrong and foolish. But it was central to Marxism as a prophetic claim—as much a moral statement as a prediction—and contemporary revolutionaries will have to understand the role it played, and provide for the needs such a claim once satisfied. By focusing on Marxism as *argument*, however, Cohen misses this whole side of the project.

The third and and perhaps most interesting reflection of Cohen's objectivist stance appears in his acrobatics in the face of the fact that capitalism plainly encourages, and indeed, in its consumer phase, *needs* rather than fetters, the runaway growth of productive forces. This contradicts his "incompatibility thesis" and its confident anticipation of systemic conflict and transformation. To rescue it in the face of unceasing increases in productivity within capitalist relations, which demonstrate that continued expansion of productivity clearly does not require socialist transformation, Cohen resorts to a value judgment: capitalism promotes increasing consumption rather than a more humane use of the forces of production; it "brings society to the threshold of abundance and locks the door. For the promise of abundance is not an endless flow of goods, but a sufficiency produced with a minimum of unpleasant toil."[8]

This shift displaces the centrality of the development and subsequent fettering of the productive forces by the much fuzzier and more subjective idea of "human optimality." Cohen accounts for the facts, but without seeing that he has begun to undermine his entire project. His reduction of Marxism to the overwhelming focus on productive forces cannot withstand its first test, the fact that the system's functioning is *not* leading to its undoing. Resting on a value judgment made against capitalism from the outside rather than on the system's self-destructive and objectively ascertainable inner dynamics, Cohen's reductionism enters into bad faith.[9]

All three of these problematic aspects of Cohen's thought, we may note, run into difficulty for the same reason. After the rise and fall of the various working-class movements, objectivistic Marxism can only have one function: to fill in the space occupied by the defunct agents of change with an argument on behalf of objective trends, rather than a project aimed at action. Instead of reflecting historically on how socialism might be achieved, given the quiescence of the working class, Cohen abstractly develops the "capacity thesis" about a willing and able working class inevitably emerging in response to the capitalist "fettering" of the forces of production. The riddles of history are conjured away by argument—almost.

Reconstructing Marxism

A many-sided development followed the pioneering analytical work of the 1970s, which delineated a new project, if not a new paradigm. Andrew Levine describes this project as follows:

> Analytical Marxists seek to clarify theoretical claims to the point where opposing views directly confront one another and become susceptible to rational adjudication. They emphasize the elaboration of conceptual structures—drawing distinctions where appropriate, collapsing distinctions where they have been inappropriately drawn, marshalling arguments in support of the positions they defend and, so far as possible, formulating questions with a view to resolving them.[10]

Thus as Marxism and analytic philosophy have become mutually congenial, new standards of rigor and clarity were introduced into Marxist theorizing, making it possible for like-minded thinkers not simply to present and defend Marxism's conceptual structure, but increasingly to subject every one of Marxism's distinct claims to "its own interrogation for meaning, coherence, plausibility and truth."[11] The reach of analytical Marxism expanded further into philosophy, and into economics and sociology as well, seriously contesting the validity of the labor theory of value, scrutinizing the theory and social reality of classes, exploring the nature of exploitation under capitalism, and developing models for an alternative, socialist organization of the process of production.

One of the essential features of analytical Marxism is its insistence that an effective radical theory must always defend itself before the bar of truth, must demand good reasons, must rigorously scrutinize itself for illusions, vagueness of thought, and unclarified assumptions. Only in this way can a politics claiming to base itself on a scientific understanding of the real world avoid becoming trapped in its own illusions, or worse, pushing its adherents as well as innocent people into catastrophe. This commitment to truth suggests, moreover, that argument, whether at Oxford or on the shop floor, is a necessary dimension of any effective politics. Understanding just how capitalism exploits its workers, and being able to explain this, is obviously a vital undertaking, as is clarifying the moral bases of political judgment and action. The widespread academic interest in analytical Marxism testifies to the importance of such questions, especially at a time when there are no major Marxist movements. Certainly it can be argued that, in the absence of movements, any and all Marxisms are theories cut off from the practice that would make them historically true. Still, analytical Marxist thinkers have managed to generate new centers of debate and discussion where otherwise there might be none.

If Cohen's restatement still contains unacceptable residues of Marxist objectivism, more self-critical efforts followed. Levine points out that "as analytical Marxism has emerged as a distinct current, sweeping philosophical pronouncements have given way in some Marxist circles to modest but tractable theorizing, positions have been carefully elaborated, assessed, revised and, in some cases, abandoned."[12] A major fruit of such labors is *Reconstructing Marxism* by Erik Olin Wright, Elliot Sober, and Andrew Levine, published in 1992. Their rendering of analytical Marxism deserves attention because it is not a general defense of Marxism but rather an effort to take the measure of Marxism in the light of its waning as a project of societal transformation, and with a critical eye turned toward removing its obsolescent features. In short, it is a systematic effort "to clarify rigorously foundational concepts and assumptions and the logic of theoretical arguments built on those foundations."[13]

Written at a time of "declining intellectual consensus coincident with the collapse of authoritarian state socialist regimes,"[14] and when "programs for social reform inspired by Marxist understandings of the social world and Marxist visions of ideal social arrangements no longer shape Left political practice,"[15] it concludes that Marxism remains "surprisingly plausible" in the contemporary world. If Cohen's defense, written a decade and a half earlier, argues for a preestablished position, Wright, Levine, and Sober sort through the arguments of Cohen and Anthony Giddens[16] and self-critically subject their own position to rigorous logical and scientific scrutiny—in order to determine what parts of the edifice may be said to remain standing.

Closely criticizing orthodox Marxism, they remove each of the weaknesses discussed in Chapter 4. What remains is a Marxism that has been freed from all teleology and inevitability, and that has been pared back to those claims that can be reasonably supported by a contemporary scientific consciousness. It can best be understood in terms of what it absorbs from Cohen and what it rejects. It is centered around Cohen's "development thesis": there is a clear and endogenous historical tendency toward techno-logical development, and such change is "sticky downward"—that is, it is usually retained and not reversed. This occurs because "there is a perma-nent, human impulse to try to improve humanity's ability to transform nature to realize human wants,"[17] and because each improvement develops interests seeking to retain its advantanges.

This "development thesis" combines with Cohen's "compatibility the-sis": "A given level of productive power is compatible only with a certain type, or certain types, of economic structure."[18] These two combine, in turn, with the "contradiction thesis," which argues that over time "the productive forces will develop to a point where they are no longer compatible with the relations of production under which they had previously developed."[19] But to these Cohen adds three further theses, the "capacity," "transformation," and "opti-mality" theses. These argue that an objective interest in transforming the production relations will bring about the capacity to do so; that compatibility thereby will be restored; and that the new relations will be optimal. In short, as we saw above, the objective trend of history is to move toward socialism. Cohen further insists that it is precisely the development of the productive forces that *brings about* such a process of change.[20]

In rejecting Cohen's last three theses after close examination, Wright, Levine, and Sober formulate what they call a "weak, restricted historical materialism." This insists that Marxism has grasped:

1. The necessary material conditions for epochal historical change: productive forces develop within a given set of production relations until conditions of instability and conflict appear.

2. The direction of this change: the continued growth of the produc-tive forces.

3. The means by which this change is to take place: class struggle leading to new production relations.

But they abandon the further claim of a "strong" historical materialism like Cohen's, denying that:

4. A class interest in epochal change implies that the class has the capacity to bring about that change.[21]

This Marxism is "weak," in other words, because it abandons all claims to necessity, and sees "the possibility of multiple routes to the future."[22] It is "restricted" because it accepts Cohen's narrowing of the traditional Marxist claim that the socioeconomic base determines the shape and character of the legal, cultural, and political superstructure, namely that not *all* none-conomic phenomena are determined by the base but *only those that serve to stabilize the base.*[23]

> Weak historical materialism is . . . not a trivial position. It provides an account of what is and is not on the historical agenda for different levels of development of productive forces. It depicts an historical map—an account of the patterns of correspondence or "contradiction" between forces and relations of production that open up and close off possibilities—and accounts as well for the direction of movement along the map. In addition, weak historical materialism makes claims about the means by which historical change (and stasis) is achieved. It is class struggle that, in the end, determines whether and how we move along the map the theory provides.
>
> Weak historical materialism is thus the orthodox theory without the unlikely and unwarranted claim that what is necessary for epochal historical change is ultimately also sufficient. Yet, in spite of this difference, both orthodox and weak historical materialism hold that there is a lawlike tendency for relations of production to correspond to forces of production in ways that facilitate the continuous development of productive forces. Orthodox and weak historical materialism are therefore historical theories in the same way.[24]

The considered tone reflects how tentative are Wright, Levine, and Sober's conclusions: they say only that "if a defensible Marxist theory of history can be maintained, it will have to be along such lines. We have already suggested that the jury is still out and is likely to remain out for some time."[25]

The Missing Frame

Is this the beginning of a reconstructed, skeptical, and humble Marxism— one that fits the contemporary world? In fact not, because in the name of "reconstructing" Marxism, Wright, Levine, and Sober create something altogether different. The problem is that they seem only half aware of this, or in any case make it only partially clear to the reader. First, after having reassembled the most enduring themes of the Marxian project's theoretical component into guidelines for a new program of research, they then acknowledge that their entire undertaking has been premised on the collapse of that project. But they do not *say* this until the last chapter's last pages. Only there do they make clear the starting points that have partially framed their analytical Marxism: Marxism is over as a "unity of class analysis and scientific socialism, forged around a general emancipatory project."[26] We are left, at best, with Marxism as "a more restricted account of particular social processes and tendencies."[27] In this very limited and specialized sense Marxism may be reconstructed, but "it is clear that a retreat to earlier Marxist aspirations is no longer possible. The world has changed and those earlier forms are irretrievable."[28]

Does this mean that Wright, Levine, and Sober conclude by explicitly acknowledging the post-Marxist character of their enterprise, seeking, for example, to find a way their still vital insights can be absorbed into new theoretical and political projects? Not quite. I say that their awareness of Marxism's end only partially frames their work—first, because this awareness is only articulated at the end of their book, and second, because even then it remains ambivalent about which aspects of Marxism are being "reconstructed." To the very end they describe this effort to rescue from Marxism's general disintegration those *ideas* that may still be valid as "reconstructing Marxism." If, from the beginning, they have been "agnostic, although optimistic" about clarifying "an agenda for future work on the problem,"[29] at the end they remain optimistic "that a reconstructed Marxism, even if less integrated, is feasible and . . . what is now experienced as a crisis will come to be seen as unavoidable growing pains."[30] But what does "less integrated" mean, if not that they have accepted, and even furthered, the dismantling of the original, integrated project I described in Chapter 2?

Certainly it is difficult to disagree with Levine: "Marxian positions *do* need to be rethought."[31] At the nadir of Marxism's existence, it is better late than never that a school of Marxists has finally gotten around to this project. An implied question behind all analytical Marxism is, "Where did we go wrong?" A related one is, "What illusions and distortions were bound up with the Communist movement?"[32] Whatever else may be needed to reconstitute the Left, surely it is necessary to clarify in a serious and tough-minded manner what can and cannot convincingly be claimed for a theory that, as a revolutionary outlook, entails a commitment to struggle and conflict.

Nevertheless, we should not deceive ourselves: in the process, the world-historical project known as Marxism is most certainly *not* being reconstructed. Rather, certain of its key theoretical underpinnings are being rethought so as to pose a new set of intellectual parameters and tasks. In the process, Wright, Levine, and Sober have changed the goal of their Marxism from transforming reality to understanding it. Their "less integrated Marxism" has been articulated not only as completely cut off from a political movement, but also from the awareness that it in some profound sense *needs* a political movement to make it true. Marxism has subtly and perhaps even unconsciously been transmuted from a theoretical–practical project of social transformation into something far more abstract and ahistorical: a "theoretical project," an "explanatory program," and a "program of research." Characteristically, the political question of Marxism's fate as a movement appears on *Reconstructing Marxism*'s first and last pages, but scarcely anywhere in between. Indeed, like much contemporary debate about Marxism the book begins by focusing on the historical movement and its "crisis," and soon winds up defending and exploring the Marxian mode of understanding and analysis, never pausing to clarify the decisive shift it has quietly carried out.

Is It Marxism?

A point is reached in the career of any movement or system of thought when the thoughts and actions of its current protagonists (their own statements aside) diverge so from the original starting points that they cease any longer to be definable in the original terms. This would be the moment when sufficient and essential features have so changed that we find ourselves stretching to use the same name for an essentially changed phenomenon. It is possible to pose this as a philosophical question, about the structure and essential features of Marxian theory. But our question—What *is* Marxism?—is not a philosophical question, about a system of ideas, but an historical one, which includes but is not limited to the Marxian structure of ideas. At what point, we may ask, has the project claiming to be Marxism changed to the point that, whatever its proponents call it, it can no longer be characterized as Marxism? Recall that the project *as such* contained a series of anticipations about history that saw the socialist revolution coming, and that these were essential to Marx's unity of theory and practice. Recall also the powerful eschatological thrust of Marxism, the prophetic sense derided by Kolakowski, which I argue was essential to the project of social transformation. And recall that Marxism's purchase on history was intimately bound up with proletarian struggles.

Although certain ideas may be regarded as Marxist and others not, Marxism itself is most definitely not a structure of ideas. One book treating Marxism this way, John McMurtry's *The Structure of Marx's World View*, itself ignores the characteristic unity of theory and practice in Marxism, and sees it primarily as an integrated set of concepts rather than as a project of social transformation.[33] This significant contribution to analytical Marxism remains rigorously true to Marxian *thought*, but has abstracted so drastically from the project that its own accuracy in terming itself Marxist might legitimately be questioned. Such a questioning depends on the judgment that, as an historical project, Marxism not only requires *action* to make it true in the full way it intended to be, but that its prophetic character generated a hope, a conviction, and a self-confidence reaching far beyond any scientifically verifiable structure of ideas. Speaking about McMurtry's Marxism, a philosophical theory lacking an orientation to action and an understanding of Marxism's emotional force, we are entitled to ask, "Is it Marxism?"

There is no question that we can define a certain set of ideas as capturing the essence of Marxist thought, and another as deviating from it.[34] McMurtry's thought—like Cohen's and that of Wright, Levine, and Sober—must certainly be classified as Marxist thought. Clearly, it makes good sense to modernize Marxist thought by removing the problematic dimensions I critiqued in Chapter 4—its eschatological character, its objectivism and scientism, and its tendency toward authoritarianism—which Wright, Levine, and

Sober have done. But as I argued there, these weaknesses happened to be Marxism's strengths. What will be substituted, for example, for its vision of universal liberation stemming from proletarian emancipation, to give a reconstructed Marxism the same galvanizing power, the same wide appeal? Would a Marxism modernized by minimizing or removing such central elements still be Marxism as a *project?* Similarly, it makes good sense to remove all of Marxism's unverifiable claims, so that we are left defending a more modest, more scientifically solid, less grandiose theory. But if we are left with *only* a theory, that theory should no longer be termed Marxism.

It may be necessary, and even desirable, to face honestly the separation of theory from practice, and to study social change without the pressures and demands of relating to a movement or project of social transformation. And it may be wise to abandon the absolute centrality of labor and the working class in a vision of social change for a more nuanced and subtle understanding that considers these dimensions extremely important, even central, but not definitive. It may be realistic and honest to face squarely the fragmentation of the Marxian project, admit that its components may never be recombined, and accept the diminished task of developing one of its fragments as a mode of explanation. But whatever it is that we have when we are finished, it is no longer what was once meant by Marxism.

What we wind up with is useful as a philosophy and mode of analysis. But by comparison with what Marxism was, it has become so eviscerated, so fragmented, so divorced from practice, that it no longer resembles the once-great world-historical project of transformation. That whole has been shattered by history, and we are left to debate over which of the pieces deserves the original name. But what we are left with are all in fact, none of which retain the sweep, the vision, the political purpose and strength of the whole. They may claim the name, as does analytical Marxism, but they do so as so many Marxisms without Marxism. They have become so transformed, so limited, so narrowly theoretical that even when their words and commitments ring true they only invoke Marxism's aura, but no more. However evocative, the ideas cannot conjure the fading reality.

The Standpoint of Analytical Marxism

By recasting Marxism as rigorous explanation and argument analytical Marxism has created a home for itself in the world of explanation and argument. This is a significant achievement. And, after Marxism, it has given us plausible arguments for believing that capitalism will remain unstable, as well as tools for understanding and criticizing our situation. But where do these arguments take place? And to whom are they addressed? In short, what is the *standpoint* of analytical Marxism? Certainly all analytical Marxists may be personally committed to a classless society, and write from deep personal convictions.[35] More important than motivation, however, is where in the world of thought and discourse a project locates itself. Wright, Levine, and Sober are explicit: as stated above, they reject Marxism's methodological distinctiveness and begin with a "wholesale embrace of conventional scientific and philosophical norms."[36]

Does radical thought differ in any significant way from "mainstream philosophy and social science?" Marxism has always assailed the false neutrality and bird's-eye view of prevailing concepts and methods, insisting both that scientists are socially situated and that their projects, objects of study, and tools are socially constructed. As I mentioned in Chapter 2, this has always made Marxism's scientific dimension distinctively different from mainstrean conceptions. To capture this difference, Dorothy Smith compares teaching "some of the major contemporary Marxist theorists of class" (including Wright) with teaching *The Communist Manifesto*:

> The text places the reader historically; class struggle is going on and you are in the middle of it. The sides are drawn up in the text itself as subjects are directly summoned and addressed. We can enter ourselves directly into its drama. Class is not objectified in the text as it is in the elaborate theoretical constructs of the contemporary Marxist theorists, needing rather careful fitting to the actualities of contemporary social relations. Rather, class emerges as a great historical process of struggle *in which the pamphlet and its analysis are situated*. The time of the text is just exactly that hinge where the past turns on a present that will be the making of the future. This is where you, as reading subject, are placed by the pamphlet. The polemic of the text is a call on you to act at precisely this juncture. But the temporal siting of reading and writing subjects in an historical trajectory of which the text itself is part isn't just a polemical effect. Though the reader isn't always being called on to act as he (I use the pronoun advisedly) is here, Marx and Engels' analyses have generally this historically situated character; the time of the text isn't separate from the historical time of which it speaks.[37]

On the contrary, Smith argues, contemporary Marxist texts neither situate the reader in time nor imply action; they avoid the language of experience and keep the reader outside the phenomena they describe. Smith's analysis perfectly decontextualized and objectified standpoint of analytical Marxists. In absorbing the approaches of contemporary science, they reproduce key aspects of the logic of contemporary social domination: its false objectivity and neutrality, its disconnection from its agents and objects. What follows, in keeping with dominant social relations, is the "objectification of processes known, lived and experienced only from within."[38] They reproduce a discursive process in which "a textually-contained world is created, standing as object, external to the writing and reading subject; the lived world is to be interpreted through the medium of the textually-contained."[39]

But this is not simply an error of perception: it stems from analytical Marxism's nature and goals. After all, it no longer is located within, or looks toward, any process and project of transforming the world. Because of their objectivist standpoint, analytical Marxists do not see their task as illuminating Marxism's protagonists and providing them with tools, or of asking themselves what it means for a Marxism to be without protagonists.

Sartre describes analytical reason as the intellectual principle and ideological reflection of a society that separates individuals and views them from the outside, in order to dominate them.[40] In this same sense, paradoxical as it may sound, analytical Marxists situate their standpoint *outside of* Marxism. Their thought processes no longer seek to erect a beacon from within the project; instead they turn to contemporary scientific reason, detached and neutral, free of any particular project, to evaluate Marxism from the outside just as it evaluates capitalism from the outside.[41]

In this sense also analytical Marxism is no longer Marxist. Sober, modest, stringent, its goal, admirable enough, is no less but no more than theoretical clarification. The historical condition for its flowering was precisely the fatal decay of Marxism as a project, the fading that enabled Marxism to be tested and embraced as explanation and argument. In this sense, analytical Marxism is a post-Marxism that has not yet acknowledged itself.

What Remains of Marxism?

I agree with Nancy Fraser: "Marxism as the metanarrative or master discourse of oppositional politics in capitalist societies is finished. So is Marxism as a totalizing theory of the system dynamics, crisis tendencies, and conflict potentialities in capitalist societies."[42] Forsaking the need to "be" Marxist in some sense that history has rendered impossible, we can now ask what remains to take with us as we bid this grand project farewell and deliberately enter the new "postMarxian field of critical theorizing"[43] and political practice. Once beyond the confusing and diverting need to maintain its original aura, we discover, as analytical Marxism and socialist feminism have both clarified, that much about it remains vital and usable and instructive. If Marxism has become relativized by becoming one project among others, its theories can still illuminate the salience of class in grasping social life, understand that social change emerges from concrete historical tendencies, offer a serviceable distinction between economic base and political/legal/cultural superstructure, supply the awareness that a central feature of social dynamics is the relationship of the productive forces to the production relations, and illuminate central features of the capitalist process of production that account for both its vitality and its anarchy.

In addition to contributing these lines of social analysis, Marxism can assert major themes of social commitment, including the conviction that the liberation of the working class must be its own work, a classless society, and a vision that communism alone can liberate the accumulated human productive capacity to meet universal needs. Reaching toward action, Marxism highlights the importance of class struggle in achieving a new society, the revolutionary and systemic nature of such a transformation, and the mutual interaction between the theory of such change and the practice of carrying it out.[44]

These remarks about what remains alive in Marxism—and may be pertinent in future radical projects—are not meant to be exhaustive. After all, the inevitable task of sifting through the Marxian heritage involves, among other things, continuing the efforts by those thinkers who have described themselves as analytical Marxists. And it involves continuing to rethink historical materialism as a theory of social explanation. My point is to avoid the sterile either/or approach that permeates thinking about such issues, and that suggests that if Marxism is over, we need no longer pay any attention to its theories, its social basis, the socioeconomic structures to which it refers, or the issues it raises.

A surprising and striking example of such thinking can be found in Jürgen Habermas' reflections on Marxism, especially in his essay "The Crisis of the Welfare State and the Exhaustion of Utopian Energies." His argument is that "what was previously a supposition or a condition of the utopian idea of a laboring society has now become a theme for discussion. And with this theme the accents have moved from the concept of labor to the concept of communication."[45] Capitalism has not solved the problems of exploitation and alienation diagnosed by Marx; are these now to be subsumed under a Theory of Communicative Action? In Habermas we see a "transcending" of Marxism that effectively dumps its concerns to one side, implicitly telling us that they have been ameliorated by the welfare state or that what remains of them can be treated under the aegis of communicative rationality. Because Marxism is no longer what it once claimed to be, namely the path of universal liberation, its understandings and visions no longer seem to have a role to play.[46]

Habermas is not alone. The pendular character of such moves "beyond" entails that issues once regarded as the essential issues, upon losing their hegemony, become nonissues. Rather than considering Foucault's work on the micropolitics of control to be *adding* a new dimension of understanding to our grasp of the modalities of oppression, many regard the Foucauldian perspective as itself an autonomous totalizing explanation. I would stress instead that the various rivals of Marxism, as much postmodern theory has been depicted, in ending Marxism's ascendancy and signaling its demise as a totalizing theory and hegemonic project, are in fact only complementing and deepening its insights into what it means to be alive today.

Any self-understandings and emancipatory projects that are sketched by such thinkers as Habermas will still have to reckon with the importance and often centrality, if no longer the primacy, of the Marxian dimension.[47] Class will return as crucial focus of analysis because even if Marxism has been relativized, class has not been abolished. The proletariat can no longer be counted on to liberate everyone or even themselves; but the fact is that they remain oppressed and exploited. The path to their emancipation may be less clear than ever, but they will still have to act on their own behalf, and with a clear, indeed revolutionary, consciousness of the system in which they are trapped. Marxism may be over as a hegemonic movement, but capitalism is not over. If historical materialism no longer gives us *the* shape of the contemporary world, it gives us some of its shapes. If it no longer is fully adequate to the demands of a contemporary philosophical or political consciousness, if Marxism is no longer our philosopher's stone, we must still remember, as we leave, to not go away empty-handed.

Why Hold On?

Before launching his extended critique of Ernesto Laclau and Chantal Mouffe's postmodern and discourse-based post-Marxism, Norman Geras frames his discussion with several paragraphs on the possible motivations of those who abandon Marxism, citing "the pressures on them of age and professional status; the pressures of the political time and environment...; and then the lure of intellectual fashion, a consideration not to be underrated by any means."[48] Although Geras later defends these remarks as having been posed "in *quite general terms*" and "misunderstood" by those who thought he meant it to apply to Laclau and Mouffe,[49] its impact has the same effect. If it is the sole flaw in one hundred pages of argument, it is a significant one. Nothing is to be gained by now applying the sword's other edge to those who remain Marxists (including Geras himself). There were, as I maintain in Chapter 1, good reasons for holding onto Marxism for so long: its synthetic power and analytical flexibility, our inability to develop any equivalent outlook or find any replacement for the proletariat, and the hope that the Soviet Union might be saved for socialism. And so in drawing this farewell to its conclusion, it is worth looking at what Marxists themselves continue to give as their reasons.

Why should we hold on? Ralph Miliband has delineated the general issue in his attack on the "new revisionism":

> The "primacy" of organized labor in struggle arises from the fact that no other group, movement or force in capitalist society is remotely capable of mounting as effective and formidable a challenge to the existing structures of power and privilege as it is in the power of organized labor

to mount. In no way is this to say that movements of women, blacks, peace activists, ecologists, gays, and others are not important, or cannot have effect, or that they ought to surrender their separate identity. Not at all. It is only to say that the principal (not the only) "grave-digger" of capitalism remains the organized working class. Here is the necessary, indispensable "agency of historical change." And if, as one is constantly told is the case, the organized working class will refuse to do the job, then the job will not be done; and capitalist society will continue, generation after generation, as a conflict-ridden, growingly authoritarian and bru- talized social system, poisoned by its inability to make humane and rational use of the immense resources capitalism has itself brought into being—unless of course the world is pushed into nuclear war.[50]

In "What Is a Marxist Today?" Andrew Levine has put the issue more personally. Although the jury remains out on a number of Marxist claims and there seems little likelihood that an explicitly Marxist mass movement will again threaten capitalism, Levine argues that "a Marxian identification . . . is a way of expressing a continuing endorsement of the radicalism of the Marxian tradition . . . [and] provides a ballast for investigators struggling to find ways of continuing the Marxian agenda by more satisfactory means than the Marxian tradition has so far provided."[51] It serves the need for a distinct radical political identity located in a coherent approach to social reality. Thus, far more than "a simple expression of dissidence, replete with historical resonances, but ultimately void of content,"[52] Marxism remains a focus of orientation and a way of objectifying a very specific approach to social life, providing an intellectual warrant for that approach as well as membership in a distinctive tradition sharing those commitments.

But what if the organized working class does indeed "refuse to do the job?" Or what if it turns out that there is more than one job to be done, spilling over into areas where class is no longer central? And what does Levine's Marxian identification continue to mean if we face fully and critically, with all of his own analytical rigor, the fact that it is "unlikely that there will ever again come a time when masses of people marching, as it were, under the banner of Marxism, will offer a realistic promise of revolu- tionary change and reconstruction."[53] Levine does not inquire into the objective basis for continuing Marxian identification in a world that he admits has gone beyond Marxism. What does it mean to "suggest that the Marxian agenda can indeed survive the demise of Marxism in any of its historically pertinent senses?"[54] Where will it survive, how and in what forms? Will it become an implicit, unstated layer of *another* movement?

Many Marxists respond to the gulf between their once-powerful and coherent theory and its failure to be incarnated in a historical movement by changing the subject. By taking the part for the whole, the idea of the project for the project itself, it is indeed possible to buy time. In this way, the whole that was once Marxism gets conveyed through its ideogram,

Marxian theory. Those who have known that whole when it was still real, promising, and powerful, live now in the half light of its diminishing relevance. They continue to draw resonance, emotional power, ethical conviction, and historical confidence from the ever dimming force of the original. It no longer has a life of its own, but the Marxian project's aura remains a memory of a world-historical movement, that once seemed to threaten capitalist civilization itself. It still lends its waning glow to the world of ideas and explanations.

This recasting of project into idea has profoundly negative consequences. Over as the universal project of human emancipation, Marxism's chance of reviving itself as a far-humbler current of analysis and action depends on its adherents frankly facing their situation, purposes, and prospects. Until that happens, post-Marxist radicals will remain unclear about their theories' standpoints and relationships to the now eclipsed project of Marxism. Continuing to fight old battles, any new radical project will remain deprived of a relativized and lower-case marxism's perspectives until post-Marxists manage to accept the eclipse of Marxism and negotiate their way, on terms of equality, into a place in future radical coalitions.

Ellen Meiksins Wood fosters the obstructions to doing so by insisting on Marxism's continued universality. Specifically, what can it mean today, in a time of environmentalism, feminism, and other new social movements, to proclaim that "the pursuit of working-class interests" is "still the only form in which 'universal human goods' can constitute a practicable political program"?[55] She is right, of course, that the place of universal goods in the socialist project is "a critical and painfully difficult question."[56] But she makes it more difficult by continuing to give priority to socialism and class. This will never allow the equal importance of other goals, or draw in those whose primary commitment is to those other goals.

In a recent argument for economic democracy, *Against Capitalism*, David Schweickart shows the pitfalls of a different approach—trying to remain "a Marxist" while in fact being a post-Marxist or perhaps even a non-Marxist in a post-Marxist world. In his concluding "Marxian Reflections," Schweickart says:

> In a fundamental sense these reflections are independent of the rest of this book. As I have tried to make clear, the basic argument against capitalism appeals to widely held values. These are values that most Marxists share, but they are by no means peculiarly "Marxist" values. These are values common to most persons of a liberal or Left persuasion, and many of them are shared by conservatives as well. In *no* way does the basic argument of this book depend on anything uniquely Marxist.[57]

In a period when it is the fashion to denigrate and sneer at Marxism, Schweickart courageously insists on proclaiming his debt to it, as well as the book's Marxian inspiration. And then he shows to what extent the arguments of this most un-Marxist book fall within the realm of Marxism, especially by spelling out how his vision of economic democracy is no different than what Marx meant by communism. This is certainly a remarkable, but symptomatic treatment of Marxism: Schweickart develops an extended argument that has little to do with Marxism except in its being based on Marxism's broad understanding of the dynamics of capitalism. But then, in the personal part of the book, he makes his Marxist convictions known, and even argues for Marxism's continuing power.

More paradoxically yet, Schweickart proclaims his loyalty to the tradition even while developing a generally post-Marxist position in these concluding pages. He argues against the primacy of labor and the working class and on behalf of the autonomy of women's concerns in relation to class concerns, and of a political organization (the Brazilian Workers' Party) that "brings together in interesting ways elements of Marxism (e.g., a concern for class and for organized, mass-based struggle) and elements to which feminist theory has contributed substantially (e.g., gender, pluralism, participation, non-violence)."[58] Schweickart relativizes his Marxism, sets it alongside feminism as one strand of a many-sided process.

What then is the point of bringing this post-Marxist approach under the umbrella of Marxism? One might say that Schweickart is connecting himself with the authority of a tradition he is going creatively beyond; but in fact, he is breaking with that tradition's claim to universality and primacy. While Schweickart may remain within Marxism in some personal or biographical way, in practice he uses it as one tool and source among many.

A Future for Relativized Marxism?

My point is that it is important to accept consciously and to admit explicitly that Marxism has been relativized, for several reasons. First, it will be helpful to dispel the comprehensive and universal aura that still clings to Marxist analyses, and to make clear that we now stand on terrain that is drastically open and only very partially charted. Recognizing that it is relativized will free Marxism's proponents from a false and counterproductive sense of totality and self-confidence. Second, Marxism has become increasingly easy to dismiss for its dogged pretensions to universality and primacy. If it can be suitably reduced, revised, and put forward as being concerned with only one major constituent of social life, to be considered alongside others, what remains alive within Marxism may point anew to the undeniable salience of social class, labor, and class struggle. Third, what remains useful in the badly frayed Marxian tradition can survive, and continue to nourish new generations of thinkers and actors, only by accepting a humbler place in the world, alongside other equally prominent traditions of resistance and struggle. In short, I am suggesting that the either/or approach of those who hold on to Marxism makes it far easier for Marxist insights to be dismissed *tout court*, and far more difficult to bring its riches into the post-Marxist field.

Facing the fact squarely that, like it or not, we are in a post-Marxist world, will make it possible to clear up confusions such as those outlined above. It will also make it possible to mitigate other harmful consequences of holding tightly to Marxism. Such tenacity, and the either/or distinctions it encourages, avoids tasks of intellectual and political reconstruction that reach far beyond the steps taken by Wright, Levine, and Sober. Above all, the fact is that a Marxism that accepts being just one project among others is no longer Marxism as we know it. It is a humble, nonuniversalizing, post-Marxist and lower-case marxism. It deals with only a single layer of social reality, it is partisan on behalf of a single social group. It is by nature coalition-oriented. Since it no longer promises universal human emancipation, its proponents can no longer claim a general hegemony for its theories, the labor process, or workers.

To find and retain what remains true and useful in their tradition, Marxists need to relativize their commitments and analysis; those who have done so implicitly need to admit this explicitly. This means many things, but perhaps above all that, after Marxism, this humble marxism no longer provides *the* overarching theoretical–practical framework. It will no longer be a world *within which* we move and think. To say that it has become relativized is to say that it is now, rather, *an* outlook, *a* set of tools, at best *one* project—one among others. Those still committed to furthering its remaining particular goals and insights and subjects have every right to do so, but they will have to negotiate for their inclusion in other and wider world views and projects. They will have to join future radical coalitions on equal rather than privileged terms. They will have to argue for the relevance of the Marxian dimension or area of analysis, rather than assuming that labor is the center of social life and its liberation everyone's central task. As Fraser says, "The only possible future for Marxism is as one contributing strand among others in this new postMarxian field. This requires a new modesty for Marxism, a willingness to open itself up to other bodies of critical thought, to reconstruct itself in the light of their insights, and generally to enter into fruitful exchanges with them."[59]

This is already occurring among some Marxist thinkers, for example in the work of Stephen Resnick and Richard Wolff. Their *Knowledge and Class* is written in the hope of "integrating the insights of specifically Marxian class analysis into the social analyses and programs of complex, multifaceted movements for social change."[60] To that end they articulate a philosophically relativistic Marxism that abandons any claim to grasp the essential social processes, rejects all reductionism and determinism, and regards the concept of class as no more than the "entry point" of Marxian social theory.

> Marx's . . . focus on class in his writings did not stem from some spurious claim that the particular process he discovered was "more important" in shaping the social totality than the myriad other processes comprising that totality. This sort of absolutist claim represented a kind of reasoning he often ridiculed. Rather, Marx's focus on class and hence on economics represented the much more modest self-awareness of someone who knew he had something particular to *add* to certain forces for social change.[61]

Absent from the analysis of Resnick and Wolff is the sense that they have grasped, and are presenting, the truth of human society and history. Using Althusser's concept of overdetermination[62] as their key epistemological tool, they stress instead that their analyses have something to add to future understandings and struggles.

Certainly Resnick and Wolff's theoretical humility is precisely the attitude Fraser calls for. However, their presentation of this shift is strikingly disingenuous. Rather than acknowledging how far their approach *departs* from Marxism, and the reasons behind this departure, Resnick and Wolff remain silent about their historic break. They act as if, while marshalling and deploying ahistorical arguments about the proper Marxist epistemology, they are simply presenting a new, more correct reading of Marx—rather than a drastically new and lower-case kind of Marxism. In fact, acknowledge it or not, their work is historically situated in the terminal crisis of Marxism as a world-historical project, and they are trying to rescue from this what they can. It is Marxism's decline that has made their reading of Marx possible and necessary. While not acknowledging this permits them to retain the aura of past Marxist movements and a continuity with other Marxist writers, it equally encourages confusion about what it is they are creating, as well as about its historical meaning. They clothe an entirely new project in the mantle of old, obsolete, Marxism. In fact, Resnick and Wolff's is a post-Marxist marxism that still needs to be freed from the old project's baggage in order to be clear about what it really is.

Marxists after Marxism

As I repeatedly stress throughout this book, much of what is appealing in Marxism lies in its view of history, its peculiar moral vision, its promise of redemption, its claim that all of these are justified scientifically—and the holistic unity among them. These are essential components of the Marxian project. If we subject them to careful analysis or remove them entirely, whatever is left—and there is a lot left, including Marxism's analysis of capitalism—lacks its customary unifying force, emotional power, scope and sweep. It is hard to imagine workers being willing to lay down their lives for "weak, restricted historical materialism." It may guide radical scholarship but will not inspire political activism. It may strengthen critical discourse and sharpen academic debate, but it will no longer be what Marxism always insisted on being, a theory *and* a practice. It may have a Marxian flavor, but it is no longer the Marxian project. It may become an important component of other political projects but they can no longer be uniquely Marxist.

When speaking of Marxism being relativized I have suggested that, suitably revised, some of its key concepts and commitments may be employed in a new and appropriate way, alongside other theories and modes of explanation. But everything about it changes when it is used to describe one social process among many needing to be altered, and to appeal to one social force among many. The reality being described becomes more complex, less easily understood. Our certainty about goals diminishes. No authority stamps our claims. Any sense of totality becomes riven with holes. We no longer see a clear path ahead indicating where we should go or where history is going. Theory seems less coherent and powerful than the stumblings and struggles of concrete practice. Each of these shifts is necessary and appropriate in this contemporary world, whether we call it modern or postmodern, because Marxism has become one theory among others, one project among others. If Marxists were to acknowledge this explicitly as many of them have recognized it implicitly, and if they were to draw the necessary conclusions, they would begin the process of transforming themselves and their tradition for inclusion in a post-Marxist world.

It is a world in which, above all, we are on our own. It is a world with no single guiding analysis, no Movement, no authority, no confident sense of history's direction. Lacking a single principle of political unity and an a priori exploratory hierarchy, it is a world with an ever-present need to make up our minds, again and again. In short, we face the fact that any future movement of social transformation, if there is to be one, will have to bring together a variety of smaller movements, individuals, causes, ideas, and points of view. Its rallying points and goals will not be given in advance, but will have to be created by its participants, argued by them, agreed upon. Will such a movement finally be immune to being distorted by myth, religion, and authority? Will it be able finally to shed the albatross of Marxism while absorbing its rich experience and insights and attention to political economy? If so, it would pick up the baton from the New Left and carry it into a fully contemporary project of social transformation.

Part Two

On Our Own

s it only sour grapes to take the next step and suggest that we are perhaps moving beyond the need for the kind of movement Marxism represented? Or is this trying to make a virtue of necessity? In the remainder of this book I explore the possibility that humans can think and act quite effectively, even toward radical change, after Marxism. I argue that this is not only necessary, because we are on our own, but also that for all its difficulties, it is an emancipation to be on our own. So long the lodestar for so many, Marxism has simultaneously been our albatross; now that it is falling from the collective necks of those who want to think and act toward radical change, it is time to move without its security, its elegant defining of terms—and, equally, without its weight, its haunting and inhibiting effect. Even if Marxism has seemed to some of us to be so much like the air we breathe, like our very skins, it is finally time to see also that it has been a burden, limiting and obstructing our movements. And it is time to shed the burden.

But what does it mean to develop radical thought and politics today, after Marxism? What does a radical project look like as we move toward the year 2000? What does revolutionary change mean anymore, philosophically and politically? If a new approach kicks over traces of not only the old project but also its expectations and its guideposts, what is it to be on our own, today, and to think and act toward radical change? In beginning to answer these questions, the second part of this book must necessarily be more tentative and uncertain than the first part. My style of presentation and argument cannot hope to be comprehensive and unified in the ways so characteristic of Marxism. Rather, it is more provisional, less certain, more open to question by both unsympathetic and sympathetic readers. The solid, heavily noted historical and philosophical argument now must take a more speculative turn, moving onto open terrain.

My task is not to invent the post-Marxist radical project, but to help find its voice. I will not attempt to develop a systematic vision, or even to speak about concrete political goals and strategies. Rather, I will answer a more immediate question: how should post-Marxist radicals see themselves? If it makes little sense today to develop "the" theory of a post-Marxist radicalism, clarifying some of its parameters may enable us to recognize ourselves. And so I will not attempt to project programmatic guidelines; instead I will argue for thinking about the contemporary radical project in specific ways.

First, it will be necessary to spell out how any new radical project will differ from those to which we have been accustomed. Chapter 7 sketches, beyond the discussions of Part I, a number of key changes and losses that have recast the objective and subjective situation of those who would become the next Left. In the face of these changes, especially the losses, Chapter 8 will ask why it is still appropriate to aspire to radical social transformation. Many readers might approve of the critical path I have followed through and out of Marxism, but resist my perseverance in trying to unite many separate activities and movements into a single one. New kinds of projects may be inevitable, and beneficial, but can we even think about a single, unified movement any more? What shared concerns will bring it together? Moreover, if a radical movement is still appropriate and possible, under what name shall we think about it, and what will be its marks of identity?

In the subsequent chapters I will explore specific defining features of the post-Marxian radical project. In Chapter 9 I describe what I regard as its single most important positive defining feature. If Marxism provided a coherent framework within which commitment, action, and strategy unfolded, after Marxism, we are no longer guided by a single vision of human life and history, a single theory. We are able to become autonomous and self-determining—that is, fully modern. What does this entail about our way of getting our bearings in the world, how is it clarified by the debates over modernity and postmodernism, and what implications does it have for how post-Marxist radicals might approach theory?

In Chapter 10 I explore the centrality of morality for a new radical project. After Marxism, it is no longer possible to act as if moral imperatives were irrelevant or as if objective social processes were fulfilling them. Instead we should be talking about right and wrong. Doing so today is fraught with difficulty, and I will attempt to develop what might be adequate moral bases for a contemporary radical politics.

Finally, in the closing chapter I will sketch sources of hope for a radical project. It must treat utopian dreams and visions as longings for a world well beyond our reach, not as scientific predictions. But as such, these dreams and visions are absolutely essential parts of any radicalism—are functional, are real. I argue that in order to keep hope alive, a new radical project must be realistic about its limits and possibities, including drastically revising our sense of how long meaningful change may take. At the same time, we must see how each of our acts and successes embodies our goals, and can thus nourish continuing struggles.

So far, these kinds of explorations have been hobbled because post-Marxist radicalism has taken shape in Marxism's shadow, compelled to define itself in its terms or in reactive opposition to it. In the first case, many of us have easily remained chained to the same script, still seeking or awaiting its current cast—knowing what the answers are supposed to sound like, waiting for those who would pronounce them. In the second case, refusing to learn from Marxism and to go beyond it, many of us have pretended that we know much less than we actually do. Playing dumb, we have flirted with regressing to, and have even celebrated, a kind of radical innocence in the face of the disappointments of the past hundred years. But as Marx once said in a heated debate, "Ignorance has never yet helped anybody."[1] In this spirit, then, I first want to clarify our situation and strengthen our resolve by spelling out in detail some ways in which we are beyond Marxism, and then talking about a new kind of radical project.

Chapter Seven

THE NEW SITUATION

New radical projects have been building for a generation. But they have not yet come into their own. Inevitably, they have been seen in the light cast by Marxism, even when their founders insist on their distance from it. Its intellectual force, its example as a coherent radical project, its place at the center of every field of serious revolutionary thought and action, its status as a kind of common sense, and its sheer historical presence, have often blinded and paralyzed other movements, stealing from their proponents the ability to talk about these movements in any but borrowed and reactive terms.[1]

As a result, new radical projects have been unable to give an adequate account of themselves, either in the now traditional ways imposed by Marxism, or on their own terms. On the one hand, these projects have always lacked precisely what Marxists have said they lacked: a coherent theory of the social system to be transformed, a clear-cut revolutionary agent, a way of showing this social force's oppression and demands as universal oppression and demand, a more or less demonstrable sense that history is moving to place on the agenda a crisis of the old order and its wholesale transformation. On the other hand, viewing these projects in a mirror where such lacks were flagrant, their proponents have been incoherent about their standpoints and purposes even on their own terms, unable to develop a satisfactory new radical language or conceptual framework.[2]

"What we need is a new Marx": this is a frequent remark, or at least a common thought, on the Left. Radical intellectuals have been haunted as if by the memory of some happy childhood, halcyon days when analysis and feeling, history and science, mass movements and societal dynamics, dream of liberation and existential task all flowed together into a single revolutionary project. I discussed in Part I how explanation, ethics, emotion, and vision formed one holistic undertaking and pointed toward the action that would fulfill it. As this has been fading, many of us have believed it only natural to replace it with a similar project, of equal unity and coherence. An understanding of the social totality, the need for a single universal agent, a sense of where history is headed, a sighting of the key underlying structures —these will be fulfilled by the "new Marx." This thinker, or political-intellectual stance, will synthesize all the swirling currents of study and action in a description of the decisive new social force(s), whose lived experience will be at one and the same time a denunciation of the system, the forecast of its transformation, and a foreshadowing of the good society destined to replace it. The new Marx will do all this while simultaneously making decisive contributions to new human sciences at the cutting edge of contemporary research, as Marx did in political economy and sociology, and will articulate a new hegemonic philosophy, social theory, and interpretation of history. But after Marxism, this is a vain dream. However we might long for such a second coming, the longing is finally trumped by a plain fact: not only is Marxism no longer on, but its *kind of project* is now just a powerful but fading memory.

No New Marx

Marxism's great strength became its great weakness: assuming and seeking to demonstrate that history itself was bringing about the revolutionary transformation from capitalism to socialism, a transformation that would be a veritable end of history as we know it and the beginning of a new stage of human life. As I argued in Part I, the formulators of such an approach were unable to examine closely its goals, and thus effectively suppressed any effort to clarify or justify the structures and meanings of socialism. Biased toward the objective unfolding of events, this approach focused attention away from trying to understand under exactly what conditions the working class might reject capitalism *in toto* and see itself as capable of seizing power and establishing a new society. And so, after effectively arguing that human labor is the source of our social and historical world, describing the dialectics of the capitalist system, and supposing (with some reason) that the workers would organize themselves to overthrow the system, Marx was unable to anticipate the powerful role human subjects and subjectivity would come to play. He did not anticipate the continuing survival and flourishing of capitalism, the success of struggles to make it more livable, or its capacity to contain efforts to reach beyond capitalism. Marxism neglected the subjective human capacities that would come to stabilize capitalism, as well as the subjective preconditions for socialist revolution. Instead, it lent the authority of its founding father, and his science, to a faith in objective developments that turned out to be no more than a pseudocertainty.

But I am far from arguing that Marxism could have or should have dealt with these "problems"; indeed, they were part of its very historical substance, its strength, its identity. I blame Marxism for nothing. But if Marxism was what it was, and could not easily have been different, today we no longer fall under the spell of its early modern hopes for social science, its eschatological expectations for social revolution and industrial technology, its nineteenth-century reverence for science, its universalizing of the role of (mostly male) workers. A revolutionary project formed under such influences, and passions, can no longer be our project. For the sake of theory and practice, philosophy and action, root understanding and radical change, we do not need a new Marx. We have become more skeptical of authority, more tentative about science and objective truth, more aware of the decisive role of subjectivity not only in history, but in shaping whatever lays claim to the mantle of objectivity, more sensitive to the different types of discourse embodied in the Marxian project and more inclined to differentiate among them. Moreover, as movements such as feminism have made clear, the labor process has ceased being the site of the main experiences of social contradictions. For at least a generation, a host of other issues has moved people into opposition while the universe of work and workers has been transformed.

A new Marx will not appear, then, because no single social group or class is making itself into *the* revolutionary subject, emancipator of itself and the rest of humanity; because neither the end nor the beginning of history can be anticipated; and because no single, decisive, and fundamental structural transformation is needed, but rather dozens of changes at dozens of sites and on dozens of levels. Moreover, we can no longer aspire to Marxism's grasp of things. In any contemporary project of understanding there is simply so much to know, so much to integrate, so many disparities and levels to reconcile theoretically, that the Marxian synthesis haunts us as a beautiful vision from a bygone and simpler world of experience. The sheer complexity of human life has increased exponentially since Marx's time. Today it seems inconceivable that a single individual or group of like-minded individuals could absorb and unify even the primary kinds of historical, economic, sociological, psychological, and political knowledge that have become necessary to formulating a meaningful radical project.

We know, moreover, too much about history, agency, and subjectivity to confidently suppose that trends are leading toward human emancipation, whether irresistibly or not. Indeed, we have scarcely begun to map the paths that must be followed before diverse groups of humans want and are ready for their liberation. Or the ways in which these paths will flow together, overlap, and conflict. No one, new Marx or not, can point toward more than a handful of emancipatory tendencies in a single very complex and shifting field in a given corner of the world.

Such considerations certainly characterize the work of the West's most comprehensive contemporary thinker, Jürgen Habermas. Even though his thought has significant political implications, as is detailed below, and even though he himself has taken positions on major issues, Habermas' theoretical standpoint remains determinedly independent of political struggles and movements. In Chapter 6 I remarked on the fact that he omits serious consideration of the working class and political economy from his analysis of life under advanced capitalism; he also seriously underestimates feminism.[3] The Third World hardly seems to appear in his writings. And finally, as discussed below, with reference to Jean Cohen and Andrew Arato's critique, the new social movements appear there largely as defensive responses to encroachments by the political and economic systems on the lifeworld, rather than as genuinely modern emancipatory movements.

The limitations bound up with Habermas' great strengths suggest that we are, today, historically beyond the possibility of the kind of holism, integration, coherence, and confidence that Marxism embodied. As we near the year 2000, both experience and knowledge point toward hesitancy and tentativeness in any project that would aim at radical change. We must, for example, critically examine each claim made for each discrete layer of social life that might become part of any new effort at synthesis. Thus it is hard to imagine any single theory performing on, and binding together, all the levels incorporated so powerfully by Marxism.

Is a new radical project possible today, after Marxism? If it is to be possible, any post-Marxist radical movement will first have to absorb, be chastened by, and respond to, the fact that Marxism is over. The terrain in which any new radical projects take shape today, and the ways in which we might view these projects, have both been transformed decisively by the spectacular changes leading to, bound up with, and entailed by the end of Marxism. After Marxism, the world is a different place, drastically altering how those of us who have been and would be the Left voice our historical and social experience—in Raymond Williams' words, the contemporary "structures of feeling."[4] In this chapter I want to explore the losses contained in these changes. Along with Marxism's passing we have lost a sense of universality and of an alternative, a faith in progress, history, and human nature, as well as our specific points of orientation.

Losing Universality

The first change, cause and effect of Marxism's decline, but also source and consequence of other transformations, immediately affects what can be said from here on, as well as how it can be said. We can no longer say "we." That is, we no longer assume that it is possible to speak universally. In Marxism, for example, working-class emancipation was to bring general emancipation: "The International will be the human race." Instead, says Jean-François Lyotard, the very "notion of reaching unanimity has been abandoned."[5] The modern "we" is tied to the modern world's great narratives of emancipation, and each of them (Marxism, democracy, free enterprise) has "been invalidated over the last fifty years."[6] Having "represented itself as a universal discourse of emancipation," Marxism, says Michèle Barrett, "has been shown to speak with a very particular historical voice." It has been exposed as "both masculinist in content and Eurocentric in context."[7] In practice in the Soviet Union and Yugoslavia, Marxism's universalism became the rationale for the forced union of several peoples under a "new class," which happened to be dominated by a single one of those peoples. As the empires disintegrated, so did the universals, leading to the virulent resurgence of the suppressed particularities.

Today there are as many collectivities as there are potential ways of grouping people, or, rather, of people grouping themselves, and there is no reason to assume that they share the same experience or bear the same outlook. Thus we cannot take Williams' conception to refer to a single structure of feeling, reflecting *the* lived experience and *the* contradictions of a given society at a given movement in time.[8] Whose lived experience might this be? How dare we speak universally and sweepingly, as if there were one structure of feeling, a single society, one mood? Not merely a mistake, such discursive practice is always a politics, generalizing colonially from a single kind of contemporary experience—in recent history that of white heterosexual male intellectuals. Their reflection on "our" contemporary experience simultaneously silences other experiences and points of view, so that the experience of one group comes to be passed off as that of every group.[9]

Anyone trying to make such discursive generalizations in a world affected by the deformation and decline of working-class universality and by black, native peoples', Third World, gay and lesbian, and feminist insistence on being heard and seen, as well as by multicultural and postmodern insights, is now fundamentally challenged. This means that anyone who would speak today has lost something in the process: an easy sense of generality and universality that was once thought to come with speech and language themselves. The ability has been lost to say, unreflectively and without careful justification, "we" in a way that wants to embrace the wider world. The "we" so often thought and said, especially by people with power to shape social discourse—and then mimicked by those without power—turns out to be, as Meaghan Morris puts it, "that embarrassing macro-binary from the days of unity and solidarity." When it is spoken, "How many disparate and displacing 'you's and 'I's are being dispossessed?"[10] That throwback is now derided as the "we" of a certain class, of a certain society, of a certain gender, of a certain ethnicity, of a certain race. It is the colonizing "we."

This means, of course, that the loss I am speaking of may be only a loss for certain white males. For all others, it is no doubt a gain to no longer be spoken for while remaining silent or unheard. The "loss" of being able to assume that there is one coherent single structure of feeling may in fact be the beginning of a wider emancipation.

Can we talk about *the* world then? The problem with doing so is an extension of the "we" problem: we cannot speak of the world if we thereby uncritically assume a privileged white male experience of Europe and North America to stand for all other experiences of the world. That game is over. We can do so only if we mean, literally, the whole world, and all people in it, and are willing to back this up with argument: for example, we face catastrophe if nothing is done about the ozone layer, or to curtail and balance energy consumption. But if this necessarily common concern can be argued for, it is less possible to presume to speak universally and sweepingly about *the* experience of the world, *the* historical period, or *the* contemporary structure of feeling, when in fact what is meant is the emphases and concerns of one gender, a certain social class, and/or a very specific, usually Western, cultural milieu.

Still, after all hesitancies and qualifications, in the next several sections, I argue generally: that during the last quarter of the twentieth century, in response to the lived history of the century, a fundamental change in mood has taken place, perhaps across the world. Am I doing no more than (to take the narrowest possibility) stating one white male's sense of loss, in fact that of an American academic, indeed, that of a Jewish radical philosopher and historian of ideas who was born and works in Detroit and lives in its near-northern suburbs? But reducing my sense of a wider mood to this most minute particularity would be as distorting as claiming the most sweeping universality for it. Obviously, I am seeking to speak about a wider change in mood and sense of loss that I have perceived around me, shared with many others, read about, and thought about, as well as experienced personally. The individual experience itself took shape in a milieu of Western (and also non-Western) intellectuals and political activists, all of whom have shared in a broad Left community and culture, including as many women as men. This particular "world" of the Left—which contains people who simultaneously and with equal attachment belong to other worlds—has been marked by, and has been trying to register, a powerful sense of loss. It is no secret that the loss seems even more widespread, extending to significant numbers of university students in the West as well as to the broader constituencies that the Left has seen itself mobilizing. To speak of this "we" is henceforth to do so cautiously and reflexively—to make an argument that can be countered and tested, rather than speaking from easy assumptions of universality. But the point remains, this collectivity has arguably experienced, and is still experiencing, a profound loss.

In the rest of this chapter I will discuss the specific "we" articulated above and only that group, except in one or two places where I am clearly and deliberately making a wider argument about universal world-historical changes. And even within this "we" I will propose rather than assume. This caution and self-consciousness, loss and gain, testifies to an exciting fact: many subjectivities have newly entered that objective, public, political space, the "stage" on which history is played out. They are quite able to speak for themselves, and will be heard. If this restrains what anyone can say and how, it frees many to speak who have hitherto been silent. And if in the long run it may indeed make possible a new kind of "we"—more diverse, more mutual, more genuinely embracing than the "workers of the world"—it also forces arguments for any point of view to confront other arguments for other points of view. It acknowledges that all of us are fundamentally, inescapably, specifically situated. No one can be quite so self-confident anymore—nor, on the other hand, so silent.

Loss of Alternatives

Losing a sense of universality also entails losing faith in the collective human capacity to create a wider, fuller, harmonious "we"; in short, we have lost the belief that a radically better social life is not just desirable but possible. As I argued in Chapter 3, the collapse of Communism is the most spectacular recent event to undermine this belief. We have lost the sense of alternative. Not because Communism was the alternative, although many embraced it until the end, and because it was capitalism's Other used its positive features to build illusions about it. Rather, its sheer existence as being other than capitalism meant that more than one kind of industrial civilization was possible. For all its oppressions and weaknesses, it demonstrated that a noncapitalist modern society could be created.

If the Soviet Union was one alternative to capitalism, why could there not be others less oppressive, more democratic, more genuinely egalitarian? Communism's sheer existence defined the world as a space of antagonism between two social systems. This space, psychological as well as political, allowed more than a choice between two ugly alternatives. It encouraged projects for creating other alternatives, such as "third ways" that might borrow from both. With the end of Communism, those who would seek such space now find capitalism on the one side, and on the other side— nothing. Thus after 1989 and 1991 almost every one of the world's remaining Communist parties changed not only their names but their ideologies overnight. Everyone, Left and Right, now embraced the "free market" and privatization; the Left was distinguished from the Right only by how fully, at what pace, and with what safeguards it embraced Capitalism. Alternatives like workers' control and market socialism were unable to resist the stampede.

This means that the world of states and societies is without an alternative vision of social life for the first time since the birth of capitalism.

Is this finally the advent of the one-dimensional society that Herbert Marcuse spoke of, a society without (explicit, systemic) opposition?[11] If so, movements are forced to assert their particular claims in particular terms, without nurturing hopes or fears about far-reaching transformations that are simply not in the cards. Yet if movements in the most advanced societies for women's rights, majority rule, and minority rights have expanded the numbers and identities of those included *within* the system, they seem to offer less and less of an alternative *to* it. Jorge G. Casteneda's study of the decline of and possible future role for the Latin American Left gives up on "the extinct socialist model" for solving the region's enormous problems, while insisting that "another type of market economy, contrasting starkly with the one currently being hailed throughout Latin America, is preferable to the status quo."[12]

Such a narrowing of perspective was hailed as a positive outcome by Francis Fukuyama's famous essay and book on the "end of history." If Marxism and its projection of working-class revolution is over, due to the "unabashed victory of economic and political liberalism,"[13] this absence of an alternative is to be celebrated. "What we may be witnessing," Fukuyama wrote in 1989, "is not just the end of the Cold War, or the passing of a particular period of postwar history, but the end of history as such: that is, the end point of mankind's ideological evolution and the universalization of Western liberal democracy as the final form of human government."[14]

But surprisingly little cheering accompanied this victory. Capitalist civilization's near-magical power to create environments and forms of gratification, to reconstitute selves and nature, is unaccompanied, astonishingly, by enthusiasm or optimism. Whatever became of past rhapsodizing about human powers, exponentially expanded, creating plenty, overcoming uneven development, removing atavistic enmities, and bringing the world under conscious collective control? Since the 1970s doubt has become widespread about where the world is headed, accompanied by cynicism about human capacities to create a genuinely humane social life. After all, what kind of progress is it that makes human life seem worth *less* in a moral and political sense, the planet *more* fragile, animal species and natural beauties *more* endangered, human conscience and values *less* vital, racism, nationalism, and irrationality *more* explosive?

Loss of Faith in Progress

Correlatively, we no longer believe that human life is improving. Communism is over and the Marxist project has come and gone as the "next wave" of history. Earlier, fascism and Nazism came and went, disastrously. Liberal and social-democratic welfare-state capitalism triumphed on the basis of imperialism and a consumer society built on reformism amid endless expansion of needs and productivity, but entered into a crisis and abandoned much of its original optimism and ameliorative bent. Thus twentieth-century experiences of capitalism, Communism, and fascism leave us not with faith in the future, but rather with memories or fears of catastrophe. Whether because of the Gulag or Auschwitz, of Hiroshima or Vietnam, of Chernobyl or Three Mile Island, or of the shrinking ozone layer, it seems that Enlightenment hopes based on promises of steady amelioration of human suffering or on revolutionary visions, have become scattered among the century's rubble.

This disintegration of hope, accelerating as we have been stumbling through the century, is inseparable from the fate of the idea of progress. As Marxism began to fade, so did this great Enlightenment belief.[15] Whether viewed through Marxist or bourgeois lenses, the advance of science, technology, productivity, education, and democracy was supposed to lead—either directly, or dialectically and through revolutionary action—to general well-being. Today we radicals are not alone in having lost our faith in the ultimate benevolence of history; the belief in progress is in tatters almost everywhere. We have seen astonishing scientific, technological, and economic progress, so much so that we stumble toward the next century only in spirit: physically, the majority in the industrialized world hurtle toward it in blinding speed and sophisticated comfort, beyond the reach of even past ruling classes. Our technical capacities are truly mind-boggling, but we have become the first generation that no longer sees them bringing happiness. This is the Janus face of human achievement: constant technical change, growth in productivity, genuine progress in knowledge and human self-understanding, accompanied by unprecedented cynicism.

And why shouldn't this be the case? After forty-five years of the world's least harsh Communism, with its attention to modernization, national and regional economic development, and education, the former Yugoslavia now lies divided and devasted, by the bombardment of Dubrovnik, "ethnic cleansing," the mass rape of Bosnian women, the siege of Sarajevo. After so many other avowals of "never again," the whole world still watched the nationalist paroxysm slowly erupting and stood around twiddling its thumbs. The Serbian–Croatian war, followed by the dismemberment of Bosnia by these opponents, have dashed any sense that progress toward tolerance accompanies modernization, that a meaningful international order characterizes the post-Cold War world.

Thus a stocktaking after Marxism, after Communism, after the Holocaust, and after progress finds little sense of hope or liberation of energies. The world's most fortunate people, those enjoying the fruits of advanced capitalism, seem rather surrounded on three sides by seductive glitz and brilliant technical possibility, and on a fourth by massive decay, destruction of community life, and poverty. Some live lives surrounded by the amenities of economic and educational privilege, others in the cruelest Third World deprivation—yet we are all ensconced in a single world economic system whose efficient functioning still turns on systematic exploitation and inequality. Its corrosive force erodes traditional sources of identity and community, its never-ending disruptiveness generates constant instability and growing pessimism.

Losing a Sense of History

Any future radical movement can rest on nothing like the sense of history that animated Marxism: that we are all within one history, unfolding in an intelligible and meaningful way, and heading in a positive direction. The very notion of *a* history is being contested today, as artificially unifying the multiplicity of histories that people actually live, of majorities and minorities, of different social classes, of men and women, of various societies, classes, ethnic groups, groups, and subcultures. Over the past generation, Western history, after so successfully passing itself off as universal history while the West was imposing its order on the globe, has become relativized.

It is worth stressing the limitations intrinsic to replacing the old false universalism with an equally false particularism. First, if, for example, Afrikaners and Zulus each have their own histories, as do particular groups within each and crosscutting between each, and if they also shape each other's histories in quite different and asymmetrical ways, it is no less true that they all simultaneously participate in European, African, South African, and world histories. From certain points of view each group can be seen as no more than a component of a larger history; from other points of view each group can be seen as living its own unique and irreducible experience.

Second, the new stress on multiplicity comes at a time when capitalism has imposed a single world economy as never before, when rapid transportation and electronic media have erected a global village, and when the penetration of the human order into nature makes it seem as if everything is constituted by structured human activity.[16] We have become more responsive to ever more local histories just as we have recognized the extent that we are bound together in a single, ever more global history. In the end neither History nor histories can be avoided: every individual can be seen as participating at multiple levels, to be revealed only through close study. We all simultaneously live within the stream of History's grand "metanarratives" *and* within more particular and individual narratives.

But however it is construed, the decline of progress changes our sense of history's directionality. It is no longer possible to believe that a good future is unfolding. At best, the future seems to promise a negative for every positive. It seems subject to a radical indeterminacy, because we now recognize the extent to which outcomes depend on a plurality of human decisions and actions, on struggle, on the ways human actions are bounded by systemic demands, on unintended consequences that almost inevitably deviate result from intention, or by chance. Moreover, the "we" who would support or oppose radical change is constantly being reshaped and reshaping itself. Even if it is not a random flux, history can no longer be read as a single story of human emancipation working itself out through its varied actors.[17] If it remains legitimate, as I still believe, to talk about aiming at a conscious and collective history—and if, as I explore in the final chapter, this goal, however distant, should remain part of any future radical project—what has been decisively shipwrecked in our century is the belief that history is actually heading in this direction. Any future radical movement will have to be characterized by a radical openness to the future as well as to a neverending reappraisal of the past.[18]

Losing Faith in Human Nature

Marxism projected a vision of human emancipation based on the capacities of a specific class. This faith—at its core a faith in human nature—has disappeared beneath the piles of bodies created by revolution, war, and genocide. Most of the millions died in the aftermath of the Bolshevik Revolution and Hitler's rise to power, so we cannot help but focus on the social logic behind Stalinism and Nazism. Both reveal fundamental structural irrationalities, and not simply the calculable effects of dominant material interests or the individual personalities of their rulers. Yet neither the Holocaust nor the Stalinist terror can be understood without being seen as widely supported human decisions taken under certain pressures at specific moments in the history of specific social forces, to perform certain actions. That is, even if they seem to defy comprehension, they were human projects like any other, and demand understanding like any other. Which is to say, "the final solution to the Jewish problem" and the related Nazi murders of millions of others, as well as the "liquidation of the kulaks" and the great terror of the 1930s, took place because large numbers of humans *chose* murderous purposes.[19] Even when understood in terms of specific societal tensions that made such choices and actions possible, these acts caution those who would dare to entertain radical hopes after Marxism. In certain situations people may be capable of the best; in others they are capable of the worst.

At issue is not only the death of over one hundred million people since the outbreak of World War I, but also the continued planning and preparation for nuclear war—today, without an enemy. At issue are primitive nationalisms such as those that accompanied the disintegration of Yugoslavia. These past, present, and still-impending disasters speak to, and in some ways stem from, a side of humanity that cannot be ignored by any hope for radical change. In *The Dialectics of Disaster* I have explored the societal dynamics behind some of these catastrophes. Whatever their causes, anyone searching for hope in the late twentieth century cannot help but be struck by the fact that tens and hundreds of millions of people continue to tolerate total threats to their security, continue to accept war as an instrument of national policy, and continue to act out of atavistic fears and manipulated national identities.[20]

No one can even begin to imagine lands of milk and honey without wondering: under what conditions will people, willing to endure the nuclear threat and environmental destruction, be willing to undertake what is apparently even more frightening, namely, make whatever sacrifices are necessary to eliminate these dangers and the authorities and systems standing behind them? Why is it that increases in prosperity, in literacy, in societal development, even in psychological sophistication, have not led to irresistible ecological demands, calls for the dismantling of nuclear weapons and the revival of a politics of emancipation? Why do people in the wealthiest countries patently not believe that the "pacification of existence" (Marcuse's phrase) is possible? And the more frightening question cannot be avoided: is there some internal connection between technological progress and our willingness to tolerate the threat of total destruction?[21]

Abandoning a faith in human nature *a fortiori* means forsaking faith in the liberating capacities of any particular group or class. Marx believed that those who were most oppressed by the social order and most excluded from its rewards, were accordingly, as outsiders, the most free from its corruptions.[22] Weakness gave strength, oppression gave vision. Thus the proletariat was "a class in civil society which is not a class of civil society."[23] Through their labor, these ultimate outsiders are the source of social life: this paradox is the basis of the proletariat's revolutionary role and its universality. But, as Sherover-Marcuse points out, the proletariat requires a protracted subjective practice of emancipation because the most oppressed are indeed *within and not outside of* the social order, dwelling precisely at its bottom rungs, thoroughly subjected to their place. Accordingly, they need to develop new strengths and new habits of thought and feeling, as part of any and all struggles to liberate themselves and transform the society.

"Human nature" needs a long and difficult process of being understood and reshaped if fundamentally democratic and egalitarian societies are ever to be created. Long-ingrained habits of deference and renunciation will have to be replaced by new kinds of strength, self-discipline, and self-confidence. Within the recesses of subjectivities that accept national, class, racial, and gender domination lie structures of feeling that will permit no liberation until they are (self-)understood and (self-)transformed. Why did so many Germans, including German workers, come to see the Jews as dangerous parasites needing to be exterminated? What are the underlying bases for ethnic and national and racial hatreds? What are the inner sources of patriarchy? Why are millions of citizen soldiers willing to kill and die in orgies of mass destruction? What motivates the massive public and private acquiescence to threats of nuclear destruction, the childlike passivity and dependence on authority figures of the most educated and technically sophisticated peoples?[24] No future radical project is possible that passes in silence over such facts, which have destroyed an earlier century's faith in human beings and their evolution and enlightenment. A new radical project must seek causes and changes on the subjective level as part and parcel of seeking causes and changes on the societal level.

Losing Our Bearings

If we have learned from history's harsh school that reality is more complex and refractory than it once seemed, genuine progress in knowledge is further increasing our collective sense of complexity, to the point marked by Lyotard's postmodern "incredulity" about describing main trends of social or historical life—that is, toward "metanarratives."[25] Certainly the new critical cultural projects—be they philosophical, linguistic, historical, psychological, or anthropological, to name only a few, and deeply marked by feminism, multiculturalism, and an interdisciplinary spirit—are extensions of the work begun by the Enlightenment, and carried further by Marx, of deconstructing all seemingly fixed and finished forms of knowledge into their historically rooted human and social sources. I stress the Enlightenment here because it has come into such disrepute recently that writers who proclaim their abandonment of it are accused of not going far enough.[26] Each of the changes I will now mention are continuations of, and developments from, Enlightenment efforts to critically understand human realities.

First, claims to truth have had their pretension to objectivity and external solidity assaulted, and now are taken as being no more than specific and situated insights into highly subjective and unstable constructs. At best, truth is seen by such a stoutly Enlightenment thinker as Habermas as the product of intersubjective consensus, developed as needed to adjudicate differences and create agreements necessary for social life. Second, identities and social positions (such as the working class) are no longer seen as given, established, and stable essences, but are now discovered to be complex (and discursive) creations, amenable to change, shifting with variations in perception, social and linguistic constitution, and political hegemony. Third, not only does every dimension of social reality now appear as constructed, shaped by prevailing forms of power, but so do the fixed and finished forms of apparently any and every reality. Under methods of scrutiny learned from modern science and social science, even the body, human needs, the self, the psyche, and the person are dissolving into their social, historical, and linguistic processes of constitution. Behind once firm social categories we can now glimpse the vital places occupied by power, by rhetoric, by discourse. Fourth, as I mention above, certain forms of objectivity and universality imposed highly specific gender, class, and cultural projects on those who were thereby silenced about *their* experiences and identities. It should come as no surprise that the undermining of objectivity as a fixed and finished realm existing independently of us has also displaced loyalty to other settled standards, for example, those of the traditional Western literary canon. How can "civilization's" great works not be seen as springing from the same relationships of power discovered at the core of so many other once-stable social realities?

This new wave of understanding enhances our sense of complexity and highlights the awareness that no single way of grasping the world compels assent today. If we have any hope of arriving at *an* understanding of our world and its problems, it will only come about through combining and working through new insights as well as old, and by creating new kinds of syntheses that manage to hold together widely divergent elements. Driving another nail in the coffin of the Marxian project, this cannot help but bring confusion to all those accustomed to its single overarching narrative, with its sense of reductive clarity, of scientific and objective truth.

In being employed in all the ways I described in Part I, Marxism gave direction to millions, but ironically only by being treated as a kind of secular religion: queller of doubts, guarantor of certainty, provider of security, promoter of unity. A friend tells the story of his father, son of an immigrant to the United States, born into orthodox Judaism, who broke away from his moorings completely. The young man became an atheist and a Communist. Rushing to embrace modernity and its promise of liberation, he did so through a new faith and set of observances, in which History replaced God, where new sacred texts replaced Torah and Talmud, where new ritual obligations replaced the old, where an all-embracing ethics under rabbinical authority was succeeded by an all-embracing politics under "scientific" party authority. In exchanging old certainties for new, his sweeping liberation turned out to be an exchange of one authoritative system for another.

Marxism provided orientation, not always as the "ruthless criticism of everything existing" or as a self-critical and self-conscious project, but equally often as a holistic outlook virtually guaranteeing success. Insofar as it distorted reality by making it appear more consistent and coherent than it really was, Marxism often provided a sense of direction *by feeding illusions*. It allowed orthodox Jewish boys to become Communist men without completely abandoning their starting points. Today, however, the old sense of direction no longer exists. Even nonreligious Marxists are at a loss; and finding bearings is a task to be started all over again.

Parameters of a New Radical Project

Today's disillusionment, however, is rooted less in Marxism's errors than in the experience of a century. Since it stems from far-reaching objective processes, the bases of disillusionment are arguably universal, and it is spreading and deepening.[27] We are surrounded by good reasons for being disillusioned: the apparent scarcity of human goodness; the destructive foibles that attend "progress"; the incredible difficulties of building a new human social order; how little of human reality we adequately understand; the deep grip in which capitalism, racism, nationalism, and patriarchy continue to hold people; and the obstacles to enlightenment, including especially people themselves. Compared with Marxism's optimism, our pessimism seems a remarkable retreat, but it is responding to how the world has evolved since Marx's death. Writing after the failed revolutions of 1848, he drew what appeared to be a stern conclusion for the workers: "You have 15, 20, 50 years of civil war to go through in order to alter the situation and to train yourselves for the exercise of power."[28] How times have changed.

But an unsparing look at our losses can do more than depress. It gives us a sense both of what a possible post-Marxist radical movement *won't* and *can't* look like, and what, if there is to be one, it *will* look like. As a conclusion to this tallying of losses, then, we can at least make some preliminary judgments about the parameters of any possible future radical project.

First, it will be without historical certainty. It will not appeal to any veiled or hidden forces that remove the burden of change from its participants. But it will also focus on the objective balance of forces and on the extreme difficulty of bringing about significant change. Participants in social struggles will be spared illusions about the "necessity" of victory, and they may perhaps learn how to avoid making their defeats into disasters.[29]

Second, a movement aiming at significant change will be a politics of identity as well as a politics of social structures and power. In significant ways it will turn on its participants' experience, including assessing, and making provision for, the *subjective* obstacles to achieving its goals. It will stress its subjects' responsibility for bringing about the changes it projects, and they will focus on dealing with, and overcoming, internalized forms of oppression and making themselves able and willing to transform society. The development of capacities and self-confidence will become central to any movement that seeks to mobilize those who are oppressed, especially if its goal is their empowerment. Consciousness raising and deepening will have to extend not only to racial but also to class attitudes and feelings, not only to attitudes toward sexuality but also to ways of experiencing life and death.

Third, the theories and explanations that a new movement will draw on will have an open character, rather than being passed off as a single and certain revolutionary science. They will not avoid scientific analysis, but where appropriate, and combined with openly prophetic but contestable visions of the future, with self-consciously moral exhortation combining ethical motivations and personal needs, and with a deliberately tentative sense of history's direction.

Fourth, a new radical movement will abandon the notion that it is theoretically and practically focused on a single decisive area of human oppression and a single social agent who can pull the lever to transform it. Instead, it will call for dozens of changes at dozens of levels and sites, only some of which rest on state power. Some of its demands will sight what might be regarded as basic social and economic structures, others will focus on social and political policies, others on the practices of individuals and groups, and still others, on individual and group attitudes. A post-Marxist movement will be made up of many varieties of individuals and groups, active on their own behalf not simply to change the system but also to change themselves, including their behavior and attitudes.

Finally, if there is to be *a* movement, it will have to become one as a coalition of groups and forces each seeking their own changes. It will be based on a plurality of needs and demands, will have to focus on changing a plurality of structures and practices and attitudes, and its various component groups will have to learn how to interact collectively and with mutual respect. Its general appeal—its unity—if it is to exist, will have to be built group by group, block by block.

In short, if there is to be a new radical project, it will scarcely resemble what we children of Marx have come to expect. But should there be a new project? And can there be one?

Chapter Eight

A NEW RADICAL PROJECT

Tentative, open, plural, aiming at and stressing a variety of subjective needs and changes: these thoughts are not original. Radical theorists have been drawing similar conclusions for a generation. Haven't most of these lessons, therefore, already been learned, and put into effect? Haven't I been implicitly talking about the new social movements of this past generation? If so, these comments about losses and new parameters might well end this book. Marxism is over, we might say, and there is not much more to be said right now. It would perhaps only remain to bow toward the new forms of political activism—either to let them define themselves over time, or to listen to their advocates and theoreticians describe and explain the new social movements. Why go further?

Why, after the first four conclusions ending the last chapter, should we press on to a fifth, to talk about how several new movements can become one? Why still presume that future radical politics will involve a single movement? Indeed, why speak of a new kind of *radical* project, as if it were both necessary and possible? In *Social Movements and Political Power*, Carl Boggs poses the goal of a new, unified movement based on multiple paradigms.[1] But perhaps, after Marxism, such a movement no longer makes sense. Synthesizing the conclusions of Fukuyama and Lyotard, one could argue that historical conditions have moved us beyond the possibility of a coherent project of radical change, and that our immediate task is to work through this loss. If the new movements remain separate and individual (and if they have not yet come to terms with, absorbed, and genuinely gone beyond Marxism)[2], this may well mean that nothing more is possible. If the new social movements have not become a unified new movement, perhaps this is because they do not actually point in that direction. No doubt some movements will continue, others will fade, new ones will be created. As Alberto Melucci says, perhaps they will continue to point out areas in our complex societies that need attention, and will demand and provoke changes, some of them specific, some more general.[3] Perhaps our movements may catalyze some kinds of radical changes, and perhaps they will improve social life within its existing parameters. Why assume that any more is really possible today?

In continuing to search for a radical new unity, don't I risk denying the ways in which this self-assigned role of radical intellectual, of movement theoretician, has been marginalized by the very processes this book has described? If a few of us have developed a considerable personal investment in the role, this does not keep it relevant, unfazed by what happens in the surrounding world. Beyond or within personal need, it is necessary to ask whether a larger claim is still warranted. Is there a legitimate reason to continue hoping and working for some sort of new collectivity and new radical project?

Bases for a Single Movement: Collective Identities

Beyond nostalgia, beyond Marxist reflex, beyond clinging to a comfortable stance in the face of irrelevance, there is a basis for arguing that in spite of the crisis of universality discussed in the previous chapter a larger "we" might still be both analytically sound and the goal of a meaningful political project. Such a collective identity is *real*. Large social collectivities can be pointed to across our common social space: in economic cooperation, in political systems and practices, in values, cultures, and in a collective relationship to nature. In *Civil Society and Political Theory*, Jean Cohen and Andrew Arato restate this argument against theorists of endless multiplicity and uncommon spaces. If they stress the differentiation that accompanies modernity, it depends on "webs of relationships of mutual recognition" that can only develop through protecting group identity across a *common* social space:

> [In spite of] our differences, we have discovered, reaffirmed, or created something in common that corresponds to a general social identity (which is itself open to change). A public discussion can show us that, after all, we do have something in common, that we are a *we*, and that we agree on or presuppose certain principles that constitute our collective identity. These become dimensions of the content of legitimate legal norms and the foundation of social solidarity.[4]

Drawing upon the work of Habermas, Cohen and Arato insist that at the core of such a collective identity, making solidarity possible, are modern procedures of rational agreement, based on individual rights. "Even modern societies characterized by value pluralism and a plurality of groups with distinct collective identities would not be societies if there were no shared principles regulating their interaction, and if there were no common (political) identity shared by their members, however different from one another they may otherwise be."[5] No matter how radical our pluralism may be, it would be on principle impossible if it excluded "meaningful normative coordination and commonality, however minimal, that is recognized, at least implicitly, by all of us insofar as we communicate and act together."[6] Thus in modern social life, a plurality of groups, each having a specific vision of "the good life," share among themselves at least "a minimal or 'weak' collective political identity."[7]

Solidarity is not something that is added later, or a value imposed from the outside: it is based on the "intersubjective communicative infrastructure of everyday social life."[8] It is "rooted in the experience that each must take responsibility for the other because as consociates they all share an interest in the integrity of their common life context—in short, a collective identity."[9] This is precisely the identity of those who, even when differing from each other, "share in the political culture of the society at large. This kind of collective identity is capable of asserting a *we* while fostering solidarity among the many group identities that compose a modern civil society."[10]

However we may differ, we are connected in the most basic conditions of our survival, in facing our common dangers, in protecting our pleasures, in our fears and our suffering, in our privileges and our victimization. Indeed, we are connected through the tools we use, the machines we operate, the words we think, the food we eat, perhaps even in our dreams and nightmares. Every particular "we" that can think of itself as such shares also larger collective identities that are the very condition and possibility of its particularity. But solidarity refers not only to protecting and extending the common ground of our uniqueness. It suggests that not only women but also men have a stake in women's liberation; that not only blacks but whites as well have a stake in black liberation; that the peoples of the South need a transformed relationship with the North not only for their own sake, but also for those living in the North; that not only homosexuals but also heterosexuals have a stake in gay liberation. Both our common and our particular identities may not only be enriched by, but *depend on*, solidarity with others.

In short, the notion of a single radical movement, understood as a new radical coalition, is based on the expectation of seeing and experiencing links, interdependencies, a common sociality. It would say "we" on account of these, but at the same time would be saying it projectively, hopefully. It would, among other things, pose the project of creating a societal "we" and an international "we," based on the intention, discussed in Chapter 7, of expanding the broad circle of the Left into wider and more inclusive collectivities building from these interconnections. I say "building from" because the interconnections do not normally contain the explicit sense of us deliberately acting together, but only a sense of separated and perhaps isolated individuals in relation to others to whom we do not relate. We act *serially*, linked, by matter, by the results of our actions, but linked passively rather than deliberately.[11] To transform this into an active and self-conscious "we" requires a deliberate project.

We see such moments of choosing to make or acknowledge connection—voluntary associations, political actions, emergency help, moments of solidarity—in political movements, in crisis situations, in great public celebrations. As social bonds normally taken for granted become renewed, are freely established, and implicit human links momentarily become visible, they are consciously felt and shared. Meaghan Morris's "embarrassing macro-binary from the days of unity and solidarity" mentioned in Chapter 7 turns out to be a real experience with a genuine basis, even if it is always *about* something: the threat of nuclear annihilation, a strike, an assassination, a sports victory, a war, a concert, a life-threatening storm. At such moments the otherwise formal, usually abstract—implicitly felt and always presupposed although unacknowledged—collectivities come alive to remind us of a collective identity that we had almost forgotten was there.

How Wide a "We"?

Within the largest social collectivity the potential for radical change consists of all those who are subjected to one of what Iris Young calls the "five faces of oppression": powerlessness, exploitation, marginalization, violence, and cultural imperialism.[12] Included are those whose lives—whose physical, social, and mental spaces—are dominated and disfigured by the irresistible force of capital. In Marxian theory all forms of oppression were reduced to the economic exploitation and class domination at the heart of capitalism; Young retains exploitation as a key term, but correctly refuses the reduction and gives independent and equal status to most of the other specific oppressions against which the various movements of the last generation have been struggling. The effect of seeing oppression structurally, as with Marx's focus on exploitation, is to give analytical precision to what was heretofore largely a rhetorical term, and to recognize each type of oppression in its specificity.

According to Young, exploitation involves "a steady process of the transfer of the results of the labor of one social group to benefit another."[13] Marginalization is the expulsion of a whole category of people "from useful participation in social life."[14] Powerlessness entails the inability to make decisions over the conditions of one's life and actions and, conversely, being subject to others endowed with authority and status, who are empowered to make those decisions for one. In turn, this means occupying "a position in the division of labor and the concomitant social position that allows persons little opportunity to develop and exercise skills." Young continues, "The powerless have little or no work autonomy, exercise little creativity or judgment in their work, have no technical expertise or authority, express themselves awkwardly, especially in public or bureaucratic settings, and do not command respect."[15] The category of cultural imperialism calls attention to "how the dominant meanings of a society render the particular perspective of one's own group invisible at the same time as they stereotype one's group and mark it out as the Other."[16] Finally, violence, treated as a systemic social practice, refers to actions that are socially tolerated, accepted, and directed at members of a group simply because of their group identity.

These categories of oppression, singly or jointly, seem to account for most of the demands of most of the movements of our generation. To them I would add another: the systemic societal oppression the capitalist system exerts on *all* of its subjects insofar as it invades and reshapes all possible spaces, subjective as well as objective, in its search for profits. As André Gorz describes it, it involves the increasing subjection of all areas of social life to economic rationality.[17] This is akin to powerlessness, but distinct in that it is a very specific kind with a very specific origin and outcome: in terms drawn from the work of Habermas, the economic subsystem colonizes and transforms the human lifeworld according to *its* logic.

A new radical project would address each oppression, would seek to unite those who are experiencing them, and would describe and oppose each in concrete and specific terms. A new radical project would appeal to those experiencing the most brutal forms of violence and exploitation, those who are scarcely surviving, and those who make ends meet but under enormous strain. And it would appeal to those who suffer from gender and racial oppression—in which all of the five oppressions may intersect. And it would not forget the organized working class in the advanced industrial societies, whose relatively comfortable members are nonetheless culturally and psychically dominated, exploited, and ultimately powerless.

The new radicalism would seek to include those who are marginalized on account of sexual orientation; whose voice and identities have been stifled by processes of cultural imperialism; whose long-term well-being is undermined by the exploitative nature of North–South relations; who are threatened by continued militarism. And its net will also be cast to include those kinds of oppression not easily included within the specific defining features of the five oppressions: those whose lives take place within the systematized irrationality and pervasive domination of consumerism; who suffer from contemporary capitalism's processes of needs creation and infantilization; who are endangered by ecological devastation. While powerlessness is central to each of these forms of oppression, they also contain kinds of domination, in the interest of an economic system beyond democratic control, not immediately reducible to exploitation, cultural imperialism, marginalization, or violence.

Thus described, a new radical movement would mobilize a vast number of different "we's," mobilized to seek both multiple liberations and common liberation. I am using "we" in a deliberately provocative way, to propose. If I self-consciously speak above from a specific and limited standpoint, I am arguing here for using "we" to describe an ever larger potential coalition of all those who are oppressed in a variety of specific ways, and in common ways. This coalition's project would be both to address collective issues and to assist its various groups in advancing their own struggles. Obviously, building a new kind of collectivity, based on multiple oppressions, voices, and identities, will be one goal of a new radical movement. Using "we" projectively, then, means not only *describing* actual links and commonalities but also *building* a global community of equals attacking their particular and their common oppressions—a coalition that respects difference, collectively aiming at classless societies that are free from racial domination, patriarchy, and other forms of oppression, in which the free development of each is the condition for the free development of all. We know that such a kaleidoscopically variegated, egalitarian, democratic "we" does not exist and has never existed, that we have only inklings of it, a few moments, brief glimpses, its abstract principle. Nevertheless, as I will explore in Chapters 10 and 11, this "we" lives as goal, as project, even as hope and utopia. Talking about it, indeed, talking "from" it and "to" it, is to call for its creation—and to invite others to join in.

The problem, of course, is that there is no basis for assuming in advance that blacks, women, Greens, socialists, gays and lesbians, peaceniks, native peoples, and other and future activists will be struggling against the same structures or on behalf of the same goals. Just as they have been oppressed in separate and diverse ways, so have they manifestly pursued diverse and independent projects. Indeed, arriving at this point of particularizion may be regarded as a major achievement. It is reassuring to conceive of the various movements as corresponding to "layers" of the same social space— as, for example, does Nancy Fraser[18] —or as all responding to the oppressions of advanced capitalism, as do many Marxists. But their very separateness and plurality challenge the assumption that they are oppressed in the same ways or by the same structures.

This means that creating one movement from these various movements, creating a single "we," is itself a task that must be taken up consciously. Rather than assuming, for example, that each of the movements is responding to the depredations of capitalism, or to any of the same basic features of the same social entity, a project of finding bases for unity must be hatched *in the case of each link to be forged and each oppression to be combated.* It will not involve, as did the proletarian movement, unifying the individual members of a preexisting group that is already socially identifiable, but rather creating a coalition of widely different groups and individuals, aiming at multiple transformations. Thinking in the plural, *transformations*, is essential. Young's "five faces of oppression" help us to see that there is no single source, and that there will be no single cure for, the various kinds of systemically practiced and encouraged dominations.

As a result, each step in the creation of this "we" would be an act of reaching agreement among equals: a coalitional movement that privileges any one of its participating groups is unthinkable. If a new movement, as a radical coalition, is to exist at all, each of its participants will have to willingly redefine themselves as members of that larger coalition. In relation to each other they will have to discover vital new dimensions of identity, understanding, or ability to achieve goals that escape them as long as they remain by themselves. Solidarity is a task, and a discovery. From movements into *a* movement: this itinerary, so long in the making in our generation but so decisively hindered by the Marxian claim for working-class hegemony and reactive one-sided assertions of particularity, may now become fully conceivable for the first time.[19] Our first success and ongoing challenge, then, would involve transforming ourselves into the "we" of a new movement.

Taking Oppression Seriously: Dionne's *Why Americans Hate Politics*

But why does combating the various oppressions I mentioned above require a *radical* movement, one which seeks to subvert the existing social system's most fundamental priorities, values, structures, and relationships, and which refuses to limit itself to acting within the channels provided by the system? After Marxism, don't the various losses of faith, and the rigorous new parameters they impose, rule out the very idea of radical change? Why not projects of reform, strategically and ideologically accepting the rules of the game, which call on the system to honor its own promises and fulfill its own obligations, and which accept using conventional forms of struggle? What is the basis for arguing that such liberal change is not sufficient?

We can move toward answering these questions by looking at two major recent efforts to rethink the politics of change. E. J. Dionne's *Why Americans Hate Politics* and Cohen and Arato's *Civil Society and Political Theory* are pitched at two distinctly different levels. The first is a practical attempt to propose a new "coalition for social reform that could command broad support in the middle class"[20] of the United States, the second a theoretical reconceptualization of the trajectory of advanced societies in terms of modernization and the new social movements. But each remains sympathetic to many radical goals while trying to establish the terrain on which social and political change is likely to henceforth take place and should take place.

Dionne seeks to lay the foundation for a new "common civic endeavor"[21] that would listen to what liberals and conservatives have been saying for a generation and, for the first time, "end the phony polarization around the issues of the 1960s"[22] that has so dominated politics in the United States. He proposes concentrating on "the practical concerns of the broad electorate"[23] by solving problems that can be dealt with across the cultural divide that has sprung up since the 1960s, as opposed to aggravating the great and irresolvable cultural issues that have so split contemporary American society. He is proposing the kind of post-1960s "end of ideology" liberalism that Bill Clinton brought to Washington: "It is a demand for steadiness, for social peace, for broad tolerance, for more egalitarian economic policies, for economic growth."[24] Perhaps this new, supremely realistic liberalism is the best we can now hope for, prodded by a shifting congeries of social movements seeking to redeem unfulfilled promises.

Dionne's goal, honorable enough, is to work within the system to improve it by concentrating on "the basics—educating children, delivering health care, building roads and mass transit, fighting crime."[25] In concentrating on "common citizenship" he deliberately avoids questioning and seeking to transform the society's fundamental structures and relations. Still he approaches the various potential insurgent constituencies sympathetically, seeking to integrate their concerns into this new politics of the middle class. The problem, however, is that he accepts oppression.

He ignores oppression by passing in near-silence over the stifling heritage of colonialism and slavery, effectively leaving the majority of people of color marginalized and without adequate resources to improve their condition, or even to hold their own in mainstream society. He does so by refusing to question the relentlessly overpowering thrust of a consumer capitalism that eventually subjects all spaces, all relations, all traditions, to its bottom line. Indeed, although he calls for "a vigorous public life," he celebrates "the efficiencies of markets."[26] He accepts oppression, although being sympathetic to feminist issues, by not touching the ways gender formation systematically subordinates women to men. He does so as well by remaining silent about how consumerism shapes collective "needs" for a culture of thrills, quick fixes, and social death.

Dionne passes over the United States' imperial role, which makes it impossible for the rest of the world to determine their own economies according to their own needs. And he approaches U.S. society by using only rarely the words "class" and "inequality," never mentioning "homophobia," "patriarchy," or "capitalism." In short, for all his genuinely good intentions and his realism, his search for a new, moral community, a "politics of the restive middle," Dionne does not take oppression seriously.

Taking Oppression Seriously: Cohen and Arato's
Civil Society and Political Theory

Cohen and Arato see themselves not only as comprehending advanced
societies on a theoretical level, but as doing so from a position of sympathy
with the new social movements and a commitment to "radical democracy."
Their starting point is Habermas' analysis of modernization as the process
whereby differentiated and autonomous subsystems emerge from the disintegration and disenchantment of traditional world views. The economic
subsystem, capitalism, and the political subsystem, the modern state, begin
to become rationalized according to their own autonomous logics (the one
being steered by money, the other by power), and art, science, and morality
equally develop each according to its own logic. Habermas stresses that the
lifeworld within which subjective experience takes place likewise under-
goes a developmental process and begins to be affected by the characteristically modern evolution of communicative rationality. Lifeworld institutions, relationships, and practices increasingly become subjected to
standards of rationality and noncoercive and nonmanipulative consensus
formation. Purposive–rational action, governed by its own internal standards of effectiveness (e.g., the logic of market economies), becomes distinguished from communicative action, based on equality and mutual respect
and oriented toward reaching mutual understanding. While on one level
Habermas thus presents a historical picture of modernity that emphasizes
human and social development leading to increasing differentiation and
rationalization, on the other hand, the lifeworld becomes increasingly
colonized by system imperatives, such as the logics of profit and power. The
rationalization of the lifeworld in the direction of communication rationality, already spotty and uneven, is further menaced "when systemic imperatives force their way into domains of cultural reproduction, social
integration, and socialization."[27]

For Cohen and Arato, Habermas' lifeworld is the terrain of civil
society, which includes families, all manner of informal, voluntary organizations, institutions of culture and communication, and private spaces in
which individual ethical choices and self-development take place. While
Cohen and Arato acknowledge the colonization of the lifeworld, they
stress a contrary but distinct trend not appreciated by Habermas, namely
the rationalization—or modernization—of civil society that takes place
through the action of new social movements. For Habermas it would seem
that such movements are above all *defensive* reactions to the colonization
process. But Cohen and Arato stress that such movements attack, and
transform, premodern forms of social relations such as patriarchy, which
depend on traditional forms of domination, and in their place assert
modern forms of communicative interaction. Habermas' sense of human

progress is thus complemented, and strengthened, by Cohen and Arato's exploration of new social movements as the agency of this progress.

As partisans of Habermas' sophisticated picture of social evolution, Cohen and Arato stress the gains won through the processes of differentiation and rationalization, as well as the need for continuing these processes. On the one hand, the modern economy (capitalism) and the modern state are both most effective when functioning autonomously and according to their own logic; on the other hand, their invasive force must be kept under control. Social movements are vital forces for solidifying and spreading rights, the institutionalization of which expands human powers, dignity, and freedom. Cohen and Arato stress that such movements must be "self-limiting," as are those that are concerned, say, with demanding specific rights for women, homosexuals, and blacks— rather than seeking massive and total change through political power and hegemony. Movements seeking larger change threaten to regress into radical fundamentalisms that look to undo the differentiation that has been the hallmark of modernity. The ultimate in "dedifferentiation," according to Cohen and Arato, was Marxist totalitarianism, Communism, which sought to govern all areas of life politically, from a central location. On the contrary, Cohen and Arato's program of radical democracy involves everywhere building on the achievements of previous generations, accepting complexity and differentiation, extending the reach of modernity's rationalizing processes, while mobilizing against and removing carryovers of traditionalist domination.

They try to retain what they consider to still be valid in radicalism after Marxism and Communism by presenting a coherent theory of modern society that accounts for its problems and possibilities, as well as its achievements. Their analyses take place from a bird's-eye standpoint that is not that of politicians nor of the new social movements, but neither is it passive or detached. Seeking "a common normative project"[28] they are partisans of continued differentiation, plurality, modernization, and of the new social movements insofar as these continue struggling to overcome traditionalist forms of domination and institutionalize new forms of rights.

It is striking, however, that any animus in their text is directed not so much against capitalism or undemocratic rule or even against patriarchy or racism, but rather against the Left—insofar as movement "fundamentalism" projects a kind of totalizing radicalism that refuses to accept limits to what might be brought under collective social control. In contrast, when stressing the "new" of the new social movements, they have in mind "a self-understanding that abandons revolutionary dreams in favor of radical reform that is not necessarily and primarily oriented to the state." This self-understanding involves accepting a "self-limiting radicalism" and developing "projects for the defense and democratization of civil society that accept structural differentiation and acknowledge the integrity of political and economic systems."[29] In this spirit, they advocate the "reflexive continuation of liberal democracy."[30]

Like Dionne, Cohen and Arato's respect for capitalism's economic rationality ignores the irrationalities. Radical and liberal critics alike have traditionally pointed out its notorious wastefulness, for example, or its unequal ways of distributing its material benefits, or the absurdity of collective economic life being motivated by the drive for individual profit. Moreover, they appear largely unmoved about contemporary societies increasingly subordinating their other social goals to economic priorities, about social life becoming dominated by making a living, and making a living by its capitalist form. They say not a word about how the pursuit of profit tends to commodify everything that can be bought and sold, to disempower its citizens, to destroy elemental bonds of citizenship and solidarity, and to deposit its isolated, separated, cynical, inhuman humans in the market place. Indeed, in affirming the marketplace as the primary way of coordinating economic life, they ignore the ways in which, shaped by work whose main meaning is to serve the commodity system, people buy back, in the form of drugs and other escape-oriented commodities, the powers they have surrendered at work, at home, and in the voting booth.[31]

Discussions of power seem strangely missing from Cohen and Arato's effort to theorize contemporary social life, as are discussions of First World economic and political domination over the Third World, as are discussions of class and privilege. For all their effort to strike a balance between the competing claims of "economic rationality and societal solidarity,"[32] it is remarkable that they should neglect even considering whether such terms as power, class, privilege, and domination are still relevant. Indeed, if these are structural concomitants of "economic rationality" as we know it, do they not continually undermine "societal solidarity"? Why is it that the "fundamentalist" Left, Marxism, and Communism provoke their denunciation, but not the dominant forms of oppression? To be sure, they seek to avoid the domination of civil society by both the political and the economic subsystems, and to aim for the primacy of a "well-defended civil society."[33] That is, they seek to limit the "colonizing tendencies of the administrative state and market economy."[34] But beyond this, Cohen and Arato's main agenda for a "radical but self-limiting politics" seems restricted to continuing to modernize the incompletely modern civil societies.

Like Dionne, Cohen and Arato do not take contemporary forms of oppression seriously. Even more than the work of Habermas from which it derives, Civil Society and Political Theory seems remarkably sanguine about where the world is headed. Its point of view, that of preserving, and extending, modern, differentiated societies, with their plurality, complexity, and respect for rights, stems from a place where consumer society is not relentlessly swallowing up the rest of social life, where there is no Third World and no mass poverty, and where patriarchy and racism appear doomed as traditional forms of domination that the new social movements seem bound to sweep away.

Taking oppression seriously mandates adopting the point of view of the oppressed. And this entails the task of highlighting certain relationships of power that normally are evaded, rather than joining the dominant social order in ignoring them. Perhaps this determination to voice the pain of oppression, and to name its sources, helps explain why the world seemed so much more grim a place to someone like Herbert Marcuse than to writers like Cohen and Arato.[35] For all its synthetic power, conceptual sweep, and provocative analyses of major issues, *Civil Society and Political Theory* calls for a counter weight, a book like Marcuse's *One-Dimensional Man*.

Why *Radical* Change?

Much of Marxism's force came from the deep moral sense that it was *right* to end exploitation being absorbed into the historical sense that it was now *possible* to do so. When morality becomes historical possibility it gains a new strength, a new urgency. Radical politics seeks to transform the existing social order, so fundamentally based on oppression, into one based on equality, dignity, social justice, and mutual respect—because material and technical prerequisites exist today for creating a world where the well-being of some no longer depends on the misery of others. This is why taking the point of view of the oppressed leads to demanding radical change.

It may have always been true that every form of oppression was wrong, because of its fundamentally unequal, nonreciprocal, stunting character: the various forms of oppression have always limited or restricted or hurt or deprived some for the benefit of others. But today, when rights are increasingly regarded as universal, when we have created the means for general well-being, poverty and wealth can be no longer justified by any kind of moral, distributional, practical, or historical necessity. Equality would not result in generalized poverty and thus would put an end to "the same old shit" described by Marx and Engels. Whatever may be said about the past, today the civilization of some no longer need depend on the servitude of the many. The effective functioning of a wealthy social order no longer need depend on exploiting its vast majority for the sake of its powerful minority. However genuinely interesting and important may be their concerns, neither Dionne nor Cohen and Arato take such issues seriously.

But they should be taken seriously. Patriarchal and racial capitalism presides over enormous powers for the "pacification of existence" but it continues social life as a war of all against all, thereby exacerbating every form of group intolerance; it maintains the domination of humans by their product, keeping contemporary societies organized around scarcity. There are no longer any material barriers to freedom from want, for all, and no material reason for perpetuating the millennial harshness of existence. But if contemporary industrial societies produce enough to go around, for the first time in human history, their capitalist organization insists that there is never enough. Certainly, a society whose functioning and survival utterly depend on the constant creation of the most frivolous needs, while simultaneously subjecting all human purposes and goals to the grim bottom line of profitability, declares its own historical obsolescence in this very paradox. After all, economic and technical development has obviated the necessity for all social life to be dominated by the economy. But capitalism is the most successful oppressive society that has yet existed; it turns the enormous capacities it generates into new fetters, to the astonishing point of reshaping psychic and physical space according to its own need for profit. Instead of its people rising up against its blatant irrationality, *it* reshapes *them*, so that its irrationality becomes its people.

In this sense, oppression is vicious: wrong in itself, it has the most harmful consequences for both individuals and societies. When justified ideologically, as it always must be, it becomes consolidated and stabilized, creating classes of the better and the worse, whether by biological or cultural (but equally "inborn") traits, or by "achievements." In either case, it diminishes people as it constitutes them, making the results of power appear to stem from the inadequacies of those upon whom it is exercised. In this sense, all social victims are always blamed for their own victimization. Oppression corrupts not only the oppressors, giving them "rights" over the oppressed, and allowing social orders to elaborate endlessly on these rights; it also corrupts the oppressed, by making them into people who internalize their oppression and then seem to deserve it.

Not only capitalism, but patriarchy, neocolonialism, and racism distribute the burdens and the pleasures of life according to logics of domination that designate women, people of color, and Third World societies as less valuable, intelligent, or worthy than those who dominate them. Ending these major forms of oppression would pose, for the first time in history, the possibility of using the capacities that generations of humans have created, and that our own powers and labors continue to create, to liberate *all of us* from toil, poverty, inequality, domination, and subjection to the commodity system and its stupefying and deforming culture. This is materially possible; is it not morally necessary?

Realism and Radicalism

This leads us to another argument for answering radical change: the liberals' and reformists' argument on behalf of realism. Speaking realistically, the kinds of liberal reform supported by Dionne and Cohen and Arato are incapable of removing most of the oppressions that characterize contemporary social life. A structural analysis might show how systemic priorities reproduce and generate each oppression; a description of each oppression might show its tenacity, as well as the force required to dissolve it. But since Dionne and Cohen and Arato pride themselves above all on being realistic, it would be most appropriate to stress that drastic changes in policies, structures, and attitudes follow from taking oppression seriously.

What would it take to end specific oppressions? What transformation of global economic power, or of dominant economic systems, would reverse the South–North transfer of resources and wealth that stems from the existing world economic system? What reallocation of resources and priorities in the Western hemisphere will overcome the heritage of slavery? What cultural and social changes are necessary in the countries once conquered by Europe to end the marginalization of their native peoples? Can consumer society's hold on personal development be broken without attacking the commodity system as such? And, after a generation of the second wave of feminism, what cultural, political, and social changes are still needed to bring women to positions of genuine equality with men? What kinds of structural, attitudinal, and daily-life changes will be required to meet the various ecological crises in the making?

Is it conceivable that any of these changes might be described as being only reforms, to be carried out *within* prevailing priorities, power, and distributions of wealth and entailing only relatively small-scale changes of structures, attitudes, and forms of life? At issue is not only the scale of change, but also the effect it would have on existing social relations, institutions, and values. Pointing in an ecologically viable, nonpatriarchal, nonracist, postconsumer direction would amount to a transformation of social life as we know it.

The main accusation against radicalism today is that a radical solution—an ecological society that does away with the oppressions of class as well as those of gender and race—is a utopia. But it is not utopian to see possibilities of radical change everywhere we turn, from movements expressing gay pride and demanding gay rights to new medical techniques such as laser surgery and new ways of operating on cancer, from new computer technology used in daily life and space travel to hundreds of years of struggles for human rights and the enormous distanced traveled by women and blacks in a single generation. And it is not utopian to insist, in a world filled with the technological wizardry of our own creations out of our control, that our chances for emancipation are not stifled by anything innate in human nature, or inherent in society, or mandated by history—but rather by concrete interests of domination, oppression, exploitation, and privilege, and by the bottom-line rationality of an irrational system.

But let us, after all, be realistic. Such struggles are not about to break out in the unified and massive way that would be required for radical social transformation. And, while such radical change is barely even an idea any more, it is worth noting that within a month of Bill Clinton's inauguration in the United States, Dionne's effort to script a new liberalism had already found its way deep into the new administration's outlook and practice.[36] Thus, even if Dionne were to yield to every point I have just argued, the nagging question would remain: why pursue a radical project when it seems so far-fetched today? Be realistic: a "radical coalition" may arguably correspond to the needs of millions, but this matters little unless they themselves see it that way; unless they see their separate oppressions as linked together; unless they can create a meaningful vision of an alternative to the existing order; and unless they come to see *themselves* as agents of revolutionary change.[37] Justice and morality may argue for radical change, but let us, above all, be realistic.

Nevertheless, as we have already seen when talking about the limits of reform, realism can cut both ways. What characterized Marxism so powerfully, and what any future radicalism can learn from, and improve upon, was its proclaimed commitment to realism. From this point of view, I would stress that the last third of the twentieth century has been demonstrating the utter unrealism of anything but radical solutions. Contemporary social systems like the United States have been characterized by growing and structurally irresolvable difficulties—including problems of racism, of family life and child rearing, of unemployment, of unmet aspirations, of social disintegration. They are systemically unable to cope with any of these. The consequences of avoiding radical change now severely impair both daily life and long-term societal functioning. Similarly, it is utterly unrealistic to imagine perpetuating an increasingly global economic system in which three regions with just over 10% of the population consume most of the world's resources and enjoy most of its wealth, while the vast majority suffer an inequality that shows no signs of abating.

Not all of the destructive and costly consequences of repressing systemic social problems are felt directly—for example, through economic stagnation and racial confrontation. Core social problems also, and increasingly, become displaced onto other terrains and areas. Are not such processes of repression and displacement at work when young Arab Islamic fundamentalists bomb the great symbol of U.S. wealth and power, New York's World Trade Center? What after all is the social logic of such horrible and costly problems as rampant crime, drugs, teenage pregnancy, and mass illiteracy, but the displacement of more basic problems? Speaking realistically, unresolved problems such as the heritage of racism, combined with unresolved problems of economic stagnation, and with systemic paralysis, are likely to continue to deteriorate U.S. society's physical and moral landscape, and the human and financial cost can only continue to sky-rocket. Being realistic, the overall social costs of growing structural unem-ployment, and of growing employment at inadequate pay, will continue to create two tiers of workers, only one of which will have full social citizen-ship.[38] The various social costs of an ever-growing pool of the poor already drain the overall quality of life and quantity of available resources in advanced capitalist societies. Can it possibly be unrealistic to insist on tackling such problems fully and directly—and realistic to play at half measures that fail to bring into question the system that produces them?

Claus Offe focuses on this "enormous capacity for conflict displace-ment"[39] of contemporary societies. Societies can solve concrete conflicts "by imposing the costs of the solution upon external actors or shifting it to new dimensions of privilege and deprivation." He explains, "In this sense, the solution of a wage conflict may result in regional imbalances, or new health hazards at work, or inflation, or cuts in social programs for certain groups, etc."[40] But racial or class oppression do not just disappear into the shadows when they become transmuted into drug or crime problems. Successfully displaced, social oppressions wind up being experienced far from their original source, hidden and misunderstood, leading to thorough-going mystification and social demoralization. When this happens, as with crime, the "remedies" pursued and the people harmed have usually lost all touch with the underlying issue. Disoriented, societies become preoccupied with the displacements and their consequences, as phenomena unto them-selves, no longer able to name their starting point.

Radical politics in this sense depends on being realistic about what those who dominate the society have hidden. It is inseparable from the correct naming of underlying problems, and those who hide them. It is dedicated to unveiling all mystifying displacements—reaching its illumi-nating power into interpersonal relations, illness, disease, or intrapsychic problems. When and as it is created, the future radical movement will lift the scales from many millions of eyes, showing a widening constituency what the problems really were all along.[41]

Realistically speaking, then, what does the future hold if we fail to create a new radical movement and drastically alter the system of social relations and the prevailing civilizational direction? In 1974, Robert Heil-broner, voicing the decline of Western belief in progress, reflected on the threats of runaway population growth, nuclear proliferation, and ecological danger, and concluded that meeting these threats may well depend on drastic civilizational transformations, including increasing authoritarian-ism, economic as well as political centralization, and the curtailing of economic growth while redistributing wealth from North to South.[42] Since then, the curve of worldwide population growth has been brought into greater equilibrium with worldwide food production and nuclear terrorism has not yet happened. However, ecological problems—especially the dangers of toxic wastes and climatic deterioration—have increased. Nothing at all has been done about the North's (especially the United States') overconsumption of resources relative to the rest of the world, and so economic development continues, unabated and uncontrolled.

Within the advanced industrial societies we can anticipate ever-greater social deterioration, manifested in epidemic crime and disease, vast abandoned areas, increased social conflict, governmental paralysis, and even more visible segregation of the haves from the have-nots. As apartheid, the ultimate form of Northern domination over the South, vanishes from South Africa, societies like the United States come to be characterized by more informal and privatized versions, complete with a force of security guards that exceeds the public police force. Within the Third World, we can anticipate increasing urbanization and modernization side by side with increasing breakdown of ever more fragile economies and polities. Although more and more people may leave traditional forms of life whose meaning has been drained away and enter directly and fully into the world economic system, they will find themselves there not as its beneficiaries, but as its hewers of wood and drawers of water. In addition to the ever more visible inequality, growing ecological destruction and scarcities of nonrenewable resources will only intensify the possibilities of conflict between the South and the North. And so, we can anticipate increasing struggles, perhaps repressed and then displaced on to other terrains, perhaps giving rise to new waves of terrorism which, sooner or later, will go nuclear.

In such a world radical analysis, such as diagnoses of the deep origins of social problems in advanced societies, and radical prescriptions for relieving the problems, are arguably far less utopian than proposals for moderate reform that fail to touch basic problems. Thus we may continue to insist, after Marxism, that it is not a pipe dream to imagine, and work toward, radical transformation. It is not arbitrary or historically meaningless to hearken back to radical goals that have surfaced in various twentieth-century struggles against oppression: a classless society, an end of patriarchy, democratic and collective control over economic life, a steady state economy, a nonracial society, North–South equality, an end to neocolonial domination of the Third World, restitution for native peoples. Each of these has come to be demanded by important movements. These are not idle dreams, no matter how far off they now seem. Indeed, believing they are unattainable may create the largest single obstacle to making them real.

And so it is not arbitrary to suggest connecting these various goals within a single, international movement. After all, a global ecological and economic crisis, rooted in the global economic system that now dominates people's daily lives virtually everywhere, may make necessary and possible the kind of global radical vision needed to combat it. Surely, then, this is as worthwhile a goal as creating a new reform politics. Such a radical project would be deeply rooted in a history of insurgencies, and could base itself on a differentiated structural grasp of the contemporary world's most basic problems. Such a perspective, and its movement, would have to have its eyes wide open. It would have to be as scientific as it is possible to be: based on close and careful study; not daring to speak about necessity, but insisting on trends; proposing plausible changes that are based on real historical possibilities.

We must indeed keep our eyes wide open. I am not saying that such a project is already happening, much less suggesting that its success is assured, but merely that it would be based on actual social groups, their identities and interests, and would be responding to societal dynamics and lived experience. And that it makes sense on several levels—as a continuation of emancipatory trends, as a meaningful theoretical possibility, as an unsparing critique of the existing order, as an ethical goal, and as a vision and basis for hope. If we can no longer talk about such a project obeying a dialectic of history unfolding before our eyes—as some of us thought plausible in the 1960s, as Communists have always thought plausible, as Marx thought plausible one hundred years earlier—we do not need to remain silent. We can talk about possibilities and tendencies that can be pointed to, and the real sufferings of real people, which are not taken fully seriously anywhere else on the political spectrum. Thus, with a sense of humility and of our own limitations, but also being moved by a sense of outrage, justice, and solidarity, it is not absurd to insist on working to make this real.

What's in a Name

A new kind of movement, self-consciously coalesced from separate movements, one that has fully absorbed the negative lessons of our century yet that is grounded in a radical vision: these are some of the preliminary defining features of the new radical movement. How then will this new movement be known?

If anything should go without saying, it is that it will not be called "socialist" as its main claim to identity. The reason is not merely the massive revulsion against the negative meanings of Soviet socialism, nor our own cynicism about the "socialism" of parties and governments claiming the name in, say, France, Spain, Italy, and Germany. More deeply, the kind of socialism appropriate to contemporary conditions *has not yet been defined.* Or, to put it more sharply, after a century of socialisms, we do not yet know what socialism means. Beyond welfare-state reforms that leave the system intact, and beyond the nationalization of industry and the party domination of society, its forms, meanings, and purposes can be expected to be undergoing development and clarification for some time to come.

Even in being party to this process, however, and in deeply feeling and being willing to argue that an emancipated humanity will require a classless society, we also know that any new radical movement will not primarily be characterized as socialist for an even more central reason. Not every group belonging to a future radical coalition will see whatever may be regarded as socialism as its overriding priority. If socialism does become the main goal of a significant component of the coalition, its centrality will then have to be argued to other members, especially those whose natural and immediate concerns lie elsewhere. This movement will no longer be dogged by the certainty—and, it must be said, the arrogance—of Marxists assuming that all struggles should be brought under socialist hegemony. Accordingly, it will be more able to negotiate real alliances between possible components and to encourage them to produce and share their own self-understandings, perhaps en route to agreeing on common self-understandings. In the process, lower-case marxists, their status relativized to that of a single component of a larger but always fragile movement, will learn to see themselves as being no longer in possession of the master discourse, but now forced to argue, defend, and negotiate their partial understandings among all the others.

Many radicals have begun to use the term "democracy," or even "radical democracy," to describe their project. Originally meaning rule by the common people, the *dêmos*, democracy historically has meant a commitment to them. As Raymond Williams points out, the term had a genuinely radical meaning until the middle of the nineteenth century, when it evolved into meaning "representative democracy" based on a redefined and more limited sense of "the people."[43] In accepting the identification *social democracy*, Marxists were saying that the bourgeois parties were satisfied with more limited and exclusive representative forms of political democracy, but that the parties of the workers sought economic and social democracy. This was an attempt to retain the thrust of pre-nineteenth-century radicalism, and was a clear expansion and critique of the limits of political democracy. Within its more limited bourgeois usage, democracy expanded into a commitment to building social institutions and human relations that are genuinely universal as well as plural and tolerant; and radicals have become clearer and clearer that a genuine people's democracy must have protections that previous generations of radicals scoffed at as being "bourgeois." As used by radicals today, democracy, then, embraces the old radicalism of "rule by the people," the rights and practices of bourgeois democracy, and the newer radicalism of economic and social rights and power.

To radical democrats today, the term democracy has thus the meaning, the historical roots, and the contemporary reach to mark, contain, and absorb the collapse of Marxism. And it has the advantage of not setting out a single, fixed end, but of expanding with people's aspirations. Which is why many see it as the appropriate rubric for future struggles of the Left: for more public control over economic life, including nationalizations, collectivization, and socialization where necessary and appropriate; for an immanent critique of capitalism demanding greater democratic control over political and economic decisions and structures at all levels, from local to national; for the fullest possible expansion of human rights so that every person is guaranteed adequate housing, health care, a genuine education, and employment; and for social, collective, democratic control over the appropriate collective areas of human life.[44] And since one of the decisive links among all categories of oppression is an undemocratic, wide, and penetrating system of power, a new movement will not merely organize itself as pressure groups seeking to influence those in power. Rather, it will aim at both coming to and transforming power. Thus it will have to develop visions of, and work toward, a society characterized by new forms of collective and democratic control, where power is "taken" by the people in such ways that it winds up being dispersed among them and thereby destroyed by them, beginning to lose the character of power as we know it.

There are, however, problems with using *democratic* as the name of a radical movement. First, there is a danger of conceptual as well as political opportunism in using the most central and fetishized term of mainstream politics to describe the essential character of a movement seeking societal transformation. But isn't this a way of making radical politics more widely acceptable in a nonradical time? Isn't the underlying goal to promote continuity between radical projects and the received political wisdom? After all, "democratic socialism" appeared in the 1980s not only in order to assert properly the connection of socialism with democracy, but also to reassure its intended audience by distinguishing its proponents, presumably from "undemocratic socialists." Not that we should avoid such continuity with the mainstream: radical politics will stand or fall on its critique of presumably democratic societies' inability to fulfill their own promises. The point is, however, to avoid bending over backwards either to become acceptable to or different from dominant political institutions. Much of the radical talk about democracy admits to doing the former.

"Democracy" offers a second potential problem: like socialism, democracy is only one of the many goals of the project. Ecological issues and struggles against racism and patriarchy and on behalf of gays and lesbians and native peoples all have clearly democratic dimensions, but they have other dimensions that will resist being brought under this rubric. Antihomosexual ordinances are one example of apparently democratic decisions, as is legislation banning abortions or supporting nuclear power. Clearly any meaningful conception of democracy, as expanded by radicals, will include space for rights. But the potential intellectual tangles suggest that a term used so sweepingly and on all sides may no longer have useful resonances for mass organizing.

As Samuel Bowles and Herbert Gintis show,[45] employing the term "democracy" successfully requires a critical redefinition of the dominant discourse: the predominately political meanings of "democracy" have to be first expanded on their own terrain and then joined by new social, economic, and cultural meanings. I am not suggesting that proponents of a new project should avoid spending the time and energy required to lay claim to an identity that then risks constant confusion with all of its received meanings. Rather, even if it holds promise, attaching "democracy" to a new radical movement is a significant, long-term effort of theory and practice, and cannot be assumed in advance.

Of course, it would be helpful to invent or appropriate a name that makes completely clear the unique thrust of the movement. In this vein some intellectuals have been writing about "communitarianism." The problem with this is not so much the specific term as the fact that any attempt at naming seems premature: the thrust of the movement will only emerge as it is created, in practice. Some of the new radicalism's parameters can be anticipated, including commitments to socialism and to democracy, but no one can today foresee how it will conceptualize and verbalize its unique claims to identity. Will it above all demand self-determination or autonomy? Will it stress equality? Will it indeed seek a new radical redefinition of democracy? Will it have a primarily communitarian orientation? Thinking about its possible demands concerning the environment or nuclear disarmament suggests one set of possibilities; thinking about its commitments to women or native peoples suggests others. What will unite them? At early stages, a major goal is to avoid foreclosing possibilities. And this leads us to the one term that suggests the requisite openness and commitment to fundamental change: *radical*.

This protean term has a long history, varying much in meaning according to place and time. Its first political use in English, Williams tells us, came in the late eighteenth century. After coming to characterize extreme changes, and begetting "radicalize" and "radicalism" in the early nineteenth century, "The words then have a curious subsequent history."[46] By the second half of the nineteenth century "radical" and "radicalism" became almost as respectable as "liberal" and "liberalism," but also sometimes were meant with their original edge. And then, in the twentieth century, matters became more complicated. First, "radical" became an alternative to the dogmatic implications of "socialism" and the violent implications of "revolutionary." Then, the term came to be applied in describing conservatives of the "radical Right." Subsequently, especially during the 1960s, "radical" recovered its original sense. Williams explains, " 'Radical' seemed to offer a way of avoiding dogmatic and factional associations while reasserting the need for vigorous and fundamental change. At the same time it avoided some of the difficulties in 'revolutionary,' making a necessary distinction between an armed rising and militant opposition to the *political system*."[47] As such, its partisans in the 1960s distinguished "radical" from "reformist" and equally from "moderate." By 1976, however, Williams wrote that its use in these ways was "probably fading," due in part to intrinsic problems of definition, which were presumably not shared, for example, by "socialism." [48]

Of course, this was before the collapse of Communism and before it began to be clear that Marxism was over. Today, the very openness of "radical" may be of use to us in negotiating the current period. Even after the rise and fall of the British Radicals, of Bentham and Mill, of the French Radical Party and the American Radical Republicans—to mention only a few—the uncapitalized term "radical" is still with us, indicating a commitment to far-reaching, still unspecified changes in the social order. In the United States it came to life in the 1930s and again in the 1960s, and today still means root-and-branch opposition and profound transformation, usually on behalf of the system's victims, and seeking changes and using methods that fall outside of the social consensus. Its openness allows a wide space under which the various movements can gather themselves. Until then, and until they work out their own relations (and thus the historically most appropriate terms of self-definition), it is at least a useful provisional name. It is the best we can do—and certainly useful—to speak of the coming radical movement.

Chapter Nine

EMANCIPATING MODERNITY

We are on our own.

First, as we have seen, as a result of losses. Deprived of faith in history and human nature, we know that if there is ever again to be a unified radical project, radicals will have to create even the "we" it begins with.

But if taking possession of our own terrain means registering losses, it also means acknowledging gains. It means assuming what we have and are—by way of ideas and experience, of disillusionment and hope, of unclarity and complexity, of heterogeneous social bases and irreconcilable constituents, of historical achievements and tasks to be completed. This is our terrain. These are our tools. There is no reason to apologize for the only authentic radical identity available to us.

Being on our own is no curse. It is our condition and our strength. There is no reason to avoid positive assertions from within this identity, nor to fear argument on its terrain. If certain things can no longer or cannot yet be said, other things can and indeed should be said forcefully today. Within our situation lie its appropriate virtues: of being open, experimental, and pluralistic, of working at connections rather than assuming them in advance, of seeing the history we suffer and make not only as tendencies and inertia, but also as choice and chance. Having actively assumed and taken responsibility for our situation, we must call for another step: to *embrace* it. This means openly and enthusiastically assuming its key features, including new kinds of radical goals, new forms of political action, and new approaches to theory and practice.

I am talking about wholly and decisively taking steps that have been separating the modern radical project from being fully and finally modern: accepting its contingency, putting its actors in the center, retaining their skeptical and critical edge, and seeing their theories as nothing more than their tools. In doing so we avoid setting up new temples to replace those that have fallen down. We embrace the radical potential and positive meanings of being on our own—our sense of autonomy, our hunger for self-determination, even the giddy sensation of being free.

Toward an Emancipated Modernity

The specific autonomy occasioned by Marxism's end offers an inkling of the exhilarating self-determination promised by modern life. Embracing it as a main feature of the new radical project means accepting postmodern skepticism while rejecting Lyotard's postmodern "incredulity." It means working and struggling toward an emancipated modernity, one that would make it possible for us to preside over, rather than cower before, the objective and subjective forces called up by modern life. It means being willing to use the strengths modernity gives us to quell its oppressions and liberate its possibilities. It means enjoying rather than dreading our freedom to shape ourselves and our surroundings. Any future project of emancipation will seek to calm the maelstrom of modern life while accepting that nothing will ever again be fixed and firm, and will seek to bring modernity's hysterias under control while tolerating its instabilities.

It is striking that not until this late moment of modern history are we finally able to embrace certain key features of the modern condition—its contingency and uncertainties, our skepticism and need for autonomy, its plurality of meanings and voices, the decisive role of subjectivity and the dethroning of theory. Apparently, we had to wait until modernity's catastrophes had stripped us of its premodern and early modern illusions, until Communism and progress were no longer believable, until Marxism was over, in order to see how, in the past, every deicide contained the seeds of a new religion, and how bracing it is to be fully on our own.

Somewhere at the origins and at the core of modernity, suggests Stephen Toulmin, lay its radical skepticism and openness, the acid bath of its rationality, and a democratic freedom from authorities old and new.[1] And yet, as if to betray its own deepest impulse, its commitment to human autonomy, modernity easily fell into its own dogmatism and illusions, its laws and certainties. Now that we are able to stand back from modernity and look at it and question it,[2] we can see how incredibly contradictory it was that a grand narrative of progress should claim to guarantee the victory of human autonomy and self-determination. Imagine the absurdity of a hidden god steering us toward being completely, self-confidently on our own. Freed from comforting but also debilitating illusions of a bittersweet modernity, we can now begin to see not only the terrors but also the riches they concealed. The terrors, often bound up with the illusions, have of course been played out repeatedly in the twentieth century's great disasters. These spring from modern as well as premodern social and psychological layers and relations, and the tensions between them. The riches, paradoxically, are no more than ourselves—and our capacities for conceiving of and living out an emancipated modernity.

Free of the illusions of history and science, of the early modern need to surrender ourselves to (the best of) authorities and (the surest of) frameworks, we are left to confront what postmodernism, but also any genuine modernism, leaves us with: being on our own. The secret of postmodernism is precisely that it removes the last intellectual barriers to the fully modern comprehension that we are on our own. Life-experience becomes disillusioned, and oppressions lose sanction—revealing crisscrossing paths without markers and conflicting choices without guidelines. Moving along these paths, as the century comes to its turn, our appropriate posture is not passivity or cynicism, but a renewed sense of acting on our own, drawing energy from new freedoms, new identities, and new uncertainties. We can gain courage from Marshall Berman's wonderful, troubled words about modernity:

> [It is] a mode of vital experience—experience of space and time, of the self and others, of life's possibilities and perils—that is shared by men and women all over the world today . . . . To be modern is to find ourselves in an environment that promises us adventure, power, joy, growth, transformation of ourselves and the world—and at the same time that threatens to destroy everything we have, everything we know, everything we are.[3]

Berman's unsettling last words demand that we clarify the ambivalence of a modernity that can be both emancipating and catastrophic, liberating and terrifying, energizing and corrosive. This entails beginning by responding to the critique of modernity by Max Horkheimer and Theodor Adorno, and to that of Michel Foucault. And it equally entails responding to the overly positive views of modernity developed by Jürgen Habermas, and by Jean Cohen and Andrew Arato. In the process, we must ask what are the vital radical principles to be found in modernity. We need also to determine whether, on the contrary, Perry Anderson is correct to argue that Berman is barking up the wrong tree, because such a notion is "completely lacking in positive content" and its confusions will be abolished by a socialist revolution.[4] Above all, I must answer the skepticism with which many readers will respond to a return to modernity as the curtain descends on this most catastrophic of centuries.

Modernity's Dark Side: *Dialectic of Enlightenment*

Why champion, at this late moment in history, a radicalization of modernity as the solution to what more and more people are seeing as modernity's intractable dilemmas? In *The Dialectics of Disaster* I traced the catastrophes of the Holocaust and Stalinism back to the explosive tension between modernizing and tradition-bound social forces. It now will be said that I am recommending the illness as therapy, that modernity's illusions are being prescribed anew to rescue us from their wreckage.

Modernity, the frame of Western experience over the past two hundred years—and ultimately the frame of world experience—has become a much-vexed theme. One source of contestation has been the history indicated in Chapter 7, the experience of a century of catastrophe. Even within the Marxian tradition, the failure of advanced industrial proletariats to play their assigned role, along with the disastrous fate of the Bolshevik Revolution and the catastrophe of Nazism, led to questioning Marx's optimistic dialectic of modernity. "In the most general sense of progressive thought, the Enlightenment has always aimed at liberating men from fear and establishing their sovereignty. Yet the fully enlightened earth radiates disaster triumphant."[5] As these opening sentences of *Dialectic of Enlightenment* indicate, Horkheimer and Adorno placed Nazism and the destruction it unleashed squarely within the tradition and development of Western reason. As Max Weber had pointed out, the fact that the tradition's instrumental rationality dissolves all particularities before it makes all individuals into equally manipulable and interchangeable integers. In this sense the Enlightenment is the ideology of a capitalism that subjects everything to the rule of increasingly abstract and overwhelming forces.

Most of the text deals with the link between reason and domination—in the *Odyssey*, in the Enlightenment, in de Sade's *Juliette*, in the culture industry. In the process Western reason becomes unreason, reveals its essence as domination. The dominant direction of *negative progress* leaves little ground for supposing an alternative, nonrepressive conception of reason and an emancipated modernity. This sustained meditation on modernity and progress, written in 1944, asks "why mankind, instead of entering into a truly human condition, is sinking into a new kind of barbarism."[6] On the one hand, Horkheimer and Adorno continue to believe that "social freedom is inseparable from enlightened thought"[7]; on the other, they and the world are witnessing "the self-destruction of the Enlightenment." Their starting point is that the conflagration is rooted in both Enlightenment thought and its accompanying social institutions:

> The fallen nature of modern man cannot be separated from social progress. On the one hand the growth of economic productivity furnishes the conditions for a world of greater justice; on the other hand it allows the technical apparatus and the social groups which administer it a disproportionate superiority to the rest of the population. The individual is wholly devalued in relation to the economic powers, which

at the same time press the control of society over nature to hitherto unsuspected heights. Even though the individual disappears before the apparatus which he serves, that apparatus provides for him as never before. In an unjust state of life, the impotence and pliability of the masses grow with the quantitative increase in commodities allowed them.[8]

This remarkable statement encapsulates the vicissitudes of modernity that Horkheimer and Adorno see leading to Nazism. The growth of productivity and social power take place within relations of, and within a logic of, domination, its fruits presided over by a privileged few: "Under existing conditions the gifts of fortune themselves become elements of misfortune."[9] The masses fail to become a social subject with the power to determine themselves or the society: "Today, because of the enthronement of power-groups as that social subject, it produces the international threat of Fascism: progress becomes regression."[10]

Technological progress within class society leads to human regression: this stands alongside the critique of Enlightenment rationality as a second (and less noticed) main theme of *Dialectic of Enlightenment*. A third appears in a series of analyses and aphorisms arguing that the fundamental dialectic of Western civilization leads directly to anti-Semitism. Where economic domination is no longer objectively necessary but is maintained socially, "the Jews are marked out as the absolute object of domination pure and simple."[11] Absolute irrationality, focused as hatred for the Jews, is the response to a social order that simultaneously offers and suppresses the possibility of total liberation.

Although it is manipulated by those in power, Horkheimer and Adorno argue that the roots of anti-Semitism lie in the "dialectical link between enlightenment and domination, and the dual relationship of progress to cruelty and liberation."[12] Dominated in the process of production, swindled out of happiness and blinded about the causes of the swindle, the powerless masses turn against those who seem to enjoy "happiness without power, wages without work, a home without frontiers, religion without myth." They continue, "These characteristics are hated by the rulers because the ruled secretly long to possess them. The rulers are only safe as long as the people they rule turn their longed-for goals into hated forms of evil."[13] The anti-Semites "gather together to celebrate the moment when authority permits what is usually forbidden, and become a collective only in that common purpose."[14]

Of course, this quintessentially modern regression is irrational to its core. In a pathological yet political act of paranoia the masses project onto the Jews their own hatreds and fantasies, "and the mad system becomes the reasonable norm in the world and deviation from it a neurosis."[15] Seeking destruction of the hated object, this social sickness remains rooted in the basic attitudes and practices of Western civilization. It is a "rebellion of repressed nature against domination, directly useful to domination."[16]

Horkheimer and Adorno began in the hope that their critique might free enlightenment "from entanglement in blind domination."[17] Was it merely a residual hope, surviving from their earlier Marxism but of no consequence in their analysis? Toward the end of their discussion of anti-Semitism they return to the thought that the Jewish question might "prove in fact to be the turning point of history."[18] But this is possible only if "the ruled see and control themselves in the face of absolute madness and call a halt to it."[19] Only this revolutionary possibility, nowhere explored in their discussion, would permit a "redemption of the hopes of the past,"[20] an end to domination and privilege, leading to a democratic and equal society. Instead, events unfolded in Germany to reveal not the revolutionary abolition of violence, but its consummation: Auschwitz. Rather than liberating itself from the disease of modernity, humanity had succumbed to it.

What then has become of the dialectic of history, and the efforts of human reason to grasp and realize it? Any hopes that the dialectic is moving toward emancipation are decisively quashed by Adorno's *Negative Dialectics*, published in 1966. Dialectical reason has become severed both from history and the prevalent forms of reason in the West; philosophy has missed the moment of its realization. The Marxian revolution, the attempt to change the world in accordance with reason, misfired. And so, today, "philosophy offers no place from which theory as such might be concretely convicted of the anachronisms it is suspected of, now, as before."[21]

Thus Adorno, mocking Hegel's optimism, concludes that the only world spirit is "permanent catastrophe." "After the catastrophes that have happened, and in view of the catastrophes to come, it would be cynical to say that a plan for a better world is manifested in history and unites it."[22] There is indeed a unity in history, drawing together the various strands and moments: "the unity of the control of nature, progressing to rule over men, and finally to that over men's inner nature. No universal history leads from savagery to humanitarianism, but there is one leading from the slingshot to the megaton bomb."[23]

Modernity's Dark Side: Foucault

Adorno's bitter verdict on modernity is absorbed and extended by the powerful critique of Michel Foucault. Foremost among modernity's illusions, according to Foucault, is that it genuinely promotes autonomy, self-determination, equality, and freedom—or even the capacity to struggle for them. Foucault studies the processes of domination by which modern individuals are constituted, body and soul. His early studies seem to leave little space from which to mount struggles to overcome these oppressions. "Humanity does not gradually progress from combat to combat until it arrives at universal reciprocity, where the rule of law finally replaces warfare; humanity installs each of its violences in a system of rules and thus proceeds from domination to domination."[24] In this view, so reminiscent of Adorno, it is difficult to imagine individuals "liberating" themselves who are shaped by "normalizing" processes of surveillance and control. This is the case for two reasons: there is no single site from which domination emanates, and the very individuals themselves are products of this power.

Thus from Foucault's perspective, the autonomous subject is a meaningless concept. The individual is not a starting point for his analyses, one that we might argue is repressed in the interest of domination and thus on principle is able to rebel in the name of that which has been repressed.[25] Foucault thus reverses a dominant theme of modern thought, namely, the celebration of the individual's growing autonomy, self-determination, freedom, and rights.[26] Rather, he demonstrates the ways in which the individual is produced by power. In *Discipline and Punish* Foucault explores the connection between modern forms of domination and a social order based on new forms of freedom.

> Historically, the process by which the bourgeoisie became in the course of the eighteenth century the politically dominant class was masked by the establishment of an explicit, coded and formally egalitarian juridical framework, made possible by the organization of a parliamentary, representative regime. But the development and generalization of disciplinary mechanisms constituted the other, dark side of these processes. The general juridical form that guaranteed a system of rights that were egalitarian in principle was supported by these tiny, everyday, physical mechanisms, by all those systems of micro-power that are essentially non-egalitarian and asymmetrical that we call the disciplines. And although, in a formal way, the representative regime makes it possible, directly or indirectly, with or without relays, for the will of all to form the fundamental authority of sovereignty, the disciplines provide, at the base, a guarantee of the submission of forces and bodies. The real, corporal disciplines constituted the foundation of the formal, juridical liberties. The contract may have been regarded as the ideal foundation of law and political power; panopticism [Bentham's vision of an ideal system of surveillance] constituted the technique, universally widespread, of coercion. It continued to work in depth on the juridical structures of society, in order to make the effective mechanisms of power function in opposition to the formal framework that it had acquired. The "Enlightenment," which discovered the liberties, also invented the disciplines.[27]

In this paragraph, Foucault uses "form," "formal," and "formally" in similar ways no less than five times, to contrast with the actual and substantive processes of micropower. These processes insure that modern society is neither an actual nor a potential field of emancipation, but rather a strategically designed and controlled terrain. On this terrain, individuals are constituted who are "normalized" by hierarchies, powerlessness, surveillance, and domination.

As we see above, Foucault is quite aware that he is depicting *bourgeois society*. Although he looks it squarely in the face, he does not depict what he sees as a particular social order, dominated by certain ruling groups and their interests, even though he clearly indicates that the techniques he describes are trying to solve the central constitutive problem of bourgeois society: how to reconcile domination with freedom, inequality with equality, submission with popular sovereignty, freedom of labor with wage labor. How can people move about freely, speak out freely, vote, and be equals, in a society based on exploitation, privilege, domination, and oppression? How can an economic system, and a mode of industrial production that *requires their freedom*, transform people used to living according to the rhythms of nature and the seasons and direct forms of oppression into disciplined appendages of the machines they operate?

These questions point us to the ambivalence of bourgeois society, and to the society's perpetual challenge. In a famous passage of *Capital* Marx had addressed the same problem: how do liberty, equality, and self-interest become the worker's subordination to the factory owner?[28] Marx suggests that need, lack of property, and the absence of any alternative will drive the worker to submit freely to capital. Foucault continues this critical thrust, looking more deeply into the individual. Only if specific forms of oppression are introjected, to the point of becoming spontaneous and self-sustaining, can the worker freely submit to his oppression. In the Enlightenment world described by Foucault, a new class regime of political equality and liberty instituted new controls just as its people, increasingly equal in formal terms, were becoming free to come and go as they pleased. Eventually they would even become formally capable of voting for or against their rulers and their social regime. And yet their submission would continue. Foucault grasps many of the processes in which old forms of subjection were replaced by new ones, and became the subjects' very identity.

Going beyond Horkheimer and Adorno: Marcuse

Horkheimer, Adorno, and Foucault reflect the enormous distance traveled during the past two hundred years, as the pendulum has swung from an overwhelmingly optimistic to an overwhelmingly bleak vision of modernity. The paramount tension described by early nineteenth-century thinkers of modernity such as Saint-Simon and Comte was between the newly dawning modern industrial world and the dying epoch that continued to hold it back. Once humanity was released from the obsolete old world and its no longer functional rulers, it would harvest the enormous fruits of new forms of productivity. Thinkers of progress following Saint-Simon and Comte celebrated the modern world's development of science and technology, education, gradual democratization, and productivity. They foresaw an improvement in human life culminating in general well-being. Since Comte, these visions of progress have often involved hidden or open appeals to natural law, resting on pseudoscience, or to Providence. In the crudest of modern visions, history seems to unfold in a positive direction virtually all by itself, carrying humans along into a promised land of plenty.

As I discussed in Chapter 4, the responsibility for this objectivism lies not only with Comte. Even Marx, the proponent of proletarian revolution, can sound as if he is suggesting that history moves on its own and that social contradictions have a life of their own.[29] Criticism of such optimism has become one of the hallmarks of postmodernism, inspired by writers such as Horkheimer, Adorno, and Foucault. But their works, in turn, contain and foster their own negative biases. One way of elaborating on this criticism of Horkheimer and Adorno is to follow the road they abandoned. The alternative to their bitter verdict on modernity was developed by Herbert Marcuse, who equally sought to acknowledge the catastrophic character of Western civilization—but in relation to its intertwined potential for liberation.

As we look back over its history, Marcuse argues, reason may well have to be defined "in terms which include slavery, the Inquisition, child labor, concentration camps, gas chambers, and nuclear preparedness."[30] These horrors "may well have been integral parts of that rationality which has governed the recorded history of mankind." But this rationality is thereby false, partial, and demands to be critiqued "by driving Reason itself to recognize the extent to which it is still unreasonable, blind, the victim of unmastered forces."[31]

In other words, the domination of reason discussed by *Dialectic of Enlightenment* must be evaluated by alternate historical possibilities, in keeping with yet another conception of reason—both of which were suggested in sections of *Dialectic of Enlightenment* itself. This, after all, was Marcuse's program.[32] It corresponds to a radically different sense of modernity than the one with which Adorno concluded, an equally explosive one containing positive as well as negative trends. Indeed, its meaning was the conflict between the two.

Progress, according to Marcuse, has become deformed by domination and thus become a force of domination, even while its potentialities for liberation remain alive and continue to gnaw away at their restraints. "Progress becomes quantitative and tends to delay indefinitely the turn from quantity to quality—that is, the emergence of new modes of existence with new forms of reason and freedom."[33] All scientific, technological, and productive progress occurs within prevailing social, political and ideological systems that predetermine, direct, and transform it in system-serving ways and for system-serving reasons. These are, fundamentally, systems of domination: domination of nature, domination of human beings. Reason and science develop within such systems in keeping with their structures and premises of privilege and domination. This is precisely what we have come to know as progress: scientific and technological transformations within social orders that only spread their fruits in ways that serve the dominant interests. The paradox of modernity is that its technological progress and economic progress are used to avoid the human progress that the Enlightenment promised. Modernity's explosiveness is the tension between the two; it generates, and tries to suppress, the social struggles that will transform its direction.

Going beyond Foucault

If seeing beyond the limitations of Horkheimer and Adorno's critique of modernity means stressing and developing one of their less-fashionable themes, Foucault himself reaches beyond his sweepingly negative conclusions, especially in his later works. In spite of their ground-breaking descriptions of modern processes of domination, many of Foucault's earlier studies say little about the resistances that have equally characterized the modern world. In this respect, these studies resemble Marcuse's *One-Dimensional Man*. But, like *One-Dimensional Man*, they became employed in acts of resistance, allowing an understanding of domination that was found nowhere else. Readers who stop with his writings on normalization, caught in the conundrum of where individuals whose identities are constituted by power can locate bases for struggling for emancipation, may not notice Foucault's passionate commitment to resisting the process he describes. As Deborah Cook indicates, Foucault's account of resistance cannot be missed by anyone who reads his numerous interviews, articles, and essays.[34] This concern to contribute to the "insurrection of subjugated knowledges" also appears in his lectures and writings on sexuality.[35]

Steven Best and Douglas Kellner defend Foucault against the charge that he presents individuals as no more than passive objects of power: this viewpoint, they maintain, "fails to observe his emphasis on the contingency and vulnerability of power and the places in his work where he describes actual resistances to it."[36] His later works, especially on sexuality, and the "technologies of the self," reflect his growing theoretical concern with processes of self-creation "as moral subjects of our own actions."[37] As Foucault says in a reevaluation of the Enlightenment toward the end of his life, "What is at stake then is this: How can the growth of capabilities be disconnected from the intensification of power relations?"[38] His own goal ultimately coincides with that of the Enlightenment: "the constitution of ourselves as autonomous subjects."[39]

Nevertheless, as Kellner and Best point out, "the overwhelming emphasis in Foucault's work is on the ways in which individuals are classified, excluded, objectified, individualized, disciplined, and normalized."[40] We get nothing in Foucault resembling the genuinely two-sided explorations into working-class history presented by Edward P. Thompson. In a discussion of the conditioning of English factory workers to the new industrial order, for example, Thompson explored the imposition of a new sense of time, now viewed as the universal rhythm of factory work and as the universal self-discipline of industrial capitalism. Yet elsewhere, Thompson describes even more fulsomely how the English working class, shaped by the transformation to capitalism, in turn *created itself*, shaping its modes of experience, culture, and combat.[41]

Nor is Foucault influenced by Jean-Paul Sartre's equally two-sided explorations into how humans make themselves from what has been made of them. Sartre concludes that even the most conditioned modern individual retains a decisive measure of freedom: "the small movement which makes of a totally conditioned social being someone who does not render back completely what his conditioning has given him."[42] This is, of course, Sartre speaking late in his life, when he had accepted the force of both class and psychological determination and modified his earlier extravagant claims about freedom. As Foucault was writing *Discipline and Punish*, Sartre was writing his biography of Flaubert, which showed how one such deeply conditioned individual, Gustave Flaubert, made himself into the author of *Madame Bovary*. While in *Discipline and Punish* Foucault does discuss illegalities and struggles, he never places them on a plane remotely equal to the conditionings he describes, nor does he seek their logic with the tenacity and force guiding his explorations of normalization. Taking resistance seriously on the theoretical level means exploring the uniquely subjective process in which determinations and conditionings, domination and normalization, become absorbed into, and transcended by, subjective praxis.[43]

Modern movements for emancipation reveal, at the heart of modernity, an intentionality contrary to the one captured by Foucault's descriptions of the web of domination. These movements reveal another major historical praxis besides control, surveillance, and normalization. As the eighteenth and nineteenth century saw a concerted effort to treat and reshape humans as the *objects* of power, so did it also see great uprisings and movements, as well as theories, insisting that they must be *subjects*. As such, they sought to actively determine their own identities and shape the conditions of their existence. This was one of Marxism's major thrusts and—experienced far beyond just the proletariat—has remained one of the great themes of modern life, recurring in all the new social movements.[44] But if these struggles have been amply described, they lack their own

Foucault; neither fundamentally Marxist nor postmodernist in character, they have not yet received the kind of sustained and general exploration of their microprocesses, nor the interpretive attention, that Foucault gave to the praxis of domination.

Foucault himself was aware of this: in speaking of a "historical knowledge of struggles"[45] he calls for "a multiplicity of genealogical researches, a painstaking rediscovery of struggles together with the rude memory of their conflicts."[46] But Foucault insists that this "combined product of an erudite knowledge and a popular knowledge" is premised on *eliminating* the "tyranny of globalizing discourses," while in fact they draw from, and contribute to, processes of theoretical generalization, for example, talking about fundamental human rights. Moreover, Foucault tends to see particular moments of resistance, but to ignore their successes, and the cumulative character of these successes. Reading Foucault gives us no sense of the *emancipatory* side of modernity, including the struggles of its subjects to define themselves.

Certainly the new forms of freedom, autonomy, and self-determination are contradicted and often fatally undermined by the new forms of control and surveillance. Equally certainly, the new institutions of civil society are often no more than formal. In these ways Foucault agrees with, and deepens, Marx's analyses. Seeking to go beyond both, Cohen and Arato argue that "it is precisely the new forms of publicity, association, and rights that will become the key weapons in the hands of collective actors seeking to limit the reach of state and other societal forms of disciplinary power."[47] But Foucault does not explore collective actors, or their successes. As he explores the microprocesses in which new forms of domination are introjected, his interest in describing these becomes so great, and his conclusions about them so sweeping, that even when mentioning, and supporting resistance, he pays no attention to exploring its processes or bases.

If he is celebrated for glimpsing, and describing, the power flow as it constitutes its human subjects, Foucault misses the power flowing in the other direction, *from* those who have been subjected and subordinated. "The system of right," he argues, "the domain of the law, are permanent agents of these relations of domination, these polymorphous techniques of subjugation."[48] But aren't rights and laws also supports for the modern world's polymorphous techniques of *resistance*? Don't they also empower people? Without rights, Cohen and Arato ask, could we conceivably have had workers' movements, socialist movements, women's movements, Civil Rights movements?[49] Indeed, in spite of pervasive forms of organization, discipline, and surveillance, the history of the modern world up to and including the present can also be told in terms of continuing, and expanding, struggles against oppression. These are not simply, as Foucault might suggest, struggles that are coopted or defeated and reintegrated into the system of domination, or that never touch its essential structures; rather, they have yielded substantive and cumulative gains in power, material conditions, autonomy, equality, and dignity.

Modernity at Century's End: Habermas and Cohen and Arato

Much of this argument against Foucault builds on Cohen and Arato's Habermasean and unabashedly modernist *Civil Society and Political Theory*. While Habermas himself does not deny the processes revealed by Foucault, they are one side of the much more complex and many-sided development I sketched in Chapter 8.[50] Habermas faults Marx for not seeing "that capitalist production methods ushered in not only a new apolitical form of class domination, but a new level of system differentiation [that] had enormous evolutionary advantages over the level reached in state-organized societies of pre-bourgeois periods,"[51] and promises to give us modernity in its full complexity.

As we have already seen, Habermas regards the key steps toward the creation of the modern world as stemming from the process of "disenchantment" that took place between the fifteenth and eighteenth centuries: an independent economy was one aspect of the new posttraditional world; realms of social life and experience traditionally bound together and regarded normatively now began to be differentiated and to develop each according to its own autonomous logic. The economy becomes a semi-autonomous system freed from traditional forms of normative regulation and "steered" by the abstract, impersonal medium of money, in the market—and functions alongside the semi-autonomous political system "steered" by power.

These systems thus become uncoupled from the lifeworld of social experience, both private and public, which consists of "action systems keyed to cultural reproduction, social integration, and socialization."[52] Lifeworld processes, including science, morality, and art, are modernized through communicative action, based on mutual respect, discourse, and individual autonomy. The more this happens, "the more interaction contexts come under conditions of rationally motivated mutual understanding, that is, of consensus formation that rests in the end on the authority of the better argument."[53] In the ideal speech situation, which is based on equality and mutual respect between free and rational people, arguments can be questioned for their reasons. Action becomes oriented toward mutual understanding no less than toward achieving a practical result.

The essential problem of modernity is that the powerful social, political, and developmental potentials of this process become blocked: "The rationalization of the lifeworld makes possible the emergence and growth of subsystems whose independent imperatives turn back destructively upon the lifeworld itself."⁵⁴ The lifeworld becomes "colonized" by the other systems—that is, subjected to their logic, pressures, and demands, including "the monetarization and bureaucratization of everyday practices both in the public and private spheres."⁵⁵ This restricts and distorts the development of its intrinsically egalitarian and democratic relationships, which otherwise would increasingly be coordinated communicatively, both among individuals and among cultural and social institutions and practices. Any deformation is not, as late eighteenth-century conservatives argued, due to modernity as such—due, for example, to the abandonment of traditional forms of social integration. Habermas contends instead that such restriction and distortion is the result of a more specific process:

> Neither the secularization of worldviews nor the structural differentiation of society has unavoidable pathological side effects per se. It is not the differentiation and independent development of cultural value spheres that lead to the cultural impoverishment of everyday communicative practice, but an elitist splitting-off of expert cultures from contexts of communicative action in daily life. It is not the uncoupling of media-steered subsystems and of their organizational forms of economic and administrative rationality into areas of action that resist being converted over to the media of money and power because they are specialized in cultural transmission, social integration, and child rearing, and remain dependent on mutual understanding as a mechanism for coordinating action. If we assume, further, that the phenomena of a loss of meaning and freedom do not turn up by chance but are structurally generated, we must try to explain why media-steered subsystems develop *irresistible inner dynamics* that *bring about* both the colonization of the lifeworld and its segmentation from science, morality, and art.⁵⁶

But just as the ghost of Marx seems to rear its head, Habermas, yet one more time, details the insufficiencies of Marxism for explaining the contemporary world, and avoids answering his own question as to the reasons for the development of these *"irresistible inner dynamics."* Nearing the end of Volume II of *The Theory of Communicative Action*, he now reformulates his colonization thesis with uncharacteristic rhetorical force:

> When stripped of their ideological veils, the imperatives of autonomous subsystems make their way into the lifeworld from the outside—like colonial masters coming into a tribal society—and force a process of assimilation upon it. The diffused perspectives of the local culture cannot be sufficiently coordinated to permit the play of the metropolis and the world market to be grasped from the periphery.⁵⁷

The Theory of Communicative Action delimits little space from which those in the periphery can challenge the metropolis. Indeed, radical political activity takes a decidedly second place to the kinds of learning that advance the differentiation process, along with, presumably, the "irresistible inner dynamics" that subject social life to the rationality of economic and political subsystems. The prospect of changing the world to advance, or even restore, freedom and meaning seems utopian as we reach the end of this massive study.

Accordingly, on the very last pages of Volume II, having dispensed with Marxism and the relevance of social class, Habermas briefly reflects both on feminism and the new social movements.

> The struggle against patriarchal oppression and for the redemption of a promise that has long been anchored in the acknowledged universalistic foundations of morality and law gives feminism the impetus of an offensive movement, whereas the other movements aim at stemming formally organized domains of action for the sake of communicatively structured domains, and not at conquering new territory.[58]

In other words, the new social movements are primarily aimed at *defending* the besieged lifeworld, and represent nothing new. And even feminism shares in their limitations, being also a response to systemic encroachments on lifeworld processes.[59] Habermas has sought to absorb but also to go beyond both Marxism and Weber by presenting a multidimensional understanding of modernity. In the simultaneous but increasingly opposed evolution of system rationality *and* communicative rationality, the former remains the more dynamic, and in the ascendancy.

Cohen and Arato disagree. In fact, they focus on processes that Habermas ignores—specifically, both the new social movements that grow up in the lifeworld (civil society) and carry modernity's work forward on the foundation of the rights institutionalized there, and the broad expansion of human rights in the past two centuries.[60] "Fundamental rights," they argue, "must be seen as the *organizing principle* of a modern civil society."[61]

As discussed in Chapter 8, Cohen and Arato stress the "positive potentials of modernity that are worth defending and expanding through a radical but self-limiting politics."[62] The primary goals of this politics are "the democratization of civil society and the defense of its autonomy from economic or administrative colonization."[63] But, contrary to that of Habermas, their emphasis falls on the modernizing role played by social movements in "the detraditionalization and democratization of social relations in civil society."[64] Racial, gender, and colonial domination come under increasing pressure from movements seeking to modernize the social relationships of civil society.

Starting from these analyses, three interdependent lines of modernization can be traced: the creation and expansion of a semi-autonomous economy (capitalism), the expansion of an independent state, and the growth and strengthening of civil society with all its attendant rights (and with its growing attack on traditional forms of domination such as patriarchy). If the expansion of the first two realms, in following their autonomous developmental logics, also diminishes and invades individual and collective experience, the third is *a no less dynamic* feature of modern social development. It issues in modern social movements that struggle against the subsystems and win new rights within civil society, modify the subsystems, and develop new and more equal cultural and social forms.[65]

By focusing primarily on the task of completing modernity within civil society, and on the new social movements as its main agents, Cohen and Arato manage to throw light on what Ernst Bloch called the "nonsynchronous contradictions" of the contemporary world—the tensions between current and obsolescent social relations coexisting in the present. Their main concern is a modernization process in civil society that, as Habermas understood, has been only "selectively" carried out: "Even if the normative development that represents the positive side of modernity is only selectively established in stable institutions, such partial achievements create the space for social movements to renew and reestablish the relevant principles in less selective ways."[66] As this process continues, so does the differentiation that modernity began, leading to further self-determination, mutual respect, and new forms of rights. It "allows democracy and democratization to be defined according to the different logics of these spheres,"[67] and encourages a new awareness of the need for political struggles to be self-limiting in order to protect the gains of prior development and struggles in these spheres. Radical movements seeking total systemic change court the danger of regression insofar as they move toward a fundamentalism that would undo processes of differentiation. It is precisely the differentiation process that must be protected, along with the identities and rights it has created, as the greatest fruit of modernity.

But as I stressed in Chapter 8, Cohen and Arato (as well as Habermas) largely ignore power, privilege, and oppression. They do convincingly convey complex processes of contemporary life—the ongoing creation of modern social, economic, and political relations in the West—including, as their critique of Foucault indicates, the role of social struggles and of rights in the process. But by neglecting powerful oppressions at the heart of modernity, they appear as latter-day Condorcets, trusting modernization too much, supporting on principle the struggles to complete it.[68]

We have seen that Habermas is more nuanced and ambiguous than Cohen and Arato. While he misreads the new social movements as primarily defensive reactions, he focuses on contemporary social problems as being fundamentally problems *of* modernity. His stress is far less on completing the transition than on intrinsically modern tendencies of colonization, and on the relative weakness of lifeworld institutions against system incursions. Still, as I indicated earlier in this chapter, his one-sided effort to go beyond

Marxism omits its essential issues and analyses from his powerful explorations of modernity. And, like Cohen and Arato, Habermas' determination to see modernity primarily in terms of rationalization makes it difficult to appreciate how inherently irrational it has also been.

Emancipating Modernity: Tasks and Complexities

Indeed, what are the fundamental irrationalities of modernity? The analyses of Horkheimer and Adorno and of Foucault brilliantly lay bare, but stress one-sidedly, negative features. Habermas' ambiguities notwithstanding, his and Cohen and Arato's resolutely modernist analyses, in contrast, brilliantly lay bare, but stress one-sidedly, positive trends. Absorbing critically these appraisals of modernity into the radical perspective that informs this book—and integrating them with Marxism's still vital descriptions of capitalism—yields a complex, multilayered task for a future radical movement: that of emancipating modernity. This entails analytical tasks that become political: separating modernity's liberations from its oppressions and then, as far as possible, bringing the latter under control so that the former can flourish. Only in this way might we be able, for the first time in history, to live modernity's emancipations without its terrors and catastrophes.

The goal of emancipating modernity imposes at least four distinct tasks, however intermingled and confused they may be at present: (1) working through the explosive tensions between modernity and traditional forms of life; (2) overcoming the oppressions of modernity imposed on traditional societies; (3) struggling directly against, and becoming emancipated from, uniquely modern forms of oppression; (4) freeing the productive and emancipatory possibilities of modernity from the capitalist system. Only then will it be possible, finally, to confront the characteristic tensions and problems of an emancipated modernity. I explore each of these tasks individually below.

1. The transition from traditional to modern social, political, and economic forms turns out to be protracted and explosive, even within the European and North American societies that are themselves centers of modernity. Trotsky's law of uneven and combined development suggested that a "privilege of historic backwardness" allowed the less developed societies to recapitulate several steps of development at once—giving, for example, one of Europe's most backward societies in the early twentieth century, Russia, its most advanced proletariat.[69] But Trotsky failed to see the potential for catastrophe in the kinds of combined development imposed on virtually every society that industrialized after Britain.

As Ernst Bloch noted, "Not all people exist in the same now."[70] As a result, some of the most explosive conflicts of the twentieth century involve "nonsynchronous contradictions," where social groups under conditions of enormous strain seek to block or undo historical development, or to force the pace of history. These become catastrophic when such groups—the Bolsheviks and the Nazis, for example—achieve power on behalf of goals, urgent to them, that their societies are not or no longer ripe for; thus they are impotent to realize them. Oriented toward the future, as were the Bolsheviks, or the past, as were Hitler's lower middle-class supporters, such groups find themselves in the impossible situation of holding political power while being unable to fulfill the goals that brought them there.[71]

No leaping of historical stages is really possible, as the catastrophic Soviet experience demonstrates; nor is turning back to the past really possible, as the catastrophic Nazi experience demonstrates. When political power, urgently seized, does not translate into the kind of meaningful social hegemony that would enable its holders' project to be carried out, this profoundly irrational situation leads to profoundly irrational policies. Each catastrophe of modernity began when modernity's social institutions were imposed on traditional social groups. The resulting kinds of explosive tensions still permeate the modern world. In ways not discussed by Habermas and Cohen and Arato, modernization continues to push social groups into situations allowing no possibility of an adequate response.[72]

2. Those who defend modernity today tend not to appreciate that outside of the privileged zones in Europe and North America most of the world's people have been dragooned into it as providers of resources, hewers of wood, and drawers of water. Modernity has come to them on the tips of bayonets, on the slave block. It has come to them in the form of geographical uprooting, of the destruction of native cultural and social patterns, of the religions imposed by Christian masters, of second-class citizenship, of townships and shanty-towns. For most of the world's peoples, being objects and not subjects of Western instrumental reason has made their world into a hellish inversion of "advanced" society. The modern calculating spirit has been inseparable from new and vicious forms of racism, which render impossible the equality it also proclaims, and from colonialism and imperialism, which render laughable its promises of material wealth. If modernity proclaims self-determination and new power over the natural and social world, this has meant primarily white, European, and male self-determination and power.

Like Condorcet, Marx saw Europe transforming the rest of the world, using the "cheap prices of its commodities" as well as the "rapid improvement of all instruments of production" and the "immensely facilitated means of communication." He details this invasion: "It compels all nations, on pain of extinction, to adopt the bourgeois mode of production; it compels them to introduce what it calls civilization into their midst, i.e., to become bourgeois themselves. In one word, it creates a world after its own image."[73] But Marx did not foresee that the image would be shaped in so distorting a mirror: most of the world became developed *for* capitalist societies and modernized *by* them, in grotesque ways. As objects and not subjects of bourgeois modernization, they became targets of its overseas expansion and sources of its slaves, its raw materials, and its plantations. They developed in partial, inhibited, and deformed ways, not wholly of their own making, not wholly European and bourgeois. Apartheid is only the most bizarre example of this nightmare from which the world has not yet awakened.

But if direct rule by Europeans is only now at an end, domination of the former Third World by the advanced industrial world has never been more thorough and entrenched. The kind of modernization that would permit most of the world's people access to the modernity whose praises Marx sang seems as remote as ever: it requires overcoming the inhibiting, one-sided, and oppressive modernization, still shaped by and profitable to the West, in which they remain locked.

3. Those fully launched into modern life, in the privileged zones of the North, are subjected to uniquely modern forms of oppression. Foucault stresses processes of normalization and domination, and Habermas explores the colonization of the lifeworld by the economic and political subsystems. These diagnoses must be continued and completed, to the point of exploring the dynamics and interests driving these oppressions, as well as locating sources of resistance to them. Are patriarchy and racism modern as well, or do they involve no more than old patterns of oppression, reworked and adapted to evolving conditions? While patriarchy may have deep historical roots, contemporary versions, as Linda Nicholson says, demand understanding as the "most recent manifestation of a longer story."[74] New forms of economic exploitation and the separation of family life—as constituting a private realm—from the public world entailed new, characteristically modern forms of women's oppression. Similarly, it is important to comprehend the modernity of colonial forms of exploitation such as racial slavery, developed in response to unprecedented opportunities and powers.

4. Then, of course, we must not forget Marx. His analysis focuses on a world characterized by modern forms of exploitation, modern processes of production, and modern forms of emancipation. Capitalism rests on and calls into being the new constellation of modern emancipatory practices, habits, energies, and attitudes, just as it rests on and calls into being enormous productive capacities—but its modern forms of privilege and exploitation ensure that they will be diverted from their liberating possibilities. It keeps them under such structural constraints and alienations, Marx argues, that a fundamental relationship of tension exists between the modern economic system and the modern energies and habits and outlooks it calls forth. In the *Communist Manifesto* he details this process in particularly lyrical terms:

> The bourgeoisie cannot exist without constantly revolutionizing the instruments of production, and thereby the relations of production, and

thereby the whole relations of society. . . . Constant revolutionizing of production, uninterrupted disturbance of all social relations, everlasting uncertainty and agitation distinguish the bourgeois epoch from all earlier ones. All fixed, fast-frozen relations, with their train of ancient and venerable prejudices and opinions, are swept away, all new-formed ones become antiquated before they can ossify. All that is solid melts into air, all that is holy is profaned, and man is at last compelled to face, with sober senses, his real conditions of life, and his relations with his kind.[75]

For Marx it is *capitalism* that dissolves, changes, rationalizes, modernizes relentlessly, uprooting everything that stands in the way of profit and yet more profit, turning everything to a commodity, every space that can be made to pay, every wish that can be bought and sold. And, in the process, "it has created more massive and more colossal productive forces than have all preceding generations together."[76] It releases truly staggering human powers: "Subjection of Nature's forces to man, machinery, application of chemistry to industry and agriculture, steam-navigation, railways, electric telegraphs, clearing of whole continents for cultivation, canalization of rivers, whole populations conjured out of the ground—what earlier century had even a presentiment that such productive forces slumbered in the lap of social labor?"[77]

The Marxist project intended to free these forces released by capitalism from their class character and the pursuit of profit by bringing them under the conscious control of collective humanity. This would entail two sharp breaks with capitalism that a new radical project must incorporate: on the one hand, the relentless systemic pressure to constantly expand production, devise new products, and relentlessly turn everything that can pay into profit would be replaced by consciously set priorities amenable to collective democratic control; on the other hand, freed from capitalist-systemic pressures, a wider range of conscious human choice and experimentation would open up, permitting people to pursue self-determined change while maintaining stability. Even after Marxism, to fulfill these modern goals requires abolishing the capitalist class character of modernity—that is, freeing modernity from capitalism.

In sum, an oppressive weight is at the core of modernity as it has come to the world. It compels us as it frees us. It drives us to live by and serve a social order that commodifies everything, even ourselves. Its marketplace, driven by a kind of systemic hysteria—constant creation of new needs, endless "development," ever-expanding invention of new commodities, constant novelty, growing commercialization—colonizes the entire society. And it does so in the interest of profit, privilege, and domination. No free and self-determining people has chosen this modernity, and certainly none guides or controls it. As energizing as our modernity is, it is built on domination, and thus paradoxically contains imbedded within it (and promotes) age-old habits of genuflection and resignation, practices of inequality and brutal exploitation. It equally contains new forms of impotence and stupidity intertwined with amazing power and genius, new forms of impoverishment amidst amazing riches. Thus burdened, it is driven forward inexorably to level or dissolve or master everything that stands in its way. No wonder then, as we know and experience it, modernity is every bit as threatening as it is liberating, every bit as destructive as it is invigorating. No wonder that its blessings and terrors, often experienced in the same lives, are even more often experienced differentially, according to class or race or gender or geography.

If Marxism first provided the critical way of thinking about modernity, we have seen how how important are its understandings, yet how simple and optimistic it now appears. In our experience, emancipating modernity involves a plurality of struggles. There are deep historical connections among our post-Marxist, "post-" or "high" modern situation, the new social movements that have risen to prominence in the past thirty years, the demands they have already made and won, those that are likely to be drawn into the future radical movement, and some of the major contours of future forms of emancipation. One way of describing such struggles is to say that their goal is to remove the terror from modernity while fulfilling its promises.

The Ambivalence of Emancipation

Taken together, these reflections indicate the vast changes it will take to end the nightmare of modernity and realize its promises: the end of capitalism; an overcoming of the structural oppressions that accompany modernity (as well as of the premodern oppressions it inherits); definitively moving beyond the colonial encounter of Europe with the rest of the world; an evening out of modernization processes until different societies' and regions' development trajectories become roughly equal and freely chosen. But the fact remains that a modernity freed from its negative structural features would still bring its liberation as a loss. An emancipated modernity would still be ambivalent. In *Modernity and Self-Identity* Anthony Giddens ignores the tensions and oppressions explored above to present the features of "high modernity" that occur independently of its processes of domination—as if emancipation had already been achieved.[78]

Modern patterns of social life not only destroy the assured, the given, the secure, the structured, but also they fail to replace them. The once-stable self embedded in local institutions and their traditions, freed from its moorings, becomes an endless project of definition. Thus modernity entails the joys and exhilaration of a perpetual contestation of what is handed down, but also the fear and dread of endless change. A social order whose truths and values are no longer guaranteed from on high and by daily routine is initially no longer experienced as an order.

Where experience is increasingly mediated by abstract systems, as for example in air travel, new kinds of trust are needed, and new forms of anxiety become inevitable. Where intimate love relationships are severed from economic and other traditional bases, new "pure" relationships, chosen for their own sake, are constantly beginning, changing, and ending. Where the norms embedded in tradition and authority no longer provide well-traveled paths for action, all action needs to justify itself. Where the possibility of creating, prolonging, or terminating life is a daily occurrence, new and unprecedented issues like assisted suicide become pressing political concerns. In short, modern life intrinsically involves risk, anxiety, and reflexivity.

The hope is that, once free of oppressions, it may be encountered by human beings capable of accepting, and flourishing within, such conditions. Change and novelty would be central features of an emancipated modernity, but their dynamic source could become conscious, free, and centered in human beings, rather than alienated and operating behind their backs. Projects of self-development could be conceived independently of the current corrosive influence of market and media. Instead of being the objects of changes imposed from the outside by an economic system driven by their alienated powers, and thus fated to respond ever more submissively or defensively, humans in control of their social life could experience *themselves* as vital centers and approach their world positively, with greater self-confidence.

Even after modernity is rigorously criticized, even after postmodernism has undermined Enlightenment universals, even after we reject the Marxian project, something remains of their essence, and it is decisive: self-determination as idea, as principle, as value, as need, as right. Exported from Europe with colonialism, the idea of self-determination within a framework of mutual recognition and respect takes hold in traditional societies and contests them to their roots, even while it becomes a weapon for contesting the colonialism it traveled with. It decomposes patriarchy even in patriarchy's most modern forms. Almost inextricably intertwined with the racism and cultural imperialism used to justify Europe's expansion in Africa and the Americas, the peculiarly modern commitment to individual and collective self-determination becomes the watchword of those whom Europe subjugated, as they battle for their emancipation. As their idea, as their right, as the idea and right of us all, it has become a universal need and a fundamental force of local and world history.

A New Paradigm?

Are we ready, then, to develop a new paradigm for radical thought and action? For years, radicals have been calling out for a new synthesis, for an outlook uniting the insights of the last generation into a new analysis capable of issuing a new call to arms. Habermas, starting by self-consciously "reconstructing" historical materialism, has been constructing a new paradigm of communicative action. With greater political focus, Cohen and Arato present their theory of civil society as the new matrix for understanding how modern society has developed and how new social movements have emerged. An alternative, or even complementary perspective might add, say, the work of Offe and Melucci on the new social movements, as well as that of Alain Touraine and Carl Boggs. In moving toward an evolving synthetic theory we might also include Young's discussion of the "five faces of oppression." Were I doing the synthesizing I would stress the modern character of any new radical project, as well as the parameters I presented in Chapter 7. I would also insist that a new paradigm must make room for the key unresolved issues of the old one, and that accordingly capital, labor, class, and imperialism will remain decisive terms as long as capitalism survives.

Beginning with the many materials available to us, there is much to say for moving toward a new paradigm: it will allow a potential movement to have a coherent sense of itself; it will provide for constructing an overall strategy of goals and paths for achieving them; and it will permit a clear litmus test to ascertain which groups and goals belong and which do not. It would seem appropriate, then, to join in dialogue over a new paradigm.

But an essential consequence of the new situation described in Chapter 7 is that it calls for new relationships with theory, and new meanings of theory. These must be explored *before articulating the theory*. We have already seen some of the questions it imposes on us. What is the standpoint of radical theory today? Will we have nothing more cohesive than multiple theories? Is a single coherent theory any longer possible? What conclusions do we draw from the fact that the very act of saying "we" is meant performatively, an act of trying to constitute a new movement? How can we take account of the multiplicity of radicalisms? In a situation in which the insights of each relativize each other, how can we develop a coherent discourse between potential constituents of a radical coalition? How to think about our awareness that radical change takes place on multiple levels, from the most individual to the most global? How to absorb the new sense of autonomy as experience and as goal, while making sense of the larger picture?

Taking all of these tasks and questions into account, don't the analyses of this book suggest that, instead of a new paradigm, we need to work without a paradigm? Certainly it is too early on the one hand to speak with confidence about its contours, or on the other to declare that a new paradigm is forever inconceivable. It is too early to argue that today's required openness should be the permanent disposition of all those who hope for radical change.[79] Nevertheless, these chapters contain an argument about some key features of a new project. As we draw these together and see the picture they form, do they lead us to conclude that the absence of a paradigm is in fact the new paradigm?

I am not sure. I am tempted to assert this boldly, and to marshall my forces in argument. I am tempted to follow with several chapters detailing precisely what such an argument entails, showing how I have been constructing a permanently open outlook throughout this book and revealing how it hangs together. I am tempted to assert this kind of theoretical strength because these chapters contain philosophical points worth arguing for, and because such assertiveness seems to go along with the very notion of radical politics. I am even tempted to look for a better name than "radical" for this project, both as a way of provoking debate about it and of minimizing its ambiguities and inherent tentativeness.

On the other hand, an irrepressible voice says that there is no reason to hurry, says not to be impatient. It will take time to absorb the implications of the astonishing world-historical eclipse of Marxism and to find new points of orientation. We are still in mourning. If some of the needs themselves that Marxism focused and gave voice to are becoming obsolete, then getting our bearings and answering the questions above involves learning to experience the world and ourselves differently. It will take time.

But both arguments are partially true. As we have seen, a new orientation has already been taking shape—expressed in theorizing about postmodernism and the new social movements. The New Left and the new social movements it catalyzed are already a generation old, and their many new intellectual and political currents have spread widely and penetrated deeply. Their new orientation is important and exciting and should be argued for, even if still in its beginnings. Indeed, this book is meant to contribute to the new project's identity.

But this does not mean creating a new radical theory. Rather, I have been sketching losses, parameters, and outlines, arguing that they point to a new kind of project, new radical identities, and a new way of seeing radical theory. In the process of clarifying these, I have been suggesting that for now it is urgent to begin where we already are, embracing being on our own without a coherent theory, a defined agency, or a historical promise—and to ask what this implies. If we need to change the ways we think about political change, we must also reconsider the ways we think about thinking.

The remaining two chapters of this book will attempt just this. They will not try to avoid the tentativeness and openness that an entire generation of radical thinkers and activists cannot surmount. They will not seek to replicate a now traditional kind of grand radical theory. Indeed, if we are on our own, and if this sense of autonomy embraces the end of Marxism, the heritage of modernity, as well as the orientation of a future radical movement, the absence of a paradigm may well turn out to be the new paradigm. But today it is neither necessary nor possible to proclaim being on our own as a new holistic philosophy or as the finished form of the new paradigm. It is necessary, and possible, to explore how a new radical movement, on its own, will construct its relationship to theory.

Theory as Tool, Not as Framework

What will be the role of theory in a new radical movement? Since Marx, a rational, theoretical, totalizing comprehension of the social order and its main tendencies has been the *sine qua non* of any radical political project. Since human struggles unfold within a given society's history and structures, these must be systemically understood. This gives a central role to the project of developing a synthetic overarching comprehension.[80] But if conditions leading to the obsolescence of Marxism call for a different kind of project, they also call for an altogether different approach to theory. The transformations I stressed in Chapter 8 lead also to the transformation of the relationship Marxism envisioned between theory and practice.

It is no longer appropriate to see ourselves *within* a certain history and a certain framework of social structures and dynamics, all to be grasped theoretically. Our lives may unfold within a number of historically produced (and intertwined) sets of relations—of class, of ethnicity, of nationality, of gender, of race, of sexual orientation, of psychology—and we may choose a number of narratives to help us make sense of them. We can no longer see ourselves as dwelling within a single grand narrative—in this sense, we are radically *outside* all frameworks. Once we realize that we are situated in a multiplicity of ways, living with a plurality of historical relations, in order to understand ourselves we are forced to consider ourselves from a number of points of view and move among the relevant frameworks. This fluidity forces us again and again to decide from what angle to consider our situation: is it appropriate to stress social class here, or national history, or issues of gender, or ethnic and religious origins, or, more broadly, questions of our relations with nature, or, more particularly, one's own individual psychology? At any given moment we may choose to place ourselves within a given framework, all the while knowing that no single one gives us the entire picture.

It begs the question to say that all frameworks, taken together, promise a synthetic understanding. Relations will continually shift between component theoretical understandings, some will alternately become more important than others, and someone, somewhere, will always have to adjust the lenses in order to keep the situation at hand in focus. That is to say that once we abandon a theoretical monism, such as Marxism, as indicating to us which relations in the world are *the* decisive relations, then we are faced with the inevitable and unending question of which theory to use when. We have placed ourselves in the position of deciding which framework and which history to insert ourselves within, and when. When do we choose a feminist analysis, when a class analysis, when are we at the intersection of two different kinds of explanation, when do we decide to synthesize them, when do we set out in search of other explanations?

Looking past the frameworks to the active and deciding agent requires us to say, and gives us the freedom to say, that we are no longer in the interior of a single framework and history, but are rather ourselves the sources of interpretations as well as of actions. And once we insist that we choose, and must justify, specific paths for our theoretical self-understanding, we can no longer see ourselves as fundamentally and essentially within the structures highlighted by any particular theory. Theory per se can no longer occupy the role as privileged illuminator of the situation in which we act. Inasmuch as we choose and argue for the relevant frameworks, they become our tools, not our environing and defining reality, and we who choose, justify, and use the tools, like it or not, must replace the primacy of theory with ourselves.

Marcuse's noble conception of theory, giving it the privilege of guiding practice, cannot be ours. Under contemporary conditions, to elevate theory over reality is to diminish the reality, not to clarify and illuminate it. No longer a kind of context or home that gives stable wider meanings or directions, theory is rather the vital tool of actors who seek to understand, clarify, and change their situation. No longer within Marxism, we will not take up residence within any theory. The rise of the New Left has dramatically demonstrated this. Theory simply did not anticipate the Civil Rights and student movements, the women's movement, or the new social movements that followed. Later, theories might be called upon to explain the movements to themselves, each other, and the wider world, but they will serve as analyses and arguments, not as homelike frameworks.

What, then, is the relationship of political actors to the verbal and conceptual structures they use to explain their action? To regard any structure as our home base, today, rather than using such structures as parameters and tools, is to mythologize our fragments of scientific understanding, narrative, argument, wish, and self-justification into something else—into a living social structure that we unproblematically share and within which we collectively function. Of course, we are each and all historical and social beings, and as such live within histories and societies. And as capitalism tends to create a single world economy, we live, increasingly, within its structures and history, affected by its problems and possibilities. But this must be explained and argued for, and used to illuminate the other structures and histories within which we have also taken shape. The day is past when we can speak unproblematically about a single history and a single set of meaningful social structures, as if everyone shares them equally. If these are constantly being redefined and are constantly up for grabs, in stressing the ongoing act of interpretation is it not time to change focus from theory to interpreters? Once we agree that the interpreters must create and intersubjectively agree on their frameworks of interpretation, is it not time to acknowledge in some fundamental sense that radical theory has heretofore missed the fact that we are on our own?

One consequence of this demotion of theory is the promotion of experimentation. First, for an entire generation, political activism has sprung not from theory but directly from people's experience, need, and anger—often in spite of theory and illuminated only later by theoretical analysis. No one knew where the New Left would break out, or when, or why. Indeed, the almost despairing tone of Marcuse's *One-Dimensional Man* reflects the high point, and also the end, of the old kind of theorizing: lacking a subject, critique nevertheless insisted on its validity, but abandoned itself to Walter Benjamin's hope for the sake of those who have no hope. But, as I discussed earlier in this chapter, although Marcuse did not experience it this way, for many of those maturing into it, the enclosed universe he described was an unlivable place. Even if Marxian theory was unable to foresee it, that closed universe would soon generate an opposition needing to resist simply in order to survive. Of course, this strand of the New Left was different from, and responded to different realities than, the Civil Rights and then the black movements. But this only sharpens the point: Marxism could not anticipate the enormous explosion of movements of the past thirty years, and as a result they would emerge outside of its theory, lacking its motivations, creating themselves, and standing on their own.

Another reason for giving priority to experimentation lies in the fact that, even after generations of radicalism and revolution, we simply do not have a clear understanding of what it means to consciously bring about fundamental social change. We know that institutional changes do not necessarily change the habits of those who operate the institutions; we know that attitudinal and behavioral changes can be swallowed up by institutional priorities and leave things much as before. Clearly, the classical "reform versus revolution" debate needs rethinking in light of our understanding of the multiplicity of struggles and sites needing change, and of the effects of specific radical movements like feminism. But just as clearly, a focus on structural change and political power cannot be abandoned without giving up all hope for ending capitalism, racism, and patriarchy.

The point is that a future radical movement will have to see itself as a vast experimental force, trying to effect change, but at the same time trying to understand what change is, and how to bring it about. Theory can be useful here, as everywhere, as guideline and parameter, as a tool of radical understanding and action, but it can no longer decree in advance that, as Marcuse said, "There is only one truth and one practice capable of realizing it." Our situation rather demands us to carry out what Mao called for, but betrayed: "Let a hundred flowers bloom."

Chapter Ten

WE SHOULD BE TALKING
ABOUT RIGHT AND WRONG

No new radical project is possible that is not constructed around a unifying and compelling vision of a different social order. Any new movement, to be effective, will have to provide a convincing account of the major problems caused by the existing order, principal structures to be changed, and groups of people likely to struggle for such changes. It will have to nourish powerful convictions about the kinds of changes being pursued and about its participants' ability to achieve them. It will have to *mobilize* people—by generating wide solidarity, giving people a sense of political and personal direction, and by simultaneously promoting self-confidence and realism. Its members will have to be sustained by a clear understanding of being wronged, deep convictions about being right, an awareness of being strong, a sense of building a new future, an effective understanding of the present, and a sense of hope and of possibility.

In the early modern universe of Marxism these requirements were met, spellbindingly, by a single, powerful, unified outlook. Its appeal was inseparable from the fact that it contained a repressed eschatology, fostered the belief that the new society was being brought about by objective processes, encouraged the anticipation that social revolution was happening with the force of inevitability, and rested these marvelous expectations on a single social group—all with the authority of science. Indeed, two interconnected features run through Marxism's various claims, weave together its many layers: its scientism and the conviction that its scientifically grasped changes were being brought about by objective historical processes. But a radical project arising in the contemporary world no longer needs, and no longer is able, to take shape under the aegis of science. It can no longer claim that a beginning or end of history is at hand. It no longer needs, nor can it appeal to, Marxism's sense of authority. And it can no longer rest on confidence in history's unfolding.

If any new radical project still must meet certain needs, if it still requires sufficient emotional cement to mobilize, coalesce, and inspire masses of people, it will have to do so without such illusions. After Marxism, after progress, after the century's catastrophes, no radical movement is possible without a sense of skepticism, of contingency, of realism about the ebb and flow of movements and people's commitments, of awareness that the desired changes may take hundreds of years.

Yet is a new radical perspective possible without Marxism's dazzling unifying power, and thus without its or similar illusions? Is it really possible both to keep our eyes wide open and form a coalition for radical social transformation? Is it possible to take each dimension of a possible radical project on its own terms, allowing (and testing) scientific claims for areas where such claims are appropriate, while taking prophecy seriously *as* prophecy, treating utopian expectations *as* utopian expectations? Is it possible to allow a movement's moral claims to be made *as* moral claims, rather than as sweeping assertions about what is unfolding in the latest stage of history? Is it possible to regard appeals for individual existential commitment as what they are, and sift through them in the personal and even psychological terms appropriate to them, rather than hiding them behind rigorously objective processes?

If all this is possible, then a movement can be constructed whose members know how varied and plural they themselves are, and on how many quite different levels they are required to function. They will have to know when they are speaking scientifically, when prophetically, when personally, when they are making moral judgments, when they are talking about history, when they are hoping, and when they are engaging in wishful thinking. They will have to find solid grounding from which to launch radical politics, and to know when they are talking about utopia. And they will have to know how important it is to talk about utopia.

In these final two chapters, I will explore two essential bases of any future radical project, its moral and its utopian dimensions, two of the "places" where a new radical project can find strength. I will stress that it is possible to find radical nerve and even confidence—in our histories, in our moralities, in the justice of our struggles, in our hopes. This chapter will argue that, no longer drawing assurance from the unfolding of historical and social processes we inhabit, we can still find strength in acknowledging and exploring the moral basis for radical politics. We should be talking about right and wrong—for the sake of our politics, and for our own sakes.

Morality in the Center?

Why oppose racism, whether in acts, in habits, or in structures? Because it is wrong that a person's position in society, and chances in life, should be in any way tied to the color of his or her skin. Why oppose patterns of patriarchy? Because it is unjust to create and sustain relationships which systematically dominate and diminish people. Why, more topically, favor universal medical care? Because everyone living in a society with the capabilities to provide it has a right to adequate medical care. It is wrong to deprive them of it. Why demand a housing policy that ends homelessness? Because it is wrong for a society to force some of its members to live on the streets, or even in run-down and inadequate housing. People have a right to be adequately housed. Why struggle against capitalism? Because it dominates people, fosters inequalities and privileges and waste; it is an oppressive and exploitative system. As G. A. Cohen says, "property is theft, theft of what morally speaking belongs to all of us in common."[1]

"Right?" "Wrong?" "Unjust?" To our ears these are certainly strange sounding terms to employ in sophisticated societal analysis. After a century and a half of Marxism, after two hundred years of secularization, after generations of turning the acid bath of critical analysis on social institutions, after recent cross-cultural encounters and study as well as generations of science, after so much education and experience accustoming us to other points of view—it now strikes many of us as quaint or intolerable to speak of right and wrong. It strikes many of us as a vain attempt to invoke a vanished cultural apparatus to dignify what are, after all, wholly personal or undeniably culture-bound expressions asserting what *we* feel and value. Furthermore, don't moral judgements open the door to the fundamentalist kinds of intolerance exercised by those who "know" the truth that everyone should follow, and have no hesitation imposing it on them?

Speaking the language of morality is, as many of us have learned during our process of radicalization, speaking ideologically. It is unscientific, idealistic, rhetorical, and, perhaps above all, a mere cloak for self-interest. As Cohen describes it, ideology "is thinking which is not just incorrect but which is systematically deflected from truth because of its conformity to the limited vision and sectional interests of a particular social class."[2] The binding power of its universal claims, concealing particular interests, performs a vital legitimizing service for the dominant social class. Many on the Left have experienced the moment of blinding insight when we peered beneath the apparent universality of moral and legal claims and saw contending forces deploying apparatuses of right, wrong, and justice as part and parcel of their struggle for hegemony. Most recently, women have furthered the process of such demystification by unmasking the patriarchal bias contained in the very words we use, starting with the seemingly most universal and neutral of pronouns: "he." For generations deflating ideological forms of thinking, and showing the interests underlying them, has been an important political task.

This has led the Left to be uncomfortable with moral discourse, preferring instead to think economically, historically, or politically, to use the language of self-interest or, more recently, to insist on the fact that no speaker is universal and all are situated. In the United States, perhaps the last great political figure to base an appeal on morality was a minister: Martin Luther King, Jr. The Civil Rights movement was buried with him; neither the black movement that replaced it, nor the anti-Vietnam War movement, the women's movement, or most of the new social movements to follow, have made morality their dominant chord.

But how can politics, especially radical politics, be separated from morality? In some fundamental sense it is about morality. Movements form out of interest and out of need, but these anchor themselves in a belief in what is just and right. The norms of justice become goals and, as Sartre says, it is in light of the goal that one's sufferings become intolerable. If in Chapters 8 and 9 I described some oppressive features of contemporary societies, my intention was not simply to indicate their dysfunctionality, but also to enumerate their evils. If I searched for the basis of a new radical coalition, every term I used has a moral coloration without which the project would lose its point. Critical social theories and radical politics always move in several directions simultaneously: to identify areas of systemic malfunctioning; to evaluate these with reference to some standard of adequate functioning, based on (explicit or implicit) norms of social morality; to propose systemic changes to bring about more adequate and more just functioning; and to locate the social force able to bring about change. Without being underpinned by a strong sense that the existing society is fundamentally wrong, and can only be set right by radical change, radical politics would be unthinkable.

Marxism's Ambivalence toward Morality

Is radical politics possible without an explicit moral basis? Marxism is the test case, because it has systematically argued against morality as a form of ideology. Yet Marxism has also been based on a postcapitalist humanism, a classless and universal ethics; Marxists have rallied to the vision of a good society. Generations of Marxists became radicalized for a number of reasons, but one of the most important involved taking morality more seriously than those willing to tolerate an unjust social system. Kai Nielson summarizes Marx's moral critique of capitalism as follows:

> Capitalism alienates robs, needlessly exploits, and makes miserable countless human beings in circumstances in which it is no longer necessary for the advancement of culture or science or the sustaining of the material culture necessary for human well-being to maximally flourish. Capitalism generally dehumanizes great masses of people while a few live in positions of privilege and control. The great masses of people have little in the way of possibilities for leisure or (far more importantly) for

control over their own lives. Such a social system with its distinctive division of labor makes a life of commodious, even idle, living possible for the capitalist class and some of its hangers on, while workers are characteristically driven to a stunted and one-sided development.[3]

For Marx and subsequent generations the steps toward radicalization have always included: an awareness that the society violates its own values; a deep commitment to equality, dignity, democracy, and the fullest human rights for everyone, both in the society's own terms and in terms that reach beyond these but seem historically attainable; and a belief that social transformations to create a just society are necessary and possible. Are moral evaluations of capitalism, which Marx obviously frequently made (even in *Capital*), inherent in Marxist theory, or are they the personal utterances of someone who (as Marx said of communism) broke "the staff of morality?" Marxists such as Kai Nielsen, Norman Geras, and G. A. Cohen stress both Marx's ambivalence toward morality and, above all, the centrality of morality to Marxism. In so doing they refute the older argument that the radical mode of understanding and politics developed by Marx *does away* with morality, casting it aside, for example, as irrelevant to the proletarian struggle.[4]

For most of its career, Marxism suppressed its normative foundation. It drew enormous power from the fact that it made its promises in the name of science and history, which did not appear debatable, rather than morality, which did. It called for action, not discussion, to realize the good. And it insisted that the good *was coming about*. In this sense it seemed infinitely more solid than any morality-centered politics. Its basis for action, the deep security it gave people about being right, was certainly underpinned by moral conviction, but *as absorbed into the very movement of history*. Indeed, as I argued in Chapters 2 and 4, the ability to point to real events and processes that were making its project come true is precisely what allowed Marxism to stress objective processes and the importance of understanding them through science. But this positivism depended on a profound Hegelian faith that the world-historical dialectic was bringing about human emancipation—that the good was being realized by history itself.[5]

A fundamental confusion lay within this structure of belief: Marxism drew on, and fed, moral conviction, while being ambivalent at best, and in bad faith at worst, about doing so. As long as morality seemed immanent in history—in the growing size and organization of the working class, in the cycles of capitalism, in the fact of class struggle and possibility of proletarian seizure of power, in the spread of Communism or the growth and power of Social-Democratic welfarism, in the rise of national liberation movements in the colonies, in the upsurge of New Lefts—as long as all this was happening, no separate moral clarification or foundation was necessary. The dialectic was, after all, the historical process itself; powerful ethical commitments and judgments were lodged in or hid behind "history," "the class struggle," and "the proletarian mission." As long as this seemed plausible there was little need for radicals to clarify goals or even means, to face their ambivalence toward morality, or to confront the paradox of an ethical commitment that simultaneously asserted and denied itself. In Cornel West's words they could be "radical historicists" who seek not to articulate moral ideals but to realize them in practice.[6] Whatever reassurance was needed was displaced from the philosophical to the practical plane and supplied by history itself.

But today history can no longer be seen as realizing the good society. The particular societies claiming to embody the dialectic have nearly all collapsed, the proletariat is not leading the way to either its own or a more general emancipation: Marxism is over. After Marxism, the Left no longer can project the realization of good in history. Unable to point to a social class or a movement, there is little reason to claim that radical change is "necessary" or even likely. The old bases for radical conviction have vanished as history and morality have gone their separate ways.[7]

However more tentatively, new bases will have to be constructed, but only if the moral dimension, no longer contained within or hiding behind history, is now made explicit and posed for its own sake. Radical morale, no longer resting on the objective unfolding of events, will depend on a sense of possibility, of achievements, and, perhaps above all, of right and justice. It will depend on morality. A new project will base itself morally on its commitment to declaring oppression wrong, and to ending it. If it will still try to draw heart from goals that are in some sense "necessary," it will no longer find this necessity in the contours of history, but rather in the conviction that its struggles are morally right.[8] Movements for justice may be defeated again and again, their numbers may wax and wane, but they will be strengthened by the deep conviction that their goals "must" succeed because they are right. If Communism was defeated, ultimately, by demoralization, this was rooted both in the awareness that history was against, not with, the project, and that its many corruptions and evils had eviscerated its moral strength. By constituting itself explicitly in terms of right and wrong, and by functioning according to ethical norms built into its self-conception, a contemporary radical project will be nourished by a more stable, if less dramatic, moral core.

The Contemporary Crisis of Morality

If a contemporary radical project *depends on* the renewal of moral thinking and discourse, how ironic that it is driven to this not only against old habits but precisely at the moment when moral thinking and discourse are beset by crisis. The terrain of thought and action about right and wrong is not in good repair, waiting to be rediscovered by a Left in search of new anchoring. Rather, it is contested and half abandoned, shot through with holes, itself needing revival. Not only has any divine sanction for morality long since dried up, but so has any transcendent basis for morality, and, as Alisdair MacIntyre points out, the modernist, Enlightenment search for a *rational* basis has failed. Marxism's most reductive view of morality as ideology is not far from the prevailing "emotivism" that MacIntyre describes in *After Virtue*: "the doctrine that all evaluative judgements and more specifically all moral judgements are *nothing but* expressions of preferences, expressions of attitude or feeling, insofar as they are moral or evaluative in character."[9]

The Left's moral feebleness turns out to be part of a more general modern ailment, which may help explain why the Right, so abstract and hollow in its moralizing, has found its appeals so successful. There seems to be no living language, no network of concepts, available for use today. Talk about right and wrong, MacIntyre points out, operates with "an impoverished moral vocabulary."[10] Because the Enlightenment tradition tried, but failed, to find a rational basis for morality, we are left today with claims for individual autonomy but without the ability to rationally demonstrate, or even seriously to argue about, right and wrong. Rather, our "interminable" contemporary moral debate turns on incommensurable and unprovable claims. We are left with what MacIntyre describes as

> fragments of a conceptual scheme, parts of which now lack those contexts from which their significance derived. We possess indeed simulacra of morality, we continue to use many of the key expressions. But we have—very largely, if not entirely—lost our comprehension, both theoretical and practical, of morality.[11]

We seem to be caught up in a general civilization-wide malaise, an inability to talk about right and wrong in a meaningful way. What are its causes? Certainly in drawing us to look behind moral claims and structures, Marxism, psychoanalysis, and social science in general have all had a powerful corrosive effect on traditional morality. So has the widespread secularization and replacement of traditional forms of authority and community in modern societies by a kind of value-free modern democracy and individuality. So has the existence of economic and political systems that, in Habermas' terms, colonize the rest of social life and *on principle* exist beyond morality. So, increasingly, has the contact among, and growing awareness of, a variety of cultures and their points of view. For MacIntyre what seems at first blush to be primarily a philosophical problem (modern philosophers have failed to find a rational grounding for morality) is really a consequence of the specific features of our modernity, and perhaps above all, the loss of the religious center that governed previous societies.

But MacIntyre's history of ideas, while bewailing modernity's effects, makes scarcely any effort to understand its processes—above all, the relationship of modern ideas to modern social realities. As both Marx and Foucault detailed, seemingly autonomous "modern" moral subjects have simultaneously been shaped as systematically dominated. As the bases for traditional morality have declined, oppressive social orders have systematically deprived their subjects of resources needed to develop new bases for morality as well as moral vocabularies appropriate to free and self-determining people. Autonomy entails, according to Len Doyal and Ian Gough, intellectual capacity, confidence, the ability to act and understand the empirical constraints on action, and the awareness of acting and being responsible.[12] In turn, they argue, achieving these depends on possessing physical health, opportunities for economic activity, and being free from cognitive deprivation and mental disorder.[13] And these presuppose that certain vital needs have been met for food, housing, health care, safe work and physical environments, as well as for security in childhood, significant primary relationships, and physical and economic security.[14] Following from this analysis, the moral infirmity MacIntyre explores can be seen as stemming from modernity's oppressions, which defeat its own promises of autonomy.

Whether it is for these reasons, or for the ones given by MacIntyre, or because of the cultural influence of science, Marxism, and psychoanalysis, or because of a growing multicultural sensitivity, or because modern democracy has made anyone's morality worth no less but no more than anyone else's—or, more likely, for all of these reasons—it is more difficult than ever to speak authentically about right and wrong today. And this at the very post-Marxist moment when we need morality more than ever. If moral bases for politics are more and more necessary, they seem less and less accessible. Today's common question is captured in the title of MacIntyre's sequel to *After Virtue—Whose Justice? Whose Rationality?* If morality varies according to who is speaking, how can we hope to anchor a new radical movement?

The question is, without a transcendent authority or universally binding norms, how do we answer the challenge Thrasymachus hurls at Socrates in Plato's *Republic* when he asserts that justice is the interest of the stronger? How do we avoid the kinds of moral relativism that make it impossible to talk about right and wrong? What sort of moral argumentation is available for a radical project? What are its premises, aims, goals, and structures?

In what follows I will begin with conventional appeals to a given society's own values, which are quite compatible with our contemporary moral embarassment. As Michael Walzer demonstrates in his frankly relativist *Spheres of Justice*, demands for justice lose no strength when we stand firmly within our own society and insist that it remain "faithful to the shared understandings of the members."[15] Societal promises, however, often are intertwined with a given society's possibilities, and exploring this opens the door to more objective and universal kinds of demands. In the West, for example, the Industrial Revolution for the first time makes social orders possible that devote themselves to the well-being of all their members. Introducing history into the argument, I will also argue that social morality advances over time. History sees an expansion, through struggle, of what it means to be a human being. A developing sense of human dignity and possibility and rights, codified in the Universal Declaration of Human Rights, suggests that humans themselves have been collectively and over time producing the kinds of moral anchoring needed by a radical project. Finally, I will suggest that the current stress on difference is a vital step in this historical process.

Moral Bases for Radical Change: Immanent Critique

"Appeals to justice," Iris Young says, "still have the power to awaken a moral imagination and motivate people to look at their society critically, and ask how it can be made more liberating and enabling."[16] The reasons why lie less in the realm of moral philosophy than in that of actual social practice, in which the various relativizing currents described above have not made universalizing appeals to justice any the less important. The moral philosophers MacIntyre discusses, as well as MacIntyre himself, register the profound problems of morality intrinsic to modern societies, but neglect the ways in which new moral resources have been *created* by struggles against oppression. As modern societies have proclaimed their rootedness in human equality and dignity, their subjects and citizens have taken them at their word and demanded that they live up to these values.

In the case of African-Americans, for example, with what moral anchoring have struggles been mounted against slavery, against segregation, for equal rights, for political power, and for equal opportunity? First and foremost the moral attack on slavery, based on appeals to justice, was an *immanent critique*. The society was castigated for its failure to live according to its own professed values. Abolitionists were fueled by the fact that "all men are created equal; they are endowed by their Creator with life, liberty, and the pursuit of happiness." Slavery contradicted the social morality upon which the United States was based and that was meant to be valid for all Americans: slavery denied the fundamental principles with which American democracy justified itself.

Any modern radical movement holds a mirror up to its society that asks, "Does it keep its promises?" As we have seen, modern societies especially depend on a legitimacy drawn from a citizenry that is legally and politically free—the consent of the governed. Insofar as modern societies are based on universal citizenship, each may be interrogated about whether all citizens do in fact have the privileges and powers and freedoms they are supposedly guaranteed to have (and that some of them certainly have). Equality of opportunity, for example, is a fundamental principle of modern society; but equality of opportunity is denied by patriarchal, racist, or capitalist structures and practices. A society promising such rights to everyone is vulnerable to an immanent critique that points out the realities of social class, sexual, racial, and ethnic discrimination, inherited wealth and poverty, and class power. In appealing to the guiding principles according to which the society claims to be organized, such a critique points to discrepancies between promise and practice, emphasizing that the society does not treat people fairly *on its own terms.*

Basing their claims on those promises one hundred years after the end of slavery, African-Americans demanding no more but no less than the rights granted to all others, attacked segregation in the South and other forms of inequality in the North. For several years this demand was galvanizing and mobilizing, drawing support from white radicals and liberals, as well as from the courts and the federal government, because it was based on universally shared premises. But then, after legal segregation ended, civil rights were achieved, and political equality was won, African-Americans largely still found themselves economically and socially unequal to whites, and subsequently ran into strategic and tactical barriers from which they have not yet recovered. Vast numbers of blacks had achieved legal and political rights without corresponding changes in their living conditions. That is, they found themselves both handicapped by the heritage of slavery and race oppression and by the built-in limits to equal opportunity in a society systematically built on racial, class, and gender oppression. Although free and equal in new ways, large numbers of blacks remain mired in poverty and inequality.[17]

Given what Walzer terms the "shared understandings" of political discourse in the United States, it was possible to struggle for equal rights and equal opportunity (including adequate schooling) but *not* to talk seriously about the right to adequate housing or employment. The society's premises and values offered little space from which to mount a campaign for such demands. And so, for many blacks, political equality has been swallowed up by economic inequality—in part because of the difficulty of finding an adequate moral basis from which to maintain blacks are *still* being treated unjustly. After all, the argument goes, a generation after the attack on segregation, no one is keeping blacks from finding better housing or a better job, and they have won the same political and civil rights as anyone else. No one in mainstream politics wants to consider the extent to which these rights will never be enough to end poverty or entail meaningful social equality.

Is it possible to argue that African-Americans, still impoverished, deserve assistance that the society provides to no one else? Or can one argue that all who are poor should have government guarantees of housing, jobs, and decent education—or indeed that everyone has such a right? These demands extend beyond the moral–political consensus of American society, and thus constrain any politics based on demanding that the society keep its promises. Similarly, on what basis can we make a claim not simply that women have a right to equal pay for equal work, but that the entire educational system needs transformation so that it ceases to inculcate the underlying assumption that women should live for men? Many movements sooner or later run into the same wall as the black movement, and are faced with the same concerns. How to move beyond immanent critique, to demand fundamental changes that reach past the prevailing moral consensus? How to justify societal changes that look beyond, far beyond, the promise of equal rights? From within a consensus that so one-sidedly stresses the individual, how to appeal to collectivity and community? On what basis can one claim not just that capitalism systematically tramples its own promise of equal opportunity, but, to renew an old idea, that capital itself is theft?[18]

Moral Bases for Radical Change: Judging Societies by Their Possibilities

Herbert Marcuse sought to formulate a way to go beyond the limitations of immanent critique by judging existing societies not only in terms of their promises, but also in terms of their *possibilities*. Given the social goal of pacifying everyone's existence, Marcuse argued that a given society might be judged in terms of how adequately it deploys its existing level of technical and material resources to do just that.[19] This involves explorations, and arguments, along two axes simultaneously: what does it mean to talk about the resources a society has at its disposal, and how can we justify the far-reaching notion of a social obligation to improve *everyone's* well-being? What does it mean to lay claim to a "society's total resources" for the good of everyone?

The first point turns on the full material network of productive forces, including skills and techniques, that the entire society presides over. Since these inevitably develop and change over time, so do objective possibilities of human development and needs and conceptions of what it means to be fully human. Indeed, what is right and just in social relations, and the needs and demands through which they are expressed, thus develop in intimate interdependency with the other ways in which humans develop over time. Since each society contains definite objective possibilities—mines, farms, factories, transportation and communication networks, schools—for organizing and ameliorating the struggle for survival, and for permitting further human development, each society can be judged according to how well and how fully it makes use of its possibilities. In a sense then, judgments on societies are always historically relative—contingent on a given society's concrete material capacities for creating the best possible life and the fullest possible development for each of its members. And yet, judgments on societies can also be rigorously objective: how adequately does a society make use of these available technical and material capacities for all of its members? Who decides how they are used?

What underlies this judgment of "adequate" use is precisely what movements put forward as the basis of their demands: given contemporary expectations, which always fall within and yet are spurred by contemporary material possibilities, our society does or does not allow us to realize ourselves fully. The extent of any gap between what is materially and technically possible (and what we *know* to be possible) for everyone, and what is socially available, diminishes us as human beings. It is the index of how we are kept from developing as fully as we might. This standard, the fullest possible human development, is the basis of radical critique put forward by one movement after another.

Moral Bases for Radical Change: The History of Freedom

But how do we get to the point of demanding the pacification of existence, the fullest possible development, for *everyone*? After all, although Plato included women among the rulers of the *Republic*, he excluded the overwhelming majority of the population. Aristotle, mirroring Greek practice, thought that civilized life depended on the existence of a group of people permanently denied the status of citizens. How do we move from the first civilized societies' dependency on servile labor and women's subordination to contemporary demands that everyone has the right both to participate in the political process and to pursue a good life?

Hegel, in such bad repute today, presented one of the most appealing visions of history, as the unfolding of reason and universal freedom. Of course he deserves criticism for looking exclusively at Western history, and for looking at it with the most abstracted gaze. Moreover, in his metanarrative reason is the active force, imposing itself on people, working through them and behind their backs: the teleological power of the dialectic drives history forward, terminating in Prussia in the early years of the nineteenth century. Still, for all its faults, Hegel's approach to history has something to tell us. It tells us first that philosophy must be, ultimately, the self-comprehension of the age, and second, that history can be looked at as the development of freedom. The historical experience of people struggling for freedom, lived and remembered, provides our deepest and most powerful bases for radical morality.

I have mentioned how little comprehension of the age there is in MacIntyre's history of ideas. If we have become unable to think morally, he tells us, it is because of modernity. I argued, in response, that we have to think of modernity's specific oppressions—seeing how, for example, by freeing people without giving them the resources to be free, it makes a consistent approach to morality impossible. But, as I also pointed out, MacIntyre limits himself to describing moral–structural problems characteristic of these societies, and ignores the ways in which humans have struggled against prevailing structures, institutions, and practices, on behalf of a richer, fuller, more meaningful freedom. An authentic self-comprehension of our age would capture both the oppressions of modernity (including seeing how most of them are *not* generic problems of modernity) and the great assertions and expansions of social morality that have marked modern struggles for freedom and equality. Hegel's philosophy of history finds a kind of corroboration in the concrete movements for freedom that have so shaped, and characterized, much of modern life. His abstract vision finds its real meaning in the demands of movements. They have sought more and new forms of power, more and new forms of democracy, equal dignity and respect, equal treatment, wealth and security more widely distributed—in short, more freedom.

Hegel's second lesson for us is that freedom has a history, if not a teleology; this history has much to tell us if we are only willing to listen. As I mentioned in Chapters 8 and 9, amidst continuing and even strengthening oppression, major struggles against slavery, colonialism, patriarchy, nondemocratic forms of rule, racism, and homophobia have not only been mounted but have won significant successes. New rights have been created. Indeed, in this period of labor's decline, it is worth stressing that some of capitalism's most outrageous irrationalities have been softened by workers' struggles leading to the creation of rights that still give workers in advanced societies a measure of benefits, protections, and dignity, if not power, unheard of during Marx's time.

What has been the moral basis of such struggles? How does it happen that it *becomes wrong* to discriminate against blacks, to deprive them of political rights, to deny women the vote, to sexually harass women? How does government-provided social security become a right? How does universal medical care become a need? How do homosexuals come to win the right to have their identities and relationships treated as socially legitimate? And why is it that such rights seem to accumulate over time, so that groups that win them tend not to relinquish them, and others tend to be inspired to struggle for *their* rights by the successes they see others have won? Why is it that, like human learnings and technological development, rights tend to be "sticky downward"?[20]

This of course is the terrain of the study I called for in Chapter 9, an "anti-Foucault" that would explore how both identities and social morality

develop—indeed in important respects advance—over time through struggle. It would explore what Samuel Bowles and Herbert Gintis call "the
expansionary logic of personal rights," which along with "the expansionary
logic of capitalist production" are the two key tendencies of modern social
life.[21] Again and again, oppressed human beings refuse to accept their
oppression and change fundamental social relationships. Each such transformation depends on specific groups of humans deciding that a specific
form of oppression has become intolerable. Multitudes of such decisions
take place, preceded by, accompanied by, and causing oppressed and oppressors to regard themselves and each other in new ways. These shifts are
intertwined with other cultural, political, technological, social, and economic changes. Redefining a once-stable relationship of oppression and
contesting it, struggles grow, frequently become violent, are partially lost,
partially won, until new stable relationships are formed. Changes in social
practice are accompanied by, and often consolidated by, changes in law. A
new social morality, once part of the culture of struggle, once only a demand,
before that only a hope or an idea, becomes generalized. A specific form of
oppression now generally comes to be believed to be wrong; it only becomes
illegal because its victims refused to permit it any longer. Having succeeded,
they have now changed the prevailing social morality. Social morality
follows, and consolidates, social struggle.

As those who are oppressed enter into struggle, they insist not only
that they will remove this or that form of oppression or acquire this or that
kind of freedom. They also insist that it is their *right* to do so. They imply
that they are *capable* of achieving and enjoying new forms of freedom, that
they *need* them, and that it is historically *possible* to achieve them. Such
statements of will, right, capacity, need, and historical possibility redefine
what it means to be a human being in general, and what it means for any
specific group to be human beings. They articulate new frameworks of rights
a human being ought to have, including more and more concrete demands
for conceptions of universal rights and universal dignity.

A "Negro" child born toward the end of slavery in the United States
might have given birth to a "colored" child who grew up under segregation,
whose "black" child in turn might have participated in the Civil Rights and
black movements of the 1960s. The stereotypical great-grandchild might
be either the contemporary African-American success—professional or
politician, civil rights leader or athlete—or member of the urban under-
class—incarcerated or dead young male, teen-age single parent or school
dropout. Or, more likely, he or she would be a member of the vast majority,
living unspectacular, hard-working lives. For any of them, a comparison
with their three earlier generations reveals striking changes. Slavery has
long since been abolished. It is no longer politically, legally, or morally
acceptable for whites to treat blacks as less than fully human. However
difficult their lives may still be, and however still beset by racism, the

current generation of African-Americans faces no statutory, and far fewer informal and cultural, restrictions on their right to work, live, be educated, shop, eat in restaurants, move about physically, and travel. Along with all the limits shared by other citizens, African-Americans have political rights and basic civil liberties, and have access to political power. Above all, they no longer live lives whose defining trait is a fundamental and systematic subordination to any and all whites.

Of course, their lives, and U.S. society in general, remain poisoned by unwillingness to act affirmatively to end racism and the heritage of slavery; but just as certainly the half empty cup is half full of painfully won freedom, dignity, and opportunity. Because it is only half full we can too easily ignore how much has changed. Because so much remains to be done it is easy to pass over how much has already been done. Yet despite the rantings of the occasional racist demagogue, the next wave of African-American struggle will start from and presuppose positions already won, no less than the horrible conditions in which so many continue to make their lives.

How do such histories supply the kind of moral anchoring needed by movements for radical change? The answer begins with the continuing redefinition and expansion through struggle of who human beings say they are, what they say they need, are capable of, and have a right to. Above all, when they speak about rights and wrongs, their very presence, their very voice, refutes any justification for denying their freedom and equality. Originally, their oppression depended in part on their own submission to it, and this fact meant that oppressors have always devoted enormous energies to legitimize the relationships of domination and subordination. Hegemony over the oppressed has always entailed some degree of acceptance of the oppressor's definition of them. To say no, to stand up and assert one's freedom and equality, is to destroy the intimate bonds of complicity that are central to any form of domination. To refuse oppressive self-definition is to change the status both of the oppressed *and* the oppressor—who can never again be quite so universal, or whose voice can never be quite so loud. It is to claim the full status of human, formerly monopolized by the oppressor, for oneself. And it is to insist on redefining that status so that, from now on, it encompasses a broader collectivity.

Such redefinitions through struggle have occurred throughout history, but at no time so frequently, and in as many geographic places and social sites, as during the twentieth century. These acts become a profound existential argument on behalf of freedom, justice, and self-determination: the oppressed rise up, the invisible are seen, the voiceless are heard. The voice of the oppressor can no longer be proclaimed as the sole, the legitimate, the normal, the one perspective. Whatever we might argue about ultimate rights and wrongs, oppression becomes historically wrong from the moment when, both in their pain and in their resistance, those who are oppressed testify that it must end. As the struggle against apartheid in South Africa demonstrates, nothing so powerfully refutes the ascription of second-class status to any group of human beings than that group itself standing up, denying this status, and thereby asserting their own humanity. And nothing generates as powerful a sense of morality and, as a consequence, of morale.

Such histories supply moral anchoring to movements for radical change that reach far deeper than criticizing a society in terms of its own promises. At stake is a new definition of proper social relationships, of human beings themselves. But if these constitute an argument, doesn't it seem circular? After all, a given pattern of social relationships becomes wrong insofar as the people subjected to it say it is wrong. Colonialism becomes wrong when its victims resist. Doesn't this imply a kind of moral positivism, leaving relationships to be regarded as morally acceptable as long as they are accepted? And don't percentages or numbers or the idea of a critical mass become relevant here? How many have to articulate a new right or reject a form of oppression to make it wrong? What if it is accepted by a majority even when a significant minority contests it?

Such questions imply that these moral redefinitions by oppressed people in struggle are arbitrary, and that they are reversible. But they are neither. The expanding discourse of rights reflects, and redefines, what has become historically possible, due, among other reasons, to evolving technical and material possibilities, skill levels, and forms of economic organization. Human aspirations develop along with other forms of development, as do human needs and the pain of oppressions (now) felt to be unnecessary.[22] People respond to new conditions and create new possibilities, new rights, against which old oppressions appear intolerable. In this sense, freedom has both a logic and a history. Increasingly humans have struggled for equality, for an end to oppression, and for self-determination; and their struggles, and the self-redefinitions they entail, tend to yield results that are cumulative. While we cannot see where the processes will end, or make them independent of the people who struggle, in retrospect we can see that they form a particular process, whose complex logic moves from place to place and time to time, from rejecting the harshest and most brutal forms of oppression such as being others' property, to rejecting permanent and inherited relationships of dominance and subservience, to demanding equality, self-determination, and a share of the social product adequate to live lives fit for human beings. Included in the most recent stages of these processes are demanding national self- determination, equal political and civil rights, a share of political power, and greater equality in life chances. As Bowles and Gintis describe it, the logic of expanding rights has a next step. "A commitment to the progressive extension of people's capacity to govern their personal lives and social histories," they argue, "requires establishing a democratic social order and eliminating the central institutions of capitalist society."[23]

Shouldn't we be embarrassed to speak, in this fragmented and cynical world, of a *historical logic*? It may be supremely unfashionable to say it, but enough has happened in history that we can point to specific forms of oppression, such as slavery, and the definitions of human power and subservience they entail, as having become flagrant violations of contemporary ethical norms. Enough has happened in history that we can name other forms of oppression, such as colonial rule, as being in the process of ending. Enough has happened that we can describe still other forms of oppression, such as patriarchy and homophobia, as having been placed on the agenda of struggles around the world, and as being in various stages of retreat. Indeed, enough has happened in human history that we can be specific about the recurring, persistent, and growing character of demands for universal citizenship, for social and political relationships of equality and self-determination, protected by civil rights and civil liberties and underpinned by material social guarantees such as housing, education, health care, and employment. And enough has happened that we can project, as a meaningful goal, the extension of these trends to their limit: a world where the major categories and sources of institutional oppression have been abolished.

Universal Rights

Our notions of enfranchisement—what constitutes it, who has a right to it—have broadened considerably over the centuries, resulting in recodifications reflecting the belief that more and more people deserve possibilities formerly enjoyed only by a few, and lowering that few to more ordinary, if still privileged, status. Hegel's schema, however intolerably abstract, becomes (with corrections) confirmed by humans struggling within a world in which some are free, to one where all become considered spiritual equals, to the point where all, increasingly, demand to be free in concrete social and political ways. Whatever radical transformations are still needed to implement this demand, it has increasingly become the prevailing norm. An increasingly shared conception of universal human dignity has evolved over thousands of years of struggle, and is presupposed in much contemporary social life. As such, it becomes a starting point for any radical politics.

The classic recent codification of such shared values is the United Nations Universal Declaration of Human Rights, written in 1948. It begins with a now highly conventional "faith in the dignity and worth of the human person and in the equal rights of men and women," which would have been inconceivable as a basic belief anywhere on earth as recently as, say, three hundred years ago. Often sounding very much like the American Constitution, the Declaration is largely addressed to separate individuals abstracted from history and nationality, says nothing about the importance of collective rights or communities, is silent about colonialism, and affirms the right of property. Yet it reaches considerably beyond the promises made by any particular contemporary nation-state, to call for equal rights for women, equal pay for equal work, the right to work, and the right to an adequate standard of living.[24]

Who is saying what to whom in this universal vision? One way to interpret its words and demands is to treat them for what they are, namely, as the highest of generally acceptable human aspirations articulated by governments in 1948. "Generally acceptable" implies a series of relationships of power, yielding compromise between the various governments forming the United Nations, not only between the capitalist societies and the Soviet Union, but perhaps more significantly, between a handful of recently colonial societies and their former imperial rulers, and no less significantly, between the imperial powers and their client states. The Universal Declaration expresses what *they* could all agree to say about what kinds of human rights could be collectively agreed to. On a deeper level, it reflects a compromise between the governments and their people about what might be regarded as the acceptable horizon of promises allowed to be promulgated in full view of the whole world. As such, the declaration reflects a kind of lowest common denominator, not only of ideas, but perhaps above all of the range of historical possibilities that rulers and ruled, oppressors and oppressed, were willing to avow immediately after World War II, as the norms by which they could agree to have their societies be judged.

The Universal Declaration placed a series of demands on the agenda that have not yet been met, except perhaps in the most advanced Scandinavian social democracies. Its first two thirds articulates the civil and political rights generally contained in democratic constitutions (including the prohibition of slavery and torture, the right to citizenship, property, equal protection under the law, democratic participation in government, and freedom of religion). Its last third also includes a series of economic, social, and cultural rights including work, social security, education, and participation in the cultural life of the community. As C. B. MacPherson points out, the first two categories "go back to the seventeenth and eighteenth centuries; they were the main objectives of the English and French and American revolutions of those centuries. The third category, the economic and social rights, is much more recent: they began to be talked about by some nineteenth-century socialists, but only become respectable during and after the Second World War."[25]

Since then, groups of people have continued to redefine what it means to be human—in thinking, writing, and teaching, in response to new technical, political, and cultural possibilities, and most sharply and dramatically, in political struggles. The process of redefining what "we" need is always a process of redefining who "we" are. Previously excluded and subordinated groups become part of, and expand, a previously narrower discourse. Many who were at first voiceless, especially colonial peoples in Africa and Asia, demanded entry, which explains in part why the Universal Declaration of Human Rights was followed, in 1966, by two International Covenants, on Civil and Political Rights, and on Economic, Social, and Cultural Rights.

Colonial people demanding to be politically free, and then to be seen and heard for themselves, produced some interesting shifts from the original Universal Declaration. The right to property is not mentioned in the Covenant on Economic, Social, and Cultural Rights. Both it and the Covenant on Civil and Political Rights stress that "the ideal of free human beings enjoying freedom from fear and want can only be achieved if conditions are created whereby everyone may enjoy his economic, social, and cultural rights, as well as his civil and political rights." The earlier emphasis on individual rights, moreover, is now corrected by a new stress on national and collective rights. Article I of both Covenants begins as follows:

> 1. All peoples have the right of self-determination. By virtue of that right they freely determine their political status and freely pursue their economic, social and cultural development.
> 2. All peoples may, for their own ends, freely dispose of their natural wealth and resources without prejudice to any obligations arising out of international economic cooperation, based upon the principle of mutual benefit, and international law. In no case may a people be deprived of its own means of substance.[26]

In these changes the West's individualist bourgeois (and even welfare-state) universalism has clearly been offset by a new collective universalism. Whatever the historical, and even logical problems in reconciling these different emphases—Bowles and Gintis correctly stress the clash between property rights and personal rights[27]—they represent a further expansion of rights humans are supposed to have. In war and revolution, economic and technological interaction, a new "we" has constituted itself, consisting of all people and all peoples.

Certainly these are just promises, broken as often as honored. The Universal Declaration and the Convenants still use the pronoun "his." Certainly some of the most brutal social orders and governments have been among the most pious in calling for the honoring of human rights. There is no need, in this argument for a new radical project, to rehearse the hypocrisy and cynicism of the powerful and the privileged, or the outrageous inequality of their world system. "Yet properly interpreted," as Doyal and Gough say, "the international discourse of rights provides a powerful yardstick with which to evaluate the performance of different societies in providing the material and procedural conditions for improving need-satisfaction."[28] And Macpherson notes that "the demand for human rights is itself one of the forces already working to put inequality, and war-oriented governments, and the worship of economic growth, on the defensive."[29]

It is worth stressing, then, that the Universal Declaration and the Covenants reflect something new afoot in the world, and unheard of only a few generations ago: the previously incredible idea that every person in the world has political, economic, civil, and social rights equal to every other person. Every person deserves to be treated with respect by his or her society and its institutions. No person should be treated as an inferior. "All people have the right of self-determination." As Macpherson says, the world is still "short of human rights,"[30] but they will remain intentions, promises, starting points for an ever expanding discourse, moral anchors for new generations in struggle.

Difference

Are we then on the threshold of a more inclusive universalism, one which might eventually embrace the freedom of sexual preference, self-determination for native peoples, a commitment to protect the environment, the superceding of property rights by an expanded and fully democratic notion of human rights, and changing the "his" of the Universal Declaration to "his and her"? Have the new social movements been seeking to broaden the "we" that is humanity to the point where talk of universal rights becomes genuinely inclusive?

Instead, social and political struggles have more and more involved women stressing their difference from men, gay men and women coming out of the closet, natives and minority ethnic and cultural groups asserting their long-subjugated identities with a new pride. This process of identity politics gained theoretical force from Foucault's attack on the "tyranny of globalizing discourses." Under the influence of postmodernism, the very notion of universal human rights has become viewed with skepticism, regarded as the Enlightenment-based outlook of Western, straight white males, habituated to claiming universality for themselves and silencing all others. And, as Anne Phillips puts it, the Enlightenment itself has turned "into a code-word for everything we ought to distrust."[31]

Thus has the new banner of *difference* been unfurled, seeking to delegitimize universalizing pretensions and to argue instead for a fundamentally pluralistic cultural, philosophical, social, and political outlook. This new relativism demands rejection of general discourse and respect for every group's identity and point of view, celebrates diversity, and theorizes about multiculturalism. At first blush it seems to pose a grave threat to the possibility of a unified politics, as I discussed in Chapter 7. As I stressed there, any new radical project will embrace pluralism and diversity, and will develop its universal demands only as a radical coalition of very different groups with very different starting points and agendas.

But even if such a radical coalition could somehow be created, doesn't its heterogeneity deprive it in advance of the kind of moral anchoring I have been exploring in this chapter? Doesn't its multiplicity defeat the project of finding a common radical moral foundation? In stressing *many* goods, no one better than the others, what becomes of the struggle for a common good? In fighting many oppressions, what becomes of a collective vision of liberation? In struggling against many injustices, don't we lose the possibility of uniting to struggle for universal rights or justice? If we feel defensive about saying "we," then how much more defensive will we be about talking about right and wrong? Where can we possibly discover moorings for a new, pluralistic, radical coalition?

If we take the themes of difference and identity politics as they are sometimes presented—as expressing pendular opposition to Enlightenment themes such as universal rights, citizenship, and equality—then we appear to be adrift in a relativism that gives us no clear standards, no sense of justice, no coherent view of right or wrong. But everything changes if, taking these themes fully seriously, we place them in historical context. They are only the latest in a two-hundred-year wave of liberation movements that have been stirred and also frustrated by the abstract universalities enshrined in such bourgeois emancipations as the British, American, and French revolutions. The abstract universalities very consciously left out slaves, workers, women, and colonial peoples, and have had to be challenged again and again—held to their promises and expanded—to be made more socially, economically, and politically inclusive. The wording of the Covenants discussed above are tokens of these struggles, which aim not at the kind of fragmentation and particularism that would generate new wars of all against all, but rather at extending the previous liberations until the universalities are made concrete.

Second, they correspond to a very particular world: the contemporary internationalized societies in which, as never before in history, people of different cultures rub elbows. We now coexist in ways that reveal the relativized status of *every* identity—forcing any particular group to admit that theirs is only one identity among others. At the same time, in this one interdependent world, each identity depends on every other. Mutual respect is at the core of the politics of difference, but it in turn depends on equal universal citizenship and rights. It is only *as equals*, within a universalist framework of equality, that we can call on each other to respect our difference. Indeed, as Charles Taylor points out, the current stress on difference presupposes, builds on, and appeals to the principle of universal equality, as its next stage.[32] This entails a politics that does something other than simply adding identities and demands to identities and demands—the familiar "laundry-list" radical coalition—or than submitting a variety of groups to the particular universality of a single group, be it the proletariat or the impartiality and value-neutral efficiency of the existing bourgeois order. It rather entails a politics reaching toward a new way of connecting people, building a wider collective identity, culture, and tradition based on genuinely including and mutually respecting different identities, cultures, and traditions.

Today, committing ourselves to overcoming any and all forms of institutional oppression and domination entails a fierce commitment to the flourishing of particular freedoms and self-determinations. But this in turn requires something new, not present, for example, in the tolerance of John Stuart Mill's *On Liberty*: a fundamental awareness of the relative nature of our own identities and practices, an appreciation of the equal legitimacy of everyone else's. Freedom entails difference. A contemporary argument for diversity is thus as sweeping as possible, involving only a single caveat, one intolerance: that no identities or practices be permitted that violate the norms of mutual respect and universal emancipation. Everything is tolerated except behaviors that destroy the tolerant community—that is, acts and structures that oppress others.

Connecting Difference and Universality

Diversity is not babel. It implies creating forums for passionate disagreement and, as Iris Young points out, a participatory politics in which people bring their whole selves into debates, rather than submitting to traditional discussion norms of unsituated rationality and impartiality.[33] But they must be welcome to do so, and they must be prepared to do so. Under what conditions is this possible? First, difference has no chance of flourishing without elemental solidarity among people who differ; and, second, retaining any form of oppression creates inequalities that stifle difference. Thus does the argument for difference join the discussions in this and Chapters 8 and 9. Only a new radical coalition, determined to create a new "we," is capable of groping toward a genuinely new social order, based not simply on the old negative ideal of tolerance, but on a new multicultural vision of difference guaranteed by universal rights and common commitments.

Theoretical support for connecting difference and universality is given by Habermas' discourse ethics, which begins from the web of communicative action of daily life: "The reciprocities undergirding the mutual recognition of competent subjects are already built into action oriented toward reaching an understanding, the action in which argumentation is *rooted*."[34] Argumentation, vital for coordinating common action, presupposes mutual respect, the absence of coercion, and freedom of criticism. How are the procedures, norms, and relationships presupposed in reaching agreement, and the discourse ethics derived from them, relevant to a situation in which some differences may never be resolved and in which our greatest achievement may involve creating the common framework and rules within which to freely tolerate diversity? As Cohen and Arato develop the theme, discourse ethics is precisely fitted to clarify the emancipatory goal of a complex, diverse, highly developed modern civil society:

> Individuals act within relationships of mutual recognition in which they acquire and assert their individuality and their freedom intersubjectively. In the dialogue process, every participant articulates his or her views or need-interpretations and takes on ideal roles in a public, practical discussion. This provides the framework in which the understanding of others' need-interpretations is made possible through moral insight and not only through empathy. It is here that the presence of commonalities is tested and respect for difference is potentially affirmed.[35]

This points toward a solidarity that involves what Cohen and Arato call the "ability to identify with the nonidentical." They explain, "In other words it involves the acceptance of the other as an other, as one who must be accorded the same chance to articulate identity needs and arguments as one would like oneself."[36] While different groups and individuals will inevitably disagree sharply over what they consider to be the good life, they will not only understand that some differences will never be transcended, but may extend the mutual respect presupposed in argument to areas of irreducible difference. Learning to live and let live in areas where individual and group values are at stake, they may come to distinguish the common frameworks and norms to which everyone must agree in order for there to be a common life, from the various particular goods that people inevitably pursue.

This involves, according to Seyla Benhabib, a vision of a community of needs and solidarity in which, beyond the liberal community of rights and entitlements (the standpoint of the "generalized other") we can take the point of view described by Carol Gilligan, of the "concrete other." This standpoint

> requires us to view each and every rational being as an individual with a concrete history, identity, and affective-emotional constitution. In assuming this standpoint, we abstract from what constitutes our commonality and seek to understand the distinctiveness of the other. We seek to comprehend the needs of the other, their motivations, what they search for, and what they desire. Our relation to the other is governed by the norm of *complementary reciprocity*: each is entitled to expect and to assume from the other forms of behavior through which the other feels recognized and confirmed as a concrete, individual being with specific needs, talents, and capacities. Our differences in this case complement

rather than exclude one another . . . . The moral categories that
accompany such interactions are those of responsibility, bonding, and
sharing. The corresponding moral feeling are those of love, care, sympathy, and solidarity, and the vision of community is one of needs and
solidarity.[37]

What kind of moral—political cement does this imply? What in this
agreement to live and let live might make people positively willing to
struggle for such a kaleidoscopic new society? The term "solidarity" has been
used, but what bonds of solidarity can be provided by identity politics?[38] Is
this only, as some have reflected, a "procedural republic" with no further
positive content than setting rules for interacting respectfully and effectively?[39] As Richard Rorty rightly asks, what about a world in which our
own point of view is relativized by others can generate a sense of solidarity
so strong that we might risk our lives for it?[40]

At this point we have no more than gropings toward the answer: a
celebration of diversity within a new common framework of mutuality *and*
universality—a multicultural community. Beyond domination and oppression, beyond tolerance, beyond abstract universality and equality—and
concretely, beyond capitalism, racism, and patriarchy—lies the prospect of
a rich and diverse world in which, secure in a stable, universal, and equal
political and economic framework, individuals and groups are free to be and
to act as they wish. A complex world of highly developed humans, freely
determining themselves as well as the common conditions of their mutual
self-determinations—this would be the highest achievement of a liberated
modernity.

One vision of such a society appears in Iris Young's discussion of city
life as a normative ideal. Rejecting the ideal of small, decentralized communities as a premodern dream having nothing to do with the technical,
economic, and human complexity of modern societies, Young reminds us
that "the richness, creativity, diversity, and potential of a society expand
with growth and the scope and means of its media, linking persons across
time and distance."[41] In other words, because diversity, complexity, and
cultural richness are all hallmarks of modern societies, her vision begins by
embracing "the given of modern urban life." City life—"the being-together
of strangers"—offers the prospect of social "differentiation without exclusion," of "variety," and of "publicity." Young stresses "a public in which all
participate, and that public must be open and accessible to all."[42] In an
environment that celebrates difference, freedom is a moral ideal: "Individuals and collectives should not only be able to do what they want, but they
should be able to do it *where* they want, as long as their activity does not
harm other agents or inhibit their ability to develop and exercise their
capacities."[43] The most appealing feature of this vision is its grasp of, and
celebration of, the relationship between modernity and difference: the

variety of diverse relationships and communities freely occupying and sharing the same contemporary social space.

My only quarrel with Young's vision is that she stresses the "politics of difference" to the exclusion of a universal public modeled on the Enlightenment. Although she seems to accept universality as a necessary underpinning of this normative ideal, the ideal never becomes one of solidarity. Undergirding and holding together the rich textures of such a utopia will have to be an infinity of physical, political, economic, and moral linkages: not only buses and sewers and telephones and power lines, but also ways of organizing collective survival and distributing a living to the groups and individuals; not only overarching political and legal institutions and practices, but also shared political, legal, and ethical norms; not only common, if diverse, forms of art and entertainment, but also shared cultural values. Equality and dignity and mutual respect will be among the common values, and so will difference and freedom and individuality. And, if such a society is possible, a new sense of community will be among one of its strongest values.

Community need not be the backward-looking and decentralized, small, face-to-face world that Young dismisses as "utopian"; it might just as well be a complex, modern world of strangers in which people, no longer systemically oppressed, would be capable of freely appreciating their differences and the forms of their commonality.[44] If all polities until now have been marked by oppression, it is no wonder that universal and general social forms have been rightly suspected of reflecting particular interests. But a nonoppressive polity would, for the first time in history, truly and concretely reflect *everyone's* interests. In such a setting, talking about the community would be more than ideology, it would have concrete and precise meaning: our common well-being. And under its umbrella, a multiplicity of smaller, crosscutting communities could form and flourish. Cohen and Arato stress the close, indeed causal, link between difference and solidarity, "because here one can put oneself in the place of the other, grasp what his or her needs and interests are, and discover, constitute, or reaffirm commonalities and a collective identity."[45] Diversity, mutual recognition, collectivity: the people of a fully modern free society will be the first to understand, and appreciate, that each of these terms achieves its full meaning only in intimate connection with the others.

An Adequate Moral Basis?

Do these explorations give us an adequate moral basis for a new radical project? Or do they simply suggest our task? After all, whatever the arguments, they must be argued: we are thrown back on our own resources, to make our case based on a historically relative, struggle-centered sense of universality and mutual respect. The goal of moral argument will be to illuminate, to commend and censure, and to point the way for a new radical project. It will provide a new movement with a self-understanding of its deepest commitments and motivations, which in turn furnishes both a basis for judging the present and mileposts for evaluating its past failures and successes.

This is not to deny the crisis of morality in which we find ourselves, but simply to suggest that we are capable of making moral arguments aimed at negotiating this crisis. A feminist analysis of the current impasse would quite possibly begin by celebrating it, because it may not just lead to new moral ideas, but to new styles of thinking about morality, new ways of connecting the moral and political dimensions, including being open to less abstract and more concrete and caring conceptions of morality.[46] At the same time as we are celebrating our diversity and difference we might also be looking beneath them, to see and celebrate the links of interdependency, and implicit community, that link us all.

If we struggle on behalf of a better social order, and if we work for specific social changes because they are both intrinsically important and may lead to more systematic change, we should begin by trying to articulate the reasons why—*our* reasons why—we think such changes essential, rather than avoiding debate or feeling comfortable only when we can take refuge in a larger historical logic. Our reasons become arguments, based on claims about right and wrong. It is urgent to take them seriously and see where they lead.

In doing so, we should acknowledge that it is still worthwhile to begin by insisting that contemporary societies—class and racist and sexist and imperialist societies—should live up to their own promises and principles. In addition, each society contains certain potentialities for ameliorating the collective human struggle for survival, and may be judged against how well it uses these potentialities. I grant that such a judgment shoots beyond current practices and principles, and uses human and historical possibilities as norms of judgment. If this invokes objective standards and conceptions of human capacities, as well as a certain view of reason and its ability to make such judgments, so be it.

Our arguments will also be premised on a historically evolving sense of human rights and needs. They will praise certain social practices, condemn others, and advocate still others, according to what humans themselves have learned about their equal worth, their specific needs, and their collective power. Beyond evaluating societies according to their own principles and possibilities, we can thus evoke a wider horizon of moral principles—achievements of human identity bequeathed by past social struggles. These increasingly concrete and universal principles embody actual progress in how human beings see themselves and treat each other. This is progress won in struggle and maintained only with concerted vigilance, but representing and demanding new—and better—forms of human social morality.

In our generation, civil rights and African-American struggles and feminist struggles, among others, have *changed* laws, habits, language, and, above all, how people actually treat each other. In our generation, new attitudes, legislation, and conventions toward homosexuality have emerged. All of this is progress in human social morality, as is the recent stress on difference, and a future radical project's stress on a diverse community. Moral debate has been an essential part of this progress: it is important to be willing and able to *argue* about right and wrong. We may no longer believe in transcendent, permanent moral principles, but neither is morality merely relative, a form of ideology, or a reflex of ruling-class self-interest. If each society has its own complex set of historically developed promises and principles, if over time, people in struggle have themselves created new identities and notions of what is just and unjust, these allow us to speak of right and wrong as passionately, and as rationally, as human beings ever have.

Chapter Eleven

SOURCES OF HOPE

As potential participants in the next radical project, how can we avoid being immobilized by despair? Even if we carry with us a firm sense of right and justice, our doubts remain many and deep. They start with the vicissitudes of Marxism, and fan out from there. It gives one more than pause that this once-powerful project, centered on the collective clenched fist of that class capable of bringing the old order to its knees, has been defeated and dispersed. Working-class movements since Marx have been stymied, on the one hand, by an absence of enough force to overthrow the old order, by an unforeseen timidity, a lack of collective will, and a fragmenting of interests; they have been impeded on the other hand by capitalism's strength, tenacity, and resourcefulness, its penetration into the media of communication, culture, education, and even—or especially—into people's psyches and thus their bodily desires. Power has been exercised to create its subjects long before it had to employ brute force; rebellions have been kept from becoming revolutions. We have become too familiar with the weight of resignation and despair, with people's willingness to prefer a bad reality to an unproven and undemonstrated alternative, with their susceptibility to divide-and-conquer strategies, with the absorption into the system's spectacle of those once set against its outrages, and with the inability of oppositional movements to develop strategies and programs of transformation that open the doors of structural change as well as meeting immediate needs.

In spite of their undeniable achievements, other movements not only have fallen short of their goals but have often seen their victories themselves absorbed and deflected. Women are constantly reminded how tenacious is the hold of patriarchy, but also that such equality as they have achieved often comes at the cost of absorption into patriarchal styles, behaviors, and structures; people of color have learned how stubborn racism is, but also how often they must become just like whites to win acceptance; excolonial peoples know how lasting and ever-regenerating are the effects of the original colonizer–colonized relationship, and that no society has escaped the embrace of the North's world economic system. By 1993 the great coming-out party of gay liberation, in Washington, D.C., celebrating new definitions of manhood and womanhood, was led by events to focus on, remarkably, appealing for gays and lesbians to serve in the U. S. military.

If struggles for liberation have persisted and grown, so has the system's absorptive power, especially of the capitalism against which all, at least implicitly, have been struggling. Every outpost relinquished by domination and oppression seems to be replaced by ever more intimate and ever more invisible ones—so much so that talk of ending oppression sounds utopian to our ears. At the same time, life has been worsening for much of the world, in absolute and visible ways. For huge numbers of the world's people, traditional forms of precolonial life have been exchanged for lives of greater poverty, dependency on the mercies of the market, and a position at the bottom rungs of the world economic system. Their lives have neither tradition's satisfactions nor modernity's rewards, and have been squeezed into modern nightmares like shantytowns, townships, or bidonvilles.

We live after Auschwitz and after Communism, and we live after progress—after the hope that great objective processes were either making the world better or leading to the revolution that would liberate the world. The twentieth century's afflictions include genocide and mass destruction amounting to over one hundred million deaths; the corruption and then self-destruction of the century's great hope, Communism; and the loss of faith in progress consequent on ecological and human destruction as well as the waning of the belief in the panaceas of productivity and technology. Accordingly, we face the century's end without a shadow of the blithe confidence shown on all sides at its beginning. Our children's world is not likely to be better than ours, and because of reduced expectations and diminished capacities for conceiving alternatives, they are not even likely to fret about it as clearly as we do.

Given these realities, how can we nurture movements to become broad enough, deep enough, and strong enough, to take on and overturn these evils? Especially when the parameters of any future radical project sketched in Chapters 8, 9, and 10 impose such strict limits on our hopes. Deprived of Marxism's securities, it must turn rather on its subjects' struggle to be genuinely self-determining. Deprived of historical assurance, it will have to find moral assurance. Faced with these limits, what resources of hope will it take to cohere a radical coalition powerful enough to stand against contemporary oppressions?

Any answer only underscores how far we are from even sketching a strategic outlook, a possible revolutionary program, for such a project. Indeed, just creating such a coalition will be a monumental achievement— that is, overcoming the unwillingness of movements to come together and agree that they are opposed to the *same* social order and can best act together, in solidarity. Beyond this, it will be necessary to develop strategies and tactics for a pluralistic project whose members know all too well that, if it comes to this, the system's defenders are willing to use the most violent, brutal force to defend it to the death against its enemies, to lay waste the planet rather than surrender its "civilization."

No wonder a successful revolution happens so rarely, and no wonder revolutions come undone. A coldly analytical eye will tell us this, a passionately revolutionary heart will admit it. If we stop insisting that it must happen and register the obstacles even to joining together, let alone to battling an entrenched social, political, cultural, and psychological system, then we can glimpse how flimsy, even how pathetic, our prospects must seem. Sighting our possibilities with a sober eye aggravates the problem: where can we find and sustain hope?

The Problem of Hope Today

The scarcity of sources of hope results from our collective memory of several events in recent history. After Auschwitz, what can we expect of the human capacity and desire to create a better world? After Communism, why should we believe that movements for social change have a reasonable chance of succeeding? After progress, how can we believe that technological change will make life better? As the twentieth century comes to its close, how can we sustain radical hope without illusion and blind faith on the one side, and disillusionment and cynicism on the other? How can we justify projects based on the belief that the vast majority of people might one day generate the necessary solidarity, make the sacrifices demanded, and wage the struggles required, for a truly humane world to be brought into being?

As I argued in Chapter 7, hope is historical, and depends on circumstances. Strictly speaking, our crisis of hope is a contemporary phenomenon, rooted in catastrophes, disillusionment with progress, and the defeat of Marxism. But just as the possibility of a new radical project depends on our creating a new kind of project, I suggested in Chapter 7 and I repeat here that its hope will be a *new kind of hope*, distinctly different from that of Marxism. Forced to be more limited and more tentative, to sharply distinguish utopia from reality, and to talk honestly and openly about future visions, we may paradoxically construct a more secure hope. We will have to hope for less to happen, and thus will be less dependent on events. We will have to argue more openly about, and be inspired by, goals and ends. Perhaps then we can learn to be more resilient in the face of defeat, and less inclined to disillusionment.

What kind of hope was Marxism's? As I stressed in Chapter 4, Marxism's hope was both modern and premodern, secular and religious, scientific and prophetic. What bound it together, and made its prophecy appear scientific, was not only that it stressed action and objective trends and possibilities, but above all that it was dependent on events. If a modern secularism such as Marxism had ushered faith out the front door, it was in the guise of history's unfolding that it let it in the back: objective historical trends were realizing socialism's eschatological promise.

The problem was that Marxism, in basing itself on the objective unfolding of events, depended on an assurance that reality was unable to provide. Supposedly scientific prophecy was still just prophecy, a vision of wondrous transformations that might or might not happen. And so, for the sake of its hope, Marxism insisted that its subjects were far more ready and able than they ever could have been to end class domination and become the rulers of a classless society. Like its dependency on prophecy, this was a premodern betrayal of Marxism's most modern claims. Indeed, it was never more than possible that the proletariat's struggle might succeed. Marxism's sense of security, rooted in its claims to be scientific and to be standing on the solid ground of history, turned out to be no more than a new faith, a false hope—indeed, to be bad faith. Beneath this faith lay, as always, the contingency and chance of all human projects.

Marxian hope was an amalgam of a number of elements. If it included a suppressed prophetic or utopian vision, it also included a faith that the proletariat, largely because of their place at the center of the emerging industrial society *and* their status as its outsiders, were capable of seizing power and transforming capitalism into a classless society.[1] And so it was dependent on collective action. It was also rooted in confidence in a scientific grasp of capitalism, including an understanding of its tendencies toward crisis and anarchy. If hindsight now tells us that these elements were not really united scientifically, it would be one of hindsight's outrages, an illusion of reason and progress,[2] to take the next step and argue that Marxism should have separated them and considered each according to its own logic, and that it would have been more successful had it done so. Marxism's grand sense of impending transformation, as I pointed out in Chapter 4, depended on not confronting the question of how the proletariat would develop the capacities to overcome millennia of subjection and make itself fit to rule. Doing so would have changed Marxism irreversibly, drastically reducing its expectations. Indeed, from the beginning Marxists would have faced our own problem of hope. We would then not have had Marxism, but something else, because its particular hope depended both on its particular unifying power *and* its blind spots.

Ernst Bloch and *The Principle of Hope*

Serious reflection on hope was in order once Marxism's hope entered into deep crisis, at least as the die became cast in Europe in the early 1920s, after the Kronstadt rebellion in the new Soviet Union and the defeat of the German workers' uprisings.[3] In fact, a number of Marxist thinkers have produced major works within that crisis, including Marxism's major utopian thinkers, Ernst Bloch and Herbert Marcuse. Critically reflecting on Bloch and Marcuse should not only make clear the crisis of Marxian hope; more to the point, it should help us see how an openly and explicitly utopian foundation can take us beyond that crisis by providing access to our deepest hopes. Indeed, both the limitations and the strengths of these great Marxist thinkers guide us toward the kind of educated hope without which a new radical project is impossible.

The crisis of Marxism undermines Bloch's major work, *The Principle of Hope*, a gargantuan three-volume study of well over a half million words. Bloch devoted himself throughout his life to showing that all human longings worthy of the name point toward, indeed, lead to, a socialist society. For over twenty years he spoke not only generally of the dreamed-of classless society, but specifically of the one being created there, in the Soviet Union during the years of Stalin's ascendancy. And he completed his greatest work as the most honored philosopher of its German satellite.

The Principle of Hope seeks to demonstrate how all daily longings and wishes, all of human culture, constitute a single, decipherable, comprehensible *system of hope*. Throughout history (and now ever more urgently because it is now technically possible), this hoping animal, the human being, has imagined and dreamed and foreshadowed and longed for a utopian state of existence. Every behavior, work, and idea he discusses is both (viewed from its starting point) a way of doing something about daily life and (viewed from its goal) a harbinger of utopia. All images of satisfaction, from the humblest to the grandest, flow into a single stream, the meaning of human history. The stream flows toward a better life that becomes historically realizable only in the contemporary world, as technological and social development make utopia possible. Our hopeful desire is revealed at every moment of daily life, and framing all of these expressions of "the working, creating human being"—sometimes consciously, more often not—is utopia: "Once he has grasped himself and established what is his, without expropriation and alienation, in real democracy, there arises in the world something which shines into the childhood of all and in which no one has yet been: homeland."[4]

For all its power, Bloch's magnum opus is marred by its overwhelming, often scarcely comprehensible character, and by his frequent glowing references to the Soviet Union as the place where utopia is being constructed. Much of Volumes II and III is virtually impossible to follow, but the reasons have less to do with the enormous breadth of Bloch's knowledge or his assertive writing style than with the way he presents his claims.

Why, we might ask, did Bloch dump his hope on the reader as *ex cathedra* assertion and encyclopedic tonnage? The answer is suggested in

Jan Bloch's exploration of his father's relationship to Communism. He describes how Bloch went beyond supporting Stalin against Hitler, regarding the Soviet Union as embodying the utopian dream of his philosophy. In so doing, he justified the Moscow Trials, accepted the Hitler–Stalin Pact, ignored the evidence of the bloody purge of his German exile colleagues in Stalin's Russia, had nothing to say about the workers' uprising of June 17, 1953, ignored the various witch hunts under Ulbricht—until he himself was singled out in 1956. Even then, forbidden to teach, Bloch still remained loyal until 1961, when he moved to the West. His son argues that, "just as love makes one blind," so did his father close his eyes to the Communist disaster.

But why was his heart "so much with the new Jerusalem?"[5] I pose this less as a biographical or historical than a philosophical question. As Jack Zipes asks, "Do the expressionist tones and apocalyptic pronouncements in his writings conceal the inadequacy of his philosophical categories to come to terms with the actual political conditions of his times?"[6] Bloch's son also asks whether his acceptance of the Stalin trials expresses the structure of his thought. "How is it possible that the revolutionary-utopian Humanum went along with inhuman despotism, the upright gait with the execution of the upright by the upright?"[7]

The answer begins with the error: Bloch was simply wrong about the Soviet Union. It was not a utopia in the making. The philosophical problem is not that Bloch made a political mistake; along with so many intellectuals of his century—liberals, radicals, conservatives, and fascists alike—Bloch wrongly celebrated a brutal, irrational, exploitative regime as the promised land. Rather, on a philosophical level, the notion that utopia has become *realistic possibility and current project* undergirds *The Principle of Hope*. But what can Bloch's celebrations of possibility mean if, as we now know to be true, utopia was not in sight when he wrote, and indeed is today nowhere in sight? To answer this we must look at what Bloch means by "hoping beyond the day which has become."[8] To hope, most simply put, is to anticipate a better world in the future—the "still unbecome, still unachieved homeland"[9]—and to act to create that world, based on real tendencies in the present.

The concrete meaning of latency, a key to Bloch's theory, is grasped fully only by Marxism, which as "forward-dawning" has a genuine premonition of what is coming up. Marxism makes authentic expectant emotion possible not by abstract theorizing about utopian ideals but by a "solely real realism which only is so because it is fully attuned to the tendency of what is actually real, to the objectively real possibility . . . and to the properties of reality which are themselves utopian, i.e., contain future."[10] Marxism thus contains a warm (eagerly expectant) stream and a cold (reality-based) stream. It grasps, and struggles on behalf of, the Novum, or genuinely new, contained in the Front, or the leading edge of historical movement. Bloch spurns "social-democrati: automatism," which sees a world becoming better all by itself. On the contrary, human action is required, indeed, human will and "militant optimism." But to avoid Jacobinism or putschism depends on scientific analysis of what is possible, knowing that "the real itself has a heavy gait and seldom consists of wings."[11] "The very power and truth of Marxism," Bloch maintains, "consists in the fact that it has driven the cloud in our dreams further forward, but has not extinguished the pillar of fire in those dreams, rather strengthened it with concreteness."[12]

Hope without Reason

As Bloch's son asks, "Does utopia need the eschatological horizon?"[13] Does its force depend on its *coming into being*? Bloch's subjective map of hope everywhere leans on an objective belief that the world is headed "home-ward" and that our subjective longings produce objective results. But does hoping become progressively more active and secular over time, progres-sively less individual and more social? To answer this would require explor-ing the history of hope, but, strange to say, in Bloch's work hope does not seem to have a history. With Marx it becomes real; until then, it was not. What, specifically, is the "forward-dawning" social vision that hope ex-presses? Does that vision itself develop historically? If it does so, then how, and why? What is its interaction with the concrete fruits of human social struggles—for example, the abolition of slavery, the end of colonialism, the advent of democracy?

These questions bring us to the philosophical frailty of Bloch's con-ception of hope. Bloch himself would agree that answering such questions requires more than a catalogue of subjective hopes. As we have seen, he is talking about a subjective drive united with the objective tendency of the world. "Reason cannot blossom without hope, hope cannot speak without reason," he says, in a statement that has become famous. He adds, "Both [are] in Marxist unity—no other science has any future, no other future any science."[14] Thus we can ask Bloch, must ask him: what is the reason for his hope? The problem is that he does not argue it. Rather than, as he says, using science to study the basis for hope, Bloch *assumes* it.

He does so with warrant, he would no doubt say: his entire analysis assumes that Marxism is coming true in the world. *The Principle of Hope* turns on two interconnected thoughts: "The very profusion of human imagination, together with its correlate in the world (one imagination becomes informed and concrete), cannot possibly be explored and inven-toried other than through utopian function; *any more than it can be tested without dialectical materialism*."[15] It is worth noting that he does *not* test it, and that he thinks not in terms of "historical materialism" but "dialectical materialism." In other words, Marxism–Leninism as interpreted by Stalin furnishes his reality test and basis, and Bloch's task is to develop the subjective side of the picture. This side presupposes its reason, its coming true in the world at every moment—as an article of faith.

To ask what is the reason of hope is to ask about its basis in the real world, about actual historical tendencies of social, economic, and political life. Not yet conscious of what, we may ask? How is any specific consciousness validated, and how do we know it corresponds to genuine tendencies of the real world? Similarly, Bloch assumes a teleological view of human development as forever "forward-dawning" and apparently driven by its possibilities. Are the positive capabilities alone doing the driving (which is what Bloch, in a non-Marxist Aristotelian turn, seems to be suggesting)? If so, how do we account for the catastrophic character of so much of twentieth-century history? Answering this is urgent within an historical–materialist hope seeking to unite the "pillar of fire" with concrete reality.

Writing in exile from Nazism, then under East German Stalinism, then going westward when the Berlin Wall was constructed, Bloch never stopped assuming that there is abundant reason to hope, that Marxism has amply demonstrated this, and that no such questions need to be posed.[16] Yet if we follow his own logic and seek to unite warm streams and cold, vision and reality, hope and reason, then certainly it was absurd to speak of hope without confronting the century's crisis of hope, including Nazism and Stalinism. It is astonishing that Bloch could write *The Principle of Hope* without really paying heed to the cold stream of reality, its graveyards of hope. But it avoids every negative tendency of the age except American capitalist culture (which is Bloch's great *bête noir*). As Jan Bloch says, "In the ontological claim to fulfillment at the end of man's journey, the problem of the Stalinist darkness and the question of the concrete paths to the natural home of man is lost."[17]

Others acknowledged the fact that there can be, as Bloch himself maintained, "no hope without reason": Bloch's fellow German-Jewish Marxist exiles Theodor Adorno, Max Horkheimer, and Herbert Marcuse found it necessary to rethink and expand their starting points in response to the century's catastrophe of hope. Indeed, their entire work was an exploration of the many levels of the crisis, including how to think about it. Bloch alone chose to write a study of every conceivable hope humans have ever had. In accentuating the positive rather than plumbing the negative, he buried his head in the sand. Even after leaving East Germany Bloch never confronts the brutality and irrationality of Communism.[18] His subsequent reflections on the shortcomings of Soviet Communism are not unintelligent[19]; the problem, however, is that he never rethinks, or even questions, his basic concepts.

The Principle of Hope, then, is representative of a prophetic Marxian hope that refuses to confront its own internal crisis. Written in a world in ruins, not only a Marxist world, but also a German world, a Jewish world, and a world of Western civilization, *The Principle of Hope* nervously, even feverishly—in the style of Serenus Zeitblom, Thomas Mann's narrator of *Doctor Faustus* (*his* book about the disaster)—ignores all these catastrophes and reaffirms German culture, Jewish messianic ethics, Marxism, and Western culture. No disaster appears, nothing but the highest of hopes still being realized, as if nothing terribly serious has happened. This denial can be understood as Bloch's response to the crisis: hopes soaring so high and so wide as to be beyond earthly containment, yet calling for practical, real fulfillment in a world that cruelly mocks them.

Perhaps this is why Bloch's hope is never argued. It cannot be: it no longer corresponds to the real world. History has made it, alas, into a purely subjective hope, unmediated by reality. As such, it can only be asserted, accepted on faith or authority, not validated. Moreover, as concrete antici- pation of the real tendency toward a future classless society, Marxism has long since been unable to present its reasons.[20] Perhaps this is why Bloch bludgeons us with his hope and overwhelms us with his learning.[21]

Herbert Marcuse and the End of Utopia

But do we then abandon hope? This must have been the question roiling beneath the surface of *The Principle of Hope*, the tension that, suppressed, undermined Bloch's project. Indeed, he apparently saw no alternative to intensifying his hopes, widening their claims, refusing to explore them critically, overwhelming his readers with them. But is Bloch's defeat, ironically expressed so triumphantly, the defeat of hope itself? It is also ironic that "no hope without reason" is one of Bloch's great watchwords; the other is, "to be human really means to have utopias."[22] The question is, standing on the wreckage of the twentieth century, what do these utopias mean? Anyone who, as Bloch says, would open windows rather than blow soap bubbles will see, as serious utopian thinker or exponent of radical social change, that there are indeed marvelous possibilities in our world and lying within our reach. But they exist alongside, and intertwined with, cata- strophically destructive ones, and these stand alongside other negative tendencies. Does this make utopian anticipation, such as Bloch's, obsolete? Has it now become a barrier to hope, rendering us incapable of grasping and functioning effectively in the world we seek to change? Indeed, doesn't utopian expectation itself pitch us into our crisis of hope?

The correct answer to these questions is just the reverse: properly understood and utilized, utopian hope has become absolutely essential to the next radical project. By "properly understood" I mean a utopia freed from eschatology, from expectation, from science. While Bloch retrieved utopia from the trash can to which generations of Marxists had consigned it, and made explicit the place it had always implicitly occupied in Marxism—thus permitting radicals to begin talking about dreams and ultimate goals—he also retained the eschatological Marxist assumption that utopia was *coming into being*. Bloch reaffirmed the dreams, but under the illusion that they were becoming reality.

Bloch's error, then, was not talking about utopia, but giving it the wrong status. It belongs in the realm of subjective consciousness, not that of sociopolitical reality. There, as recent students of utopia have articulated, vigorous utopian thinking sketches models of a peaceable kingdom, points us toward society's repressed possibilities, enables us to see more clearly actual tendencies, both positive and negative, strengthens our grounds for rejecting existing social forms, reactivates lost dreams and longings, and encourages political action.[23] If the end of oppression and the emancipation of modernity are to be pursued, utopian thinking can give color and timbre to these desires, can make them come alive, can connect our pain with our memories and dreams, and allow us to imagine the flavors and tones of a different future. If it is located in consciousness and not in the world, we will not be tempted to mistake utopia for reality, expect it to be realized, and watch these hopes dashed.

Is this what Marcuse, infinitely more pessimistic than Bloch, managed to achieve and avoid? Like Bloch, and unlike virtually all other heirs of Marx, Herbert Marcuse spoke openly and directly about utopia; unlike Bloch, he never fell victim to the illusion that utopia was coming into being. Rather, he tried unsparingly to confront the crisis of hope that Bloch denied, producing utopian images out of this confrontation. Marcuse tried to keep alive the conceptual possibility of a qualitatively different world, even while unflinchingly registering the full depth of prevailing unfreedom.

In *Reason and Revolution* (1941) he defended the capacity for thinking about alternatives. Then, in *Eros and Civilization* (1955), first inquiring why proletarian revolution either misfired or failed to take place,[24] he explored the philosophical and psychological basis for an alternative reality principle—a nonrepressive civilization. In doing so, he drew on images from myth, art, and literature, arguing that the aesthetic dimension gives voice to longings and possibilities that subvert the historically dominant Western performance principle. He sought to establish the possibility of a different world, a new sensibility, a transformed attitude toward need, a novel way of resolving the fundamental tensions Freud saw as constitutive of civilization itself. Indeed, Marcuse argued there and in his later writings that the success of the Western project of dominating nature (and humans) yields a productive apparatus whose enormous capacity increasingly undermines the economic, social, and instinctual bases for—and any justification of—repression. Utopia is now no longer a fantasy; it has become materially and technically possible. At the same time, advanced industrial society increasingly channels these emancipatory possibilities into intensifying, rather than subverting, a life based on irrationality, waste, toil, and brutality.

Given the new technological capacities, Marx's most utopian thoughts are not radical enough: "Freedom is only possible as the realization of what today is called utopia."[25] By the second half of the twentieth century it had become possible—and increasingly necessary for the sake of human survival—not only to imagine but also to construct a social order that would satisfy the deepest longings of humanity and remove the most stubborn oppressions. Humanity had passed through the eye of the needle and created the industrial–technological apparatus, and the skills and habits, necessary to end the age-old struggle for survival and to overcome the conflicts and alienations that had been part of it. A new sensibility, a new humanity, a new civilization, have been made possible by these capacities—and made urgently necessary by their ever more dangerous use in the interest of domination.

The great power of Marcuse's message lay in its connecting indictment with prophecy, which linked his unsparing analysis of the evils and dangers of advanced industrial society with his insistence that utopian longings for a different type of existence, indeed, a new form of civilization, were now realizable. Utopia is at an end: it is now a practical project. Marcuse firmly based himself on the tradition of Western rationalism from Plato to Hegel and drew it into Marxism; he encountered Freud and emerged with a message of liberation; he absorbed into this the most transcendent qualities of aesthetic theory and high culture. In his hands, history, philosophy, material and technological reality, and psychoanalysis all join with the deepest of human longings to announce the realistic possibility of a new form of civilization—just in time to clarify the wishes of a movement inchoately and confusedly demanding the same. No wonder Marcuse came to be regarded as the movement's prophet, insisting that we no longer need to be dominated and shaped by an obsolete struggle for survival that impoverishes the vast majority of the world's population.

A pacified existence would mean the end of the scarcity, toil, and domination that have been built into existence as unquestioned necessities; it would mean the construction of a fully human life beyond the realm of material survival. This life would be characterized by the creation of a new self-determining subject and a new sensibility, based on the liberation of the senses made possible by the end of regimes of scarcity and domination. As sketched by Charles Fourier, the greatest of utopian socialists, a society is now possible "in which work becomes play, a society in which even socially necessary labor can be organized in harmony with the liberated, genuine needs of men."[26] Marcuse contends that the aesthetic dimension, until now the focus of withdrawal and substitute gratification, comes into its own in the new project:

> The liberated consciousness would promote the development of a science and technology free to discover and realize the possibilities of things

and men in the protection and gratification of life, playing with the potentialities of form and matter for the attainment of this goal. Technique would then tend to become art, and art would tend to form reality; the opposition between imagination and reason, higher and lower faculties, poetic and scientific thought, would be invalidated. Emergence of a new Reality Principle: under which a new sensibility and a desublimated scientific intelligence would combine in the creation of an *aesthetic ethos*.[27]

Part of the power of Marcuse's message is his insistence on confronting the situation without illusions: before the eruption of the Movement, his hope (even after writing the utopian *Eros and Civilization* and postulating the end of surplus repression) was limited to the Great Refusal based on Walter Benjamin's poignant remark, "It is only for the sake of those without hope that hope is given to us."[28] He everywhere stressed the tragedy of contemporary history, the horror of Nazism, the slight chance of reversing the negative trend of civilization, the apocalyptic dangers built into contemporary society. Certainly the emancipatory possibilities are equally real, are arguably the *telos*, the end and real meaning, of technological civilization. But, he stressed, only a reversal of its direction, only a rupture with its priorities and a regression from its standard of living, will make possible the pacification of existence. Increased barbarization, brutalizing the system's enemies and those on its margin, and its people's increased banalization and immersion in false needs, are the dominant trends, and liberation is only a chance. Rosa Luxemburg's alternatives—socialism or barbarism—are Marcuse's as well: an emancipatory, utopian socialism that truly creates a new civilization and a new reality principle; or the absorption of all opposition, all partial and thwarted liberations, into an increasingly aggressive and one-dimensional system of false needs and brutality, driven by its own inner war against its own utopian capacities.[29] Utopia may be possible, but so is the ultimate civilized barbarism, culminating in genocidal and suicidal war.

The Uses of Utopia: Homage to Marcuse

As we near the end of the twentieth century, what are we to make of these reflections of a revolutionary philosopher born at the end of the nineteenth century? If his thoughts rang true for a generation, our generation, the memory of Herbert Marcuse is now no less repressed than he once thought were the possibilities for utopia. Is his vision obsolete today? Do we look over our shoulders at these ideas of an aging romantic, embarrassed by the indiscretions of our youth? Yes, it is discomfiting to have once hoped so nakedly and completely, to have embraced the possibility of creating a new order of existence. Many of us encountered these ideas as we sought to make the passage from childhood to adulthood, and they, and the political enthusiasms they nurtured, enabled us to postpone becoming realistic. Since then, reality has come to seem so harsh, so unbending, and struggles to change it so protracted, so unrewarding. Those of us who have kept on have done so with vastly diminished expectations.

Nevertheless, we cannot forget these ideas. Once they allowed us to focus and clarify our hopes, to the point where such hopes rang true. Once we tapped dreams rooted in, and not quite buried in, childhood, drew them into the adult world we were contesting, and found ourselves demanding no less than everything. Whatever it meant, however it was ringed by despair about its impossibility, we did imagine it, and we did demand it. Marcuse helped us do this, and we lodged at the core of our commitment a sense that a new reality was indeed possible. It all seems so foolish now. If we spoke and acted feverishly and exaggeratedly, it was about something so profoundly real yet so denied by the world ever since its articulation, that we were unable to abide the contradiction. In growing up and adjusting to the need to be part of the world we so despised, we let go of the demand, perhaps revisiting it occasionally at first (like the grave of a recently dead loved one) and then once in a while, and then not at all. Utopia has once more become utopian. But occasionally, for those of us who remain committed or active or concerned, a demonstration, a song, a memory will remind us of, and then flood us with, a hope so sweet and electric that it becomes impossible to bear, a dream so beautiful and besieged that we no longer want to dream it.

But does this philosopher help us negotiate our crisis of hope? After all, the vogue of Marcuse was bound up with a time of discovery, of opposition, of movement. After the ferment, lacking Marcuse's vision, without his focus on interests of domination and possibilities of liberation, a determined analysis of negative trends yields the much longer-running vogue of Foucault. Now that New Left political energies have faded and been recanted, how do we evaluate the tools Marcuse bequeathed us? By insisting on the material possibility of a new world and a new way, and by stressing the obscenity of a system that uses these very possibilities to repress liberation, Marcuse gave us approaches that can still serve as bases for hope and action to come. His end-of-utopianism, especially by linking historical and technological possibility with timeless human longings, encourages our political imagination, legitimizes our sense of the great discrepancy between humanity's immense possibilities and its sorry realities. It authenticates and dignifies our longings, and thus allows for tying them to radical politics. We imagine a peaceable kingdom because our longings connect with humanity's deepest and oldest dreams, and because it is now technically feasible.

Thus, like Bloch's, Marcuse's vision connects our radicalism with the entire range of human longings and the sweep of human history. At the same time, it permits merciless criticism of the status quo, dismissing its "realistic" justifications and betraying the narrow and ideological character of its democracy and freedom, its concern for security and reasonableness. And it proposes plausible models of a future free society, and a new reality principle, which still demand our discussion and debate. In short, like all utopian thinking worthy of the name, Marcuse's gives us hope without making any promises.

A Despairing Hope: Critique of Marcuse

Marcuse's hope was, nevertheless, always a hope ringed with despair. His vision was oddly simultaneously too optimistic and too pessimistic. He moved from the most soaring possibilities to the most disturbing sense of containment and repression and back again, and again. After *Eros and Civilization* elaborated the concept of a nonrepressive civilization, *One-Dimensional Man* (1964) argued that the dialectic of liberation had been absorbed. *An Essay on Liberation* (1969) then embraced the new forces of resistance without giving any sense of how they were being created; *The Aesthetic Dimension* (1978) retreated into art's function of preserving the possibilities of liberation in spite of and against reality.

Of course, Marcuse never believed that the good society was coming into being, only that our accumulated skills and technological capacities now make it possible, that they tend to give rise to an opposition demanding a rupture with the system, that this possibility is systematically combatted by the established order, and that if not employed for emancipation, the new technological capacities become used to stifle it. Indeed, a massive rupture is needed to bring about a nonrepressive society, which would bring a catastrophe of liberation inasmuch as it entails reversing the direction of civilization itself, especially its aggressiveness, its productivity, its increasingly artificial needs, its resignation, its alienation, and its toil.

But what is the relationship between our new technological capacities and the human capacity for creating and living in a nonrepressive civilization? How will human beings become *willing and able* to make the sacrifices necessary to create a nonrepressive society? If Marcuse is right that a reversal of values is necessary, a rupture with the trend of civilization, this means that most people will have to be liberated *in spite of* and *against* themselves. In all of this Marcuse suggests not only the New Left's countercultural self-image and self-justification but also its hostility to the mystified masses, the hard hats and the silent majority. Immersed in "their" false needs, instinctually bound to the system's aggression, they identify with their oppressors and fight off the catastrophe of liberation. This analysis, turning on terms like "rupture" and "mystified" and "reversal," easily yields a mood of contempt for those it would liberate as well as for the reconciling powers of a democracy based on misinformation and false choices.

Liberation for the masses easily becomes envisioned in spite of and *against* them: "For among a great part of the manipulated population in the developed capitalist countries the need for freedom does not or no longer exists as a vital, necessary need."[30] The solidarity that does exist in this scenario is that among the wretched, the outsiders, the blacks, the young rebels acting *against* the vast majority, but in *their* interest. In key respects the mood of Marcuse is the mood of Weatherman, of Baader-Meinhof, of the Red Brigades, and can too easily become their ideological justification. Many of us have shared this mood, and understand it all too well from the inside: a powerful feeling for the possibilities of liberation, a sense of how much of a reversal it requires, an awareness of the massive resistance, and, perhaps above all, a need to do something to break the impasse.

It yields a kind of latter-day Leninism: "All the material and intellectual forces which could be put to work for the realization of a free society are at hand. That they are not used for that purpose is to be attributed to the total mobilization of existing society against its own potential for liberation."[31] If all the "material and intellectual forces" really are "at hand," then we are being held back only by the system's control of consciousness. Those who perceive this—schooled in the texts of Fourier as well as Marx, Rilke as well as Lenin—carry the burden for all of humanity. Accordingly, Marcuse flirts again and again with the idea of an educational dictatorship. Plato's *Republic*, Babeuf's Conspiracy of the Equals, the notion of "Repressive Tolerance"—all testify to Marcuse's pervasive sense of the role of mystified consciousness in stabilizing the existing order, and the need for an imperialism of theory to break free of it.[32]

A related feature of Marcuse's outlook that needs to be highlighted —and rejected—is his urgent and single-minded focus on the *end*. Among Marxists and radicals this *endpoint*—the socialization of the means of production, a classless society, a world governed by relations of democracy and equality and functioning at the highest levels of wealth and culture, a nonrepressive society, utopia—has been the motivating force. But as long as the end is not achieved, all other victories are only partial, tentative, drawn back into the oppressive vortex of system. Rosa Luxemburg's response to Eduard Bernstein's "The goal is nothing, the movement is everything" was simply the reverse: "On the contrary the movement as such without regard for the final aim is nothing, but the final aim is everything for us."[33] A reformism without goals is replaced by an absolute end, without approaches, resting points, or way stations, and with a desperate urgency about arriving there.[34] To focus exclusively on the moment of rupture, on the reversal, means falling victim to an "endism" that rules out any celebrations short of the final one. Only then, according to the eschatology, will we all emerge from the tunnel into the light. Only then will history finally begin. In the meantime, the bleakness of the present reality gives rise to the discouraging awareness that we are not *there* yet. Our hope makes us desperate.

This mood ignores not only the long, slow process of social and political transformations that began with history itself, but also how many victories are presupposed in the final one. In particular, it ignores the kinds of specific histories I discussed in Chapter 10: of the brutal forms of subjugation with which civilization began; of the many failed and successful rebellions that led tortuously, slowly, toward first the notion of spiritual equality, then the notion, and practice, of political equality; of how many kinds of struggles and changes—philosophical, literary, and psychological as well as political, social and economic—enter into each advance in human social morality. Marcuse stresses the historical development of productive forces as *the* decisive trend—but where is the history of subjectivity? Even our most abstract forms of mutual respect have taken hundreds of years; our practices of equality between sexes and races and sometimes even classes have taken longer. I have remarked in Chapter 7 how optimistic Marx was, when he told the workers, after 1848: "You have 15, 20, 50 years of civil war to go through in order to alter the situation and to train yourselves for the exercise of power."[35] Understanding the real extent of training for the exercise of power would lead us to insist on a more realistic timetable for the reversal Marcuse talks about: maybe 150, maybe 200, maybe even 500 years.

Who can help us to make this correction? In Chapter 4 I discussed Erica Sherover-Marcuse's treatment of some of the central issues involved in transforming "those attitudes, character traits, beliefs and dispositions"[36] essential to human emancipation. She sketches "prolegomena" to the practice of emancipatory subjectivity that would seek to transform explicit beliefs and values, underlying assumptions embodied in daily experience, and "the affective underpinnings of oppressive character structures and behavior patterns." She calls for "a practice of subjectivity [that] would seek to implement the *affective unlearning* of the habits of oppression." This kind of political activity would seek to undo both the internalized dominator and the internalized victim.[37]

Clearly, the creation of an emancipated human sensibility, already long in the making, will only result from patient, long-term action on many levels. As suggested by Sherover-Marcuse, this action must appreciate the full extent of internalized human subjugation, and take the slow, deliberate steps needed to overcome it. If it takes one hundred and fifty, two hundred, or five hundred years before the reversal is prepared, so be it.

Herbert Marcuse, however, does not point to this kind of a continuous (if uneven and manysided) emancipatory process, taking place over time, but rather to "a break rather than a continuity with previous history, its negation rather than its positive continuation, difference rather than progress."[38] To be sure, the great Hegelian knows his dialectics: the new morality will be "heir and negation of Judeo-Christian morality"; the break with the struggle for survival "inheres in the development of the productive forces themselves."[39] But why does it not inhere in human development? Must there not be a subjective process of *increasing* human power, self-confidence, consciousness? If freedom is "something that is nowhere already in existence,"[40] doesn't the end of slavery, of serfdom, of segregation, of colonialism count for something? Rather than granting equal importance to the long process of developing emancipatory consciousness, it seems as if Marcuse remains stuck within Marx's stress on objective trends. He sometimes sounds as if a single objective change would suffice to initiate the reversal, rather than the thousands of subjective *and* objective changes, molecular as well as cultural and institutional—until people and situation intersect in a quantitative change become qualitative.

Such a process must be guided by human, not institutional or structural ends, by strengths to be achieved, powers to be won, oppressions to be dissolved. Instead of the single overarching end Luxemburg, and apparently Marcuse, have in mind, the struggle must pursue a rainbow of ends: strengths here, structures there, skills, attitudes, and spaces won. Marcuse's opposition between break on the one hand and continuity on the other must be overcome. We will seek to continue certain progressive strands of our history and break with that which restrains them, to continue emancipatory processes *and* negate processes of oppression. We can only move forward from stations constructed by those who have come before us, and we must protect, understand, and celebrate their achievements, and strengths, even as we try to move beyond them.

Marcuse suggests that the productive forces that now make utopia possible can be measured and calculated in advance, but there is no way of knowing how far human beings can go toward emancipation without first entering into struggles, and then seeing what is possible. But even if subjectivity cannot be measured with precision, certain emancipatory steps presuppose others, and their preconditions can indeed be evaluated. For example, as I mentioned in Chapter 10, contemporary talk about difference *presupposes* a society in which equality has become a universal principle, and takes the next step beyond it.

If Marcuse minimizes partial struggles, the preparation of subjectivity, many long marches to emancipation, it is no doubt because he stresses the absorptive and cooptive power of the system to turn all partial emancipations to its profit. But as long as its hegemony lasts, which will be until just before its overthrow, it will successfully turn to its own advantage every step toward liberation, as these steps are being taken. While he was writing, the Vietnamese, supported by vast numbers of North Americans, won their war to expel American imperialism, and they have lost the peace ever since. Still, for all their subsequent problems, they did succeed in driving out the world's great imperial power. In the years since, the political structures of apartheid have been abolished, but not its manifold economic and social inequalities. Still, for all the profound problems that remain, colonialism in Africa is over; *that* stage in Africa's history is past. Every struggle short of the ultimate one may be coopted in these ways, but can we ignore that short of total transformation, many battles have been fought, and some of them won? Marcuse pointed toward, and spoke about, the need for a dramatic rupture, an overcoming of false consciousness, a breaching of the system's hegemony. He left us no way of appreciating these specific struggles, and their victories, or of connecting them with larger goals. Understood and evaluated properly, as inevitably coopted and undermined, but as absolutely necessary emancipatory steps, the effects of these specific struggles are grounds for hope rather than despair.

A Five-Hundred-Year Perspective

I want to emphasize the importance of understanding and evaluating the effects of specific struggles: each reason to hope becomes recast and refocused within the context shaped by the other reasons until, together, they add up to a new kind of hope. If in spite of their shortcomings, Bloch and Marcuse clarified the age-old longing for utopia, and Marcuse stressed the maturation of productive forces that provides its new technological possibility, how do we absorb these marvelous thoughts into a vision that is not inherently hopeless? At least two other themes enter into, and shape, a new sense of hope: understanding that achieving the good society is not possible in our lifetimes, but rather will take several hundred years; and the commitment to act to further it.

If our deepest dreams are not coming true, this is no catastrophe—as long as we can overcome the desperate urgency that often goes along with experiencing utopian longings. They do not have to be realized in order to be real. Their sheer presence gives a sense of authenticity that springs from strong hopes and wishes, rooted as these are in earliest childhood and the most ancient histories. Access to these resources, freed from the urgency of bringing them into being before our eyes, can be encouraging and invigorating, as well as consoling, as many of us experience so often when movements sing their anthems. These remind us of who we are and why we are, recall us to our original and deepest purposes.

They also remind us of all who have struggled before us for dignity and in solidarity, and how much they have achieved. This anti-Foucauldian sense of past struggles and victories, one of the main themes of Chapter 10 and one of the main sources of radical morality, is a vital dimension of the five-hundred-year perspective. Not only need we look ahead, hopefully and yet realistically, but we need to look back. As we do so, we can take ownership of the painful and yet impressive history of struggles, and take our place *within* it.

The most long-term perspective makes what we can hope for at any moment more modest, perhaps minimal. But it thereby becomes more solid: it enables us to link daily sacrifices with the expectation of achieving specific victories, skills, powers, and emancipations that become part of this history of struggles and may eventually make it possible to achieve our most long-term ends. Within frameworks that stretch out before and after our lives it may be conceivable to connect rigorously realistic actions with ultimate goals, to wage struggles, as Rosa Luxemburg once said, with our feet firmly on the earth and our heads in the sky. To be able, that is, to participate in radical activity without harboring illusions of impossible success and then, inevitably defeated, growing cynical.

We want to believe that our goals are being realized, but reality is a dasher of dreams. It takes visionaries become activists and torments them into letting go of either the vision or the action. It remakes people who act with hope to achieve a meaningful social goal, repeatedly pitching them into impossible situations until they change into cynics or idealists. A five-hundred-year perspective allows us to dream fully, to allow that dream its own reality, and to act with the rigorous determination to win the kinds of victories that may one day realize it. It may help us to persevere with hope—finding resources in the justice of our causes, in the strength of our goals, in a rigorous understanding of the limits of our actions, and in a tough-minded understanding of how these struggles link up with, and further, the prerequisites for a good society.

The world of ex-radicals is peopled with cynics who learned the hard way about hoping too much; the world of activists is peopled with potty idealists who pretend to themselves and others that dreams are becoming reality; and with grim realists who, having abandoned all hope, persevere dully. As Bloch and Marcuse stress, keeping up hope means, rather, retaining the full original desire, and feeling fully its authenticating and invigorating force. Alongside this, we need the realistic sense of how far and in what little ways it might be worked toward, and we need the commitment to do so.

Action

This most long-term perspective, and its openness to utopia, depends on the commitment I addressed in Chapter 8: to act against oppression, and to act on behalf of creating the conditions for the good society. In this sense, the future radical project need only absorb this fundamental feature of Marxism's hope, its commitment to struggle, based on observable events and trends. Marxism made achieving the deepest longings of humanity into a conscious, collective project. As we saw in Marx's "Theses on Feuerbach," it is action that redefines the terrain from one we observe to one we seek to *change*. And this alters everything.

A radical project may be inspired by dreams, but it itself is not a dream, and it needs both to remain real and to see far beyond reality, into the world to be created, and to draw inspiration from it. But we cannot do this if we let go of trying to understand what our action can achieve at a given moment. Because their visions of utopia were not intimately connected with action, both Bloch and Marcuse fell victim to this. If individuals need to know that what they are doing is good, and if they need to have a strong sense of how it joins up with what others have achieved, they also need to know not only *that*, but *how*, the good society will eventually be possible. Unlike every other politics, radicalism must connect not only the present with the achievable, but utopian vision with hard analysis, pessimism with hope, looking forward to the future with a grounding in the present, the soaring resources of the spirit combined with the demands of the intellect. And we have to avoid confusing these as we act.

Still, if a truly human society may take five hundred years, how will the generations of "we's" sustain themselves to bring it about? Are the resources of hope I've sketched adequate to encourage people to persist in the struggles, to make the transformations, to recover from the defeats, to make the step-by-step changes that are necessary before we end oppression? Perhaps the best way to answer this question is to begin without hope, in situations with no possibility of achieving a meaningful result. I am thinking both about certain extreme situations, such as Auschwitz and the Warsaw Ghetto, and political actions without the ghost of a chance of achieving their goals, such as the earliest American Civil Rights movements or anti-Vietnam war demonstrations. In such cases, where significant results are inconceivable, when we act against oppression all we can hope to do is to bear witness.

The remarkable fact is that, again and again, people choose to act in this way—to struggle to arrange their remaining belongings on a concentration camp shelf, to die with dignity, to stand up and fight, to let it be known that they resisted, to do the right thing—rather than to submit to evil. When occupants of the Warsaw Ghetto decided to fight rather than passively submit to continued deportations and the liquidation of the ghetto, their action contained a number of meanings. To the Nazis they were declaring themselves as their equals as human beings, and that they would not submit to their oppressors.[41] To other Jews, and to the rest of the world they were saying, "We will die fighting." To everyone, including themselves they were maintaining their right to be heard and seen. To posterity they said, "We are right, and what the Nazis are doing to us is an intolerable evil."

No positive results were possible, and yet by simply acting, there were positive results: a handful survived, German soldiers were killed, a spirit of resistance was kindled elsewhere, the plight of the Ghetto became known. All who come after will have the possibility of feeling solidarity with the Ghetto fighters and of being inspired by their spirit. Acting alone and without hope, even in impossible situations, can create new possibilities. Acting in this sense of bearing witness, even without hope, creates hope, and creates results. It creates facts, it creates solidarity, it creates morality. And it modifies even the most hopeless situations.

Creating Utopia

To hopeless action, action that creates hope, I would add one final source of hope: the peaceable kingdom momentarily experienced in the movements for change, the utopias people fleetingly live. As anyone knows who has been part of a movement, a demonstration, a campaign, or a strike, struggles undertaken for the most limited and prosaic goals have a way of opening the most profound and lyrical sense of possibility in their participants.[42] To experience even briefly a movement's solidarity, equality, reciprocity, morality, collective and individual empowerment, reconciliation of individual and group, is to have a foretaste of the peaceable kingdom. In the midst of the most frenetic strike, with its threats, with its tensions, with its angers, individuals find themselves becoming part of a collectivity and together experience moments that will mark their lives forever. It is the moment of another reality, a glimpse of utopia that Bloch or Marcuse, had they been activists, would have found irresistible to describe.[43]

It can't last, of course. We're only human. Reality makes it impossible. And, what's worse, those with political power won't let us live. It may take five hundred years for us to be capable of actually living this way for more than a moment. And yet, the cat has been let out of the bag, as it were. Once we have experienced solidarity, we can never forget it. It may be short-lived, but its heady sensations remain. It may be still largely a dream, but we have experienced that dream. It may seem impossible, but we have looked into the face of its possibilities.

One reason why the subsequent disillusion is so overpowering—and we know how bitterly, after their particular god fails, ex-radicals regret their illusions—is precisely because the experience reaches so deep, feels so wonderful, is so disarming. What has happened is that we have dared to hope. This means that for a moment we want everything that we have ever repressed and reconciled ourselves to living without. For a moment, we dare to open ourselves to what we really wish the world were like. As Sartre describes, seriality collapses, and we momentarily become part of a group, nurtured in reciprocity. Does this begin with a vision, a theory? Not at all: rather, it gets produced by a community in struggle, creating itself, pursuing its goals, defending itself. On strike, we suddenly produce utopia, and live in it. On a demonstration, we bring justice to life, and we dwell in it. Struggling alongside people who thereby become our comrades, we live fully through solidarity, community, collective action, morality, authenticity, the overcoming of alienation. Standing up together, we are momentarily what we want to become, we throw off subjection and humiliation, we live centered in the deepest human needs and desires, we reject the system's control over us, we share and share alike. And then—because the movement turns in on itself, loses, succeeds, because the wrong kind of leaders take over, hardship becomes too much, divide-and-conquer tactics succeed, the war continues, the essential nature of collectivities asserts itself, bureaucratization sets in, and for a dozen other reasons—it comes crashing down, or just fades. And, ironically enough, we hurt far more than if we had never experienced it. But might not this experience, if we could understand it *as* a moment, a foretaste, unstable, bound to vanish but in some deep sense our most long-term goal—and, above all, as unmistakably real—sustain rather than destroy hope?

But how might this occur? We need to understand that, when we speak about keeping hope alive, the goal is not socialism, or a rainbow society, or such and such a vision of social structures: the end is rather being fully human, fully alive, fully free, fully respected, fully a community, fully self-determining. This is what must be kept alive, this is what hope keeps alive. This is what struggles keep alive. While to institute fully this community of free people may take us five hundred years, it does not have to wait to be experienced: it can be present, and felt, in each and every struggle. Such moments open ontologically onto the free society and the realized individual. The experience of ourselves they give us is active, empowered, and self-determining, universal but different. We are free, with others. Our hope is lived through, but not reducible to, a specific situation; it is brought to life in our relationships, our practices, and our selves.

Being infected with "endism" breeds despair and discouragement. It makes it difficult to say: Yes, we hope to win this particular goal but we are also fueled by a world-historical sense that much more is at stake; we are struggling for this or that goal but we will measure its results by whether and how it empowers people for further struggles; we are also being human, hoping actively and acting within a millennial human struggle against oppression.

Hope

Immanuel Kant thought that all of reason's concerns are embraced by three questions: What can I know; what should I do; and what may I hope.[44] Integrated into a single project, these are precisely the questions that have been addressed by the critique of radical hope that I present in this book. In exploring how we radicals should think about ourselves after Marxism, I have been suggesting what we can know, how we should act, and what we can now hope. In a sense, hope is the central issue throughout this discussion, framing every page. I have sought to develop a sense of hope that does not depend on the need to believe that our vision is *coming true*. And yet at the same time, we still need some sense that our actions are connected to, and may perhaps further, our radical vision. Beyond all faith, we must ascertain possibilities and likelihoods, and act in relation to them. Hope involves desire for certain goals, belief that these are on principle attainable, and the conscious and self-critical constructing of actions aimed at formulating the approaches to these goals by achieving what can be achieved at this moment. In the process, we can formulate such approaches by acknowledging the collective utopian experiences that may momentarily accompany our struggles.

This suggests a new kind of hope. It does not depend on being able to point to the good society coming into being. It turns on action, action that recognizes its possibilities and limitations, but that seeks to create new realities. It lodges at its center stirring visions of utopia, but has no illusion that they are coming into being. These are, rather, norms, models, inspirations, sources of clarity, authenticity, and solidarity. Our utopia is a necessarily unreal—because not immediately achievable—horizon of our daily activity. It is an ideal to be inspired by, to argue about, to compare with others, and to take completely seriously, as ideal.

As discussed in Chapter 10, maintaining hope entails a good deal more than action in the real world, even action inspired by utopian visions. It requires appreciating what humans have achieved through struggles and over time. It turns on a sense of justice, and righteous anger. As Bloch and Marcuse present it, hope also turns on being in touch with the deepest of human well-springs and desires, which connect us with earlier generations and other cultures. It entails solidarity. And, as Marcuse insists, it means having a sense of possibility. Rooted in what is greatest in humanity, moved by visions of the good, by deep needs, by human solidarity and a sense of right and wrong, it is in hoping and acting on our hopes that we achieve our full height as human beings.

I have been sketching the kind of hope appropriate to the new radical project. Yet is it enough to lead us beyond the crisis of hope in which the project itself begins—to nourish and guide this project? Compared to the hope of Marxism, with its conviction about the new society being brought into being, ours seems paltry indeed. How, for example, can we solve the Sphinx's riddle of tying long-term goals to immediate actions, when Marxism at its strongest had trouble answering this programmatic challenge? Nevertheless, as I argued in Chapter 4, Marxism itself always reached far beyond what was really possible: its inspirational force depended on proposing a liberation brought about by the actions of people who would need much more than fifteen, twenty, or fifty years to become fit to rule. In other words, if Marxism was an historically indispensible project of struggle, in hard fact it never actually pointed to a classless society. Its sense of power and security turned out to lack a solid foundation.

A new radical project's sense of hope will not be based on "tendencies working with iron necessity toward inevitable results,"[45] but rather on possibilities and contingencies. Instead of claiming predictive power it will at most talk about what may happen and what can happen. But neither will it rest covertly on a quasi-religious faith that can nowhere be argued, and that undermines its own proud scientific claims. Our more modest hope will also be less subject to disenchantment.

The International

We have acted and we can see the results of our action. Alas, we have not achieved the peaceable kingdom, anywhere. We have not transformed the system or ourselves. But we have modified it, made it live up to its own promises a bit more, felt our own strength time and again. We have gained strength, and we have lost it. We have helped to end apartheid, but not made living conditions better for most black South Africans. We have helped to end the war in Vietnam, but were powerless to prevent the disasters that followed. We have helped to integrate the United States racially but we have been unable to improve the material conditions of most African-Americans.

In short, we have lost repeatedly, but we have also won. We can give some reasons for hope, but no sense of certainty, of necessity, even of probability. We know both that our struggle requires a rupture with the direction in which all of civilization is moving and that this may take as long as five hundred years. We will nourish ourselves on the fleeting utopias we produce without being seduced into believing they will last, just as we will be inspired by utopian hopes without believing they are likely to be met in our lifetimes. We will have to learn what changes are needed truly to be prepared for self-determination, an end of patriarchy, racism, and class society, and to guide our struggles so that we can gain the necessary strengths. We will have to understand the nature of consumer capitalism's hold, and mount struggles designed to weaken it.

This chastened hope, expecting such a long struggle but willing to win small victories and celebrate along the way, is embodied in a close comrade and friend, the revolutionary whose name appears on this book's dedication page, Saul Wellman. He worked to organize truck drivers while still in his teens, served in the International Brigades in Spain while in his twenties, was a paratrooper in World War II when he turned thirty, organized automobile workers in Detroit for over ten years, became acting chair of the Michigan Communist Party in the early 1950s, was jailed and then freed in a sensational Smith Act trial, and then left the Communist Party and became a printer and, later, a local union officer. In his sixties he became a New Leftist and helped form the Detroit chapter of the New American Movement. With the exception of his involvement in World War II, his every major purpose had been defeated by the end of his life, yet after rethinking his commitments during his eightieth year he remained, as always, a revolutionary.

Why was this the case? His major hopes had been disappointed, but he had seen, and participated in, many lesser victories. But no end-of-life accounting could justify being a lifelong revolutionary. Something else had to explain why—even after the collapse of Communism, which he had spent so many years fighting for and with a small "c" never stopped believing in—he spent painful months of confusion, and still decided, whatever the next radical project's features, that he would be part of it. He was a revolutionary in the fullest sense of the word: a lifetime of commitment to solidarity with the oppressed, of anger against all forms of oppression, of living the moral commitment to struggle against injustice, of identification with past and present struggles, of refusing to be kept down, of being determined to act, and of always maintaining a sense of possibility.

Why have three generations of radicals been so drawn to those foreigners who fought in Spain on behalf of the Republic between 1936 and 1939? What makes their heroism any different from that of others who fought to organize factories and farms, who risked their lives in the Southern United States, who joined various resistance movements during World War II, who infiltrated into apartheid South Africa during the 1970s and 1980s? There was no difference of courage, to be sure, and none of commitment. But unlike the others, the volunteers in Spain left their country to join a cause that was supposed to belong to *someone else*. Like Eugene Debs in response to his country's entry into World War I, they declared, and demonstrated by their actions, that their country mattered less to them than *other human beings*. They dared to say "we" and mean the whole world, and in pursuit of this International, one third of them died, and were buried, on the battlefields of Spain.

Saul Wellman was wounded in Spain, but he returned to the fight again, and again. He has been one of those to keep alive the project of creating the widest possible "we," the International. He has been one of those to incarnate this project in his words and deeds. He kept on saying "we"—when it claimed to designate hundreds of millions, when it only seemed to designate hundreds, when using the very term met with ridicule. Nearing the end of his life, he could not point to this "we" increasing, to the International having become the human race. But that human race now, self-consciously, included blacks as well as whites, women as well as men, homosexuals as well as heterosexuals, formerly colonized people as well as former colonizing people. At least he and those like him had won some battles, and in so doing they, we, have kept a revolutionary hope alive, and inspired others to do so. It will be kept alive, until its time.

NOTES

Introduction (pp. 1–5)

1. See my "South Africa as Apartheid Unwinds," *Socialist Review*, vol. 92, no. 2, 1992.

Chapter One (pp. 9–39)

1. Allen Ginsberg, "America." *Collected Poems: 1947–1980* (New York, 1984), 146.

2. Karl Marx, "Letter to Arnold Ruge, September, 1843." In Robert C. Tucker (ed.), *The Marx–Engels Reader* (New York, 1972), 10.

3. Herbert Marcuse, "Repressive Tolerance." In Herbert Marcuse, Barrington Moore, Jr., and Robert Paul Wolff (eds.), *Critique of Pure Tolerance* (Boston, 1965), 81.

4. Ronald Aronson, "The Movement and Its Critics," *Studies on the Left*, vol. 6, no. 1 (1966).

5. Ibid., 10–12.

6. Ibid., 19.

7. Ronald Aronson, "Reply to Oscar Berland." *Studies on the Left*, vol. 6, no. 5 (1966), 55.

8. Ibid.

9. Ibid., 57.

10. Ibid., 58.

11. Ibid., 60.

12. Ronald Aronson and John Cowley, "The New Left in the United States." In Ralph Miliband and John Saville (eds.), *The Socialist Register* (New York, 1967).

13. Ronald Aronson, "Dear Herbert." In George Fischer (ed.), *The Revival of American Socialism* (New York, 1970), 273.

14. Ibid., 272.

15. Ibid.

16. Ibid., 273–274.

17. NAM *Political Perspective* (n.d.), 2.

18. Detroit NAM discussion paper, 1976.

19. Edward Said, "Zionism from the Standpoint of Its Victims." *Social Text*, no. 1 (Winter, 1979); reprinted in *The Question of Palestine* (New York, 1980). My response is "Never Again? Zionism and the Holocaust." *Social Text*, no. 3 (Fall 1980); reprinted with changes in *Dialectics of Disaster: A Preface to Hope* (London, 1983), Chapter 6.

20. Of course, this has changed significantly, as since 1967 the Palestians from the West Bank and Gaza have become day laborers inside Israel. See my *The Dialectics of Disaster* (London, 1983), Chapter 6.

21. Perry Anderson, *In the Tracks of Historical Materialism* (London, 1983).

22. Ronald Aronson, "Historical Materialism, Answer to Marxism's Crisis." *New Left Review*, no. 152 (July–August, 1985).

23. See my "The End/s of Socialism." *Theoria*, no. 76 (October 1990).

24. Ronald Aronson, "Is Socialism on the Agenda: A Letter to the South African Left." *Transformation*, no. 14 (1991); a considerably revised version was cited above, Introduction, n. 1.

25. *Sartre By Himself*, transcript of the film by Alexandre Astruc and Michel Contat (New York, 1978), 72.

Chapter Two (pp. 40–68)

1. For an exploration of social irrationality in the twentieth century, see my *The Dialectics of Disaster* (London, 1983); on denial, see "Deciphering the Israeli–Palestinian Conflict." In Ronald Aronson and Adrian van de Hoven, *Sartre Alive* (Detroit, 1991).

2. Karl Marx, "Theses on Feuerbach." In Robert C. Tucker (ed.), *The Marx–Engels Reader* (New York, 1972), 109.

3. Karl Marx and Frederick Engels, *The German Ideology* (New York, 1947), 26.

4. The possible exception is Belgium, for a brief moment eighty years ago. See Adam Przeworski, *Capitalism and Social Democracy* (Cambridge, England, 1986).

5. Herbert Marcuse, *One-Dimensional Man* (Boston, 1965), 29.

6. Immanuel Wallerstein, *Historical Capitalism* (London, 1983).

7. See my "Socialism, the Sustaining Menace." In K. T. Fann and Donald Clark Hodges (eds.), *Readings in U.S. Imperialism* (Boston, 1971).

8. Gilles Deleuze and Felix Guattari, *Anti-Oedipus* (London, 1977).

9. Vincent Navarro's spirited effort ("The Limitations of Legitimation and Fordism and the Possibility for Socialist Reform." In *Rethinking Marxism* [Summer, 1991]) to see the facts of recent history as showing the Left's growing strength, is worth reflecting on in this regard. This useful article gathers all the positive evidence and arguments one might consider, showing, for example, how consumerism is less a capitalist strategy than a product of class struggle. The importance of such a study serves to remind us of the continuing analytic strength of Marxism and to alert us to the class dimension and class struggle dimension of social reality. But

in the end, we are still left with wild and unsupported claims that over the past generation the struggle for socialism has actually *advanced*.

10. In *Hegemony and Socialist Strategy* (London, 1985, 8–14) Ernesto Laclau and Chantal Mouffe argue that Rosa Luxemburg was unable to bridge the gap; almost thirty years earlier in *Soviet Marxism* (New York, 1961; orig. ed. 1958, 13–22), Herbert Marcuse described Leninism as an effort to do just that.

11. Perry Anderson, *In the Tracks of Historical Materialism* (London, 1983), 86–87.

12. See, for example, Maurice Cornforth, *Historical Materialism* (New York, 1954).

13. See Thomas S. Kuhn, *The Structure of Scientific Revolutions* (Chicago, 1970).

14. Daniel Little, *The Scientific Marx* (Minneapolis, 1986), 3.

15. Ibid.

16. Fred M. Gottheil, *Marx's Economic Predictions* (Evanston, IL, 1966).

17. Gottheil presents his "Compendium" of 172 predictions on pages 192 to 200.

18. Gottheil, 193–194.

19. Letter to Arnold Ruge, September, 1843. In Tucker, op. cit., 8.

20. "Contributions to the Critique of Hegel's *Philosophy of Right*." In T. B. Bottomore (ed.), *Karl Marx, Early Writings* (New York, 1963), 52.

21. Ibid.

22. Ibid., 53.

23. Ibid., 54.

24. Religion is "the sigh of the oppressed creature, the heart of a heartless world, and the soul of soulless conditions. It is the *opium* of the people" (Ibid., 43–44, tr. changed). For a critical view of Marx's discovery of the proletariat see Timothy McCarthy, *Marx and the Proletariat* (Westport, CT., 1978).

25. Nicholas Lobkowicz, *Theory and Practice: History of a Concept from Aristotle to Marx* (Notre Dame, 1967), 276.

26. After winning the Civil War, the Bolsheviks found themselves faced with the task of industrializing the Soviet Union, not with socializing an already existing industrial base. Marxism provided few guidelines for this wholly unanticipated task.

27. See Georg Lukacs, *History and Class Consciousness* (Cambridge, MA, 1971), 27–45.

28. Maurice Merleau-Ponty abandoned Marxism in part because its objective, scientific side—which captured the full weight and density of material reality—led to a determinism he found bound up with Stalinism, while its willful, active side led to a dialectical Marxism (e.g., that of Lukacs) that was as impotent to change reality as it was appealing. In other words, the fluidity of human transformative action and the weight and necessity of material reality were fated to remain polar opposites, never to be united, while Marxism in power was fated to be authoritarian and oppressive. Rather than continue to look for, or await, the historical conditions under which human action could grasp and transform the full weight of social reality, Merleau-Ponty abandoned Marxism altogether. See my *Sartre's Second Critique* (Chicago, 1987), Chapter 1.

29. Lobkowicz, 376.

30. See Little, op. cit., 24–29.

31. There is absolutely no room for it in contemporary efforts to create a

defensible historical materialism—as attempted, for example, by G. A. Cohen in *Karl Marx's Theory of History: A Defense* (Princeton, 1978) and *History, Labor, and Freedom* (Oxford, 1988); or Erik Olin Wright, Andrew Levine, and Elliot Sober, *Reconstructing Marxism* (London, 1992). See Chapter 5, this volume.

32. See Karl Marx, "The Eighteenth Brumaire of Louis Bonaparte." In Tucker, op. cit., 436–525.

33. What Anderson (op. cit., 87) has in mind above all in this formulation is that only Marxism unites "practical efficacy" and "radicalism of achievement."

34. See Leszek Kolakowski, *Main Currents of Marxism*, vol. I (Oxford, England, 1978); see also the review of this by Ralph Miliband in *Class Power and State Power* (London, 1983), 215–229, and *Divided Societies* (Cambridge, England, 1989).

35. For a sophisticated anti-Marxist appreciation of the prophetic dimension of Marx, see Joseph Schumpeter, *Capitalism, Socialism and Democracy* (New York, 1950), 5–8.

36. It is important to stress that Marxism has always seen itself not as *a* project but in some fundamental sense as *the* project—because it illuminates the main structures and tendencies of modern social reality itself, and the main forces making for its transformation. It was in this sense that Sartre once claimed existentialism to be an ideology *within* Marxism, which he regarded as the "philosophy of our time" (*Search for a Method* [New York, 1976], 7). Similarly, all Marxists have considered its particular approach to social reality, and the anticipated political and social transformations, to be the overarching ones, rather than as one specific project among others. Marxism, it has always been argued, is the privileged framework because it *is* reality itself in its main tendencies and actions.

37. See Herbert Marcuse, *Reason and Revolution* (Boston, 1960), 318–320.

38. See G. A. Cohen, "Historical Inevitability and Revolutionary Agency." In op. cit. (1988). Cohen makes the mistake of treating Marx's claims to inevitability as serious, and valid, scientific statements. The question thus becomes, in what sense is socialism inevitable, and what are the consequences of this for individual action? At this stage in Marxism's career, however, it should be clear that as a scientific claim, inevitability was always without basis and always foolish, and that today it should be rejected. As a prophetic claim, in contrast, inevitability was central to Marxism, and serious revolutionaries need to understand the role it played and to provide for the needs such a claim once satisfied. By focusing on Marxism as *argument*, analytical Marxism misses this entire side of the project. See Chapter six, this volume.

39. Laclau and Mouffe (op. cit.) seem to be saying just this.

40. These are among the criteria developed by Brian Fay in his *Social Theory and Political Practice* (New York, 1975) and *Critical Social Science* (Cambridge, MA, 1987).

41. Kolakowski, op. cit., 363–376.

42. These facts were the basis for Marcuse's *One-Dimensional Man*, (Boston, 1965).

43. This is the situation giving rise to Eric Olin Wright's study, *Classes* (London, 1985).

44. André Gorz, *Farewell to the Working Class* (London, 1982); Harry Braverman, *Labor and Monopoly Capital* (New York, 1975).

45. See André Gorz, *A Critique of Economic Reason* (London, 1990).

46. Claus Offe, *Disorganized Capitalism* (Cambridge, MA, 1985).

47. Ibid., 129–150.

48. See, for example, Stanley Aronowitz, *The Crisis in Historical Materialism* (New York, 1980).

49. See Wallerstein's conclusion, op. cit.

50. See Wright, op. cit.

51. Miliband, op. cit. (1989), 23.

52. David Harvey, *The Condition of Postmodernity* (Cambridge, MA, 1990).

53. See Miliband, op. cit. (1989), 48–50; and Stephen Wood (ed.), *The Transformation of Work?* (London, 1989), 1–43.

54. This is, in part, because class struggle from above is unceasing. Miliband, op. cit. (1989), 50, 203–224, 207.

55. Ibid., 110.

56. Ibid., 100.

57. Ibid., 18.

58. "These include non-unionized unskilled workers; most migrants; rural laborers; those employed in the formal sector, and the millions of unemployed." ("The Role of the SACP in the Transition to Democracy and Socialism" [discussion paper, 1993]).

59. Ibid., 13.

60. Ibid., 8.

61. But an accommodation with capitalism would only be acceptable if it were done "in such a way as to develop the leading role of the working class" (Ibid., 13)

62. Ibid., 5.

63. Ibid., 7.

64. Ibid., 8.

65. Ibid., 16.

66. André Gorz developed the notion of "strategic reforms" in the 1960s: *Strategy for Labor* (Boston, 1967).

67. See, however, Stanley Aronowitz, *False Promises* (New York, 1973).

68. See, however, Guy Debord, *The Society of the Spectacle* (Detroit, 1967).

69. Gorz, op. cit., 8.

70. See, however, Michael Goldfield, *The Decline of Organized Labor in the United States* (Chicago, 1987). This is discussed in Chapter 4, this volume, where I will argue that it was probably too much to expect in an early modern movement of the oppressed and exploited that they would become able to rule within the short time span assumed by Marx. As Erica Sherover-Marcuse argues in *Emancipation and Subjectivity* (Oxford, 1988), Marx perceived as unproblematic what is actually one of the most problematic aspects of modern political thought.

71. See Goran Therborn, "A Balance Sheet of the Left." *New Left Review* 195 (July–August 1992).

72. In 1967 David Herreshoff wrote:

Every American generation since the eighteen-twenties has witnessed a significant expression of labor radicalism. It seems likely that there will be new expressions of it and that labor radicalism will be one of the forms of revolt to attract the generation now of college age. The great uncertainty would seem to lie in whether the next labor radicalism will be more conscious and more powerful than its predecessors. When the future dispels this uncertainty one of two historical estimates of the modern working class will be vindicated: Thomas Jefferson's or Karl Marx's. Jefferson thought that the class of wage workers created by capitalism would prove politically and morally impotent, but Marx had faith that the victims of modern society would learn to free themselves. The scales of prophecy are still balanced. Experience has battered the consciousness and depressed the self-confidence of the labor movement, but in the waves of reform turbulence which occasionally sweep the United States the role of labor has grown. Unless this pattern has finally fulfilled itself, the story of the Americanizers of Marx is not yet at an end. *American Disciples of Marx: From the Transcendentalists to Daniel De Leon* (Detroit, 1973), 192.

Nearly three decades later, it seems that the pattern has fulfilled itself.

73. Aronowitz, op. cit., 219.

74. Bertell Ollmann, *Dialectical Investigations* (Routledge: New York, 1993), 148.

75. Ibid., 157.

76. Ibid., 164.

77. Ibid., 158.

78. Ibid.

79. Ibid., 159.

80. Ibid.

81. Ibid., 166.

82. Ibid., 167.

83. See Michael Mann, *Consciousness and Action among the Western Working Class* (London, 1973).

84. Miliband (op. cit, 18), for example, talks about Marxism as follows: "this notion of a new society, far from being a *vision*, spun from idle dreams, is in fact a *project*, solidly grounded in material conditions, human will, and historical experience."

85. Sartre, op. cit., 7.

86. For one hundred years, in the face of recalcitrant reality, there have been many efforts to save the theory and its revolutionary possibilities by *redefining* the workers, the nature of their oppression, why they are being held back from their revolutionary mission, and how contemporary movements relate to the political economy of capital. During much of this period, the classical effort to rescue Marxism *from* reality has been under the banner of Trotskyism; it begins with the claim that the Bolshevik Revolution was betrayed. For a contemporary restatement see Alex Callinicos, *The Revenge of History* (College Park, PA, 1992).

87. Ollmann, op. cit., 159.

Chapter Three (pp. 68–86)

1. See Karl Schorske, *German Social Democracy, 1905–1917* (Cambridge, MA, 1955).

2. Quoted in E. J. Hobsbawm, *The Age of Empire 1875–1914* (London, 1987), 133.

3. Was this a genuine revolution or a putsch? I discuss the issue in *The Dialectics of Disaster* (London, 1983), Chapter 2.

4. This was the basis on which Leninism became universalized to apply to full-fledged colonial societies struggling to overthrow foreign rulers.

5. Herbert Marcuse, *Soviet Marxism* (New York, 1961), 17.

6. See Jean-Paul Sartre, *Critique of Dialectical Reason*, vol. I (London, 1991); and my *Sartre's Second Critique* (Chicago, 1987). Bukharin did in one sense grasp the implications more fully than Lenin, Trotsky, or Stalin, as is argued by Steven Cohen in *Bukharin and the Bolshevik Revolution* (Oxford, 1980). But the fact remains that he was correct *in the abstract* only: he was unable to forge a coalition to stop Stalin and, until very late he was blind to the necessity of doing so. See Aronson, op. cit. (1983), Chapter 2.

7. Joseph Stalin, *Dialectical and Historical Materialism* (New York, 1969), 15.

8. See Perry Anderson, *Considerations on Western Marxism* (London, 1976).

9. Max Horkheimer, *Critical Theory* (New York, 1972), 226.

10. See Ernest Mandel, *The Meaning of The Second World War* (London, 1986).

11. See Jean-Paul Sartre, "Czechoslovakia: The Socialism that Came in from the Cold." In *Between Existentialism and Marxism* (London, 1983).

12. Alex Callinicos, *The Revenge of History* (College Park, PA, 1992), 2.

13. This is described in detail by Isaac Deutscher, *The Prophet Armed* (New York, 1954), Chapter 14, and *The Prophet Unarmed* (New York, 1959), Chapters 1 and 2.

14. Indeed, the vicissitudes of the Soviet Union in the 1920s and 1930s can be studied (as I have in Chapter 2 of *The Dialectics of Disaster*) as an increasingly irrational and brutal effort to realize the original Bolshevik project *in the circumstances created by its victory and under the control of those brought to power by those circumstances.* Or, as Jean-Paul Sartre described it in *Critique of Dialectical Reason*, vol. 2 (London, 1991) the deviation of Bolshevism at the hands of Stalin, including the fact that all power came to be concentrated in Stalin's hands, resulted from the Revolution's struggle to survive. Deviation is the key analytical theme and political question. It is a praxis process in which, Sartre says, "these men have become other men intent on attaining other objectives by other means—yet they do not even know it" (238). Called upon to save the Revolution, Stalin finds himself caught up in, and shaped and transformed by, the praxis-process he has set in motion (see Aronson, op. cit. [1987], Chapters 5 and 6). Sartre argues that Bolshevism–Leninism–Stalinism were in a profound sense a single praxis unfolding *and* being created in context, changing hands in the process and deviating according to the new vicissitudes they had to confront. Stalinism was Bolshevik praxis in the impossible situation in which the isolated, exhausted, but victorious Revolution found itself.

15. See, for example, Isaac Deutscher, *Russia in Transition* (New York, 1957), 83–100.

16. Callinicos, op. cit., 2–3.

17. Ibid., 2.

18. Well before Solidarity, this was Isaac Deutscher's hope; see his *The Unfinished Revolution* (New York, 1967).

19. Isaac Deutscher, *Russia: What Next?* (New York, 1953), 230.

20. Aronson, op. cit. (1987), 241–243.

21. For comments on this see Marcuse, op. cit., 121–178.

22. For a discussion of this see Perry Anderson, *In the Tracks of Historical Materialism* (London, 1983).

23. Aronson, op. cit. (1987), 242–243.

24. "The Role of the SACP in the Transition to Democracy and Socialism" (discussion paper, 1993), 4.

25. Ibid.

26. Callinicos, op. cit., 21–66.

27. Ibid., 118–133.

28. The following thoughts are from a conversation with Daniel Singer, June, 1991.

29. Callinicos, op. cit., 136.

30. Ibid., 106.

Chapter Four (pp. 87–123)

1. Karl Marx and Frederick Engels, *The Manifesto of the Communist Party. Collected Works*, vol. 6 (New York, 1976), 487.

2. Speech at the Anniversary of the *People's Paper*. In Robert C. Tucker (ed.), *The Marx–Engels Reader* (New York, 1972), 428.

3. Leon Trotsky, *The History of the Russian Revolution*, vol. 3 (London, 1967), 289. Max Eastman translates it as "rubbish-can."

4. Isaac Deutscher, *The Unfinished Revolution* (New York, 1967), 34.

5. Moshe Lewin, *Lenin's Last Struggle* (New York, 1968), 18–19.

6. See Isaac Deutscher, *Stalin: A Political Biography* (New York, 1967) 343–344.

7. Or perhaps, as Jean-Paul Sartre says, it is a dogmatic way of having people jettison all dogmas. See his *Critique of Dialectical Reason*, vol.II (London, 1991), 109; and my *Sartre's Second Critique* (Chicago, 1987), 110.

8. If this is true, the return to Saint Petersburg—Petersburg—may well be an act of going forward, recapturing the name of Russia's first great modernizer. Perhaps it is a return to the "window on the West" discussed by Marshall Berman, the city beloved of so many modernist Russian intellectuals, the vibrant, cosmopolitan, cultured, critical-minded link between Russia and the modern world. It was the city abandoned as capital after having been revolutionary center, whose "active and audacious masses" had insisted, in 1921, that the Revolution fulfill its promises, and who had been crushed by it (Marshall Berman, *All That Is Sold Melts into Air* [London, 1982], 272).

In discussing modernist poet Ossip Mandelstam, for whose writing the transformation of Petersburg had been a main theme, Berman writes prophetically, allowing us to see why the renaming of Leningrad may be seen as a step forward:

Mandelstam's life and death [in a concentration camp, in 1938] illuminate some of the depths and paradoxes of the Petersburg modern tradition. Logically, this tradition should have died a natural death after the October Revolution and the departure of the government for Moscow. But the increasingly sordid betrayal of that revolution by that government served, ironically, to give the old modernism a new life and force. In the neo-Muscovite totalitarian state, Petersburg became "the blessed word with no meaning," a symbol of all the human promise that the Soviet order had left behind. In the Stalin era, that promise was scattered to the Gulag and left for dead; but its resonance proved deep enough to survive many murders and, to outlive its murderers as well (281).

9. It is striking that recent Marxist writing tends to ignore or downplay this theme. For example, G. A. Cohen's *Karl Marx's Theory of History: A Defense* (Princeton, 1978) virtually ignores the starting and end point of Marx's theory, the belief that a classless society is coming about and the determination to make it happen. I emphasize "starting point" and "end point": John McMurtry's *The Structure of Marx's World View* (Princeton, 1978) manages to explore the key propositions of Marxism as a philosophy while barely mentioning these deep hopes, anticipations, and commitments—in other words, by leaving out its key terms. It is as if the Marxian mode of thought has no *goal* animating it, and is not part and parcel of a project to realize this vision. See Chapter 6, this volume.

10. Karl Marx, "Inaugural Address of the Working-Men's International Association." In Tucker (ed.), op. cit., 379.

11. Celebrated as such by, for example, George Lichtheim, in *Marxism: An Historical and Critical Study* (New York, 1965).

12. Karl Marx, "The Economic and Philosophical Manuscripts of 1844." In Tucker (ed.), op. cit., 70.

13. This is a much-controverted issue; see Paul Thomas, "Marx and Science." *Political Studies*, vol. XXIV, no. 1 (1976).

14. Frederick Engels, "Socialism, Utopian and Scientific." In Tucker (ed.), op. cit., 638–639.

15. Although Marxism can be disconnected from such sweeping claims and seen as a philosophy or mode of analysis rather than a *project*, the philosophy and the mode of analysis have always absorbed their force from the *vision* guiding Marxists, their determination to realize the vision, and their belief that our history is leading to an end that will be followed by a new beginning. See Chapter 6, this volume.

16. David McLellan, *Marxism and Religion*, (New York, 1987), has recently surveyed such attempts to hoist Marxism on its own petard by attacking its "religious" character: Robert C. Tucker, for example, in an analysis of the "religious essence of Marxism," stresses that the Marxian idea of revolution parallels the Christian promise of salvation or redemption (*Philosophy and Myth in Karl Marx* [Cambridge, England, 1972], 22–25). Such criticism, as McLellan points out, has turned on at least two central features of Marxism: "the idea that history has a purpose that is being relentlessly worked out and a powerful vision of future harmony to contrast with present discord" (161). There is no doubt, McLellan admits, that "Marx's thought has an eschatological dimension which has strong religious roots. But a conception of the world can have a religious origin without itself being religious" (Ibid.). In other words, Marxism may indeed be eschatological in a sense that must be precisely defined if we are to avoid the "conceptual wooliness" of such accusations, but it is also a thoroughly secular project that is neither dependent on God nor concerned with transcendence or other spiritual needs that only religion can fulfill. True enough, but the central question, which McLellan does not address, turns on the outrage of critics like Tucker that Marxism foresaw a turning point of history. For Marx, reflecting on this issue in 1843, religion was always the "heart of a heartless world," presenting images of our longings and hopes that cannot be satisfied because of social and economic limits. But if our

conditions of life were so transformed that the world did indeed find its heart, humans could place themselves at its center for the first time. Many of the longings heretofore satisfied only by religion can now be foreseen as being satisfied on earth. A classless society means ending the most fundamental of human conflicts; since *The German Ideology* its premise has been the fullest development of industrialization under capitalism, to achieve the world of milk and honey dreamed of since the beginning of history.

17. Leszek Kolakowski, *Main Currents of Marxism*, vol. I (Oxford, 1978), 375.

18. Karl Marx and Frederick Engels, *The German Ideology* (New York, 1970), 56.

19. Bertell Ollmann took a giant step toward this in "Marx's Vision of Communism: A Reconstruction," gathering Marx's various remarks on communism into a coherent picture (*Critique* [8], 1977).

20. As David McLellan points out (and as I have indicated above), there is a fundamental continuity between the early and the late Marx, the second presupposing the first (*Karl Marx: His Life and Thought* [New York, 1974]). Nevertheless, many commentators distinguish between the early and the late Marx, praising or blaming the one or the other as "humanistic" or as "mechanistic," as "apocalyptic" or as "mature." Thus do they praise or blame the philosophical or eschatological Marx on the one side or the scientific and realistic Marx on the other. George Lichtheim, for example, regards Marx's starting points as immature, and treats these as expressed for example, in the most impassioned parts of *The Civil War in France*, as the rhetorical baggage of socialism's earlier phases with which a mature, working-class socialist movement happened to be saddled (Lichtheim, op cit., 112–121). This "realist" approach to "rhetoric" fails to understand the project of Marxism: the verbal flourishes constitute the emotional cement holding Marxism together. They contain, as I have said previously, its starting point and end point.

21. As Ollmann says, he "was concerned to distinguish himself from other socialists for whom prescriptions of the future were the main stock-in-trade" (Ollmann op. cit., 8).

22. Albrecht Wellmer, *Critical Theory of Society* (New York, 1971).

23. Indeed, even if one agrees with Marcuse about a "determinate choice," in which specific features of the existing situation are transcended in a specific way (*One-Dimensional Man* [Boston, 1965], 221–222), the question remains as to who carries it out and how they come to do so. Since the emancipatory transformation Marx foresaw depended on human agency, it was necessarily dependent on human freedom. All the more so since, as Marcuse has expressed it, in projecting conscious human control over the world of human creations, Marxism projected a *rupture* with all previous civilization (*Reason and Revolution* [Boston, 1960], 318). Marcuse speaks explicitly of a "rupture with the continuum of domination" in "Re-examination of the Concept of Revolution." *New Left Review*, no. 56 (July–August, 1969).

24. Wellmer, op. cit., 72.

25. This is demonstrated, for example, in Marx's early vision of a class with radical chains, the universal class that would overturn all human suffering and liberate all of humanity. Was Marx talking about the actual working class, or didn't he rather come upon the proletariat, "sword in hand" while looking for the class that would fulfill his eschatological mission? See his Introduction to "Contribution to a Critique of Hegel's *Philosophy of Right*" (Tucker [ed.], op. cit., 11–23). For a

discussion see Oscar Berland, "Radical Chains: The Marxian Concept of Proletarian Mission" (*Studies on the Left*, vol. 6, no. 5, 1966.)

26. Karl Marx, Speech to the Communist League. Quoted in Boris Nicolaievsky, *Karl Marx: Man and Fighter* (London, 1973) 231; McLellan, op. cit. (1974), 249.

27. Karl Marx, *Herr Vogt*, quoted in Nicolaevsky, op. cit., 129.

28. Ibid.

29. As I have indicated in Chapter 1 and in note 23 above, Herbert Marcuse is one of the great exponents of the subjective side of Marxism, but this in turn gives his work a surprising fuzziness about the objective bases for social change; although he speaks much about tendencies, his discussion of them is rather loose and casual. See Chapter 11, this volume.

30. Thomas, op. cit., 10.

31. Ibid., 11–12.

32. Thomas is also concerned to distinguish Marx from Engels and to deny (incorrectly) that Marx ever used the term "dialectics" in describing his own work. See for example his Afterword to the Second German Edition, *Capital*, vol. I. In Tucker (ed.), op. cit., 197–198.

33. Ibid., 193.

34. Erica Sherover-Marcuse explores the issue and describes a number of passages from Marx in *Emancipation and Consciousness: Dogmatic and Dialectical Perspectives in the Early Marx* (Oxford, England, 1986), 122–128.

35. Marx and Engels, op. cit. (1970), 48.

36. Most telling is Marx's discussion of the laws of capitalism as its "laws of tendency." Because human action, struggles, and decisions are part and parcel of the economic process, as Little emphasizes, Marx's description of the falling rate of profit can never amount to a law, but rather can only indicate *tendencies* operating in a complex field. Hence the signal importance in *Capital* of Marx initiating the discussion of the "counteracting influences" that "cross and annul the effect of the general law, and which give it merely the characteristic of a tendency" (Karl Marx, *Capital*, vol. 3 [Moscow, 1962], 227). These "counterbalancing forces" result from the decision and practice of the capitalists themselves, and may also be responses to the class struggle; in the 1860s they included increasing the intensity of exploitation, depressing wages below the socially accepted subsistence minimum, and increasing foreign trade.

37. See Aronson, op. cit. (1987), Chapter 1.

38. See Sherover-Marcuse, 126–128, for her citation from the *Grundrisse* and *Capital* of passages that make it sound as if the needs of production will call up a socialist order to unfetter them.

39. Ibid., 4.

40. Ibid., 123.

41. Ibid., 124. See Tucker (ed.), op. cit., 4–5, for the text.

42. Sherover-Marcuse, op. cit., 126.

43. Ibid., 102–104.

44. Ibid., 137.

45. Minutes of the Meeting of the Central Authority (of the Communist League), September 15, 1850. In Karl Marx and Frederick Engels, *Collected Works*, vol. 10 (Moscow, 1978), 626.

46. Karl Marx, "The Class Struggles in France." In Karl Marx and Frederick Engels, *Selected Works*, vol. 1 (Moscow, 1962).

47. Sherover-Marcuse, op. cit., 184.

48. Ibid., 117–119.

49. Herbert Marcuse, *Soviet Marxism* (New York, 1961), Chapters 1 and 2.

50. This is equally true of the great proponent of workers' revolutionary spontaneity, Rosa Luxemburg. Her dogmatic vision of the workers, coupled with her critique of Leninism, has been appealing to non-Leninist Marxists. This set of issues is the jumping-off point for Ernesto Laclau and Chantal Mouffe's post-Marxism in *Hegemony and Socialist Strategy* (London, 1986).

51. Marx and Engels, op. cit. (1976), 495.

52. See Keith Michael Baker, *Condorcet: From Natural Philosophy to Social Mathematics* (Chicago, 1975).

53. See Gertrud Lenzer, Introduction, *Auguste Comte and Positivism* (Chicago, 1983).

54. In Part 2 of *Reason and Revolution* (op cit.) Marcuse stresses this difference between social science (described as positivism) and social theory.

55. Quoted in Thomas, op. cit., 6.

56. The most obvious example is his rhapsodizing about cooperatives in the International's opening Address. See Tucker (ed.), op. cit., 379–380.

57. Georges Haupt, "Marx and Marxism," In Eric J. Hobsbawm (ed.), *The History of Marxism*, vol. I (Bloomington, IN, 1982), 275–276.

58. Ibid., 268.

59. Ibid.

60. Ibid., 265.

61. V. I. Lenin, "What Is To Be Done?" *Selected Works*, vol. 1 (Moscow, 1963), 150.

62. Ibid.

63. As Marcuse says, Lenin's theses had, and were intended to have, far wider theoretical import than on Russia alone (op. cit., 14–18).

64. See my *The Dialectics of Disaster* (London, 1983), 92.

65. Wellmer, op. cit., 75.

66. Maurice Merleau-Ponty, *Adventures of the Dialectic* (Evanston, 1973); see Aronson, op. cit. (1987), Chapter 1.

67. Russell Jacoby, *The Dialectic of Defeat* (Cambridge, 1981).

68. Jean Paul Sartre, *Search for a Method* (New York, 1976), 30.

69. Georg Lukacs, *History and Class Consciousness* (Cambridge, MA, 1971), 71.

70. Ibid., xviii.

71. Ibid., xx. His 1933 recantation, he insisted in 1967, contained only a single "conformist element"—that "it was necessary to adopt the current official jargon" (xxxviii). Otherwise, presumably, the recantation expressed his own authentic criticism of his work.

72. A generation after *History and Class Consciousness*, Sartre presents his existentialism similarly as an "ideology" within the "philosophy of our time," Marxism. Sartre assumes the centrality of Communism and Soviet Marxism, and sets up shop alongside it to stress specificity, the subject, and the self-determining character of all human action. Beginning with the historical phenomenon of Marxism as embodied in the French Communist Party and the Soviet Union, he

seeks to account for its ossification, as well as to open it up and correct it. Like *History and Class Consciousness, Search for a Method* is designed to complement Marxism, not to replace it.

73. Trotskyism, for example, has always presented itself as the rational alternative to Stalinism, and makes no sense without it. See Aronson, op. cit. (1983), Chapter 2.

74. This is used by Anthony Giddens, *Modernity and Self-Identity* (Cambridge, 1991).

75. Zygmunt Bauman, *Modernity and Ambivalence* (New York, 1990), Chapter 7.

76. See Aronson, op. cit. (1983), 58–59.

77. One of the great difficulties in discussing modernity is the vagueness of the terrain; this is paralleled by a characteristic pitfall of discussions of postmodernism: to select what one is objecting to as being characteristically modern, in order to supersede it. Zygmunt Baumann, for example, calls uniquely modern the effort to bring chaos under control (see *Modernity and Ambivalence*, Chapter 1). He clearly has not been reading his Plato. The problem is that all such discussions, professing to be descriptions of cultural phenomena, become veiled *valuations* and *arguments*.

78. Immanuel Kant, *Political Writings* (Cambridge, England, 1991), 54.

79. André Gorz, *Critique of Economic Reason* (London, 1989), 1.

80. This is the Marx described by Marshall Berman.

81. Even if, ironically enough, it provided the theoretical and rhetorical base for the transformation on an almost nonexistent working class.

82. Sartre, op. cit. (1991), 111 (my translation); see Aronson, op. cit. (1987), 111.

83. Karl Marx and Frederick Engels, op cit., 506.

Chapter Five (pp. 124–139)

1. As David Schweickart says, "Marxism has been, from its inception, committed to the theoretical equality of the sexes. Marxist philosophers, looking back over their favorite texts, do not have to cringe the way most other philosophers do" (*Against Capitalism* [Cambridge, England, 1993], 350–351).

2. Heidi Hartmann, "The Unhappy Marriage of Marxism and Feminism: Towards a More Progressive Union." *Capital and Class*, no. 8 (1979), 5.

3. The *locus classicus* for this is Frederick Engels, *The Origin of the Family, Private Property, and the State* (New York, 1972).

4. See, for example, Eli Zaretsky, *Capitalism, the Family and Personal Life* (New York, 1976).

5. Lourdes Beneria, "Whatever Happened to Marxist Feminism?" Paper presented at the *Rethinking Marxism* Conference (Amherst, MA, November, 1992).

6. Alison Jaggar, *Feminist Politics and Human Nature* (Totawa, NJ, 1983), 124.

7. Ibid., 137.

8. Michèle Barrett, *Women's Oppression Today: The Marxist/Feminist Encounter* (rev. ed. [London, 1988], 8. The term "sex blind" is Heidi Hartmann's (see note 2 above).

9. Barrett, op. cit. (1988), 8–9.

10. See Lise Vogel, *Marxism and the Oppression of Women* (New Brunswick, NJ, 1983).

11. Ibid., 170.

12. See, for example, the comments of Scarlet Pollock in a review in *The Canadian Review of Sociology and Anthropology* (February, 1987), 150.

13. Jaggar, op. cit., 78.

14. Ibid., 290.

15. Ibid., 123.

16. Ibid.

17. Ibid., 127.

18. Ibid., 134.

19. Ibid., 136.

20. Ibid., 141.

21. "On the socialist–feminist analysis capitalism, male dominance, racism, and imperialism are intertwined so inextricably that they are inseparable; consequently the abolition of any of these systems of domination requires the end of all of them" (Ibid., 124).

22. Ibid., 159.

23. Ibid., 160.

24. Hartmann, op. cit., 6.

25. Iris Young, "Socialist-Feminism and the Limits of Dual Systems Theory." In *Throwing Like a Girl and other Essays in Feminist Philosophy and Social Theory* (Bloomington, 1990), 30. Emphasis in original.

26. Zillah Eisenstein, Introduction to *Capitalist Patriarchy and the Case for Socialist Feminism* (New York, 1979), 2.

27. Ibid., 5.

28. Barrett, op. cit. (1988), Chapter 3.

29. Ann Ferguson, *Sexual Democracy: Women, Oppression, and Revolution* (Boulder, 1991), Chapter 2.

30. Nancy Hartsock, *Money, Sex, and Power* (New York, 1983), chapter 10.

31. Ilene Philopson, "The Impasse of Socialist-Feminism: A Conversation with Deirdre English, Barbara Epstein, Barbara Haber, and Judy MacLean." *Socialist Review*, no. 79 (1985).

32. Lynne Segal, *Is the Future Female?* (London, 1987), 44.

33. Barrett, Introduction to the 1988 edition, op. cit., xxii–xxiii.

34. Zillah Eisenstein, "Specifying US Feminism in the 1990s: The Problem of Naming." *Socialist Review*, no. 90/2 (1990): 46.

35. Ann Froines, "Renewing Socialist Feminism." *Socialist Review*, No. 92/2 (April–June, 1992).

36. Nancy Fraser, "A Future for Marxism in a Postmarxist Age." Paper presented to the American Philosophical Association (Chicago, April, 1991).

37. See Michèle Barrett, "Words and Things: Materialism and Method in Contemporary Feminist Analysis." In Michèle Barrett and Anne Phillips (eds.), *Destabilizing Theory* (London, 1992); and Young, op. cit. (1990), Introduction and Part 2.

38. Zillah Eisenstein, "Reflections." In Sonia Kruks, Rayna Rapp, and Marilyn

B. Young (eds.), *Promissory Notes: Women in the Transition to Socialism* (New York, 1989), 333.

39. See, for example, Linda Nicholson's stress on the various pieces of the "puzzle" of the social whole of women's oppression, in *Gender and History: The Limits of Social Theory in the Age of the Family* (New York, 1986).

40. Eisenstein, op. cit. (1990), 49.

41. Ibid., 50.

42. Ibid., 333. See also Young, op. cit. (1990); and Barrett, op. cit. (1992).

43. Eisenstein, op. cit. (1990), 50; see also Young, Introduction, op. cit. (1990), 5.

44. Eisenstein, op cit., 50–51.

45. Hartsock, op. cit., 234 (my italics).

46. See Donna Landry and Gerald MacLean, *Materialist Feminisms* (Cambridge, MA, 1993).

47. See Jaggar, op. cit., Chapter 10.

48. Jaggar, 317.

49. Eisenstein, op. cit. (1990), 51.

50. Ellen Meiksins Wood, "Capitalism and Human Emancipation." *New Left Review*, no. 167 (January/February 1988), 4.

51. Ibid.

52. Ibid., 20.

53. Ellen Meiksins Wood, *The Retreat from Class* (London, 1986), 199.

54. Perry Anderson, *In the Tracks of Historical Materialism* (London, 1983), 97.

55. Barrett, Introduction to 1988 edition, op. cit., xxii.

56. Ibid., 8.

57. Eisenstein, op. cit. (1990), 51; see also Barrett, Introduction to the 1988 edition, op. cit., vi–ix.

58. Jane Flax, "Postmodernism and Gender Relations in Feminist Theory." *Signs*, vol. 12, no. 4. (1987): 631.

59. Lourdes Beneria, op. cit.

60. Ibid.

61. Fraser, op. cit., 1.

62. Barrett, op. cit. (1992), 205.

63. Flax, op. cit., 624.

64. See Barrett, op. cit. (1992), 215.

65. Flax, op. cit., 633.

Chapter Six (pp. 140–159)

1. Andrew Levine, "What Is a Marxist Today." In Robert Ware and Kai Nielsen, *Analyzing Marxism: New Essays on Analytical Marxism* (Calgary, 1989): 32

2. Erik Olin Wright, Andrew Levine, and Elliot Sober, *Reconstructing Marxism* (London, 1992), 5.

3. Ibid., 3.

4. Ibid., 2.

5. G. A. Cohen, *History, Labor, and Freedom* (Oxford, England, 1988), 17.

6. Ibid., 15.

7. Ibid., 65.

8. G. A. Cohen, *Karl Marx's Theory of History: A Defense* (Princeton, NJ, 1978), 307.

9. Ibid., 307.

10. Levine, op. cit., 32.

11. Alan Carling, "Rational Choice Marxism." *New Left Review*, no. 160 (November/December, 1986), 25.

12. Levine, op. cit., 32.

13. Wright et al., op. cit., 3.

14. Ibid., 2.

15. Ibid., 1.

16. See Anthony Giddens, *A Contemporary Critique of Historical Materialism* (Berkeley, 1981).

17. Wright et al., op. cit., 24.

18. Ibid., 19; quoted from Cohen, op. cit. (1978), 158.

19. Wright et al., op. cit., 25.

20. Cohen, op. cit. (1978), 158–165.

21. See Wright et al., op. cit., 89–93.

22. Ibid., 90.

23. See Cohen, op. cit., Chapter 9.

24. Wright et al., op. cit., 91.

25. Ibid., 97.

26. Ibid., 190.

27. Ibid., 191.

28. Ibid.

29. Ibid., 12.

30. Ibid., 191.

31. Levine, op cit., 55.

32. The fate of the Soviet Union provides the most glaring example. Cohen and the authors of *Reconstructing Marxism* agree that historical materialism requires a high degree of economic development as an indispensable prerequisite for socialism. Thus "premature attempts at revolution, whatever their immediate outcome, will eventuate in a restoration of capitalist society" (Cohen, op. cit. [1978], 206; see also Wright et al., op. cit., 32).

33. John McMurtry, *The Structure of Marx's World View* (Princeton, NJ, 1978).

34. Wright et al. raise this same question when trying to ascertain the differences between "strong" and "weak" historical materialism as well as between orthodox, neo-, and post-Marxist class analysis (op. cit., 183–185).

35. Cohen has indicated his personal starting points in the preface to *Karl Marx's Theory of History* and, more recently and more eloquently, in his reflections in "The Future of a Disillusion." *New Left Review*, no. 190 (November/December 1991).

36. Wright et al., op. cit., 5.

37. Dorothy E. Smith, "Feminist Reflections on Political Economy." *Studies in Political Economy*, no. 30 (Autumn, 1989), 44–45. Emphasis in original.

38. Ibid., 45.

39. Ibid., 47.

40. See my *Sartre's Second Critique* (Chicago, 1987), 42–44, 221–223.

41. "The contemporary renaissance of scientific Marxism is, in part, a conse-quence of the greater autonomy accorded the development of Marxist theory as the role of Marxist officialdom has waned. It is difficult to imagine the theoretical advances within Marxism of the 1970s and 1980s occurring if Marxist theoretical work had been produced primarily within the organizational structures of political parties that required party discipline of their members. The heightened autonomy of Marxist sceintific practice from direct subordination to political requirements has contributed to the opening up of Marxist discourse to wider theoretical influences and debates" (Wright et al., op. cit, 181–182).

42. Nancy Fraser, "A Future for Marxism in a Postmarxist Age." Paper presented to the American Philosophical Association (Chicago, April 1991), 1.

43. Ibid.

44. To Wright et al. continued adherence to these ideas may qualify me as "neo-Marxist" rather than "post-Marxist" because it accepts "that class and related concepts are *important*, but not necessarily the most important causes" (op. cit., 184–185). Note, as I said before, that what marks a Marxist in this passage is not adherence to the Marxist project, but only acceptance of the centrality of class as an explanatory category. Their litmus test is posed *within* the realm of theory, rather than in terms of a theoretical–practical revolutionary project.

45. Steven Seidman (ed.), *Jürgen Habermas on Society and Politics* (Boston, 1989), 298.

46. I am indebted to Christopher Johnson and his paper, "Habermas vs. the New Working Class." (Wayne State University, January 1993), for the argument in this and the next two paragraphs. See also Johnson, "Lifeworld, System, and Commu-nicative Action: The Habermasean Alternative in Social History." In Lenard Berlanstein (ed.), *Essays in Discourse and Class Analysis* (Urbana, IL 1993).

47. Iris Young's *Justice and the Politics of Differences* (Princeton, 1990) makes a welcome attempt to retain the Marxian dimension of exploitation while articulat-ing other, equally important kinds of oppression: marginalization, cultural imperi-alism, powerlessness, and violence. See Chapter 8, this volume.

48. Norman Geras, *Discourses of Extremity* (London, 1990), 62.

49. Ibid., 163.

50. Ralph Miliband, "The New Revisionism in Britain." *New Left Review*, no. 150 (March/April, 1985), 14.

51. Levine, op. cit., 57

52. Ibid., 42.

53. Ibid., 54.

54. Ibid., 54.

55. Ellen Meiksins Woods, *The Retreat from Class* (London, 1986), 178.

56. Ibid., 173.

57. David Schweickart, *Against Capitalism* (Cambridge, England, 1993), 335–336.

58. Ibid., 353.

59. Fraser, op cit., 1.

60. Stephen A. Resnick and Richard D. Wolff, *Knowledge and Class: A Marxian Critique of Political Economy* (Chicago, 1987), 280.

61. Ibid., 279.

62. Resnick and Wolff explain:

In contrast to . . . essentialistic approaches, we conceptualize each distinguishing aspect of a social relationship as a process and thereby underscore Marxian theory's focus upon the ceaseless change characterizing society and each of its parts. Such change is understood as the consequence of the interaction among processes within any social totality. Marxian theory conceptualizes that interaction by means of its concept of overdetermination. Every class and nonclass process in society is theorized as overdetermined by all the others existing within society and therefore changing it.

To generalize Marxian theory, each process in society is understood as the site of the interaction of the influences exerted by all the others. In other words, the existence and particular features of any one social process are constituted by all the other processes comprising a society. Each social process is the effect produced by the interaction of (i.e., is overdetermined by) all the others. Each process is overdetermined as well as a participant in the overdetermination of every other process in the society (Ibid., 23–24).

Part Two (Introduction) (pp. 161–164)

1. Quoted in Boris Nicolaievsky, *Karl Marx: Man and Fighter* (London, 1973), 128.

Chapter Seven (pp. 165–180)

1. As David Plotke says, the tendency of new social movement discourse is to "invert" Marxism, and thus to "restate" it. See "What's So New About New Social Movements?" *Socialist Review*, no. 90/1 (1990), 88.

2. Barry D. Adam, "PostMarxism and the New Social Movements." *The Canadian Review of Sociology and Anthropology*, no. 30 (August 1993). Alberto Melucci, one of the first to use the term "new social movements" (in 1977), reflects this incoherence at a number of points in *Nomads of the Present* (London, 1989). Asked in a concluding interview about the claim that new social movements cannot achieve fundamental change because they fail to question property relations, Melucci agrees that property, in the sense of capital, "remains one of the problems facing us today," but then insists that a new kind of property, "our biological and psychological existence," is becoming "more and more important" (211). When asked, no less than three different times, about ways the new social movements revive and continue earlier movements, Melucci avoided the question entirely, stressing rather what is new in the movements (214).

3. See Nancy Fraser on Habermas and feminism, *Unruly Practices* (Minneapolis, 1990).

4. Raymond Williams, *Marxism and Literature* (London, 1977), 128–135.

5. Michèle Barrett, *The Politics of Truth: From Marx to Foucault* (Cambridge, England, 1991), 161.

6. Jean-François Lyotard, "Universal History and Cultural Differences." In Andrew Benjamin (ed.), *The Lyotard Reader* (Oxford, England, 1989), 316.

7. Ibid., 318.

8. "In England between 1660 and 1690, for example, two structures of feeling (among the defeated Puritans and in the restored Court) can be readily distinguished, though neither, in its literature and elsewhere, is reducible to the ideologies of these groups or to their formal (in fact complex) class relations" (Williams, 134). Obviously, as a variety of social groups find their voices, a multiplicity of structures of feeling will be accessible.

9. Postmodernism has been criticized for doing precisely this. See Nancy Hartsock, "Rethinking Modernism: Minority vs. Majority Theories." *Cultural Critique*, no. 7 (Fall 1987), 196.

10. Meaghan Morris, *The Pirate's Fiancée: Feminism, Reading, Postmodernism* (London, 1988), 53.

11. From this point of view Marcuse's description may be regarded as premature. The sense of alternative, as the activism of the 1960s and 1970s revealed, was still very much alive. Only now, it seems, will we get a real test of his theses in *One-Dimensional Man* (Boston, 1965).

12. Jorge G. Casteneda, *Utopia Unarmed: The Latin American Left after the Cold War* (New York, 1993), 431–432.

13. Francis Fukuyama, "Have We Reached the End of History?" RAND Corporation paper, 1989, 1.

14. Ibid., 2. It is worth noting, however, that even at capitalism's moment of victory, ideologists like Fukuyama cannot afford to be honest and speak directly about capitalism. What has triumphed, rather, is the political form, "liberal democracy" or, at best, the "market economy."

15. This is obvious, for example, in Robert Heilbroner's bellwether book, *An Inquiry into The Human Prospect* (New York, 1975).

16. See Fredric Jameson, *Postmodernism, or, The Cultural Logic of Late Capitalism* (Durham, NC, 1991).

17. We can learn much from Sartre's attempt to understand dialectical processes within a field of radical indeterminacy—and from the fact that he got no farther than highlighting a few moments of unity, a few conflicts, and the process of totalization by a single totalizer—the sovereign individual, Joseph Stalin. See Jean-Paul Sartre, *Critique of Dialectical Reason*, I (London, 1976), and II (London, 1991); and my *Sartre's Second Critique* (Chicago, 1987).

18. I do not want to deny the existence of a Hegelian "cunning of reason"—or, rather, of many of them—that is, that human actions may be driven by goals from which we are structurally alienated, and of which we are unconscious. Thus, against our will, our own human actions may tend in directions that we experience with subtle, albeit overwhelming force. Nor do I want to deny that such "forces," acting behind people's backs, as it were, may serve the interest of those in positions of power, may express conflict, or may even express deeper, common, but unconscious goals and projects. History is hardly all pluralism and multiplicity, transparency and free action. And history's propulsions are hardly all direct and explicit. But even if we commit ourselves to the kinds of systemic analysis that might uncover precisely what forces operate behind people's backs and why, no logic can be posited in an a priori way as either single or dominant, let alone as emancipatory. We may wish to make it so, and a project of liberation may assert this, but such becoming conscious is a wish and a goal, and even more, a project. It should not, any longer, be confused with the analysis of what is actually taking place. Processes sustaining the various forms of domination

are with us constantly, perpetuated on every level; struggles against domination wax and wane, at times achieving victories but also suffering defeats.

19. For the argument see my *The Dialectics of Disaster* (London, 1983), Chapter 1.

20. For the self-invention of the Afrikaner see Dan O'Meara, *Volkskapitalisme: Class, Capital, and Ideology in the Development of Afrikaner Nationalism 1934–1948* (Cambridge, England, 1983).

21. See Aronson, op. cit., Chapter 7.

22. See Erica Sherover-Marcuse, *Emancipation and Consciousness: Dogmatic and Dialectical Perspectives in the Early Marx* (Oxford, England, 1986), Chapter 1. The phenomenon is a familiar one to those community organizers of the 1960s in the American South and then North who saw U. S. blacks as similarly free from the corruptions of the system. Rita Felski, criticizing both Marxist and feminist conceptions of a privileged standpoint, suggests that "if the master is blinded by a will to power, it is equally possible that the slave may be crippled by an internalized sense of inferiority which inspires envy and obsessive hatred of the master. Being oppressed is no guarantee of clarity of vision or possession of truth." See her "Feminism, Postmodernism, and the Critique of Modernity." *Cultural Critique*, no. 13 (Fall 1989), 40.

23. Karl Marx, "Contribution to a Critique of Hegel's *Philosophy of Right.*" In Robert C. Tucker (ed.), *The Marx-Engels Reader* (New York, 1972), 22.

24. As human beings become in some arguable sense more mature, more fully modern, as I have said, do they actually become infantilized by the forces that rule them? Does it reveal the profound limits of earlier projects, or contemporary developments, that both the "masses" and the intellectual "elite" alike seem sunk in a childlike dependency that only seems to increase with time? If there seems to be something "nonsynchronous" about this—that is, regressive—so does there seem something profoundly modern. In any case, no movement for change can avoid dealing with psychological issues, as Marcuse demonstrated in *Eros and Civilization* (Boston, 1954).

25. Jean-François Lyotard, *The Postmodern Condition* (Minneapolis, 1984), 37.

26. See Nancy Hartsock, "Modernism and Political Change: Issues for Feminist Theory." *Cultural Critique*, no. 14 (Winter, 1989–1990).

27. Alex Callinicos argues, to the contrary, that this disillusionment is rooted in the failure of the generation of 1968 to successfully carry out radical change, and in its subsequent absorption into the system. See *Against Postmodernism: A Marxist Critique* (Cambridge, England, 1989).

28. Minutes of the Meeting of the Central Authority (of the Communist League), September 15, 1850. In Karl Marx and Frederick Engels, *Collected Works*, vol. 10 (Moscow, 1978), 626.

29. For a description of how this happened in the aftermath of the great Paterson silk-workers' strike of 1913, see Steve Golin, *The Fragile Bridge: Paterson Silk Strike, 1913* (Philadelphia, 1989).

Chapter Eight (pp. 181–202)

1. Carl Boggs, *Social Movements and Political Power* (Philadelphia, 1986), 16.

2. As Barry D. Adam argues, the new movements have largely ignored the realms of political economy, workers, and class domination ("PostMarxism and the

New Social Movements." *The Canadian Review of Sociology and Anthropology*, no. 30 [August 1993]). In this sense, they continue to battle against the Marxian paradigm and create rival paradigms, rather than drawing a relativized Marxism's insights and analyses into a pluralistic framework. In distinct contrast with Marxism, Alain Touraine, for example, speaks about the "cultural" nature of the new social movements ("An Introduction to the Study of Social Movements." *Social Research*, vol. 52, no. 4 [Winter 1985]). Jean Cohen and Andrew Arato stress their "self-limiting" nature (see *Civil Society and Political Theory* [Cambridge, MA, 1992], 15–16). Alberto Melucci speaks about the new social movements' "symbolic challenge" to the prevailing system (*Nomads of the Present* [London, 1989] and "The Symbolic Challenge of Contemporary Social Movements." *Social Research*, vol. 52, no. 4 [Winter 1985]). But, as Carl Boggs says, "Surely, even a post-Marxist schema will have to incorporate an understanding of the economy and class forces into its conceptual structure. It would be absurd to think that the global crisis—or even a postindustrial issue such as environmental decay—can be grasped without an analysis of the crucial (and sometimes decisive) material factors at work" (Boggs, op. cit., 16). For Boggs, a suitably relativized Marxism becomes one of the "multiple paradigms in a situation where the prospects for a single, unifying agency (social or political) have vanished." But, as he points out, a new, unified movement based on multiple paradigms has not yet emerged; the 1970s and 1980s post-Marxist formations he studies have not yet come to terms with Marxism and incorporated it as one of their paradigms, en route to creating a coherent new movement. This is especially true for the German Greens who, in Boggs' analysis, seem as strongly shaped by their *avoidance* of Marxism and socialism as by their innovative approaches to environmental issues. See Boggs, op. cit., Chapter 5.

3. Melucci, op. cit. (1985), 810.

4. Cohen and Arato, op. cit., 368.

5. Ibid., 373.

6. Ibid.

7. Ibid.

8. Ibid., 376.

9. Ibid., 378.

10. Ibid., 384.

11. This is what Sartre called the practico-inert social field.

12. These terms, from Iris Young's discussion, allow us to include the various kinds of oppression that have been contested over the past generation. See *Justice and the Politics of Difference* (Princeton, NJ, 1990).

13. Ibid., 49.

14. Ibid., 52.

15. Ibid., 56–57.

16. Ibid., 58–59.

17. André Gorz, *Critique of Economic Reason* (London, 1989).

18. Nancy Fraser, "A Future for Marxism in a PostMarxist Age." Paper presented to the American Philosophical Association (Chicago, April 1991).

19. This, of course, is why a relativized Marxism, now willing to enter a coalition on terms of equality, is no longer Marxism as we know it.

20. E. J. Dionne, Jr., *Why Americans Hate Politics* (New York, 1991), 27.

21. Ibid., 337.

22. Ibid., 18.

23. Ibid., 330.

24. Ibid., 345.

25. Ibid., 346.

26. Ibid., 354.

27. Jürgen Habermas, *The Theory of Communicative Action: II. Lifeworld and System: A Critique of Functionalist Reason* (Boston, 1989), 374.

28. Cohen and Arato, op. cit., 2.

29. Ibid., 493.

30. Ibid., 470.

31. Their "politics of reform" would democratize civil society and defend its autonomy from the economy and political systems; moreover, they would create "sensors" in the state and economy and democratize the political sphere, in order to "open these institutions to the new identities and egalitarian norms articulated on the terrain of civil society" (526).

32. Ibid., 476.

33. Ibid., 491.

34. Ibid., 489.

35. It is worth noting that a radical like Marcuse, for all his pessimism about the existing order, at the same time entertained hopes that were much greater than those expressed by Dionne and Cohen and Arato. See Chapters 9 and 11, this volume.

36. Compare especially President Clinton's State of the Union address and subsequent policy proposals with Dionne, Part 3, "Curing the Mischiefs of Ideology," especially the detailed program on 347–348. The parallels are striking.

37. Claus Offe, "New Social Movements." *Social Research*, vol. 52, no. 4 (Winter 1985), 838. Offe points out that even if there are real bases for continuing conflicts, "there is by no means a natural or unchangeable tendency for the new social movements to form an alignment with the Left" (862).

38. See Gorz, op. cit., 65.

39. Offe, op. cit., 845.

40. Ibid.

41. Even Offe seems seduced by the phenomenon: "The systemic interchangeability of the scenes of conflict and the dimensions of conflict resolution makes any idea of a 'primordial' conflict (such as derived, for instance, from the Marxian 'law of value') obsolete" (Ibid., 845–846). On the contrary, I would argue that the structural source remains, and remains hidden. This means that we need to try to speak of "sources of problems" *and* recognize that the displacement has won functional autonomy and, after all, must be treated as *the* problem. See my "Historical Materialism: Answer to Marxism's Crisis?" *New Left Review*, no. 152 (1985).

42. Robert Heilbroner, *An Inquiry into the Human Prospect* (New York, 1975).

43. See Raymond Williams, *Keywords: A Vocabulary of Culture and Society* (New York, 1976), 82–87.

44. See, for example, Joshua Cohen and Joel Rogers, *On Democracy* (New York, 1983); and Samuel Bowles and Herbert Gintis, *Democracy and Capitalism* (New York, 1986).

45. Bowles and Gintis, op. cit., see especially 176–213.

46. Williams, op. cit., 210.
47. Ibid.
48. Ibid., 211.

Chapter Nine (pp. 203–230)

1. Stephen Toulmin, *Cosmopolis: The Hidden Agenda of Modernity* (New York, 1990), Chapter 1.
2. Zygmunt Baumann, *Modernity and Ambivalence* (Oxford, England, 1991), Chapter 7.
3. Marshall Berman, *All That Is Solid Melts into Air* (New York, 1982) 15.
4. Perry Anderson, "Modernity and Revolution." In Cary Nelson and Lawrence Grossberg (eds.), *Marxism and the Interpretation of Culture* (Urbana, IL, 1988), 332.
5. Max Horkheimer and Theodor W. Adorno, *Dialectic of Enlightenment* (New York, 1973), 3.
6. Ibid., xi.
7. Ibid., xiii.
8. Ibid., xiv–xv.
9. Ibid., xv.
10. Ibid.
11. Ibid.
12. Ibid., 169.
13. Ibid., 199.
14. Ibid., 184.
15. Ibid., 187.
16. Ibid., 185.
17. Ibid., xvi.
18. Ibid., 200.
19. Ibid., 199.
20. Ibid., xv.
21. Ibid., 3.
22. Theodor W. Adorno, *Negative Dialectics* (London, 1973), 320.
23. Ibid.
24. Michel Foucault, "Nietzsche, Genealogy, History." In Paul Rabinow (ed.), *The Foucault Reader* (New York, 1984), 85.
25. Michel Foucault, *Power/Knowledge: Selected Interviews and Other Writings 1972–1977*, Colin Gordon (ed.) (New York, 1980), 59.
26. For a critical discussion see Jean Cohen and Andrew Arato, *Civil Society and Political Theory*, (Cambridge, MA, 1992), Chapter 6.
27. Michel Foucault, *Discipline and Punish* (New York, 1979), 222.
28. Karl Marx, *Capital*, vol. 1 (Moscow, 1961), 176.
29. "What the bourgeoisie, therefore produces, above all, is its own grave-diggers. Its fall and the victory of the proletariat are equally inevitable." Karl Marx and Frederick Engels, *The Communist Manifesto. Collected Works*, vol. VI (New York, 1976), 487.

30. Herbert Marcuse, "A Note on Dialectic." In *Reason and Revolution* (Boston, 1960), xii.

31. Ibid., xiii.

32. Before writing these lines in 1960 Marcuse had already taken three enormous steps of this journey. First he explored the liberatory character of the Hegelian dialectic as absorbed into Marxian social theory; then he sought to develop, in dialogue with Freudian theory, a nonrepressive conception of reason and society; then, seeking to restore the possibility of a genuine critical theory of society, he showed how Soviet Marxism had transformed the critical thrust of Marxism into ideology. After his "A Note on Dialectic" (op cit.) Marcuse's project continued to diverge from Adorno's: toward developing the power of negation that holds up—in theory, in language—an alternative to the false rationality of the status quo; then toward finding that alternative embodied in the New Left; then toward seeking it in art. Thus did he preserve the hope, embodied in this "Note on Dialectic" for a fulfillment of progress by its reversal.

33. Ibid., viii–ix.

34. See Deborah Cook, *The Subject Finds a Voice: Foucault's Turn Towards Subjectivity* (New York, 1993), Chapters 8 and 9.

35. Foucault, op. cit. (1980), 81.

36. Steven Best and Douglas Kellner, *Postmodern Theory: Critical Interrogations* (New York, 1991), 55.

37. Foucault, "What Is Enlightenment." In Rabinow (ed.), op. cit., 49.

38. Ibid., 48.

39. Ibid., 43.

40. Kellner and Best, op. cit., 55.

41. See E. P. Thompson, *Customs in Common* (New York, 1991) and *The Making of the English Working Class* (New York, 1964).

42. Jean-Paul Sartre, "Itinerary of a Thought." In *Between Existentialism and Marxism* (London, 1974), 45.

43. See Jean-Paul Sartre, *The Family Idiot* (Chicago, 1987, 1991); see also my *Jean-Paul Sartre—Philosophy in the World* (London, 1980) and *Sartre's Second Critique* (Chicago, 1987).

44. See my "Hope and Action." In *Stay Out of Politics! A Philosopher Views South Africa* (Chicago, 1990).

45. Foucault, op. cit. (1980), 83. Emphasis in original.

46. Ibid.

47. Cohen and Arato, op. cit., 277.

48. Foucault, op. cit. (1980), 96.

49. Cohen and Arato, op. cit., 295.

50. See Jürgen Habermas, *Autonomy and Solidarity: Interviews*, Peter Dews (ed.) (London, 1986), 69; see also his two lectures on Foucault in *The Philosophical Discourse of Modernity* (Cambridge, Mass., 1987), 238–293.

51. Habermas, op. cit. (1986), 91.

52. Jürgen Habermas, *The Theory of Communicative Action: II. Lifeworld and System: A Critique of Functionalist Reason* (Boston, 1989), 261.

53. Ibid., 145.

54. Ibid., 186.

55. Ibid., 325.

56. Ibid., 330–331.

57. Ibid., 355.

58. Ibid., 393.

59. Habermas, op. cit. (1986), 61.

60. See Cohen and Arato, op. cit., Chapter 10.

61. Ibid., 442.

62. Ibid., 526.

63. Ibid.

64. Ibid.

65. Ibid., Chapter 10.

66. Ibid., 405.

67. Ibid., 419.

68. As Albrecht Wellmer says, "We have to distinguish between those irreversible differentiation processes, which signify the end of traditional society and the emergence of specifically modern, universalist conceptions of rationality, freedom, and democracy, on the one hand, and the specific form in which these differentiation processes have been articulated and institutionalized in capitalist societies" ("Reason, Utopia, Enlightenment." In Richard Bernstein (ed.), *Habermas on Modernity* [Cambridge, England, 1985], 62).

69. Leon Trotsky, *History of the Russian Revolution*, vol. 1 (London, 1967), 21–23.

70. Ernst Bloch, "Nonsynchronism and the Obligation to Its Dialectics." *New German Critique*, no. 11 (1977): 35.

71. See my *The Dialectics of Disaster* (London, 1983), 131–134.

72. See Ibid., especially Chapters 1 and 2.

73. Marx and Engels, op. cit., 488.

74. Linda Nicholson, *Gender and History: The Limits of Social Theory in the Age of the Family* (New York, 1986), 90.

75. Marx and Engels, op. cit., 487.

76. Ibid., 489.

77. Ibid.

78. Anthony Giddens, *Modernity and Self-Identity* (Cambridge, England, 1991), 196. Certainly Giddens might be criticized for failing to see these processes critically—for failing to convey, for example, specific tensions capitalism places at the heart of our modernity. He thoroughly mingles marketplace cant and profound world-historical process, pop psychology and ontological risks, self-improvement talk, and reflections on institutional reflexivity. As he makes clear toward the end of his study, capitalism has something to do with the processes he is describing, but he is more interested in describing the features of "high modernity" for themselves, as if they were not entwined with the economic system. Accordingly, *Modernity and Self-Identity* is most informative if considered as the product of an act of abstraction.

79. Cohen and Arato claim such status for their understanding of civil society (op. cit., 1); on the other hand, Alberto Melucci presents a theory of continued openness in *Nomads of the Present* (London, 1989).

80. In *Reason and Revolution*, Herbert Marcuse presented a curious version of this, arguing for the priority of theory in relationship to practice:

According to Marx, the correct theory is the consciousness of a practice that aims at changing the world.

Marx's concept of truth, however, is far from relativism. There is only one truth and one practice capable of realizing it. Theory has demonstrated the tendencies that make for the attainment of a rational order of life, the conditions for creating this, and the initial steps to be taken. The final aim of the new social practice has been formulated: the abolition of labor, the employment of the socialized means of production for the free development of all individuals. The rest is the task of man's own liberated activity. Theory accompanies the practice at every moment, analyzing the changing situation and formulating its concepts accordingly. The concrete conditions for realizing the truth may vary, but the truth remains the same and theory remains its ultimate guardian. Theory will preserve the truth even if revolutionary practice deviates from its proper path. Practice follows the truth, not vice versa.

This absolutism of truth completes the philosophical heritage of the Marxian theory and once and for all separates dialectical theory from the subsequent forms of positivism and relativism (op. cit., 321–322).

While Marcuse seems only to be formulating the Marxian approach to theory, his stress on the truth of theory, "even if " practice deviates, bears the stamp of the period in which these words were published (1941), and equally reflects the Frankfurt School's project of coming to grips with the failure of the truth to be "realized" both in the Soviet Union and the West. In such a situation, where the reality has confuted the theory, it understandably seemed to be theory, not practice, that preserved the hope for liberation. Reality had placed Marxism under siege, either invalidating Marxism or relegating it to the status of a critique lacking the chance of being realized. Thus Marcuse asserts theory *against* reality: to deny the truth of critical theory in a society without opposition is to be totally overcome by the prevailing situation's hopelessness. Measuring the reality against its own promises, evaluating the system's dynamics in terms both of the human suffering they cause and the possibility of emancipation they seek to repress—these critical acts allow theory to keep alive the space for opposition. As I argued in "Dear Herbert," this heroic view of theory shifts very easily, for the best of reasons, into an imperialism of theory (in George Fischer [ed.], *The Revival of American Socialism* [New York, 1970]). As such, those promoting its ascendency blind themselves very easily to the forces, the movements, and the needs for change that may be continuing to simmer just beneath the surface of the world around them.

Chapter Ten (pp. 231–257)

1. G. A. Cohen, *History, Labor, and Freedom* (Oxford, 1988), 302.

2. Ibid., 239.

3. Kai Nielson, *Marxism and the Moral Point of View* (Boulder, 1989), 133.

4. Nielson gives a thorough account of the debate.

5. See Norman Geras, "The Controversy about Marx and Justice," *New Left Review*, no. 150 (March/April 1985).

6. Cornel West, *The Ethical Dimensions of Marxist Thought* (New York, 1991), 92–94.

7. Perhaps this is why many Marxist academics turned toward the question of morality in the 1970s and 1980s, creating what Nielsen describes as "a minor growth industry." The irony is that morality should be restored to the heart of Marxism just as Marxism was making its exit from history. Cornel West's effort to revive the older Marxist view takes no account of these recent discussions or of Marxism's crisis.

8. The classical liberal attack on Marxist morality is that a movement believing itself to be warranted by history can easily fall prey, as did Communism, to cynicism about what *means* it chooses. This was one of the most harmful consequences of Marxism's attack on conventional morality. If morality is ideology, how then do we judge our forms of struggle? Even at its best, Communist morality left enormous space for equivocation. Leon Trotsky's *Their Morals and Ours* (New York, 1973) reveals how orthodox Marxism dismissed most discussions of morality, but also dedicated itself to reaching the consummately moral goal of "the liberation of humanity" (48). While Trotsky dismisses most talk of morality, he commends class struggle and revolution as moral acts and even develops revolutionary criteria of morality—all focused on strengthening the proletariat's capacity to struggle:

Permissible and obligatory are those and only those means . . . which unite the revolutionary proletariat, fill their hearts with irreconcilable hostility to oppression, teach them contempt for official morality and its democratic echoers, imbue them with consciousness of their own historic mission, raise their courage and spirit of self-sacrifice in the struggle. Precisely from this it flows that *not* all means are permissible. (49)

9. Alisdair MacIntyre, *After Virtue: A Study in Moral Theory* (Notre Dame, IN, 1984), 2.

10. Ibid., 59.

11. Ibid., 2.

12. Len Doyal and Ian Gough, *A Theory of Human Need* (New York, 1991), 63.

13. Ibid., 171–190.

14. Ibid., 191–221.

15. Michael Walzer, *Spheres of Justice* (New York, 1983), 313. As Raphael de Kadt has pointed out, Walzer's relativism presupposes certain univeralist commitments without which the undertaking would fall apart. See Raphael de Kadt, "*Spheres of Justice* or: How Not to Defend Pluralism and Equality," *Social Dynamics*, no. 9 (2), (1983).

16. Iris Young, *Justice and the Politics of Difference* (Princeton, NJ, 1990), 37.

17. This has been the obvious goal of the National Party in South Africa. See my "South Africa as Apartheid Unwinds." *Socialist Review*, vol. 92, no. 2 (1992).

18. One way of going beyond a society's promises is for movements to base themselves on the common stock of broad social values that form a penumbra around any particular society. Both the old and new abolitionists appealed to basic Judeo-Christian moral values, including direct appeals to shared religious traditions: if all people are created in God's image, then all people deserve equal treatment. But today this approach runs into precisely the problems sketched by MacIntyre, namely, it builds on words and concepts that no longer have their original coherence and resonance for all but relatively small religious communities. Walzer attempts to reach far beyond his thesis that "justice is relative to social meanings" (op. cit., 312) by arguing for a

"complex equality" that should be implemented in the different spheres of social experience. In the process, he undercuts his relativist determination to lodge justice in "a community's understanding of itself" as he *contests* such received social meanings—by arguing that advantages we achieve in one sphere (e.g., wealth) should not be permitted to carry over into another sphere (political power).

19. Herbert Marcuse, *One-Dimensional Man* (Boston, 1965), 219–224.

20. Every reader can think of a dozen examples of worsening situations, including free-market offensives, deregulation, the shrinking political (and even protective) power of labor unions in the United States, Britain, and France, post-Communist nationalism, new restrictions on reproductive rights, revivals of racism and neo-Nazism, antihomosexual ordinances. Of course those on the various opposite sides don't give up easily, and often manage to reverse apparent victories. I say only that rights "tend to" accumulate.

21. Samuel Bowles and Herbert Gintis, *Democracy and Capitalism: Property, Community, and the Contradictions of Modern Social Thought* (New York, 1987), 29.

22. In this sense needs are historically relative, although, as I am implying, they are also objective insofar as communities in struggle define what it means to be a human being as such, drawing from wider social meanings and adding to them, and insofar as there is, increasingly, a wider social definition. Doyal and Gough avoid a self-consciously historical definition of needs, because it appears to them as relativistic and thus defeats the kind of objectivity they correctly perceive is necessary if we are to talk about need (Doyal and Gough, op. cit., 12–13). But this gives their quite contemporary conception of needs an abstract and timeless quality that seems to deny that human needs evolve historically. Rather than seeing how this objectivity emerges, over time and through struggle, they posit it in argument. It may be that in some abstract sense certain needs—for example, autonomy—were always present. It is, however, only in the late twentieth century that it is possible to write a book such as *A Theory of Human Need* that makes a meaningful argument for universal autonomy.

23. Bowles and Gintis, op. cit., 3.

24. But its terse reference to the rights of property ("Everyone has the right to own property alone as well as in association with others") suggests that the Declaration was as much a document of compromise as it was a statement of fundamental principles, and its commitment to the traditional patriarchal family shows the limits of its universal vision. Clearly, even at their best, common cultural values have boundaries that shape in advance what may be demanded and what may not.

25. C. B. Macpherson, *The Rise and Fall of Economic Justice* (Oxford, 1985), 23.

26. See James Nickel, *Making Sense of Human Rights* (Berkeley, 1987), Appendix.

27. Bowles and Gintis, op. cit., 27–41.

28. Doyal and Gough, op. cit., 224. On the same page they quite correctly stress that it is "counterproductive and dangerous" to dismiss human rights as no more than an "ideological sham" that obfuscates real inequalities.

29. Macpherson, op. cit., 31.

30. Ibid., 22.

31. Anne Phillips, "Universal Pretensions in Political Thought." In Michèle Barrett and Anne Phillips, *Destabilizing Theory* (Cambridge, England, 1992), 10.

32. Charles Taylor, *Multiculturalism and "The Politics of Recognition"* (Princeton, NJ, 1992), 38.

33. Young, op. cit., Chapter 4.

34. Jürgen Habermas, *Moral Consciousness and Communicative Action* (Cambridge, MA, 1990), 100.

35. Jean Cohen and Andrew Arato, *Civil Society and Political Theory* (Cambridge, MA, 1992), 376–377.

36. Ibid., 383.

37. Seyla Benhabib, *Critique, Norm, and Utopia: A Study of the Foundations of Critical Theory* (New York, 1986), 341.

38. L. A. Kauffman, "The Anti-Politics of Identity." *Socialist Review*, vol. 20 (1990).

39. See Taylor, op. cit., 58.

40. Richard Rorty, *Contingency, Irony, Solidarity* (Cambridge, England, 1989), 189.

41. Young, op. cit., 233.

42. Ibid., 241.

43. Ibid., 255.

44. Young's utopia of city life is premised on solidarity in a second way: the diverse groups would have have had to create themselves into a vast we in order to overthrow the old order and its oppressions.

45. Cohen and Arato, op. cit., 383. They go on to quote Habermas to the same effect: "Without unrestricted individual freedom to take a position on normative validity claims, the agreement that is actually reached could not be truly universal; but without the empathy of each person in the situation for everyone else, which is derived from solidarity, no resolution capable of consensus could be found" (385; quoted from Jürgen Habermas, "Justice and Solidarity: On the discussion Concerning Stage 6." In Thomas E. Wren [ed.], *The Moral Domain: Essays in the Ongoing Debate between Philosophy and the Social Sciences* [Cambridge, MA, 1990], 246–247). See also Benhabib, op. cit., 351.

46. See Kathryn Pyne Addelson, *Impure Thoughts: Essays on Philosophy, Feminism and Ethics* (Philadelphia, 1991).

Chapter Eleven (pp. 258–282)

1. See page 179 and Chapter 7, note 28.

2. I discuss this concept in *the Dialectics of Disaster* (London, 1983), 115.

3. Ibid., 77–92.

4. Ernst Bloch, *The Principle of Hope* (Cambridge, MA, 1986), 1375–1376.

5. Jan Robert Bloch, "How Can We Understand the Bends in the Upright Gait?" *New German Critique*, no. 45 (Fall 1988), 24.

6. Jack Zipes, "Ernst Bloch and the Obscenity of Hope." *New German Critique*, no. 45 (Spring 1988), 7–8.

7. Jan Robert Bloch, op. cit., 15.

8. Ernst Bloch, op. cit., 9.

9. Ibid.

10. Ibid., 145.

11. Ibid., 208.

12. Ibid., 146.

13. Jan Robert Bloch, op. cit., 35.

14. Ernst Bloch, op. cit., 1367.

15. Ibid., 15 (my emphasis).

16. Bloch's Tubingen inaugural lecture (see *Sporen* [Frankfurt, 1969]) raises the issue in a vague, diffuse way, but makes no effort to come to grips with Bloch's experience of East German Communism.

17. Jan Robert Bloch, op. cit., 33.

18. Indeed, "He persisted even after the watchtowers [in Berlin], regardless of all historical experience, in Marxism and the dream of the absolute, in the same gait and plan of attack, without seriously reflecting on the conditions that made him leave" (Jan Robert Bloch, op. cit., 37).

19. See Michael Landmann, "Talking with Ernst Bloch: Korcula, 1968." *Telos*, no. 25 (Fall 1975).

20. Perhaps this is why Ernst Bloch is of more interest to religious thinkers than to students of the tendencies of the twentieth century and their possibilities (both disastrous and utopian). Bloch's thought is ultimately an all-inclusive faith in the dawning of a better world, one neither demonstrated nor demonstrable, drawing much of its sustenance from religion. It expresses this faith by taking totally seriously—indeed, more seriously than many religious thinkers—the hope bubbling up in the Jewish and Christian Bibles. But we know that this is in Bloch, as in religion, a hope without reason.

21. That is, he chooses this tactic rather than, we might say, treating his reader with *democratic* respect. Sartre once argued that the future classless society was foreshadowed in the relationship of mutual respect between author and reader (and this at a time when he was expressing his first rush of political hope and activism, in postwar France)—a striking contrast with Bloch. See Jean-Paul Sartre, *What Is Literature?* (New York, 1949); this is discussed at length in my *Jean-Paul Sartre— Philosophy in the World* (London, 1980), 122–141.

22. Quoted by Jan Robert Bloch, op. cit., 33.

23. For discussions of the function of utopia see Ruth Levitas, *The Concept of Utopia* (New York, 1990) and Vincent Geoghegan, *Utopianism and Marxism* (London, 1987).

24. See Douglas Kellner, *Herbert Marcuse and the Crisis of Marxism* (Berkeley, 1984), 154.

25. Herbert Marcuse, Foreword, *Negations: Essays in Critical Theory* (Boston, 1968), xx.

26. Herbert Marcuse, *Five Lectures* (Boston, 1970), 68.

27. Herbert Marcuse, *An Essay on Liberation* (Boston, 1969), 24.

28. Herbert Marcuse, *One-Dimensional Man* (Boston, 1965), 257.

29. For an analysis of how the revived nuclear threat of the 1980s was shaped by this deep sense of the polar alternatives of emancipation and catastrophe, see Aronson, op. cit., (1983), Chapter 7.

30. Marcuse, op. cit. (1970), 65.

31. Ibid., 64.

32. See Herbert Marcuse, "Repressive Tolerance." In *A Critique of Pure Tolerance* (Boston, 1965); and "Thoughts on the Defense of Gracchus Babeuf," in *the Defense of Gracchus Babeuf* (Boston, 1967).

33. J. P. Nettl, *Rosa Luxemburg* (New York, 1969), 99.

34. Similarly, in the minds of some South Africans, there can be little reason to

cheer the fall of apartheid when South Africa is still so far from genuine emancipation—that is, socialism. After all, it is persuasively argued, national liberation cannot be complete under capitalism: A postapartheid capitalist South Africa, like a post-1960s America, will only replace statutory racial oppression with a self-perpetuating sequel—inherited racial poverty. Or, as Fred Curtis asserts: "The more the conditions of existence of capitalism are reproduced in such a situation, the more the gains of the national liberation struggle—as expressed in the popular demands for political, economic, and property rights in the Freedom Charter— would be threatened and eroded" ("Race and Class in South Africa: Socialist Politics in the Current Conjuncture." Rethinking Marxism, vol. 1, no. 1 [1988], 129). The statement occurs in the end of an essay arguing for the importance of class analysis in South Africa. Curtis equivocates: He begins by arguing, from largely anecdotal and subjective evidence, that "Socialism is on the agenda in South Africa" (108) but ends, more realistically, with some suggestions for what must happen "if socialism is truly to be on the agenda for South Africa" (129)—namely "the analysis of class and non-class struggles." In fact a wide public mood equates capitalism with apartheid and yearns for greater equality, under the rubric of socialism, while a more Marxian definition of the working class yields a relatively small number of black proletarians. At the same time, nonclass forms of social-democratic changes are absolutely necessary to realize the barest rudiments of a nonracial democracy: health care, housing, education, employment. Clearly, then, something *beyond* capitalism is on the agenda, whether or not it means contesting "the extraction of surplus labor from productive laborers by capitalists in the form of surplus value" (Curtis, 119). See my discussions in *Stay Out of Politics! A Philosopher Views South Africa* (Chicago, 1990); "Is Socialism on the Agenda? A Letter to the South African Left." *Transformation*, no. 14 (1991); "South Africa as Apartheid Unwinds." *Socialist Review*, vol. 92, no. 9 (1992).

35. See page 179 and Chapter 7, note 28.

36. Erica Sherover-Marcuse, *Emancipation and Consciousness: Dogmatic and Dialectical Perspectives in the Early Marx* (Oxford, 1986), 1.

37. Ibid., 137.

38. Marcuse, op. cit. (1970), 65.

39. Ibid.

40. Ibid., 69.

41. No evil is quite so overwhelming once we act against it. Our relationship to it, shifting from contemplative to active, makes it an enemy to be combatted. See Aronson, op. cit. (1983), Chapter 8.

42. See, for example, Alan Lennon, "The *Critique*: A View from the Labor Movement." In Ronald Aronson and Adrian van den Hoven (eds.), *Sartre Alive* (Detroit, 1991).

43. See, for example, Steve Golin's description of the Paterson Pageant at Madison Square Garden on June 7, 1913, in *The Fragile Bridge: Paterson Silk Strike, 1913* (Philadelphia, 1989), Chapter 6.

44. Immanuel Kant, *Critique of Pure Reason* (New York, 1961), 635.

45. Karl Marx, *Capital: A Critical Analysis of Capitalist Production* (Moscow, 1961), 8.

INDEX

A

Adam, Barry D., 300, 303
Addelson, Kathryn Pyne, 312
Adorno, Theodor, 14, 72, 208, 211, 265
    and Max Horkheimer, 205–208,
        210, 211, 212, 219
Althusser, Louis, 158
Analytical Marxism, 140–151
Anderson, Perry, 35, 44, 136, 137,
    205, 289, 290
Angola, 68, 74
"Anti-Foucault," 243, 275. *See also*
    Foucault, Michel
Anti-Semitism, 206–208
Aristotle and Aristotelian thought,
    14, 242, 265
Aronowitz, Stanley, 64, 287
Aronson, Pamela, 37

B

Baader-Meinhof Gang, 272
Babeuf, Gracchus, 272
Bahro, Rudolph, 37
Baker, Keith Michael, 294
Bakhunin, Mikhael, 95, 97
Barrett, Michèle, 126–127, 131–132,
    137, 139, 169
Bauer, Bruno, 95

Baumann, Zygmunt, 120, 295
Bebel, August, 110
Beneria, Lourdes, 126, 138
Benhabib, Seyla, 253
Benjamin, Walter, 229, 269
Bentham, Jeremy, 202
Berland, Oscar, 19, 293
Berman, Marshall, 121, 205, 290–291,
    295
Bernstein, Eduard, 68, 69, 71, 272
Best, Steven and Douglas Kellner,
    212, 213. *See also* Kellner,
    Douglas
Bloch, Ernst, 5, 120, 218, 219, 261–
    266, 267, 270, 275, 276, 278,
    280, 313
Bloch, Jan Robert, 263, 264, 265
Boggs, Carl, 181, 225, 303
Bolshevik Party, 70, 77, 87–89, 112,
    289. *See also* Communism; So-
    viet Union
Bolshevik Revolution, 14, 68, 87, 175
Bookchin, Murray, 27–28
Bowles, Samuel, and Herbert Gintis,
    200–201, 244, 246, 249
Bukharin, Nikolai, 289

C

Callinicos, Alex, 77–79, 81–82, 288,
    303

Capitalism
   and patriarchy, 127–130
   as a destructive force, 221–223
   as immoral, 234–235
   as "sex-blind," 128
   as theft, 233
   beseiged by Marxism, 73–75
   displacement of conflicts under,
      196
   its development undermines prole-
      tarian revolution, 19
   unable to solve its most serious
      problems, 197–198
   victorious over Marxism, 82, 86
Carling, Alan, 298
Casteneda, Jorge G., 172
Castoriadus, Cornelius, 37
Ceausescu, Nicolae, 84
Civil society, 218
Class consciousness, as created by ob-
      jective processes, 64–66. See also
      Working class
   seen as unproblematic by Marx, 106
Clinton, Bill, 188. 195
Codrescu, André, 84
Cohen, G. A., 141–143, 144, 148,
      233, 235, 286, 291, 298, 299
Cohen, Jean, and Andrew Arato, 168,
      182, 187, 189–192, 194, 225,
      253, 255, 303, 306
   on modernity, 214–220
Cohen, Steven, 28
Collective identities, 182–184. See
      also "we," universality
Communism, 12, 23, 36, 68, 75, 76–
      78. 83, 85, 171–3, 178, 190, 235,
      236, 259, 265, 282, 295. See also
      Bolshevik Party, Soviet Union.
   as beyond capitalism, 80–81
Comte, Auguste, 95, 108, 210–211
Condorcet, Marquis de, 107–110,
      218, 220
Cook, Deborah, 212
Cornforth, Maurice, 285
Cowley, John, 21
Cuba, 16, 22–23, 44, 68, 73–74, 84, 122
Curtis, Fred., 313–314

D

Debs, Eugene, 282
Derrida, Jacques, 139
Deutscher, Isaac, 77, 78, 88–89, 122,
      136, 289, 290
Dionne, E.J., 187–188, 191–192, 194,
      195
Doyal, Len, and Ian Gough, 238, 249–
      250, 310

E

Eisenstein, Zillah, 130, 131–133, 138
Elster, Jon, 141
Emancipating modernity, 219–223
Engels, Frederick, 38, 77, 104, 110,
      117, 118, 295. See also Marx,
      Karl, and Frederick Engels
   preference for "critical and revolu-
      tonary socialism," 110
   Socialism: Utopian and Scientific, 45
England, 301
Enlightenment, 105–106, 120, 173,
      177, 205–208, 209, 212, 224,
      237, 250–251, 255
Eurocommunism, 68
Existentialism, 68, 286, 295

F

Fay, Brian, 286
Felski, Rita, 302
Feminism and Marxism, 124–139
Ferguson, Ann, 131
Feuerbach, Ludwig, 95
Flaubert, Gustave, 213
Flax, Jane, 138–139
Foucault, Michel, 139, 152, 208–210,
      211, 212–215, 218, 219, 221,
      239, 250, 270
Fourier, Charles, 95, 268, 272
France and French Communist Party,
      22, 75, 133
Frankfurt School, 68, 72, 73, 308. See
      also Adorno, Theodor; Hork-

heimer, Max; and Marcuse, Herbert

Fraser, Nancy, 37, 139, 151, 157–158, 186

Freud, Sigmund and Freudian theory, 14, 104–105

Froines, Anne, 131–132

Fukuyama, Francis, 172, 181

G

Geoghegan, Vincent, 313

Geras, Norman, 153, 235

Giddens, Anthony, 119, 144, 223–224, 295, 298, 308

Gilligan, Carol, 253

Ginsberg, Allen, 10

Goldfield, Michael, 287

Golin, Steve, 303, 314

Gorz, André, 37, 38, 64, 120, 185, 286, 287, 304

Gottheil, Fred M., 285

Gough, Ian. See Doyal, Len, and Ian Gough

Gramsci, Antonio, 23, 73, 77

H

Habermas, Jürgen, 37, 152–153, 167–168, 177, 182, 185, 189–191, 221, 225, 237, 252, 311
    on modernity, 215–220

Hartmann, Heidi, 125, 130

Hartsock, Nancy, 131, 302

Haupt, Georges, 294

Hegel, G. W. F., and Hegelian thought, 12–13, 42, 95, 208, 235, 242–243, 273, 306

Hegelian "cunning of reason," 302

Hegelian Marxism, 117

Heilbroner, Robert, 196, 301

Herreshoff, David, 287–288

Hess, Moses, 95

Historical materialism, 3, 21, 35, 38, 94, 141–151, 264–265, 299. See also Marxism.

feminist historical materialism, 135

Hitler, Adolf 175, 220, 263

Holocaust, 3, 38, 173, 175, 206

Homer, *The Odyssey* 206

Horkheimer, Max, 14, 72–73, 265. See also Adorno, Theodor and Max Horkheimer; Frankfurt School

I

International, the 108–109, 168, 281–82

Israeli–Palestinian conflict, 17, 34, 38

Italian Communist Party, 133

J

Jacoby, Russell, 116

Jaggar, Alison, 126, 129–130, 13–132, 135–136

Jameson, Fredric, 301

Johnson, Christopher, 299

K

Kadt, Raphael de, 310

Kampuchea, 85

Kant, Immanuel, 12, 279, 295

Kauffman, L. A., 311

Kautsky, Karl, 69, 104, 110

Kellner, Douglas, 313. See also Best, Steven, and Douglas Kellner

Khrushchev, Nikita, 12

King, Martin Luther, Jr., 234

Kolakowski, Leszek, 51, 55, 93–94, 95, 148

Korsch, Karl, 72, 73

Kuhn, Thomas S., 285

L

Laclau, Ernesto and Chantal Mouffe, 37, 153, 285, 286, 294

Landry, Donna, and Gerald MacLean, 297
Lenin, V. I., 38, 68, 77, 78, 89, 104, 110, 113, 118, 272
and Leninism, 69–71, 72
and minority revolution, 112
recasting Marxism, 112, 294
State and Revolution, 112
strategy of, 76
What Is to Be Done?, 69
Leninism, 23, 32, 69–71, 72, 73–74, 107, 116, 264–265, 272, 284, 289
Leningrad, 87
Lennon, Alan, 314
Lenzer, Gertrude, 294
Levine, Andrew, 141, 147, 154. *See also* Wright, Erik Olin, Andrew Levine, and Elliot Sober
Levitas, Ruth, 313
Lewin, Moshe, 290
Lichtheim, George, 291, 292
Liebnicht, Wilhelm, 110
Little, Daniel, 45, 99
Lukacs, Georg, 23, 72, 73, 117, 118, 285
Luxemburg, Rosa, 72, 77, 118, 269, 272, 274, 276, 285, 294
Lyotard, Jean-François, 139, 181, 168, 204

M

MacIntyre, Alisdair, 237–238, 239, 243, 310
MacLean, Gerald. *See* Landry, Donna and Gerald MacLean
MacPherson, C. B., 248, 250
Mandel, Ernest, 289
Mandelstam, Ossip, 290–291
Mann, Michael, 288
Mann, Thomas, 266
Mao Zedong, 118, 230
Maoism, 68
Marcuse, Herbert, 2, 3, 5, 12–16, 44, 70, 72, 74, 75, 91, 116, 117, 172, 176, 192, 211–212, 241, 262,

265, 266–275, 276, 278, 280, 285, 286, 292, 293, 294, 301
diference between social science and social theory, 294
Eros and Civilization, 25
Essay on Liberation, 26
on the role of theory, 228–230, 308–309
Marcusean analysis, 18–21, 22–23
Martov, Julius, 70,
and the Mensheviks, 87
Marx, Karl, 38, 78, 118, 164, 165–167, 177, 220, 238, 272, 273. *See also* Marx, Karl and Frederick Engels
Capital, 25, 44, 99, 103, 106, 210, 293.
as act of emancipatory consciousness, 101
Class Struggles in France, 103
conception of theory versus Comte's, 108
"Contribution to a Critique of Hegel's *Philosophy of Right*," 92, 293
"Critique of the Gotha Program," 89
Economic and Philosophical Manuscripts of 1843–1844, 92, 94
faith in workers' responses, 108–109
faith in the dialectics of history, 106
Grundrisse, 89
objectivism of, 105–106, 211
on capitalist modernity, 221–222
opposed minority rule in 1848, 112
Preface to *A Contribution to the Critique of Political Economy*, 89, 92, 102
role in International, 108–109
The Civil War in France, 89
"Theses on Feuerbach," 42, 45, 96, 276
violence as "midwife" in, 89
Marx, Karl, and Frederick Engels, 42, 77, 129
The Communist Manifesto, 40, 44, 92, 150, 221–222
The German Ideology, 92, 93, 94, 97

Marxism
    and Communism, 147
    and faith in history, 116
    and feminism, 124–14
    and hope, 260, 261, 263–266, 280
    and inevitability, 142
    and morality, 234–236
    arguments for the continued vitality of, 58–59
    as "sex-blind," 126–127
    as "the philosophy of our time" (Sartre), 66, 286, 295
    as a science of tendencies, 99
    as an idealism, 66–67, 82–83
    as depending on favorable conditions, 48–50
    as authoritarian, 89, 91
    as deterministic, 89, 91
    as early modern, 90, 114–115, 121–123, 231,
    as eschatological, 89, 91–97
    as modernizing, 87
    as objectivist, 89, 91, 98, 99, 100. 141–143, 231, 293
    as obsolete, 40–45, 56–58, 60
    as official outlook of German SPD, 110
    as predictive science, 45–46
    as a project, 43–44, 50–55, 133–134, 146–149, 158–159, 172, 222, 224
    as *the* project, 286
    as prophecy, 51, 93–94, 148, 265–266
    as religion, 93, 291–292
    as relativized, 151–153, 156–159, 304
    as scientific, , 50–55, 95, 97, 98, 150
    as scientistic, 97–99, 231
    as tending toward authoritarianism, 107–111, 308–309
    attractive to New Left, 79
    celebrates modernity, 107
    criticized as name for a movement, 110–111
    decline of, 75–76
    high tide of, 73–75
    labor as central category of, 56
    mourning the end of, 83–86
    orthodox and Soviet Marxism, 77, 78, 118, 141, 144
    recast into explanation or theory, 147–149, 155, 291
    still-useful themes of, 151–153
    weaknesses a source of its strength, 114
    Western Marxism, 73–74, 91, 118, 141
Marxists-in-waiting, 61
McLellan, David, 291–292
McMurtry, John, 148, 291
Melucci, Alberto, 181, 225, 300–301, 303
Mensheviks, 112. *See also* Martov, Julius.
Merleau-Ponty, Maurice, 100, 116, 118, 285
Miliband, Ralph, 51, 59–60, 66–67, 153–154, 288
Mill, John Stuart, 202, 252
Miller, Richard, 141
Mittérand, François, 68, 75
Modernity, 204–205, 212
    and domination, 222–223
    Anderson on, 205
    Berman on, 205
    Cohen and Arato on, 205
    dark side of, 205–210
    Foucault on, 295, 205, 208–210, 212–215
    Habermas on, 205, 215–219
    Horkheimer and Adorno on, 205–208
    Marcuse on, 210–212
Morality
    and historical struggles, 243–247
    and immanent critique, 239–242
    and Marxism, 234–236, 309
    and radicalism, 192–193
Morris, Meaghan, 169, 184
Mouffe, Chantal. *See* Laclau, Ernesto and Chantal Mouffe
Mourning the end of Marxism, 83–86
Mozambique, 68, 74, 75

N

Nazis and Nazism, 175, 206–208, 265, 269, 277
Needs, 46–49, 238, 310
Neilson, Kai, 234–235, 309
Nettl, J. P., 313
New Left, 16–29, 38–39, 68–69, 73, 83, 116, 124, 132–133, 136, 228–229, 235, 270–272, 281
New Left Marxism, 128–129
New social movements, 181–182, 217–218, 303
Nicaragua, 68, 74, 75, 76
Nicholson, Linda, 221, 297

O

Offe, Claus, 196, 225, 286, 304, 305
Ollmann, Bertell, 64–67, 292
O'Meara, Dan, 302
Oppression, 184–193, 211–212, 218, 245, 302
Owen, Robert, 95

P

Page, Margaret, 129
Paris Commune, 42
Perret, Henri, 110
Phillips, Anne, 250
Plato and Platonism, 12–13, 67. 238, 242, 295
Plotke, David, 300
Pollock, Scarlet, 296
Postmodernism, 4, 90, 119–121, 204–210, 213, 301
    and feminism, 138–139
Progress, 172–174, 211–212
Proudhon, Pierre Joseph, 95
Przeworski, Adam, 141

R

"Radical," as description of post-Marxist movement, 198–202
Radicalism vs. realism, 194–198

Red Brigades, 272
Resnick, Stephen, 157–8
Rights, expanding historically, 243–247
Rilke, R, 272
Roemer, John, 141
Rorty, Richard, 254
Rubel, Maximilien, 110–111

S

Sade, Marquis de, *Juliette*, 206
Said, Edward, 34
Saint-Simon, Henri de, 95, 210–211
Sartre, Jean-Paul, 2–3, 33, 38, 66, 73, 74, 75, 91, 116, 123, 213, 234, 278, 286, 289, 304, 313
    Existentialism is a Humanism, 12
    on analytical reason, 151
    on deviation of Bolshevik Revolution, 289
    on "Socialism in One Country," 123
    on Stalinism, 78–79, 301
Scarcity, 94
Schumpeter, Joseph, 286
Schweickart, David, 155–6, 295
Segal, Lynne, 131–132
Self-determination, 249, 224
Sherover-Marcuse, 111, 115, 176, 273, 287, 293, 302
    on emancipatory subjectivity, 101–104
Schorske, Karl, 288
Singer, Daniel, 290
Smith, Dorothy, 150
Sober, Elliot. See Wright, Erik Olin, Andrew Levine, and Elliot Sober
Social Democratic Party, 69, 71
"Socialism in One Country," 70, 80
Socialist feminism, 124–136
    as idea rather than project, 135–136
"Socialist," as description of post-Marxist movement, 198–199
Solidarity, 187, 254, 311
South Africa, 3, 34, 37–38, 43, 56, 60, 61–63, 74, 80, 174, 197, 221, 245–246, 281–282, 310, 313–314
Soviet Union, 1, 22–23, 69, 70–71,

73, 76–79, 81–82, 91, 113, 117, 122, 153, 169, 171, 220, 262–263, 298, 308
Stalin, Joseph, 70, 77, 110, 112, 118, 262–263, 264–265, 289
   Dialectical and Historical Materialism, 71, 79.
Stalinism, 3, 38, 84, 88–89, 175, 206, 265, 301
Stalinist Marxism, 77

T

Taylor, Charles, 251
Theory, its role in a post-Marxist movement, 225–230
Therborn, Goran, 287
Thomas, Paul, 98, 291
Thompson, Edward P., 213
Toulmin, Stephen, 204
Touraine, Alain, 225, 303
Trotsky, Leon, 72, 77, 88, 309
   theory of uneven and combined development, 219–220
Trotskyism, 68, 72, 82–83, 288, 295
Trotskyist interpretation of USSR's collapse, 77–79
Tucker, Robert C., 291–292

U

Universal rights, 247
Universal Declaration of Human Rights, 239, 247–250, 311
Universality, 168–71. *See also* "we," collective identities
Utopia, 5, 194, 232, 266–271, 272–276, 278–279. 281

V

Vietnam, 16, 22–23, 68, 73–74, 75, 76, 122, 124, 173, 274, 277, 281,
Vogel, Lise, 127–128
Voltaire, 105

W

Walzer, Michael, 238–239, 310
Warsaw Ghetto Uprising, 277
"We," 168–171, 182–187, 252, 277, 281–282. *See also* collective identities, universality
   redefined and expanding, 248–250
   sense of collective solidarity, 85–86
Weatherman, 272
Weber, Max, 206, 217
Weitling, Wilhelm, 97
Wellman, Saul, 281
Wellmer, Albrecht, 37–38, 96, 101, 113, 117, 307
   on Marxism's failure to appreciate subjectivity 101
   on tension between determinist and revolutionary sides of Marxism, 99–100
West, Cornel, 236
Williams, Raymond, 168, 169, 199, 201–202
Wolff, Richard, 157–8
Wood, Allen, 141
Wood, Ellen Meiksins, 136–137, 155
Working class, 19–20, 24, 50–52, 56–60, 63–66, 67, 69–71, 76–77, 98, 106, 113, 143, 154, 176, 213, 235, 258, 287–288
Wright, Eric Olin, 141, 150, 286
   with Elliot Sober and Andrew Levine, 144–51, 157, 286

Y

Young, Iris, 130, 132, 184–187, 225, 239, 252, 254–255, 299, 304, 311
Yugoslavia, 73, 169, 173, 175

Z

Zimbabwe, 74, 75, 76
Zaretsky, Eli, 296
Zipes, Jack, 263

Printed in the United States
25194LVS00003B/171

9 780898 624168